But Will It Fly?

ALSO BY IVER P. COOPER
AND FROM McFARLAND

Airships: Their Science, History and Future (2025)

Poseidon's Progress: The Quest to Improve Life at Sea (2024)

*Arming the Warship: Naval Weapons Technology
and Gunnery from the Spanish Armada
to the Cold War* (2024)

But Will It Fly?

The History and Science of Unconventional Aerial Power and Propulsion

IVER P. COOPER

McFarland & Company, Inc., Publishers
Jefferson, North Carolina

Portions of this work were previously published in the *Grantville Gazette*. For particulars, see the explanatory note at the end of the bibliography.

Use of released U.S. Navy imagery does not constitute product or organizational endorsement of any kind by the U.S. Navy.

ISBN (print) 978-1-4766-9654-6
ISBN (ebook) 978-1-4766-5545-1

Library of Congress cataloging data are available

Library of Congress Control Number 2025036728

© 2025 Iver P. Cooper. All rights reserved

No part of this book may be reproduced or transmitted in any form or by any means, electronic or mechanical, including photocopying or recording, or by any information storage and retrieval system, without permission in writing from the publisher.

Front cover images: *clockwise from top left* Ritchel's airship, depicted in flight on the July 15, 1878, cover of *Harper's Weekly*; Belgian Vincent de Groof's ornithopter, July 9, 1874, engraving, published in 1875 (© ZU_09/iStock); design drawing for Tissandier's 1883 battery powered airship (Library of Congress); the unmanned Pathfinder-Plus flies over Hawaii on July 17, 1998 (photo by Jim Ross, courtesy National Aeronautics and Space Administration [Dryden Flight Research Center Photograph Collection] NASA Photo EC96-44629-58).

Printed in the United States of America

McFarland & Company, Inc., Publishers
Box 611, Jefferson, North Carolina 28640
www.mcfarlandpub.com

For Lee, Louise and Jason.

Table of Contents

Preface	1
Introduction: Preliminary Considerations	3
Part I: Unconventional Power	9
1. Muscle Power	9
2. Steam Power	30
3. Alternative External Combustion Power	60
4. Battery Power	69
5. Solar Power	83
6. Nuclear Power	95
7. Miscellaneous Power Sources	104
Part II: Unconventional Propulsion	123
8. Buoyancy-Driven Propulsion	123
9. Wind Propulsion	148
10. Oars, Paddle Wheels and Cycloidal Propellers	164
11. Biomimetic Propulsion (Flapping and Undulating)	188
12. Miscellaneous Propulsion Methods	203
Conclusion	211
Appendices	213
Appendix 1: Author's Airship Aerodynamics Standard Model	213
Appendix 2: Aerodynamic Modeling of Buoyancy-Driven Propulsion	217
Appendix 3: Sensitivity of Aereon *Predictions to Modeling Method*	220

Table of Contents

Appendix 4: Reliability of Wind Speed Estimates by the Aereon *Flight Eyewitnesses* — 222

Appendix 5: Reliability of Estimates of the Ground Speed of the Aereon — 224

Appendix 6: Analysis of Steam (Rankine) Cycle Thermodynamics — 227

Appendix 7: Thermal Efficiency of Historical and Proposed Steam Locomotives — 229

Appendix 8: Methods of Improving Theoretical Cycle Efficiency of Steam Powerplants — 232

Appendix 9: Improving Actual Cycle Efficiency of Steam Powerplants — 235

Appendix 10: Steam Car Data — 237

Appendix 11: Condenser Pressure — 240

Chapter Notes — 243

Bibliography — 251

Index — 281

Preface

> *Two roads diverged in a wood and I—*
> *I took the one less traveled by,*
> *And that has made all the difference.*
> —Robert Frost, "The Road Not Taken" [1915]

Nowadays, most airplanes burn liquid fuel in an internal combustion engine. Expanding combustion gases move a piston (in small airplanes) or turn a turbine. The piston turns a crankshaft, which turns a propeller. In a turboprop, the turbine likewise turns a propeller; in a turbojet, the turbine powers a compressor, and the compressed air expands out a nozzle. Only piston engines were used in commercial and military airships.

This book examines the roads "less traveled by" regarding aerial power and propulsion. Some were the subject of experimental flights; others remained on the drawing board. But all exhibit the workings of the creative mind.

An important distinction must be drawn between airships (lighter-than-air vehicles) and airplanes (heavier-than-air vehicles). An airship can take off because the buoyancy of its lift gas is greater than its takeoff weight. It can take off without even turning on its engines. In contrast, an airplane ascends as a result of aerodynamic lift, a force generated by the difference in airflow above and below its wings. A shark needs to swim to breathe, and an airplane needs to be moving forward to generate aerodynamic lift and maintain its altitude.

Thus, an airship will require less propulsive power than an airplane of the same takeoff weight, and unconventional power and propulsion designs are easier to incorporate into airships than airplanes.

On the other hand, the airship will be much larger than the airplane, because a thousand cubic feet of helium will generate only about 60 pounds of buoyant lift. Hence, for a given propulsive power and weight, the airship will have a lower maximum speed.

A further important point is that the buoyant lift scales with the hull

Preface

(gas bag) volume, whereas the aerodynamic drag scales with the surface and frontal area. Hence the power-to-weight ratio of the airship's engines is less significant for a large airship than a small one.

The treatment of unconventional power and propulsion begins with an introduction that explains what is considered conventional. The remainder of the book is divided into "Unconventional Power" and "Unconventional Propulsion." "Unconventional Power" looks at powerplants and their sources of energy, and "Unconventional Propulsion" at how thrust is generated.

In most chapters, we first look at the history of the concept and then analyze its practicality (perhaps with some modern improvements) from an engineering standpoint. However, we depart from that format when it is helpful to the reader.

Introduction

Preliminary Considerations

Conventional Aerial Power and Propulsion

It is worthwhile to expand a bit upon the nature of **conventional** power and propulsion to serve as a baseline for comparison with unconventional technologies.

Airships and General Aviation Airplanes

The general aviation engine is a reciprocating piston, spark-ignition, internal combustion engine that burns gasoline and runs on the four-stroke Otto cycle.[1] The combustion is of an air-fuel mixture and is ignited by a spark (Çengel and Boles 2002, 457–459). The engine may be air-cooled or liquid cooled (Sadraey 2013, 464).

Most modern airships use four-stroke airplane engines. For example, the Zeppelin NT (LZN07) is propelled by three Textron Lycoming IO-360-C1G6 engines (Khoury 2012, 549; EASA 2014, 5), each with a compression ratio of 8.7:1 and rated 200 horsepower (hp), or 149 kilowatts (kW), at 2,700 revolutions per minute (rpm; Lycoming 2009, 2–3). These have an engine standard dry weight of 324 pounds (lb; 2–9), for a weight-to-power (W/P) ratio of 1.62.

There are also two-stroke Otto cycle engines, with just a power stroke and a compression stroke. The "latter part of the power stroke" partially expels the exhaust gases and then takes in fresh air. During the compression stroke, the air-fuel mixture is ignited. "The two-stroke engines are generally less efficient than their four-stroke counterparts because of the incomplete expulsion of the exhaust gases and the partial expulsion of the fuel-air mixture with the exhaust gases. However, they are relatively simple and inexpensive, and they have high power-to-weight and power-to-volume ratios, which makes them suitable for …

Introduction

motorcycles, chain saws, and lawn mowers" (Çengel and Boles 2002, 458–459). The GEFA-FLUG AS105GD thermal airship relies on a ROTAX 582 twin-cylinder, two-stroke, liquid-cooled engine (Gefa-Flug 2015, 1.2.2).

Commercial and Military Airplanes

These airplanes use gas turbine engines in which the working gas is air.[2] Air is drawn in, compressed, heated by a burner, allowed to expand against the blades of the turbine's rotors, and exhausted (Çengel and Boles 2002, 470). In airplane engines, the turbine powers the compressor (472).

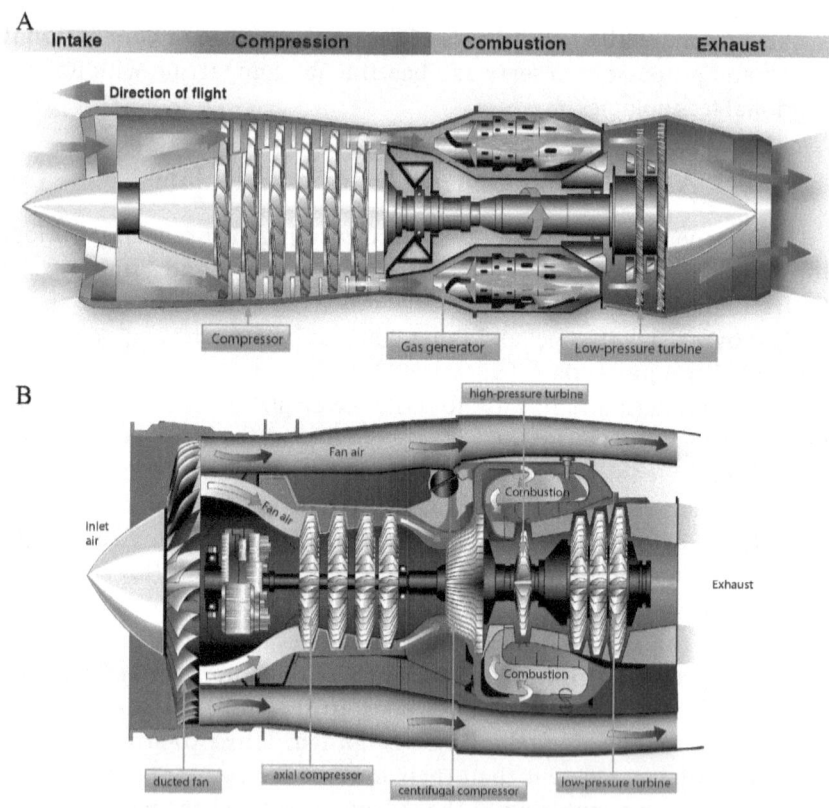

A. Schematic of basic turbojet engine (FAA 2022, fig. 16–1). *B*. Schematic of turbofan engine (fig. 16–2). https://www.faa.gov/regulations_policies/handbooks_manuals/aviation/airplane_handbook.

Introduction

In a turbojet engine, the power extracted by the rotation of the rotor is used merely to power the compressor, and the remainder of the expansion is through a nozzle, accelerating the exiting air (jet propulsion; Çengel and Boles 2002, 483–486).

A turbofan engine is equipped with a ducted fan. The turbine powers the ducted fan as well as the compressor, and some of the intake air bypasses the compressor and burner and is accelerated by the ducted fan (Çengel and Boles 2002, 487–488). Commercial airplane engines are likely to have a high-bypass ratio and military ones, a low ratio.

In a turboprop engine, most of the expansion is in the turbine, and the turbine drives a propeller. "Jet thrust usually accounts for less than 10 percent of the total engine power" (FAA 2022, 15–2).

I consider ramjet and rocket engines to be unconventional propulsion systems for airplanes and address them in chapter 12.

Performance Considerations

Required Propulsive Power

As a first approximation, we can assume that the required propulsive power for an airship or airplane is proportional to the cube of the airspeed, which is an airship's or airplane's speed relative to the air mass it is traveling in. If there is a wind (the air mass is moving relative to the ground), the airspeed and ground speed will differ.

The required propulsive power is also proportional to the air density and thus decreases with altitude. However, gasoline engine power will also decrease with altitude if the engine is naturally aspirated (supplied with air).

Power and Weight

One major concern is an engine's power-to-weight ratio (P/W).[3] The greater the engine weight, the less lift remains for payload.

In the metric system, P/W is typically expressed as watts/kilogram (W/kg). When power is given in horsepower and weight in pounds, it is fairly common for sources to state the inverse ratio, weight to power (W/P), so the value is greater than one.

Some early airships had gasoline engines specifically designed for airship use; the Maybach Mb.IVa, with a compression ratio of 6.7:1[4] and 245 hp[5] at 1,400 rpm, had an engine weight of 860 lb,[6] yielding a W/P of 3.51 (Robinson 1982, 221 n50).

Introduction

However, the 400 hp 1917 Liberty V-12 airplane engine had a W/P of 2.04 (Anderson 2002, 157). The Pratt & Whitney Wasp model R-1340-AN2 engines used on the later K-class blimps of World War II had a W/P of 2.19 (Goodyear 1943, 2, 16).

The Rolls-Royce Merlin I achieved 1.28 (McNeil 2002, 320). It's possible for a gasoline piston engine to break the 1 lb/hp barrier (the 4,300 hp Pratt & Whitney 28-cylinder supercharged R-4360–59B used in F2G-1 and F2G-2 Corsair fighters was 0.92; CAM 2018), but it's not easy.

Modern "piston engines generally weigh about 1.1 to 1.75 lb ... per takeoff shaft horsepower, while for turboprop engines the equivalent figure is between .35 and .55 lb/hp" thrust[7] (Torenbeek 2013, 99). A "bypass jet engine" (turbofan) weighs ".17 to .25 lb/lb thrust" (note the change in unit), and a "single-flow jet engine" (turbojet) "about .25 to .35 lb/lb ... at takeoff thrust" (100). Sadraey (2013, 431) provides these estimates: "piston 1.5 lb/hp; turboprop, 0.4 lb/hp; turbofan 0.2 lb/lb thrust; and turbojet 0.3 lb/lb."

Thermal Efficiency and Specific Fuel Consumption

Another major concern is fuel consumption. The fuel consumption rate depends on the energy content of the fuel (the energy released by combustion per unit mass or volume) and the thermal efficiency of the engine (the fraction of that energy that is extracted from the fuel by the engine). The specific fuel consumption is the fuel consumption rate per unit of power.

"General aircraft" piston engines typically run on avgas (aviation gasoline), which has a specific energy of about 43.71 megajoules per kilogram (MJ/kg) and an energy density of 31 megajoules per liter (MJ/L) at 15°C (Hemighaus et al. 2007).

Jet fuels in general are less volatile than avgas. Jet B (civilian, cold climate) and JP-4 (former American military) fuels are wide-cut fuels that are mixtures of hydrocarbons distilling in the gasoline and kerosene ranges. Specific energy is about 43.54 MJ/kg, and energy density is 33.18 MJ/L. The principal civilian jet fuels (Jet A and A-1) and the current American (JP-8) and NATO (F34) military fuels are narrow-cut fuels in the kerosene range. They have a higher flash point than the wide-cut fuels. Specific energy is about 43.28 MJ/kg, and energy density is 35.06 MJ/L (Hemighaus et al. 2007).

For an internal combustion engine, the theoretical thermal efficiency

Introduction

depends on the compression ratio. The working fluid is initially cool air but becomes a hot mixture of air and combustion gases during the combustion stroke. Assuming the common simplification that the working fluid is air, the efficiency is $1-r^{1-k}$, where r is the compression ratio and k is the specific heat ratio of air. The latter, at 25°C, is 1.4 (Çengel and Boles 2002, 456, 459–460).[8]

Thus, the theoretical efficiency is 57.5% for an 8.5:1 Lycoming O-320-D2J gasoline engine. However, power is dribbled away in other ways (for a breakdown, see Lowry 1999, 124–126) so that the total efficiency for that engine is 33.3% (125).

At sea level, a Lycoming O-320-A airplane engine, maximum power of 150 hp at 2,700 rpm, has its lowest propeller load specific fuel consumption (PLSFC) at about 2,350–2,400 rpm (Lycoming 2006, 3–10). Performance cruise power is 75% (2,450 rpm, 110 hp, consumption rate is 10 gallons per hour [gal/h]); economy cruise is 65% (2,350 rpm, 97 hp, 8.8 gal/h; 3–8).

The "prop-driven engines (e.g., piston-prop and turboprop) have the lowest specific fuel consumption up to about Mach 0.4" (307 miles per hour [mph]). That is, of course, faster than any historical airship. As for the jet propulsion types, the specific fuel consumption is highest for the turbojet and lowest for the high-bypass turbofan (Sadraey 2013, 430). At Mach 0.8, it is about 1.2 lb/h/lb thrust for the turbojet, 0.8 for a low-bypass (bypass ratio 1) turbofan, and 0.6 for a high-bypass (ratio 5) turbofan. At Mach 0.2, the turbojet is about 1.0 lb/h/lb thrust, and the high-bypass turbofan is about 0.4 lb/h/lb thrust; the piston-prop and turboprop are about 0.25 lb/h/hp (Sadraey 2013, fig. 8.9).

PART I: UNCONVENTIONAL POWER

1

Muscle Power

Here, we consider the use of human muscle power to rotate a conventional propulsor—a propeller—in order to propel an airship or airplane through the air. Hands, feet or both could be used to operate a mechanism that turns the propeller. Chapters 10 and 11 cover unconventional propulsors—oars, flapping wings, et cetera—activated by human muscles.

History—Airships

Hugh Bell, "a Scots doctor with a London practice" (T&T 1952, 1098), constructed an airship in 1848 or 1850. It was 56 feet (ft) long and 21 ft 4 inches (in.) in diameter, with a cylindrical midbody and conical ends. It had two hand-worked screw propellers, but it was considered a failure (Hodgson 1924, 39; Whale 1919, 61).

On October 29, 1870, Henri Dupuy de Lôme (1816–1885), a marine architect of great stature, was authorized by the French government to build a navigable balloon. At the time, Paris was under siege by the Germans. The Franco-Prussian War ended (with a French defeat) before he completed this assignment (it wasn't easy to acquire the necessary quantities of taffeta and rubber), but on February 2, 1872, his airship was ready to make its first ascent. It was 36.12 meters (m) long and 14.84 m in diameter, and it had a gas capacity of 3,454 cubic meters (cu m).[1] It held a "basket for fourteen people," and its two-bladed, 29.5 ft diameter propeller was turned by a long crank (Domański 2024; Nature 1872). The all-up weight of the airship was 3,799 kilograms (1,776 kg airship empty weight, 1,148 kg crew with baggage and provisions, 275 kg cargo, and 600 kg ballast; Leclert 1872, 284; de Lôme 1872, 23).

De Lôme (1872, 6, 9) recognized that to minimize air resistance, the gas bag must have an "oblong shape," and more particularly, he preferred one defined "by an arc of a circle rotating around its chord."

He also realized that the internal pressure must be higher than that of the outside air to maintain that shape. This superpressure was achieved by

Part I: Unconventional Power

a ballonet filled with pressurized air. As the airship ascended, the hydrogen expanded, forcing air out of the ballonet. The ballonet volume was one-tenth that of the gas bag, allowing ascent, he calculated, to 866 m without venting hydrogen (de Lôme 1872, 6–7, 24). (The correct value is 1084 m, assuming International Standard Atmosphere conditions.)

Each of the 14 crew members had an assignment: eight to turn the crank, four to control the ballonet fan, helm, ballast, valves, guide rope, and anchor, and two to be in charge of navigation. The crew was in a wicker basket 6.5 m long (de Lôme 1872, 13).

According to Domański (2024) and Nature (1872), the sailors worked in two 30-minute shifts of four sailors apiece, and the airship's speed was 9–11 kilometers per hour (km/h, 5.6–6.8 mph). However, Leclert (1872, 284) says that all eight were "employed at the screw." De Lôme (1872, 15) contemplated both modes of operation.

According to de Lôme's calculations, to achieve an airspeed of 8 km/h (2.22 meters per second [m/s]), his airship would need a motive power of about 30 kilograms-force per meters per second (kgf-m/s), about 272 watts (W). For that speed, he estimated that a flat plate would incur 0.665 kgf/m^2 frictional drag; the total drag on the balloon alone would be 6 kgf (59 newtons [N]) and that on the entire airship, 11 kgf (108 N; Leclert 1872, 281–282; de Lôme 1872, 30). The drag power (drag force times airspeed) would then have been 240 W.

De Lôme (1872, 31–32) believed that four men could sustain work (power) of 33 kgf-m/s (323 W) for an hour (50) and that with "a change of men" every hour or even half hour, "the pace ... could be sustained for ten hours if necessary."

With eight men working simultaneously, he thought the speed could be increased to 12.6 km/h (3.5 m/s; de Lôme 1872, 32), a 57.5% increase, but this is incorrect. Required power is proportional to the cube of the speed, so the speed increase would have been 26% (if propulsive efficiency was unchanged). In any event, the airspeed actually achieved with eight men cranking was considerably less than what he predicted (see table 1–1).

Unlike most early aeronautical inventors, de Lôme (1872, 45) took care to carry aloft instruments for measuring ground, wind and airspeed. For ground speed, he timed how long it took for the angular position of a sighted landmark to change by a fixed value; he determined altitude with an aneroid barometer graduated to indicate altitude directly; and he had a lookup table to avoid the need to make trigonometric calculations while aloft (46). The airspeed was determined with a suitably calibrated propeller-type anemometer (44). If the ship's propeller were stopped, the

1. Muscle Power

ground speed would equal the wind speed (46). Heading and course were determined by reference to a magnetic compass. The ship's track was also plotted on a map (49).

Time	Alt m	Relative to Ground		Angle w/ Wind Direction*		Airspeed**		Screw rpm
		Course	Speed m/s	Heading of Bow	Heading of Course	m/s	mph	
1:15p	560	NE 7° N	12			0		0
1:30	607	NE 5° E	12	97	12	2.35	5.26	25.00
1:45	580	NE 5° N	15		10	0		0
2:00	608	NE 15° E	16	85	10	2.45	5.48	26.00
2:15	660	NE 16° E	17	84	11	2.82	6.31	27.50
2:30	910	NE 6° E	17			0		0

Table 1-1: Offwind Performance of Lôme's Airship (de Lôme 1872, 46–49)

*The heading angle is expressed relative to the direction the wind is blowing **toward**, so downwind is a heading of 0°.
**with eight men cranking.

To achieve a course deviating only 10°–12° from the direction the wind was blowing toward, the airship had to head at about a right angle to the wind. The wind qualified as Beaufort force 4, moderate breeze.

Charles Francis Ritchel (1844–1911), a mechanic and professional inventor, patented an airship design in 1878. The airship he built, the Dirigicyle, or Flying Car, had, according to an 1878 newspaper article, a cylindrical, rubberized linen gas bag 13 ft in diameter and 25 ft long, "weighing only 66 lb" and buoyed by hydrogen. With the externally suspended gondola, the total weight was "little more than 112 lb." Its four-bladed horizontal axis propeller, 24 in. in diameter, was turned by a hand crank (Knotts 2014; DeLuca 2022).

For its first public flight, it was piloted by Mabel Harrington "inside one of the large exhibition halls at the 1876 Centennial Exhibition in Philadelphia." For its first outdoor excursion, a short there-and-back-again flight on June 12, 1878, it was piloted by a child, Mark Quinlan (who weighed just 96 lb). There were later exhibition flights, but the airship "never exceeded speeds of 3 to 4 mph and could only be flown in calm conditions" (Knotts 2014).

Part I: Unconventional Power

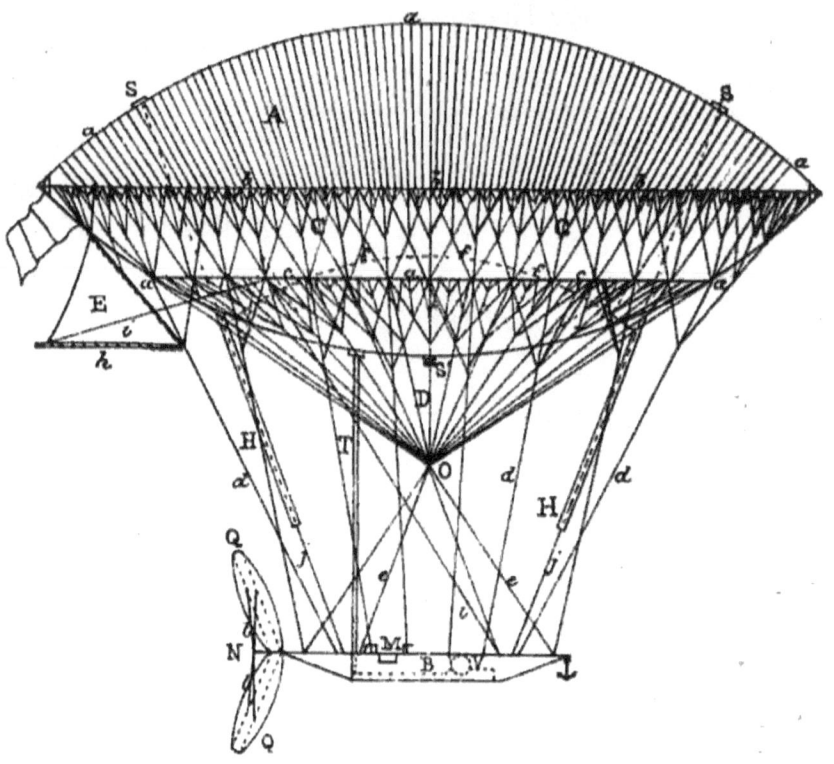

Profile view of De Lôme airship (Leclert 1872, fig. 1).

Nonetheless, "Ritchel later built and sold five of his patented flying machines, all the while envisioning a bigger, long-distance version of his dirigible that would be mechanically powered by an 11-man hand-cranking crew. That machine never materialized" (DeLuca 2022). This optimistically named transcontinental airship would have had an 85 ft long, 35 ft diameter, 81,000-cubic-foot (cu ft) cylindrical gas envelope, expected to lift 5,670 lb (70 lb per 1,000 cu ft, which would have required very pure hydrogen). The expected empty weight was 2,700 lb (47.6% gross lift), and it would have carried 15 people, including the crew (Knotts 2014). Each person was expected to weigh 120 lb, for a total of 1,800 lb, and the water ballast would have weighed 600 lb.

Carl E. Myers (1842–1923) worked variously as a banker, telegrapher, and photo studio proprietor, but he and his wife Mary (1849–1932) became interested in aeronautics. Carl built (and also flew) balloons, and his wife, under the show name Carlotta, was also a balloonist, drawing large (and

1. Muscle Power

paying) crowds for each ascent. They became interested in being able to move against the wind. Here, they seemed to proceed along two separate development tracks.

In *The Aerial Adventures of Carlotta, or Sky-Larking in Cloudland* (1882), an illustration shows what appears to be a conventional balloon basket equipped with a "screw sail and a rudder kite" (Bassett 1963, 372). In 1885, the Myers jointly filed for and received a patent on this design. Only the base of the balloon is shown in the patent figure, but the balloon likely had a conventional shape. Carlotta used this Flying Dutchman design on some of her ascents (373).

The alternative design, the aerial Velocipede, is shown in an 1881 issue of the *American Magazine of Aeronautics* (Bassett 1963, 378). This balloon had an elongated gas bag, a round-topped, flat-bottomed shape tapered at both ends. (Myers [1902] referred to it as a *capsized-boat shape*.) The gondola had a bicycle-like saddle, handlebars and pedals. The latter powered a bow propeller via a chain drive. At some point, discovering that the

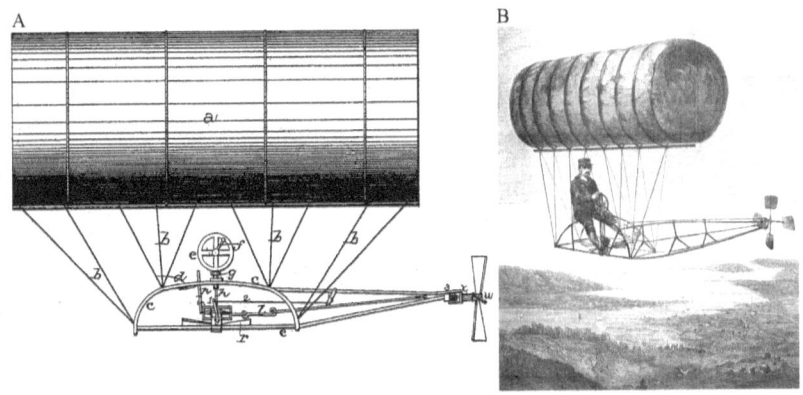

A. Figure 1 of the Ritchel patent (1878). The patent has several interesting aspects. First, the gas bag was to have "a lifting capacity sufficient to almost lift the machine, together with at least one person in it." To achieve takeoff, a vertical axis lifting propeller® was engaged, and reversing this propeller would cause the airship to descend. The direction of rotation was controlled by a hand lever. Forward motion was achieved by turning a horizontal axis bow propeller (w). This propeller could be turned by treadles. Ritchel noted the possibility of mounting the propeller (w) on a universal joint, "for assisting the machine to rise ... and to descend." B. Ritchel's airship, depicted in flight on the July 15, 1878, cover of *Harper's Weekly*. https://en.wikipedia.org/wiki/Charles_F._Ritchel#/media/File:C.F._Ritchel_in_his_dirigible.jpg.

Part I: Unconventional Power

handlebars weren't needed for steering, Myers replaced them with hand cranks. However, there is no reference to the latter in an 1890 account by W. P. Pond of his own ride on the vehicle (Bassett 1963, 376).

The aerial bicycle proper "weighed only 9 pounds" (Bassett 1963, 374). The propeller, 15 ft in diameter, weighed 2.5 lb (Myers 1897a). Myers also called the aerial velocipede a *gas kite* or *aerial elevator* because of the ease with which it rose; this is probably attributable to the cambered shape of the gas bag, which would have produced aerodynamic lift if propelled forward at a zero angle of attack. However, descent was difficult if there was a wind.

In 1895, he unveiled a new design. The gas bag had a fat, symmetrical spindle shape and sharply tapered ends. Two "bat's wings" extended from either side of the gondola (Myers 1897b). Myers allowed a *New York World* reporter to fly it from Brooklyn to Lower Manhattan to Yonkers on August 3, 1895. This craft was featured in Myers's 1897 patent entitled "Sky-Cycle." However, a 1915 photo shows the same gas bag without the bat's wings. The total weight of the vehicle was 75 lb (Myers 1902). Myers claimed that "hundreds of voyages have been made by myself and others" in this craft, and a photo shows the Sky-Cycle after a "20 miles voyage" in 1893 (Myers 1902).

In 1901, Talbot reported that the gas bag of Myers's Sky-Cycle was "39 feet in length..., 16 feet in diameter, and is inflated with 4,000 cubic feet of hydrogen gas." But Phillips says that it was 49 ft long (2009, 49). It was said to be "capable of carrying a weight of 200 lbs" (Talbot 1901, 344). Note that by ascribing the gas to a specific lift of 70 lb per 1,000 cu ft, the gross lift would have been 280 lb, and that would imply an empty weight of 80 lb.

Performance-wise, some very different numbers have been published. According to Talbot (1901), "the average velocity is eleven miles an hour, but on one occasion it attained the high speed of twenty-three miles an hour" (345). But Basset (1963) notes that "Carl usually cruised at four to five miles an hour, and by working hard he could make ten miles an hour, but he could not maintain it. This means that calm weather was essential. If a breeze came up there was a good chance that the rider could not get back home" (381). Myers (1902, 33) claimed a speed of "five miles per hour by muscular power alone."

Cromwell Dixon (1892–1911), a mechanically inclined youth, began building an airship in 1905 (age 13!) and completed it, with familial support, in 1907. The design was quite similar to Myers's Sky-Cycle, which was exhibited at the St. Louis World's Fair (1904); Dixon is known to have been there (Phillips 2009, 49–50). Dixon's *Moon* made its first flight on June 10,

1. Muscle Power

1907. The *Moon* made several additional flights before it was destroyed in a park fire (51).

Dixon "salvaged the frame from the *Moon*" and purchased a "fifty-four-foot-long balloon made by the Carl Myers Balloon Farm." With these, he assembled a new Sky-Cycle (Phillips 2009, 51). On one flight, he "reached an altitude of 3,000 feet and sailed a distance of five miles" (52). In October 1907, he flew from St. Louis to Venice, Illinois, 10 miles (mi) in 25 minutes (53), corresponding to a ground speed of 24 mph (without knowing the wind speed and relative direction, his airspeed cannot be

A. Cromwell Dixon's Sky-Cycle (Hatch 1910, 46). (Author replaced heavy moiré pattern in background with gradient fill.) B. Close-up of the fourteen-year-old Cromwell Dixon pedaling his Sky-Cycle at the international balloon race in St. Louis, October 21, 1907 (Windsor 1907, 1329). The gas bag was 25 ft long and 10 ft in diameter, and the "complete outfit before inflation weighs 75 lbs." Windsor says he reached a height of 1,200 ft and flew 8 mi (1331). C. Cromwell Dixon at 17, with his mother. At this point, he had made "more than 275 successful flights in his home-made dirigible airship" (*TWM* 1910, 115). D. Airship stock offering by Mrs. Cromwell Dixon (Dixon 1908, 144).

Part I: Unconventional Power

calculated). However, "in a wind higher in velocity than ten miles an hour, Mr. Dixon found considerable difficulty in returning to his starting point" (Hatch 1910, 37).

Tony Norton designed and built the *Snoopy*, which flew in 1976. It carried 3,500 cu ft of helium and "reportedly can do 9 mph" (Allen 1977, 131).

The *White Dwarf* airship was designed and built by Bill Watson from 1984 to 1985. It flew 58 mi in 1985 but was put in storage and not flown again until 2000. In its construction, full advantage was taken of modern materials—a polyurethane-coated nylon envelope, an open-framework aluminum alloy (2024 T3 and 7075 T6) gondola, and a Dacron-sheathed Kevlar suspension. Its teardrop-shaped (per photos) envelope had a length of 48 ft and a maximum diameter of 17 ft. Its lift was derived from 6,200 cu ft of helium, and it had an empty weight of 140 lb. The maximum takeoff weight was just 390 lb (Gleason 2019). (This corresponds to an assumed specific lift of 62.9 lb per 1,000 cu ft of helium.)

It used pedal power to produce, "via 4:1 gearing and plastic chain drive," about 10 lb of cruise thrust for a cruise speed of 6–7 mph.[2] Its maximum level speed was 12 mph.[3]

The spruce-and-Styrofoam propeller was two-bladed and could be tilted for vertical thrust (Gleason 2019).

In 1991, the engineer Graham Dorrington "pedaled Britain's first human-powered airship from Southampton to the Isle of Wight" (Wertheim 2004). Subsequently, Dorrington's students at the University of Southampton built an 18 m long airship with 165 cu m of helium lift, which first flew in May 1992. Pedal-powered, the *D2* traveled "at a sedate 8 mph." In November 1992, it made 7 mph in a 6 mi there-and-back-again flight (Southampton 1995a, 1995b).

"On 28 September 2008, Frenchman Stephane Rousson attempted to become the first person to cross the English Channel [34 mi wide] in a pedal-powered airship.... He ... made it roughly three-quarters of the way across before deciding to give up, after winds shifted and increased" (Khoury 2012, 623). His *Zeppy-1* (not to be confused with his *Zeppy-3*) had 4,591 cu ft of helium and achieved a maximum airspeed of 22 mph (624). A video shows that the pilot-cyclist is completely exposed and that the pedaling apparatus drives two propellers (Rousson 2007).[4]

We backtrack now to consider Konstantin Danilewski's 1899 airship design. Nowadays, this would be called a hybrid airship, as its buoyant lift was not quite sufficient to support its takeoff weight. Its gas bag was oriented so that its long dimension was vertical to minimize air resistance during ascent (or descent). (He also intended to use a double-pointed gas bag but was unable to do so.) "Underneath the envelope was a rectangular 'frame' ... with louvers which could be opened or closed as needed to assist ascent or inhibit descent." Below the frame was the pilot's "trapeze," and there were pedal-powered, pivotable propellers on either side of him (Akimov 2019, 41–43, 277–279).

Danilewski stated that the "propulsion was directed at the will of the aeronaut upward, downward, forward or backwards by simply turning a handle" (Akimov and Welker 2019, 250, 254). However, he acknowledged that it was "not at all suited for horizontally advancing powered flight" because of the "enormous resistance to oncoming air on its side surface" (252, 255). Hence, he recommended that the propeller just be used to provide upward or downward thrust, and the louvers could be set at an angle to the vertical so that the diverted air provided a horizontal thrust (252, 255).

History—Airplanes

There are three forms of takeoff for a heavier-than-air craft capable of muscle-powered flight: unassisted takeoff, takeoff assisted by externally stored pilot power, and takeoff by any other means—for example, a catapult launch. To purists, only the first form of takeoff is acceptable. Moreover, "minimum altitude [above the takeoff point] and duration criteria" may be imposed by contest organizers (Reay 1977, 12–13, citing Helmut Haessler).

In 1784, Karl Friedrich Meerwein calculated that the "wing area necessary to support a man" was 11.7 square meters (sq m), and later, Otto Lilienthal accepted this figure for "a machine with an all-up weight of 91 kg" (Reay 1977, 22).

Early, unsuccessful proposals generally took the form of an ornithopter—that is, the would-be aviator used his arms to flap wings. (Flapping propulsion, human or machine powered, is covered in chapter 11.)

William Gehrhardt's *Cycloplane*, with seven stacked wings (heptaplane), managed to get 2 ft up in July 1923. This was "the first attested flight by a human-powered aircraft." However, the *Cycloplane* collapsed on its next attempt (Hush-Kit 2021).

A more long-lasting success came 12 years later. "Starting with a glider of 150 kg empty weight, Helmut Haessler produced a man-powered aircraft with an empty weight of 34 kg"; the pilot weighed 65 kg (Reay 1977, 96). He pedaled from a reclining position, and the pedaling apparatus was connected to the propeller by a belt drive, which increased transmission efficiency at the price of requiring "replacement following every six flights" (93–94).

Part I: Unconventional Power

His *Mufli* airplane first flew in August 1935, reaching a height of 1 m and covering 120 m in 17 seconds. Later the same month he achieved a height of 4–5 m in a 220 m, 21-second flight (Reay 1977, 97). However, *Mufli* benefited from a catapult takeoff (Grosser 1981, 10).

On November 9, 1961, a Southampton University team achieved the first human-powered takeoff; their *SUNPAC* flew 64 m in eight seconds (Reay 1977, 164). "The *SUNPAC* could reach take-off velocity of 9.14 m/sec in a distance of 90 meters." It then climbed slowly to its cruising altitude. The maximum flight length achieved was 622 m (170). The *Hatfield Puffin* set a new record in 1962, 911 m at an average height of 2 m (Grosser 1981, 35). Neither plane could turn easily.

In 1977, the *Gossamer Condor* was able to fly a 1.15 mi figure-eight course and thus win the first Kremer Prize. It achieved a speed of 10.82 mph (Grosser 1981, 145); in 1978, pilot Bryan Allen could pedal at 0.31 hp for 2.5 hours (168).

The *Gossamer Albatross II* (the backup aircraft for the *Gossamer Albatross*) during a test flight at NASA's Dryden Flight Research Center, Edwards, CA, photographed March 20, 1980. https://www.nasa.gov/image-detail/gossamer-albatross-5/ (courtesy NASA).

1. Muscle Power

The first human-powered airplane to cross the English Channel was the *Gossamer Albatross* in 1979. The current distance record is held by Kanellos Kanellopoulos in the MIT *Daedalus 88*, which flew from Iraklion to Santorini (71.53 mi) in 1988 (FAI 2024). The current duration record is held by Lois McCallin in a Michelob *Light Eagle* (37:38 in 1987; Wilson 1986a, 356). The current speed record is held by Holger Rochelt in the *Musculair 2* (27.5 mph in 1985; Kenealey 2018; FAI 2024). It had a wing loading of 65.4 N/m^2, an empty weight of 25 kg, and a 32.5 aspect ratio (Schoeberl 2004).

The only airplane powered by *two* humans to have flown was the HPA (Hertfordshire Pedal Aeronauts) *Toucan*, but its maximum flight length in the Kremer Prize competition was 640 m (Hush-Kit 2021).

History—Human-Powered Helicopters

There was a prolonged competition among many institutions to build a human-powered helicopter that could win the American Helicopter Society's Sikorsky Prize. This required staying aloft for 60 seconds and reaching a height of 3 m. Most entries failed to lift off the ground.

The two-rotor, 44 kg *Da Vinci III* (Cal Poly San Luis Obispo) was able to fly for 7.1 seconds and reach an altitude of 20 centimeters (cm) in 1989 (Gavaghan 1989). In 1994, the four-rotor, 38 kg *Yuri I* (Nihon University) flew for 19.46 seconds and ascended to the same height (Hirschberg 2012).

Progress after that was slow until the prize money was increased in 2009. In 2011, the University of Maryland's four-rotor *Gamera II* was able to stay aloft for 50 seconds (Hirschberg 2012).

The prize was finally won in 2013 by the University of Toronto and Aerovelo's *Atlas* piloted by Todd Reichert; it flew for 64 seconds and achieved an altitude of 3.3 m (AHMEC 2022). The *Atlas* was a quad-rotor design, with a rotor radius of 10.2 m and a weight of 55 kg. The designers estimated that for a one-minute flight with an 80 kg pilot, the average power output required was 550 W. Reichert's actual power output averaged "just over 700 Watts" (Aerovelo 2016a).

Analysis

Power Requirements

The power requirements for a human-powered airship or airplane are the same as those for a conventionally powered craft if the airspeed is the

Part I: Unconventional Power

same. Just substitute *human muscle power* for *engine power*. But it is likely that because of the limits on human power, the achievable airspeed will be much lower.

DE LÔME AIRSHIP

I have modeled de Lôme's airship using my standard aerodynamic model (appendix 1). With the forebody and aftbody both set as tangent ogive shapes, the volume came to 3,488 cu m (versus 3,454 cu m for the actual airship). Assuming flight at 1,000 ft (geometric) and an International Standard Atmosphere (ISA), an airspeed of 5 mph (2.24 m/s) required a propulsive power of 0.37 hp (278 W).[5]

The propulsive efficiency of de Lôme's propulsion system is unknown, but in 1948, Brian Worley assumed that a human-powered airplane would have a propulsive efficiency of 75% (Reay 1977, 127). If applied to the de Lôme model, the required total human power output at 5 mph would be 0.5 hp (371 W). If four sailors were pedaling at one time, each would need to produce 0.125 hp.

ECONOMIES OF SCALE

De Lôme's choice of a relatively large airship powered by four or eight sailors possibly reflected hope for an economy of scale. The buoyant lift is proportional to the hull volume, but the drag force should scale with the surface area of the hull, and thus (for airships of congruent shape) with the two-thirds power of the volume. A large enough human-powered airship thus could carry passengers or sustain a longer powered flight.

For example, consider the K-class military airship of World War II. The *K-14* had a theoretical envelope volume of 425,000 cu ft (12,035 cu m) and thus was much larger than any of the historical human-powered airships. It had two 425 hp (at 1,775 rpm) engines, and its maximum speed of 67.5 knots (77.68 mph) was reached at 1,740 rpm (Goodyear 1943, 2–3). Assuming that the power requirement scales with the cube of the airspeed, propelling the *K-14* at 20 mph would require an engine power of just 14.5 hp and, at 10 mph, 1.81 hp. The normal crew of the airship was 10 men (assumed to weigh 175 lb each) (18). So if a *K-14* were modified for pedal power, eight men, each producing 0.25 hp (186 W), could achieve a speed of slightly more than 10 mph, assuming that the pedaling apparatus did not significantly reduce the propulsive efficiency.

Moreover, the *K-14*, converted to pedal power, would not need the engine (1,858 lb), starting system (84 lb), outriggers and engine nacelles (741.1 lb), fuel system (348 lb), fuel (3,930 lb), or main engine oil (390 lb),

1. Muscle Power

and as a civilian airship, it would not need its 1,620 lb of armament. There would be some increase in the weight of the engine accessories (238.1 lb), which presumably include the transmission to account for the pedaling apparatus, but it is clear that there would be a net reduction in weight. This would allow for more pedalers, if desired, or for paying passengers.

I am not proposing that anyone is going to build a human-powered airship as large as the *K-14*; I am just using this to show that economies of scale can exist.

WHITE DWARF

I modeled the *White Dwarf* as having a slightly ellipsoid (almost hemispherical) forebody (21% of the length)[6] and a tangent ogive aftbody, giving it a volume of 6,196 cu ft. With my standard aerodynamic model, at 1,000 ft and 6 mph, the required propulsive power is 0.04 hp (28 W). Assuming a 75% propulsive efficiency, the required muscle power is 0.05 hp (37 W). If the speed is increased to 12 mph, the required propulsive power is 0.29 hp (217 W), and the required muscle power is 0.39 hp (290 W). The biggest uncertainty in the calculation is the proper rigging factor (ratio of airship drag to bare hull drag); my standard model uses a factor of two.

Also, photos show the *White Dwarf* flying at altitudes very close to the ground. At 100 ft and 12 mph, my model predicts that required muscle power is increased to 0.40 hp (297 W), but it doesn't take ground effect into account. Flying close to the ground reduces the lift-induced drag (Reay 1977, 129).

AIRPLANES

Required power curves (power vs. airspeed) are available for the Bossi-Bonomi and Haessler-Villinger airplanes (Reay 1977, 127). McIntyre (2016) provides required specific power (W/kg) curves for the *Gossamer Condor, Gossamer Albatross, Daedalus 88, Monarch, Musculair 1, Betterfly, Velair 89*, and *Airglow*. As is typical for airplanes, there is an airspeed corresponding to the minimum required power (and minimum drag force).

Human Power Output

The problem is that humans can output only very limited power for a very limited time. The longer the period, the smaller the average output.

PHYSIOLOGICAL CONSIDERATIONS

Muscles make use of several different fuels. The fast-acting fuels are adenosine triphosphate (ATP) and phosphocreatine (PCr). ATP is

Part I: Unconventional Power

used directly, and PCr is used to replenish ATP. They are anaerobic fuels; the muscles do not require oxygen to use them. "Each muscle fiber stores enough ATP for about 2 to 5 seconds of all-out effort and enough PCr ... for about a further 10 seconds of ATP effort" (Wilson 2004, 52).

Carbohydrates (glucose and glycogen) may be burned aerobically (requiring oxygen) or anaerobically. Of the carbohydrates, glycogen is more important than glucose, as it is stored in the muscle (Wilson 2004, 53–56).

The aerobic processing occurs primarily in slow oxidative (SO, type I) muscle fibers. These contract slowly and can't exert much force, but "are able to contract repeatedly without fatigue" (Wilson 2004, 57–58).

Like carbohydrates, fats also serve as muscle fuels. They are metabolized slowly and aerobically, primarily by SO fibers (Wilson 2004, 52, 56).

Fast glycolytic (FG, type IIb) muscle fibers primarily rely on anaerobic metabolism. These fibers can contract quickly and exert large forces. (The third type of fiber, fast oxidative glycolytic, is intermediate in character.)

Anaerobic metabolism is much less energetically efficient and results in the buildup of lactate (Wilson 2004, 58). The lactate threshold is the exertion level at which lactate is produced faster than it is consumed, so lactate blood levels rise (Allen et al. 2019, 353). If it is exceeded for a prolonged period, the adverse symptoms of acidosis manifest themselves. These include muscle pain, fatigue, nausea and vomiting. Ultimately, the individual is unable to continue the exercise. There is individual variation in both the exertion level corresponding to the lactic acid threshold and the tolerable lactate blood level.

Besides the quantity of the different fuels, the proportions and thickness of the different muscle fibers, and the person's lactic acid threshold and tolerance, human exertion is also limited by oxygen uptake, cardiovascular status, body temperature, and ultimately, the need for sleep.

Oxygen uptake. If the rate of oxygen use is plotted against exercise intensity, it levels out at a value (VO_2max) that may vary among individuals. "For a non-athletic person, ... [it] is assumed to be about 50 ml/s [milliliters per second] or 3 L/min ([liters per minute] approximately 60 percent that of an elite competitor)." However, endurance is more likely to be limited by the lactic acid threshold than by VO_2max (Wilson 2004, 67–68, 75).

1. Muscle Power

Body temperature. Even aerobic metabolism is only about 25% efficient; the rest of the muscle fuel energy is converted into heat (Wilson 2004, 109). (In the Daedalus study, "the mechanical efficiencies among the 25 athletes tested ranged between 18.0 and 33.7%" [Bussolari and Nadel 1989].)

In still air, we are cooled mostly by the evaporation of sweat, but evaporation is slower if humidity is high. However, this is not a panacea, as perspired water must be replaced. For work done indoors at 55°F, it has been estimated that a heat load of 586 W, corresponding to about 325 W/m^2 skin area, can be sustained as a result of perspiration and free convection of air (Wilson 2004, 114).

For the Daedalus flight, it was estimated that the 68 kg pilot, doing 225 W of mechanical work, would produce 900 W of metabolic power. Of the 675 W of heat generated, 60 W was expected to be lost by radiation and convection, leaving over 600 W to be lost by evaporation of sweat. It was calculated that the pilot would "lose about 900 ml [milliliters] of water per hour. Since the ill effects of body dehydration begin to occur when the loss of body water exceeds 3% of body weight," and the expected flight duration was several hours, rehydration was necessary, and a rehydration rate of one liter (L) per hour (with fluid containing glucose and sodium) was proposed (Bussolari and Nadel 1989).

On some human-powered airships and airplanes, the pedalers are usually not inside a closed or even an open car but are completely exposed to the environment. Hence, they are further cooled by the forced convection created by the craft's motion. However, on the *Gossamer Albatross*, "Bryan Allen ... suffered from overheating ... because of insufficient through-ventilation and insufficient water" (Bussolari and Nadel 1989, 115).

It has been estimated that "a racing bicyclist producing 0.6 hp (450 W) emits heat at about 850 W/m^2" body surface area. But "heat generated at such a rate could be absorbed by air moving at about 3 m/s (7 mph)" (Bussolari and Nadel 1989, 115).

If heat production exceeds heat removal, the body temperature will increase. The time to crisis will depend on the net heat, the individual's weight, the specific heat (the amount of heat energy needed to raise the temperature of a unit mass by 1°C), and the elevation in temperature that the individual can tolerate (Bussolari and Nadel 1989, 114).

At high altitudes (or latitudes), heat loss may be an issue, and the apparent wind created by the vehicle motion results in wind chill (Bussolari and Nadel 1989, 116).

Part I: Unconventional Power

Endurance training. This training type results in "increases in the mitochondrial content and respiratory capacity of the muscle fibers" and therefore greater reliance on fat than glycogen as an energy source (Holloszy and Coyle 1984). It also results in an increase in the size of the ventricles of the heart (Parry-Williams and Sharma 2020). Finally, it reduces resistance in respiratory canals and "increases lung elasticity and alveolar expansion" (Khosravi et al. 2013). In 1992, Wilson reported that 24 40-minute endurance training sessions spread over three weeks increased critical power (sustained power) from 196 W to 255 W in "untrained male college students" (Wilson 2004, 46).

Power and Duration

Human power output may be measured directly by an ergometer. Most ergometers are of the pedaling type, but there are also those intended to mimic rowing, skiing or swimming (Wilson 2004, 38).

A standard test protocol calls for the subject to pedal at a constant rate (for constant power) until exhaustion.

Reay (1977, 143) measured cycling power indirectly by combining road race speeds with drag measurements in wind tunnels. More recently, it has become possible to directly compare racing times and power output if the competitors ride bikes equipped with crank-based power meters.

Power data are sometimes expressed in watts per kg of body mass, implicitly assuming that power is linearly proportional to muscle mass and muscle mass to body mass. Thus, Wilson (2004, 15) suggests that for a short duration, a cycling champion could produce 6–10 W/kg (an outdated figure).

Perhaps the first serious study of human power output was by Oskar Ursinus in the late 1930s, and it was specifically directed at achieving human-powered flight (Reay 1977, 90–91). This was followed by work by Nonweiler and Wilkie in the 1950s. Nonweiler, using an indirect method, reported an average power for an amateur road racing cyclist of 0.343 kW over about 23 minutes and 0.229 kW for about 4.5 hours (Reay 1977, 144). Wilkie examined power output in running, rowing and cycling (with or without also turning a hand crank) over periods of up to 100 minutes; a champion cyclist was able to sustain about 0.5 hp (0.373 kW) over the latter period (Reay 1977, 266).

A much more recent study (Valenzuela et al. 2022) of training and competition performance by professional cyclists from the men's World

1. Muscle Power

Tour and Pro Tour from 2013 to 2021 revealed the following values for mean maximal power (see tables 1–2, 1–3A, 1–3B):

	Table 1–2: Power Output of Top Male Professional Cyclists, by Percentile Group								
	Power-to-Mass Ratio (W/kg)					*Maximal Mean Power (W)*			
Time	Pctle 10	Pctle 25	Pctle 50	Pctle 75	Pctle 90	Pctle 10	Pctle 25	Pctle 50	Pctle 75	Pctle 90
5 s	15.71	16.59	17.99	19.78	20.83	995	1,091	1,202	1,344	1,529
1 min	8.87	9.51	10.10	10.74	11.33	580	617	677	744	820
5 min	6.52	6.75	7.06	7.34	7.65	432	450	472	503	531
20 min	5.47	5.79	6.03	6.29	6.59	369	387	403	426	453
60 min	4.71	4.91	5.15	5.47	5.76	310	329	350	368	398
120 min	4.23	4.47	4.70	4.91	5.12	282	296	312	330	355
180 min	4.00	4.27	4.45	4.64	4.84	266	281	297	315	338
240 min	3.83	4.03	4.24	4.42	4.63	252	268	284	298	325
(Valenzuela et al. 2022, quoted in Bonnevie-Svendsen 2022)										

The same research group collected similar data for professional female cyclists (Mateo-March et al. 2022).

At a somewhat less stratospheric performance level, there is data from Cycling Analytics. These data are from male and female "serious cyclists," all have power meters, "and about half of Cycling Analytics users race regularly" (Johnstone 2018). This group, in my opinion, would be the most likely to consider a personal human-powered airship or airplane if the price were right, and time aloft would probably be a half hour or more. Note that 95% of the 20-minute average power is considered a good estimate for functional threshold power, the power sustainable for one hour.

Part I: Unconventional Power

Table 1-3A: Cycling Analytics Power Data, Males						
	Power-to-Mass Ratio (W/kg)			Average Power over Duration (Watts)		
	Pctle 10	Pctle 50	Pctle 90	Pctle 10	Pctle 50	Pctle 90
5 s	7.66	12.14	16.74	601	930	1254
1 min	4.48	6.49	8.55	354	491	627
5 min	3.21	4.48	5.73	261	339	416
20 min	2.71	3.80	4.86	222	286	349
95% 20 min	2.58	3.61	4.61	211	272	332

Table 1-3B: Cycling Analytics Power Data, Females						
	Power-to-Mass Ratio (W/kg)			Average Power over Duration (Watts)		
	Pctle 10	Pctle 50	Pctle 90	Pctle 10	Pctle 50	Pctle 90
5 s	6.09	10.03	14.27	391	632	860
1 min	3.76	5.91	7.48	240	352	455
5 min	3.10	4.29	5.43	187	256	324
20 min	2.70	3.80	4.61	168	223	278
95% 20 min	2.56	3.61	4.38	160	212	264

To put these numbers in perspective, on the *Musculair 2* at full power, the pilot produced 315 W (0.422 hp), propelling the airplane at about 12 m/s (26.8 mph). The minimum flying speed (to avoid stall) was 10 m/s (22.4 mph), requiring 250 W (0.335 hp; Schoeberl 2004).

According to Langford et al. (1986, table 4), the *Daedalus* was expected to require 210 W (0.28 hp) for its design speed of 7 m/s, whereas the *Gossamer Albatross* required 246 W (0.33 hp) to fly at 5 m/s.

The relationship between power and duration of effort was once firmly believed to follow an offset hyperbolic curve: power (critical power) times duration equals a constant. The critical power was characterized as the low-power, long-duration asymptote, reflecting fat-burning aerobic power. However, Drake et al. (2024) assert that "the hyperbolic model is now the focus of a heated debate in the literature

1. Muscle Power

because it unrealistically represents efforts that are short (< 2 min) or long (> 15 min)."

An alternative is a power law model: this postulates that the power output is ST^{E-1}, where S is a positive constant, E is between zero and one, and T is the duration. Drake et al. (2024, fig. 9) asserted that this model was a better predictor of race time for cyclists than the hyperbolic model but unfortunately didn't state the best fit values for S and E.

An eyeball comparison of the two models shows that, unlike the hyperbolic model, there is no low-power asymptote with the power law model. Wilson's (2004, fig. 2.4) constant-power-output duration-to-exhaustion plot[7] plainly lacks an asymptote. Eyeballing

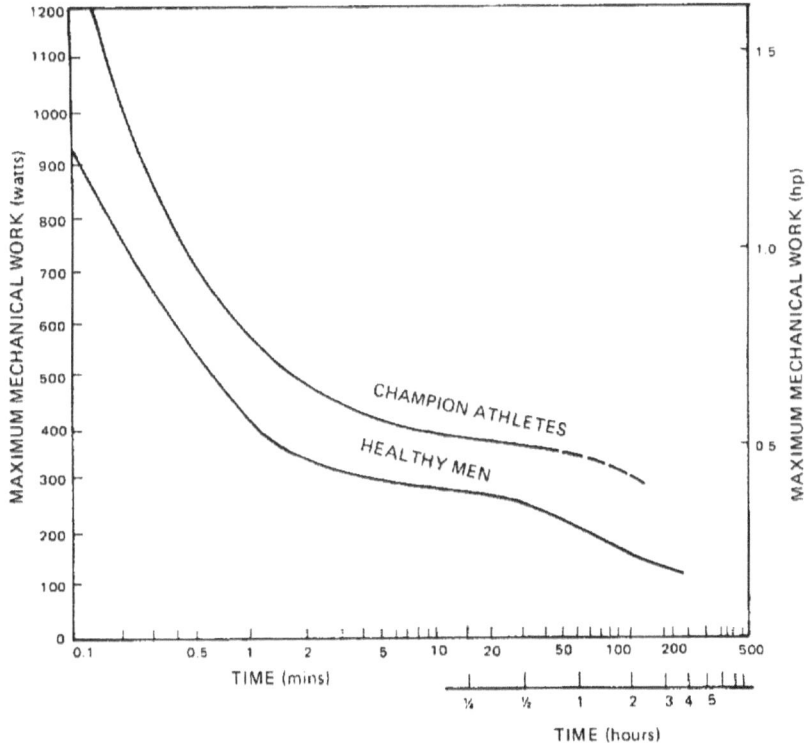

"Maximum efforts of healthy fit men and champion athletes" from a 1973 NASA report (Parker and West 1973, fig. 18-15). This understates modern capabilities (and ignores women), but the shape of the curve is essentially unchanged. Cp. Roth (1966, fig. 17), based on a similar graph in a 1962 NASA report (also used by Wilson 2004) but adding metabolic rate and oxygen consumption.

Part I: Unconventional Power

this plot, for an effort of one hour, power output is in the range of 200 W (healthy men) to 500 W (elite athletes).

Campbell (1990, 7) suggested a logarithmic decline in power with duration: the power output (hp) of human legs when pedaling was $0.53 - 0.13 \times \log_{10}$ (t min) for t = 1 – 100 minutes. In contrast, for "an adequately fed 35-year-old male European laborer," presumably making use primarily of the arm muscles, his equation was $0.35 - 0.92 \times \log(t)$ for t = 4 – 480 minutes.

Method of Work. The early human-powered submarines (e.g., the Fulton *Nautilus*, the Bushnell *Turtle*, and the eponymous *H. L. Hunley*) used a hand crank to turn the propeller (USSS 1963, 2). However, leg muscles are stronger than arm muscles. Windstream once sold a generator that could be cranked either by hand or by foot pedals. Hand cranking yielded 50 W and foot pedaling 80 W (AENews 2008). Wilson (1986b) asserts that "a person can generate four times more power ... by pedaling than hand cranking."

An additional power boost may be achievable by using arms as well as legs, as shown by Ursinus and Wilkie, but Reay (1977) suggests that this depends on whether the leg action exhausts the "heart and lung capacity" (90, 151, 266).[8] A 1978 study indicated that "for periods of up to a minute, 11–18% more power could be obtained with hand and foot cranking than with foot cranking alone" (Wilson 2004, 84–85).

Depending on the length of the flight, the power benefit of arm cranking might be outweighed by the weight cost of the hand crank mechanism. In addition, the hands may be needed for steering or other flight controls.

Turning our attention back to pedaling, "there is virtually no difference" in power production between upright and recumbent pedaling (Wilson 2004, 85). There is some variation in power production as a function of saddle height and crank-arm length (88–91).

For airship and airplane engines, an important parameter is *specific power*, the maximum sustained power output divided by the engine weight. The analogous parameter for a human-powered craft is the individual's power output (sustainable over the expected flight duration) divided by body weight.

The Daedalus team required that candidate pilots have a "VO_2max on cycle ergometer of approximately 70 ml/min/kg" body weight and be "capable of producing at least 3.3 watts per kg body weight for five to six hours" (Dorsey 1990, 198).

When comparing human-powered aerial vehicles to those with other power sources, the question of which weights should be included

1. Muscle Power

in calculating the specific power is significant. The transmission system and propeller are certainly part of the propulsion system, but if they are counted against the human-powered vehicle, they should be counted against the reference vehicle, too. The same may be said of the weight of the structural members used to support the propulsion system.

WEIGHT

Weight is the bugbear of all aerial vehicles, and an important design parameter for airplanes is the *wing loading*, the ratio of the takeoff weight[9] to the planform area of the wings. While a low ratio is desirable, too low a value may be the result of unduly weakening the airplane structure; this was an issue with several versions of the *Gossamer Condor* (Grosser 1981, 95, 136).

Weight reductions could be effectuated by using materials with high specific strength or stiffness. Historically, steel was replaced with aluminum alloys and later with carbon fiber composites (as on the *Musculair*). Redesigning components could also accomplish weight reductions. For example, on the *Musculair*, the pedal power train weighed "only 450 g (in racing bicycles 1.2 kg is normal)" (Schoeberl 2004, 3).

2

Steam Power

History—Airships

Sir George Cayley proposed a steam-powered airship in 1816. He couldn't make up his mind whether it was better to propel it with propellers or flapping wings, and hence he gave it both types of propulsors. It would have had an ellipsoidal gas bag and a boat-type gondola hanging by an external, net-like suspension (Kelly 2006, 4–5).

Cayley (1816, 326) envisioned a hydrogen gas bag with a length of 144 yards (yd) and a surface area of 11,880 square yards and attributed to it a gross lift of 163,000 lb. He estimated that a single-cylinder, 100 hp steam engine would weigh 7,210 lb, consisting of an engine (3,210 lb) and a 400 square foot (sq ft) tubulated boiler (4,000 lb). In addition, he figured that the fuel requirement would be 1,500 lb plus 5 lb of coal per horsepower-hour (hp-h), and the water requirement would be 3,000 lb plus 30 lb per hp-h. Thus, for an hour's operation, the total weight of the engine, boiler, fuel and water was 15,210 lb. Cayley speculated that the water "can be recovered again for the use of the engine to pass within the double coats of the balloon," which would provide an "extensive ... cooling surface" (327).

Twenty years later, Cayley (1837, 11) more pessimistically reported that Goldworthy Gurney had constructed steam carriages with a combined weight of the engine and boiler running 200 lb per hp. As for coke and water, Cayley allowed 30 lb for the constant quantity and then 10 lb of coke and 60 lb of water per hp-h. Thus, the combined powerplant, fuel and water weight for an hour flight would be 300 lb per hp. For a 100 hp engine, that would be 30,000 lb, about twice his 1816 estimate.

Cayley (1837, 12) nonetheless proposed a design for an airship with a gross lift (from hydrogen) of about 170,000 lb and an empty weight (**not** including the powerplant and propeller) of about 66,000 lb. He thought it might be capable of 14 mph.

Cayley's dreams were partially realized by the engineer Henri Giffard (1825–1882). Giffard, raised in a "poor bourgeois family," developed an early

2. Steam Power

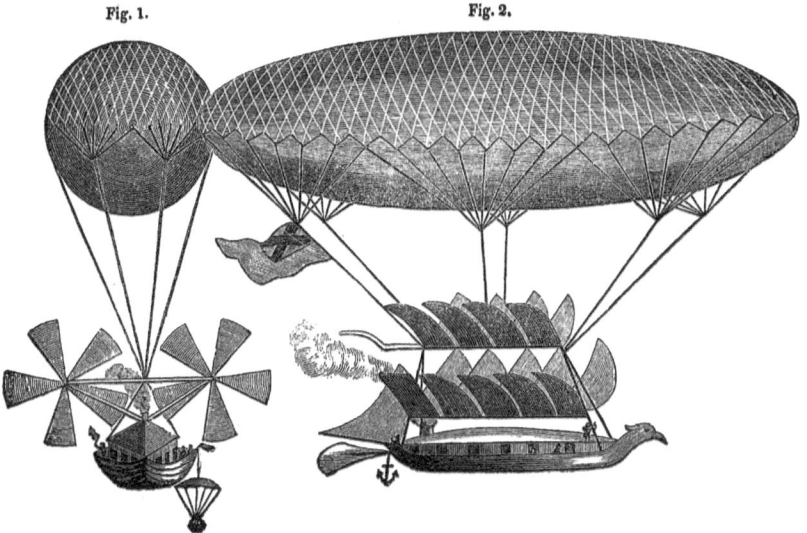

Cayley's proposed steam-powered airship (Cayley 1816; as reprinted in Cayley 1837, plate 2).

interest in steam locomotives. At age 17, he "entered the railway workshops," and in 1849, he designed and built his first steam engine, which weighed 45 kg (99 lb) and produced 3 hp. In 1850, he designed the steam injector, the device that was to make him a rich man, but he didn't patent it until 1858 (Ernouf 1884).[1]

In the meantime, he had become interested in aviation. "On August 20, 1851," he "took out a patent for the application of steam to aerial navigation." In the patent, he proposed that his "dirigible aerostat" have the shape of "a cylinder equipped with two points, the junction of which occurs gradually and without sudden deviation" (Ernouf 1884).

Giffard made his first powered flight from the Paris Hippodrome on September 24, 1852. He told *La Presse*, "The wind blew with quite great violence; I did not think for a single moment of fighting directly against him, the strength of the machine would not have allowed me to do so. This was planned in advance and demonstrated by calculation. But I was able to perform various circular movement and lateral deviation maneuvers with the greatest success" (Ernouf 1884). According to his barometer, he reached an elevation of 1,800 m. He landed in "the town of Elancourt, near Trappes (Seine-et-Oise)."

According to the reporter's account published the following day,

Part I: Unconventional Power

Giffard's original airship had a length of 44 m, a maximum diameter of 12 m, and a gas capacity of 2,500 cu m (Tissandier 1872, 3–4). He could not afford hydrogen and had to make do with "lighting gas" (mostly methane) instead (Ernouf 1884). This is confirmed by the account Giffard gave to *La Presse*: He said that with pure hydrogen gas, its gross lift would have been 2,800 kg, but he used lighting gas, giving a lift of just 1,800 kg (Tissandier 1872, 33).

Giffard provided a weight breakdown for his airship: the gas bag with valves (320 kg); the "filet" (150 kg); the crossbeam, suspension ropes, and rudder (300 kg); the empty engine and boiler (150 kg); the water and coal in the boiler (and firebox) at time of departure (60 kg); the engine frame, stretcher, boards, movable wheels (for transporting the engine on land), water and coal tarpaulins (420 kg); the drag rope (80 kg); the pilot (70 kg); and the lift force required from the start (10 kg), for a total of 1,560 kg. He said that the remaining 248 kg (*sic*, 1800 − 1560 = 240) in useful lift should be allocated to water, coal and ballast (Tissandier 1872, 33–34).

As for the engine, it produced 3 hp (Tissandier 1872, 6). The boiler weight was 100 kg; the engine proper, 50; there was no condenser (32–33). The fuel used was "good quality coke" (32).

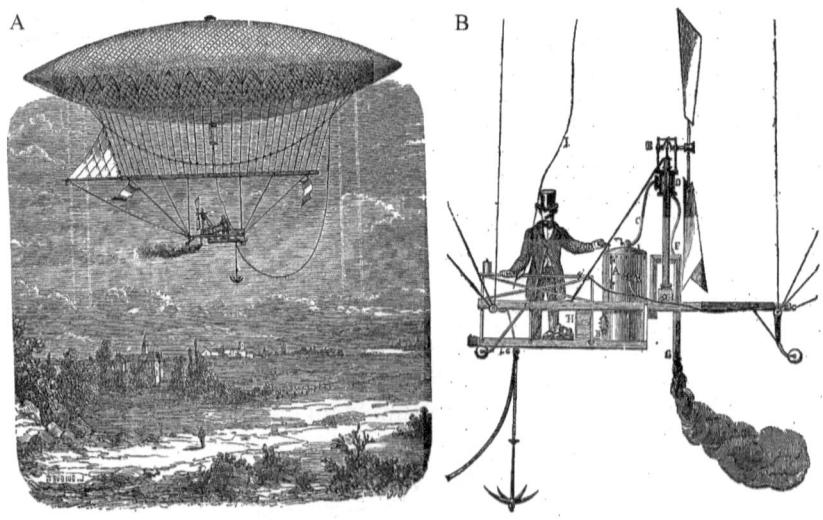

A. Giffard's 1852 airship (Tissandier 1872, 5). The original engraving appeared in *Merveilles de la Science*, de M. Louis Figuier. The artist was L. Guiget. B. Close-up view of Giffard's gondola, showing the pilot, boiler, engine, transmission, and propeller (Tissandier 1872, 7).

2. Steam Power

In 1855, he made a second attempt, having enlarged the gas bag to a length of 70 m and a capacity of 3,200 cu m. This allowed him to take on a passenger, even though he was still using lighting gas (Ernouf 1884). The new airship had an "ovoid" shape (Tissandier 1872, 10). While he was "able to deviate from the wind direction" and to have the airship "hold its own" against the wind, he still "could not obtain absolute steering with this new engine, although stronger than the first" (Ernouf 1884; Tissandier 1872, 9–10).

The steam injector invention made Giffard a millionaire, and he produced hydrogen, a more buoyant gas, by the reaction of iron with sulfuric acid. He used this hydrogen in 1867 to inflate a "tethered steam [sic] balloon, measuring 5,000 cubic meters." In 1868, he advanced to one with a capacity of 12,000 cu m. Finally, in 1878, he erected and flew a tethered balloon of 25,000 cu m in volume, with a total weight of 14,000 kg. He used this to take 38 passengers at a time to a height of 500 m. While steam was not used to propel these balloons, a steam winch was used to return them to the ground (Ernouf 1884).

Giffard remained determined to build a large airship capable of lifting a "powerful machine" engine and thus render the craft capable "to overcome not only weak winds, but currents of average intensity." He was aware that sustained flight would require a continued supply of water for the boiler, and he thought of two ways to accomplish this: One was to use "a large surface condenser." The other was to burn the vented hydrogen (Ernouf 1884). However, in 1881, he lost all or most of his sight, and in 1882, he committed suicide.

The London publisher and banker Frederick Marriott (1805–1884) partnered with John Stringfellow and William Samuel Henson to form the Aerial Steam Transit Company in the 1840s. The goal of this company was to build a steam airplane, but this was unsuccessful (see next section). Marriott moved to San Francisco (Bluffield 2014, 1–2).

While the Aerial Steam Transit Company had failed, Marriott remained interested in aviation, incorporating the Aerial Steam Navigation Company in 1866. In 1869, his *Avitor Hermes Jr.* (or just *Avitor*), a hydrogen-lift airship, made an unmanned, tethered, 1 mi, circular test flight. The airship was 37 ft long and 14 ft wide, with a 1,360 cu ft gas bag, and it had a 1 hp steam engine (Skaarup 2012, 91; Bluffield 2014, 2). Different statistics were reported in the July 3, 1869, *San Francisco News Letter*: 28 ft long and 11 ft wide, with 5 ft wide delta wings on the forebody. However, it agreed regarding the gas capacity and empty weight (uninflated) of 84 lb. Once inflated, the net static lift was negative 4 to 10 lb—that is, it was

Part I: Unconventional Power

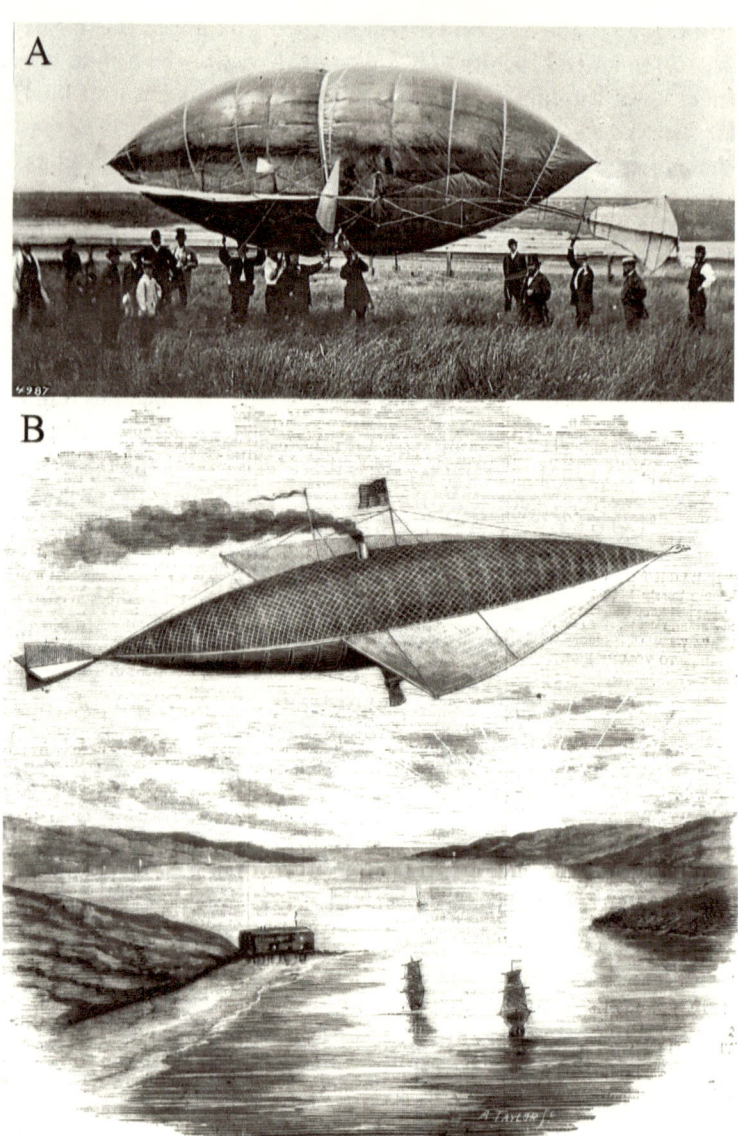

A. July 2, 1869, photograph of the *Avitor Hermes Jr.* courtesy of the University of Southern California Libraries and the California Historical Society. https://digitallibrary.usc.edu/asset-management/2A3BF-19G0Q1?FR_=1&W=1851&H=893. *B.* Artist's impression of the *Avitor* in free flight, from the cover illustration of the Sept. 3, 1869, issue of *English Mechanic and Mirror of Science.*

not fully buoyant but needed aerodynamic lift to take off. On its first flight, the air was still, and the reported speed of the airship was 5 mph (Martin 1935). The boiler carried 8 lb of steam (EMMS 1869).

In November 1869, Marriott received a patent on an aerial steam car. The patent depicted a spindle-shaped winged hull, and Marriott taught that "when fully inflated," it "does not contain sufficient gas to cause it to rise, but remains in its position until the propellers are started into operation." Thus, strictly speaking, the patent contemplated a hybrid airship. By 1881, Marriott had convinced himself that he could dispense with the gas bag entirely and rely entirely on steam-powered aerodynamic lift, but the Patent Office considered this notion implausible (Martin 1935, 318; for steam-powered airplanes, see the next section).

History—Airplanes

William Henson and John Stringfellow unsuccessfully attempted to fly an unmanned steam-powered airplane in 1847. Their one-cylinder engine was 100 pounds per square inch (psi) and provided a propeller thrust of about 5 lb. It burned alcohol, provided 0.5 brake horsepower (bhp), and weighed 12 lb. By 1848, they had been able to increase the power to 0.75 and decrease the weight to 9 lb. Stringfellow's 1868 Crystal Palace engine was more powerful (1 bhp) but weighed 13 lb (according to the Prize Award) or 16.25 lb (according to Kelly 2006, 14–15, 24).

In 1857, Felix du Temple de la Croix built a 1.5 lb (!) steam-powered model airplane that could take off and remain in the air. He went on to build a full-sized airplane, but it is unclear whether it was powered by steam or hot air, and it did not take off on its own or achieve sustained flight (Kelly 2006, 33–35).

Thomas Moy built an aerial steamer for tethered flight in the Crystal Palace. The single-cylinder, 140 psi engine produced 3 hp and weighed 80 lb. "The total weight of the craft was 214 lb which was about 1.25 lb per sq. ft of wing area." In 1875, "the maximum speed attained around the circular track was only 12 mph, and this was just enough to enable the 'aerial steamer' to lift off between 2 and 6 in. from the ground" (Kelly 2006, 40–41).

In the 1880s, the naval officer Alexander Fedorovich Mozhaiskii (1825–1890) made unsuccessful attempts to get a manned steam airplane aloft. Modern calculations suggest that for takeoff, it needed to reach 28.6 mph, and its engine was only capable of driving it to 15.6 mph. That said,

Part I: Unconventional Power

he demonstrated progress in improving the power-to-weight ratio of a mobile steam powerplant; his airplane carried two engines of 10 and 20 hp, respectively, and the total weight of both engines and boilers was 310 lb (Kelly 2006, 75).

The first manned flight of a steam-driven airplane was in 1890, by the engineer Clément Ader (1841–1925) in the Éole. His steam engine was 20 hp and connected to a multitubular boiler. Notably, it had a fuselage-mounted condenser, so it was capable of recycling its water. The total powerplant weight was 112 lb. With a pilot, the plane weighed 653 lb, and the wing loading was about 1.6 lb/ft^2 (Kelly 2006, 82–83, 86).

The astronomer and physicist Samuel Pierpont Langley (1834–1906) claimed to have wondered about the possibility of "artificial flight" since his childhood (Adler 1907, 17). While his unmanned *Aerodrome No. 5* relied on a catapult for takeoff, on its first flight in 1896, it "rose steadily..., increasing its height until it reached an altitude of about 80–100 ft before the power unit ran out of steam and the craft glided down." It had traveled horizontally 3,000 ft. It had a 1 hp engine and used petroleum as fuel (Kelly 2006, 91). His later *Aerodrome No. 6* had a 120 psi, 1.25 hp engine that "weighed in at 4.4 lb per hp." This airplane flew for "45 seconds and covered a distance of 3,900 ft" (92–93).

Johnson (1912, 131), without specifically identifying which Langley model he was thinking of, said that the engine was 1–1.5 hp, and the "weight of the complete plant" was 7 lb/hp. "The boiler was of the flash type, the steam pressure 100 to 150 [psi]."

Sir Hiram Maxim (1840–1916) is best known as the inventor of the machine gun. His two-engine steam biplane, with "an all-up weight of 8,000 pounds," was seriously damaged during its first test (1888) and not repaired. However, its engines were quite noteworthy. Each was a compound engine with 150 and 320 psi cylinders. Together they were rated at 360 hp (of which only about 130 hp was used for generating lift) and weighed 640 lb (Johnson 1912, 100–101). The water tube boiler, "with its casing and dome weighed just under 1,000 lb" (105).

H. H. Groves flew a model steam monoplane in 1916. Its significance is that it used a monotube (flash steam) boiler (Johnson 1912, 126). The advantage of such a boiler is that it is lighter in weight than a traditional boiler; the disadvantage is that there is no steam reserve if there is an interruption in the operation of the firebox.

It weighed just 3 lb, and its powerplant weighed half that. The propeller thrust was 10–12 ounces (oz). Its "soaring velocity" was "some 20 mph." (These imply an engine of 0.03–0.04 hp.) It was "capable of rising from the

2. Steam Power

ground under its own power," and "when hand launched it flew 150 yards." It ran on "benzoline" and carried fuel for 30 seconds of flight (Johnson 1912).

In 1933, William J. Besler flew a steam-powered biplane for a short flight (10–15 minutes). Multiple sources agree (with no dissents) that it had a two-cylinder, double-acting, 90° V piston engine with compound expansion, an oil burner, and a 500 ft monotube boiler. After that, it gets complicated (see table 2-1):

Table 2-1: Contradictory Specifications of Besler 1933 Steam Plane Powerplant	
Engine Power	90 hp (2, 6); 150 hp at 1,625 rpm (1, 4, 5, 9); "the propeller was driven directly at 1350 rpm" (7); 150 hp at 1,650 rpm (8)
Engine Weight	180 lb (1, 4, 5, 8, 9); 273 lb (6)
Burner Capacity	9 million Btu per cu ft firebox area (5)
Boiler	Doble Model F (2); ordinary working pressure 950 psi and steam temperature 750°F (3); 1,200 psi, water consumption 1,500 lb/h (5); feedwater preheated by exhaust steam (4); 650 psi and 399°C (750°F; 6); 1,200 psi and 800°F (8); 1,200 psi (9)
Condenser	99% water recovery (1, 4, 5) "Ten gallons are sufficient for an ordinary flight under reasonably cool weather conditions" (4).
Additional Powerplant Weight	485 lb (1, 5); 789 lb (for marine installation, 6); 300 lb (9).
References: (1) SPCN 1981; (2) FKP 2019b; (3) *SciAm* 1933; (4) Discovery 1933; (5) FKP 2019a; (6) Kelly 2006, 134; (7) Self 2022; (8) SCDSA 1934; (9) NASM 2024	

In a 1954 report to the government, Besler and Whitlock indicated that the Doble F engine used in the 1933 flight achieved an actual cycle efficiency (defined below) of slightly more than 20% with a pressure of 1,000 pounds per square inch gauge (psig; 40). With a pressure of 835 psig (and 875°F steam), the theoretical cycle efficiency was 30%,[2] and the actual cycle efficiency was 21.6% (45).

Despite the references to the high efficiency of the condenser, it has been asserted that for the flight demonstration, an automobile radiator was used rather than the condenser (FKP 2019a). A YouTube video copy of the original film footage of the flight (Airboyd 2013) shows steam venting as the airplane prepares for takeoff and as it lands. So, if the condenser was

Part I: Unconventional Power

installed, it obviously could not condense all the steam generated at those stages of flight. Hays (2015, 8) agrees.

The creator of the now-defunct Flying Kettle website commented, "It appears that Besler only flew the plane for a few short flights. After three years building it.... My steam car guru's opinion ... is that the condensation apparatus must have been inadequate, despite the explicit statements to the contrary, and that water consumption precluded longer flights."

Doble manufactured steam cars until 1932. Besler acquired the Doble patents and other assets and became the last commercial manufacturer of steam cars (Wise 1973, 87–88). During the 1930s, the Russians had at least 11 research and development projects for aviation steam turbines and purchased a Besler steam automobile "as a basis for designing a steam engine for aircraft." The projects didn't go well; the designed powerplants were too big and heavy to fit on the available airframes (Harrison 2003).

In 1934, Hüttner proposed equipping an airplane with a 2,500 hp steam turbine with a rotating boiler. Hüttner claimed that this would permit "a satisfactory ratio of weight to power," although the basis for this claim is unclear (Self 2022). Wrangham indicates that in a rotating water tube boiler, the water is "flung into the U-tubes by centrifugal force," so a feed pump and feed regulator are not needed. In addition, there is a "rapid rate of heat transmission" (Self 2008).

Rotating steam boilers were first developed in the United States in 1847, but then the rationale was that boiler explosions might be caused by "stresses set up by unequal thermal expansion" (Self 2008). (Self doubts that this was a significant problem and that the rotating boilers were at all safer.)

There is no indication that the Hüttner project was successful. Nonetheless, in 1938, Aero Turbines Ltd. designed another steam turbine with a rotating boiler, which they believed had "great possibilities as a power unit for aircraft" (Army Air Corps 1938, 38). The test unit was 30 hp with an alleged all-up weight of 60 lb for a W/P of just two (Kelly 2006, 136–137). A 1944 illustration depicts the exhaust steam as going to an external condenser. However, the same source contains text claiming first that the boiler, turbine and condenser are combined in a single unit and later that the boiler may be used as a condenser (Self 2008). I suspect that the all-up weight didn't actually include a condenser. In any event, their steam turbine was never incorporated into an airplane.

In 1942, the Breguét Aircraft Works installed a 1,200 hp steam turbine in an "experimental jet-propelled aeroplane.... The estimated speed of this aircraft was 310 mph but it has not been established whether it actually flew" (Kelly 2006, 138–139).

2. Steam Power

Historical Analyses of Airplane Steam Potential

Some preliminary development and design work for an airplane steam turbine powerplant was done by the U.S. Navy's Committee on Experimental Power in the 1920s (Wilson 1926). It concluded that to minimize weight, a flash boiler (no storage space for water or steam) had to be used. Also, the combustion chamber couldn't be insulated with firebrick; a steel-walled air jacket might be used instead. The boiler was intended to operate at 300–500 psi and 800°F–900°F. In one test, at 325 psig and 772°F, it evaporated 9,450 lb of water/hour with 80% efficiency. The committee estimated that the finished weight of the steam generator would be under 2 lb of generator weight per hp, and they contemplated that this would drive a turbine that would be 1 lb/hp.

The catch was the condenser weight. A wing-type airplane radiator then weighed about 0.3 lb/sq ft, but the putative steam powerplant required 11.5 times the cooling area per hp-h as an internal combustion engine. Why? The radiator for an internal combustion engine merely must keep the temperature within metallurgical limits (about 640 K/692°F for an aluminum alloy piston [Esfahanian et al. 2006], higher for a turbine blade). The radiator for a condensing steam engine must remove enough heat energy from the steam to convert it back to liquid form. Therefore, it was found to require over 3 lb/hp.

A typical airplane would not in fact have enough wing area, and hence there would also need to be a core-type radiator, which would increase drag as well as weight.

The conclusion was that a steam powerplant for airplane would have two to three times the weight of an internal combustion engine of the same power but be only half as fuel efficient.

In the 1930s, the Great Lakes Aircraft Corporation claimed that a 4,800 hp steam turbine plant could be built with the following component weights: steam generators (3,448 lb), turbine and gears (4,200 lb), condensers (3,468 lb), and auxiliary pumps and controls.[3] However, Burgess (1932) opined that the estimates were "unsubstantiated by comparison with existing power plants" and "exceedingly optimistic." For example, the "engine cooling system of the AKRON," which had eight gasoline engines of the same total power, weighed 3,208 lb, but the proposed condensers "have to dissipate a much greater quantity of heat at about the same temperature gradient."

Great Lakes also claimed a specific fuel consumption of 0.549 lb/hp-h at 2,986 hp and of 0.618 lb/hp-h at fuel power. To achieve the first value, the overall thermal efficiency would need to be 24.8%. Great Lakes claimed that the boiler efficiency was 90% and the "turbine efficiency" 74%. (The latter probably referred to the actual cycle efficiency as a percentage of the theoretical efficiency.) The Carnot theoretical efficiency for operation between 1,015 pounds per square inch absolute (psia; and 545°F) and 4 psia (153°F) was 38%. Ninety percent of 74% of 38% is 25.3%.

Burgess (1932) commented that "the estimated boiler efficiency seems very high, but it may be possible." As we will see, two decades later, Besler, a manufacturer of steam boilers, only assumed a boiler efficiency of 80%.

Besler 1954 Steam Powerplant Design for Airplanes

In the 1950s, the Besler Corporation designed steam powerplants for aeronautical use under a contract with the Office of Naval Research. Their intended purpose was not only to propel the airplane but also to control the boundary layer of air adhering to the airplane during flight and thus reduce drag (Besler and Whitlock 1954, 1). An airplane with four 200 hp propulsive engines (21–24) and two 100 hp boundary layer control blower engines (14) was contemplated.

We are going to examine this design closely because it is the product of an experienced steam car and boiler manufacturer, and it promised improvements in both thermal efficiency and the weight-to-power ratio. Moreover, the powerplant was actually constructed and bench tested.

The steam temperature was to be 780°F; the pressure, 1,200 psia for takeoff and 900 psia for cruising (Besler and Whitlock 1954, 3). Cruise was apparently 75% power (22). The theoretical Rankine cycle efficiency under takeoff conditions was 30.7%. Besler and Whitlock (1954) suggested that the actual cycle efficiency would be 72%[4] of the theoretical value—that is, 22.1%. They expected a boiler efficiency of 80%[5] for a gross overall efficiency of 17.7%. And if 5% of the power would be needed for auxiliaries (e.g., pumps), the net overall efficiency would be 16.8%.[6] If the energy content of the fuel was 19,000 Btu/lb (British thermal unit per pound), the specific fuel consumption would be 0.797 lb/hp-h (4).

The 1954 design was a two-cylinder, double-acting, V-type compound engine. "The crankcase is aluminum and the other parts are steel" (Besler and Whitlock 1954, 4). While the V configuration presents more frontal area (and thus would create more drag) than an in-line design, "the primary forces are inherently balanced" (5).

2. Steam Power

The steam generator was a "forced-circulation water-tube boiler" with a "combustion chamber" operating at ambient pressure and capable of producing 2,500 lb of steam per hour (Besler and Whitlock 1954, 7), but at cruise conditions (75% power), "the blowers are not operating, so the boilers would only evaporate 1500 pounds" (9).

The engine was expected to use water at a rate of 10 lb/hp-h (so, 2,000 lb/h; Besler and Whitlock 1954, 11). Condenser inlet pressure was 2 psig (3). "There were two all-aluminum condenser cores, with a total face area of 7.8 square feet, a depth of 3.5,"[7] and a total weight (including side plates and headers) of 57 lb[8]; in copper, the weight would have doubled. The heat load on the condenser was estimated at 966 Btu/lb steam or 1,932,000 Btu/h (9–11).

Both cores were of the staggered tube/continuous flat fin type, with four rows of seven tubes each per core and 12[9] fins (.006 in. thick) per inch. The tubes were .08 in. by .75 in. in cross section (i.e., flattened, with the long dimension parallel to the fluid flow), with tube walls .012 in. thick and tubes spaced ⅝ in. apart (Besler and Whitlock 1954, 9–11, 13).

The condensers themselves would be air-cooled. Based on data on a Cadillac Automobile Core with a face area of 1 sq ft, Besler assumed that the condensers would provide a heat transfer rate of 186,000 Btu/h per square foot of condenser face area if the temperature differential between the condenser inlet and the ambient air were 100°F and the airflow was 316 lb/min/ft². The necessary face area would then be 10.39 sq ft. If the saturated steam pressure in the condenser were 5 psig, the steam temperature would be 226°F, and if the ambient temperature were 90°F, the temperature differential would be 136°F. That would reduce the required face area to 7.64 sq ft (Besler and Whitlock 1954, 11–13).

The source of the airflow through the condenser face was not explicitly addressed, but presumably it was the result of the airplane's forward motion. If the airflow were 316 / 60 = 5.27 lb/s/ft², then at sea level under ISA conditions (air density 0.0765 lb/ft³), the required inlet speed is 68.89 ft/s (46.97 mph). At higher altitudes, the required inlet speed would be higher to compensate for the reduced density.

"The principal auxiliaries are the water pump, the fuel pump and the combustion air blowers" (Besler and Whitlock 1954, 16). The total dry weight of the 200 hp powerplant was expected to be 372 lb, including the engine (133.7 lb), boiler (102.8 lb), two condensers (total 57 lb), feedwater pump (20 lb) and piping (16 lb). To this, add 50 lb of water and 10 lb of lubricating oil for a wet weight of 432 lb and a W/P of 2.16 lb/hp (28).

Part I: Unconventional Power

Besler 1958 Design

Besler's 1958 report was somewhat vague about the preferred pressure and temperature of the engine. In figure 7, the top of the power curve is 880 psi,[10] 750°F, and a water rate of 10.65 lb/hp-h was experienced at 755°F (no pressure stated). Figure 9 presents test data at 690 psi and temperatures of 625°F–775°F. A preference was expressed for "operation at 800°F," presumed to allow a water rate of 10 (Besler 1958, 13), but elsewhere it was said that "it was found desirable to limit the steam temperatures to 700–720°F … as cylinder lubricating oil with high temperature ability obtainable some years ago was not located for these test runs" (7). Because of that limitation, the fuel consumption was slightly higher than expected: 0.812 lb/hp-h instead of the previously estimated 0.797 lb/hp-h, and allowing 4% for auxiliary load, fuel consumption increases to 0.8475 lb/hp-h (13).

There were minor changes in the weight breakdown. According to Besler's 1958 report, the principal component weights were the engine (134 lb), boiler (118 lb), condensers (50 lb), feed pump (17.5 lb) and steam separator (17 lb); the total dry weight, including miscellaneous plumbing and fittings, was "about 417 lbs" (Besler 1958, 5). If the water and lubricating oil requirements were unchanged, that would bring the wet weight to 477 lb, for a slightly increased W/P of 2.39 lb/hp.

As built, the powerplant used four smaller condensers (Besler 1958, 4) instead of the two originally contemplated. These were aluminum tube-fin condensers with 15 fins per inch (Besler 1958, fig. 15). Besler suggested that the condensers be "installed so that the slipstream of the propeller is directed toward their inlet and that a pressure drop of 3" H_2O is available."

At takeoff (ambient temperature 59°F), the airplane was to climb at 60 mph. The expected "heat transfer rate" was "29.2 Btu/min/°F/ft^2" for the previously stated airflow rate (Besler 1958, fig. 15) for a 100°F difference that corresponds to 175,200 Btu/h (a little less than the 1954 estimate). "If condensing took place at atmospheric pressure, the temperature difference would be 153°F, a total of 8 sq ft of surface is installed and the heat transfer would be 2,280,000 Btu/hr." Assuming that condensation required the removal of 1,000 Btu per pound of steam, according to Bessler (1958), that would be sufficient to handle a water use rate of 11 lb/hp-h (11–12).

Under cruise conditions (160 hp), "the drag of the condensers in this case would consume about 14.7 air hp. This drag is comparable to the cooling drag of an air-cooled reciprocating engine" (Besler 1958, 12).

"All major components" were "fabricated and tested," and "preliminary design had started of an installation in an aircraft nacelle." However, the Navy decided instead to install it in a "28-foot Navy personnel boat" (Besler 1958, 3).

In the Besler (1954) design, the condenser contribution to the W/P was just 0.285 lb/hp, far less than the 3 lb/hp assumed by Wilson (1926). And the weight of the 1958 condensers was slightly smaller.

History—Helicopters

A helicopter is an aerial vehicle with a powered propeller mounted on an essentially vertical axis. "In 1863, the Vicomte Gustave Ponton d'Amecourt built a model helicopter with counter-rotating propellers and a steam engine." However, it was a failure (USCoFC 2024).

The Italian civil engineer Enrico Forlanini "is credited with manufacturing the first helicopter to make a sustained flight" in 1878. While it was steam powered, it did not have a complete steam powerplant; the boiler was "heated by means of a fire on the ground."[11] It was thus comparable to a "fireless locomotive"—that is, one using stored steam provided from an outside source. The 160 psi twin-cylinder engine was ¼ hp and weighed 6 lb (Kelly 2006, 61).

Analysis

There is no doubt that airships and airplanes can employ steam propulsion; the 1852 Giffard airship and the 1933 Besler plane stand as proof. A large enough steam powerplant could produce as much horsepower as any airplane's internal combustion engine. Rather, the question is whether steam engines could ever be light enough and efficient enough to be competitive with internal combustion engines for aerial use, especially in airplanes.

First, here is a quick recap on how steam engines work. A fuel is combusted in a furnace. The hot combustion gases heat the water in a boiler, producing steam. The steam expands and works by pushing a piston in a cylinder (in a reciprocating engine) or the blades of a turbine (in a rotary engine). For propulsion, a transmission system uses this reciprocating or rotary motion to turn a propeller.

Steam engines may be characterized as condensing (the spent steam is condensed into liquid water and returned to the boiler) or noncondensing (the spent steam is exhausted into the atmosphere). Most steam

Part I: Unconventional Power

locomotives had noncondensing engines and thus required water towers along their route if their range was not to be water limited. Clearly, steam engines for airships and airplanes would need to be the condensing type for them to have a practical range.

Because steam engines use water as the working fluid, they have two important operational limitations. First, heat must be used to vaporize the water, and the heat—so used—doesn't generate power. This results in low thermal efficiency. Second, water freezes at a temperature that is encountered in the normal working environment, and it may be necessary to supply additional heat to the water tank to keep it liquid.

Other potential weaknesses of aerial steam are a low power-to-weight ratio (relative to gasoline engines) and high maintenance costs. The weight of the condenser has been a particular concern. We will explore just how serious these weaknesses are and whether they can be alleviated.

Steam propulsion also has its strengths, notably low initial costs, an ability to use a greater variety of fuels (including coal, wood, and heavy oil), and relative insensitivity of power delivered to altitude.

However, the fuel diversity advantage comes with a caveat: using fuel with low energy density requires carrying a greater weight of fuel to maintain range (and thus less payload). Also, while steam engines are able to exploit solid fuels, notably wood, coal and even agricultural waste, solid fuels are difficult to handle. In contrast, fluid fuels can be pumped.

The effect of altitude on conventional (non-condensing) steam locomotives is somewhat complex. If a locomotive boiler were operating at 200 psig pressure at sea level (air pressure 14.7 psia, so boiler pressure 214.7 psia), moving it to 10,000 feet would mean that the air pressure was 10.1 psia, and the boiler pressure would be 210.1 psia. That's just a 2.1% reduction in cylinder inlet pressure. On the other hand, it will be exhausting against 10 psia. Assuming zero superheat, the theoretical non-condensing cycle efficiency at sea level is 23.81%, whereas at 10,000 feet, it is 18.45%. Thus, steam engines on locomotives actually run **better** as the altitude increases, as they exhaust steam against a lower pressure. However, aerial steam powerplants must recycle their water, via a condenser, so altitude doesn't alter their cycle efficiency.

However, there are three other considerations (the first two of which also apply to conventional locomotives). At higher altitude, there will be a greater temperature differential between the powerplant and ambient air, so a greater rate of heat loss from the firebox, boiler and cylinders (hence higher fuel consumption) if not addressed by additional insulation. Also, there is less oxygen available, and so the rate of airflow into the firebox must be increased to compensate if it previously was only enough to support the desired combustion rate at sea level. Finally, the reduced air temperature will increase the effectiveness of an air-cooled condenser.

Thermal Efficiency of Steam Propulsion

Stationary steam-electric powerplants can achieve relatively high efficiencies, but they also use much higher pressures and boiler temperatures than any vehicular plant and are equipped with subatmospheric condensers and other refinements that add weight and cost.

The Rankine cycle is the idealized thermodynamic process by which a steam engine extracts heat energy from steam and converts it into mechanical energy (work). The efficiency of this process (work done/heat energy content of the inlet steam) is known as the *cycle efficiency*.

However, to generate the steam, the chemical energy must be extracted from the fuel and transferred to the water inside the boiler. The efficiency of this process (heat energy content of the steam at the boiler outlet/chemical energy content of the fuel) is known as the *boiler* or *fuel-to-steam efficiency*. The overall thermal efficiency of the production of work at the crankshaft is thus the product of the boiler and cycle efficiencies.

The rate at which work is done at the crankshaft is the powerplant power. Some of the generated power may be used for purposes other than propulsion; for example, to power the compressor used by the engine, the fan used by the condenser, or accessory electrical systems (cabin lighting, air conditioning, etc.). Hence a distinction may be drawn between gross and net power.

The product of the transmission efficiency and the propeller efficiency is the propulsive efficiency, the ratio of the propulsive power to the powerplant net power.

The overall propulsion efficiency is the product of the thermal (pre-transmission) efficiency, the net power-to-gross power ratio, and the propulsive efficiency. The overall efficiency, together with the specific energy (energy/mass) and energy density (energy/volume), determines the specific fuel consumption (mass or volume per unit power and time).

The steam locomotive evolved in a period in which fuel (wood, coal or oil) was cheap, and therefore little concern was given to thermal efficiency. As Ennis (1915, 354) aptly states, "The aim in locomotive design is not the greatest economy of steam, but the installation of the greatest possible power-producing capacity in a definitely limited space."

Part I: Unconventional Power

In the mid-20th century, a typical steam locomotive had an overall boiler efficiency of 72%, an actual cycle ("cylinder"[12]) efficiency "bordering on" 14%, and a transmission efficiency of 90% (Wardale 1998, 491, citing Cox 1969, 178). However, we will ignore the transmission efficiency because it would be the same regardless of whether a gasoline or steam engine was used if the revolutions per minute were the same. Thus, the steam locomotive had a pre-transmission efficiency (fuel to crankshaft) of at best 9%. Appendix 7 has detailed efficiency data for several locomotives.

Data for commercial steam cars are limited, but a Doble Model E automobile steam engine was tested in 1929, exhibiting "125 shaft horsepower, with a brake specific fuel consumption of 0.916 lb. fuel oil per shaft horsepower hour" (Luchter and Renner 1977, 10). This corresponded to an actual "brake thermal efficiency" (overall pre-transmission efficiency) of 15% (13).

Theoretical Cycle Efficiency

The cycle efficiency is generally much lower than the boiler efficiency. Let's look at what theory tells us is the highest possible value to put this in better perspective.

Steam engines are true heat engines; their working fluid (water) cyclically receives heat from a high-temperature source (boiler), converts some of the heat energy to work (steam-driven piston movement), and rejects the remaining waste heat to a heat sink (condenser or outside air).

The thermal efficiency of a heat engine is its net work output (work done during expansion minus work done during compression) divided by the total heat input. It may also be expressed equivalently as 1 − (heat output/heat input).

The theoretical (Carnot cycle) maximum efficiency is expressed by the equation

$1 - (T_{sink}/T_{source})$

with temperatures in K.

The ideal Rankine cycle is less efficient but provides a more accurate model of what happens in a real steam engine. Calculating the efficiency of a Rankine cycle is much more complicated than doing so for a Carnot cycle, as the enthalpy and entropy of the steam at various temperatures and pressures must be considered, and steam under typical conditions does not behave like an ideal gas. One limitation on the efficiency of the Rankine cycle is that some heat must be used to change water into steam, and this heat doesn't do any useful work.

2. Steam Power

If a steam engine continually takes in new water, it is operating on an open cycle, and if it recycles its water, it is a closed cycle. In general, a closed Rankine cycle—that is, one with a condenser—will have a higher theoretical cycle efficiency than one with an open cycle. For example, with the boiler at 2,000 psia and 1,000°F, the ideal closed cycle with condensation at atmospheric pressure is 34.93% efficient versus 31.33% for an open one with feedwater at 59°F.

The theoretical efficiency of the Rankine cycle may be increased by a variety of means (see appendix 8). Three expedients—increasing boiler pressure, superheating the steam, and heating the feedwater to the boiler—were used reasonably frequently as the steam locomotive evolved. It may also be increased by reheating the partially expanded steam (depending on the extraction pressure) and the use of a subatmospheric condenser.

The pressures and temperatures used in steam cars have generally been higher than in steam locomotives. In a survey covering auto engines tested between 1951 and 1976, pressures ranged from 600 to 2,500 psia and temperatures from 700°F to 1,100°F (Luchter and Renner 1977, 14). The higher pressures and temperatures would tend to increase the theoretical cycle efficiency.

Atmospheric temperature and pressure decrease with increasing altitude, and this results in an increase in the cycle efficiency of a steam powerplant with an air-cooled condenser (Marcy and Hockway 1979, 11).[13] (The temperature decrease will also reduce the condenser weight, as the greater temperature difference between the steam entering the condenser and the air side of the condenser will increase the heat transfer rate.)

Actual Cycle Efficiency

A real-life steam powerplant doesn't achieve the theoretical cycle efficiency because of various irreversibilities, such as fluid friction, incomplete absorption of heat from the combustion gases, and heat losses from the steam to the surroundings (Ennis 1915, 301ff; Çengel and Boles 2002, 519ff). Methods of reducing these irreversibilities are discussed in appendix 8.

An ideal expansion (or compression) is isentropic,[14] so its actual efficiency, as a percentage of the theoretical one, is called the *isentropic efficiency*. The work done during expansion will be the work done by the piston or turbine if the cycle were ideal, multiplied by the isentropic efficiency of the expansion.

An isentropic efficiency of 65%–90% is typically assumed for steam turbines. It's much more difficult to find numbers for reciprocating steam. For early stationary plants, the actual efficiency was typically 40%–80% (more often 50%–70%) of the theoretical one (Ennis 1915, 398); figure 60%–70% if high superheat is used (399). In the case of the locomotives for which I have both actual and theoretical cylinder efficiencies (see appendix 7), the former was 68%–85% of the latter.

Condensers: Overview

With the possible exception of a seaplane or an airship operating primarily over water and equipped to suck water up from the ocean as needed, a steam-powered airship or airplane requires the ability to recycle its water for sustained operation. And that means it needs a condenser.

A condenser removes heat from a gas in order to change it into a liquid. Basic thermodynamics textbooks teach how to calculate how much heat is being removed by the condenser (the heat load). The design of the condenser to handle a particular heat load is taught in a more advanced course on heat transfer.

With a mobile powerplant, when rejecting heat to the ambient air, it is best to minimize air resistance. The weight of the cooling system and the volume it occupies also have to be considered.

Historical Condensing Steam Powerplants for Vehicles

Generally, locomotive steam engines weren't equipped with condensers and thus operated on an open Rankine cycle. The few exceptions were those operating in arid regions or close to a front line (where the concern was that the exhaust plumes could be spotted by enemy aircraft). South African Railways had the 25C locomotives, which were equipped with condensing tenders (Smith 2001; Reefsteamers 2018). However, their condensing capacity was insufficient, and the condensers were later removed (Valentine 2015).

While condensers are common in stationary plants, "it is much harder to accommodate an adequate condenser on a locomotive which has to be mobile and whose size is constrained by the loading-gauge" (Semmens and Goldfinch 2000, 155). And "there is an element of danger involved in returning condensed steam from reciprocating engines to the boilers, on account of the cylinder oil it contains" (Ennis 1915, 431).

These problems with condensing locomotives apply mutatis mutandis to steam airships and airplanes.

Normally, a locomotive will use the exhaust steam, funneled into blast pipes, to create a strong draft and thereby achieve a high rate of combustion. With a condensing plant, an alternative source of forced draft is needed. For the SAR 25C condensing locomotive, the source was a turbine driven by the exhaust steam before it was condensed (Smith 2001). There will, of course, be some degree of forced draft for an airship or airplane in motion, but it might need to be supplemented.

There were several commercially manufactured steam cars with condensers, including models from White, Johnson, Lane, Stanley, Doble and Detrick. These are believed to have been *atmospheric* condensers—that is, the inlet pressure was at or slightly above atmospheric pressure. They were apparently structurally similar to automotive radiators. They only recovered part of the steam; hence, water had to be added periodically.

As Luchter and Renner (1977, 19) observed, "the cooling requirements of an automobile Rankine engine condenser were three to five times greater than that of a conventional internal combustion engine (ICE) radiator."

There were also several proposed experimental designs of automotive condensing steam powerplants. These sought to recover all the steam. The particulars of these designs are given in appendix 10.

The 1933 Besler steam plane had or was intended to have a condenser, but it is likely that it didn't recover all the steam. Finally, from 1954 to 1958, Besler designed a fully condensing powerplant for an airplane.

Condenser Specific Heat Loads and Heat Rejection Rates

The specific heat load is the amount of heat that must be dissipated per pound of steam entering the engine. In general, the higher the theoretical cycle efficiency, the lower the condenser load.

Also, the higher the isentropic efficiency of expansion, the lower the condenser load.[15] However, an isentropic efficiency of expansion of 50% does not double the condenser load. In one case I looked at, the condenser load increased by 21.5%. And an isentropic efficiency of 70%, in the same case, increased the condenser load by 12.9%. The exact effect depends on the engine inlet pressure and temperature.

If the condenser's specific heat load (Btu/lb/cycle) and the power at which the engine is operating are known, the necessary heat rejection rate can be calculated. Power is energy (work) per time. Multiply the shaft horsepower by 2,546 to convert it to Btu/h and divide that by the work

Part I: Unconventional Power

done (Btu/lb) per cycle to get the steam demand (lb steam/h). Then multiply that by the specific heat load (Btu/lb/cycle) to get the condenser's heat rejection rate (Btu/h).

Achievable Thermal Performance

Table 2–2 shows my calculations of various thermodynamic parameters for several historical vehicular steam powerplants (including those in appendix 10). This used the methodology explained in appendix 6.

The table provides the theoretical Rankine cycle efficiency and the cycle efficiency if expansion and compression are actually at 70% isentropic efficiency. Making this calculation requires knowing the engine (expander) inlet pressure and temperature. The engine outlet (condenser inlet) pressure is assumed (except for Fleischer and Zafran [1957]) to be one atmosphere; therefore, the temperature is 100°C. (In the case of Besler [1933], since there was inconsistent data, the highest quoted pressure and temperature were used in the calculation.)

The table also shows steam quality (at 70% and 100% isentropic efficiency). Dry steam is defined as having a quality of 100%. Water droplets in steam can accelerate corrosion and erosion. The inefficiencies in a real-world Rankine cycle translate into waste heat; this increases the steam quality (the steam dryness) at the condenser inlet. Some steam powerplants collect the steam at an intermediate stage in its expansion and reheat it to improve the steam quality.[16]

The table also shows the specific load and, if engine gross power is available, the corresponding heat rejection rate at both 100% and 70% isentropic efficiencies.

In terms of thermal efficiency, the Besler 1933 and subsequent designs are fairly close together. We see, however, from Fleischer and Zafran (1957) and Hypothetical #1 that the use of a subatmospheric condenser improves actual cycle efficiency by several percentage points and from SES and Hypothetical #2 that the use of a superatmospheric condenser makes it worse.

It is also evident that increasing pressure and temperature increases cycle efficiency, with the highest values being those for Gibbs and for Hypothetical #3 (which gives Gibbs the temperature of the Strack (1970), Carter and SES designs). However, increasing the temperature also increases the specific heat load on the condenser. In addition, increasing pressure and temperature, after a point, require the use of more expensive materials in constructing the powerplant and result in increased maintenance costs and a shorter worker life.

Table 2-2: Cycle Efficiency, Steam Quality, Condenser Load, Heat Rejection Rate

Case (condenser pressure if not 1 atm)	Boiler Pressure (psia)	Engine Inlet Temp (°F)	Suppl Heat (°F)	Gross Power (hp)	Steam Quality %		Cycle Efficiency %		Specific Condenser Load (Btu/lb/cycle)		Condenser Heat Rejection Rate (Btu/h)	
					100%	70%	100%	70%	100%	70%	100%	70%
							Isentropic Efficiency					
25C Locomotive	224.70	691	299	2,600	96.50	Dry	21.14	14.76	936.85	1,012.41	24,624,287	38,014,678
Stanley Steamer[7]	600	600	113	?	84.50	93.50	26.02	18.10	820.28	907.36		
Besler 1933[18]	1,200	800	231	150	85.00	Dry	30.95	21.47	825.78	937.92	843,668	1,368,921
Besler 1954 Takeoff[19]	1,200	781	214	200	84.40	95.80	30.79	21.36	819.15	929.58	1,133,167	1,837,050
Besler 1954 Cruise	900	781	214	150	87.30	98.30	29.43	20.46	847.06	953.87	908,649	1,461,750
Williams	1,014.70	1,000	454	150	92.70	Dry	31.97	22.23	900.25	1,028.12	806,663	1,316,057
Fleischer and Zafran (5 psia)	1,100	660	103	100	76.90	88.60	33.34	23.16	770.36	886.94	504,754	830,197
Hypothetical #1 Fleischer and Zafran (1 atm)	1,100	660	103	100	80.4	90.50	29.44	20.41	780.10	878.76	603,985	971,956
Gibbs[20]	2,000	850	213	60	81.20	93.70	33.54	23.15	788.59	909.83	298,091	491,317
Strack;[21] Carter	1,100	1,000	364	175	92.00	Dry	32.35	22.48	893.37	1,022.53	924,569	1,511,773
SES (20 psia)[22]	1,000	1,000	455	158	94.40	Dry	30.67	21.32	906.62	1,027.88	902,373	1,461,514
Hypothetical #2 SES (1 atm)	1,000	1,000	455	158	92.90	Dry	31.91	22.19	901.49	1,029.12	852,438	1,390,178
Hypothetical #3	2,000	1,000	364		86.50	Dry		24.15	839.08	976.03		

Part I: Unconventional Power

The use of expedients such as reheating and regeneration (feedwater heating with residual heat) increases system complexity and cost and increases the system weight (Hays 2015, 55–56).

If a reasonable actual cycle efficiency is 25%, and it is multiplied by a boiler efficiency of 80%, then overall brake efficiency would be 20%. That is less than two-thirds of what is achievable with an internal combustion engine, so higher fuel consumption may be expected. While a steam engine may use cheaper fuels than gasoline, those are likely to also be cheaper because they are lower in energy content than gasoline. Hence, the steam-powered airship or airplane will likely have higher fuel costs than its conventional counterpart.

Power-to-Weight Ratios

Another important goal for an aerial powerplant designer is to obtain a high specific power: the ratio of power to weight (mass). For airships, the heavier the powerplant, the greater the buoyant gas volume must be, which in turn increases drag and thus the required power of the engines, so there is a multiplier effect. For airplanes, the heavier the powerplant, the greater the necessary dynamic lift, which is obtained either by increasing the wing area or the airspeed (and thus the required power of the engines).

If imperial units are used (horsepower and pounds), the P/W ratio tends to be less than one, and consequently, the reverse ratio (weight to power, specific weight) may be used, as it is in this section. The lower the W/P, the better.[23]

The weight of an aerial steam powerplant would be the combined weight of the boiler (including the combustion chamber), engine and condenser, and the related controls and tubing. It might also include a feedwater heater and water recovery apparatus for the exhaust combustion gas.

Weight was a problem for early aerial steam propulsion; W/P (lb/hp) for the powerplant on the Giffard airship was 50:1. The aeronautical pioneer Alberto Santos-Dumont (1973) wrote, "Giffard's primitive steam engine, weak in proportion to its weight, ... had afforded that courageous innovator no fair chance." He conceded that the weight of the steam engine proper could be less than that of the internal combustion engine, but "the boiler always ruins the proportion." And for a prolonged flight, the pilot either needed to carry a great deal of water or add a condenser to the powerplant. Santos-Dumont noted that the 60 hp Clément internal combustion engine weighed just 4.4 lb/hp (30). And the W/P ratio for internal combustion engines has decreased since then (see introduction).

To complicate matters further, Marcy and Hockway (1979, 11–12) assert that there is an inverse relationship between Rankine cycle efficiency and specific power, at least for a steam turbine. He predicts that at 35% efficiency, the engine will be 8 lb/hp, and at 45% efficiency, about 13 lb/hp.

Condenser Sizing

Given the concerns expressed over condenser weight, we look at that issue more closely. The necessary heat rejection rate is proportional to the engine power. The greater the necessary heat rejection rate, the greater the heat exchange surface area that the condenser must provide and thus the greater the weight. The weights of some vehicle condensers are given in table 2-3.

Unlike condensers for stationary or marine plants, those for land or air vehicles cannot rely on water as the ultimate cooling medium. They must use air, which at sea level temperature and pressure has only about one-fourth the heat capacity per unit weight and 1/3,500th the heat capacity per unit volume. The faster the engine is running, the greater the steam flow rate and, therefore, the greater the cooling rate needed. A condenser must remove enough heat to restore steam to its liquid state, whereas a radiator must only get rid of enough heat so that the engine doesn't overheat. Moreover, the heat conductivity of air is less than one-tenth that of water, which reduces the efficiency of heat exchange (Valentine 2015).

The slowest part of the overall heat transfer will be the convective heat loss when the heat is ultimately dumped into ambient air, whether the condenser is air-cooled directly or is cooled by water that in turn is cooled by a radiator. The radiator will need a large air-side surface area, and its weight will be a substantial part of the overall weight of the steam powerplant cooling system.

Condensers are heat exchangers. In a surface heat exchanger, a fluid-impermeable barrier separates the hot and cold fluids. The flow of the two fluids may be in the same direction (parallel flow), opposite directions (counterflow), or perpendicular directions (cross flow). Counterflow provides the highest average temperature difference between the fluids and is thus the most thermodynamically efficient, whereas parallel flow is the least efficient. The disadvantage of counterflow is that it requires the most

Part I: Unconventional Power

complex header and distributor layout of the three arrangements. Hence, cross flow is often favored.

In a pure tubular exchanger, the primary heat transfer surfaces are the tube walls, and one fluid runs inside the tubes and the other outside them. Such exchangers usually aren't compact. In a plate exchanger, the primary heat transfer surfaces are parallel plates spaced to create fluid channels, each carrying a single fluid, and these are further subdivided by the fins (discussed below) into narrow passages. Usually, the hot and cold streams alternate.

Typically, one fluid has better heat transfer characteristics than the other (e.g., water is better than air), so the designer will want to extend the surface area on the "bad" side by adding fins. These are secondary heat transfer surfaces (structures not directly between the hot and cold fluids); they receive heat from the tubes or plates. Thus, there are plate-fin and tube-fin heat exchangers.

Fins are thin, so the heat transfer surface they provide is determined by their length and width, with length deemed the direction away from the tube. The longer they are, the thicker they must be for mechanical reasons. There are several fin types (plain, offset, wavy/corrugated, louver, pin, perforated).

The heat transfer characteristics of these various designs are affected by the particular dimensions: tube diameter, thickness and spacing, plate thickness and spacing, fin length, fin type (which introduces further parameters), and so on.

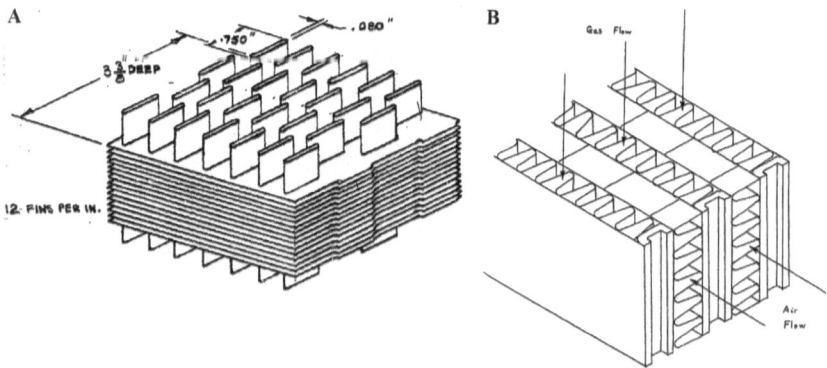

A. Besler (1954, 11) tube-fin heat exchanger; the steam travels through the flattened tubes and the cooling air between the plate fins. B. Fleischer (1957, fig. 17) plate-fin heat exchanger; the fins are wavy (corrugated), creating numerous small fluid inlets between them and the separator plates. Both are cross flow heat exchangers.

For some designs, there are published correlations. Perhaps the largest of these collections is in Kays and London (1998). Those, unfortunately, take the form of graphs, which are inconvenient to work with. Some published correlations set forth formulae. In either case, one must be careful to ensure that the geometric and flow parameters are within the bounds of validity set forth in the publication. For example, for a plate-louvered fin design, I was not able to find a published correlation that covered airflow Reynolds numbers as high as those an airship or airplane would encounter.

Much heat exchanger design data are proprietary; Besler (1954, 1958) was fortunate to have access to Cadillac data on a flattened tube-fin geometry. I was not able to find published data for that.

The correlations are used to calculate the overall heat transfer coefficient, referenced to the air-side surface area. This is divided into the specific thermal load to obtain the required air-side heat transfer surface area.

The condenser weight will depend on the density, surface area, and thickness of its component structures (tubes, sheets, etc.). Copper is denser than aluminum but has higher thermal conductivity.

Achievable Power-to-Weight Ratios

The first experimental steam cars date back to the late 18th century, and commercial manufacturing began in the 19th century. A complication in looking at steam car data is that the engines were often rated in *boiler horsepower*, a measure of the maximum rate at which the boiler could supply steam. In 1876, testing showed that "it took approximately 30 pounds of steam per hour to produce 1 horsepower of mechanical work" (i.e., to supply enough steam that the engine could perform 1 hp of work). In 1889, *boiler horsepower* was defined as the ability to evaporate 34.5 lb of water in one hour at 100°C—that is, to supply 33,475 Btu/h (ABMA 2015).

However, the relationship between steam production and engine power depends on the efficiency of the engine. In 1917, Gebhardt wrote, "One boiler horsepower will furnish sufficient steam to develop about four actual horsepower in the best compound condensing engine, but only one-half horsepower in a small non-condensing engine" (150).

Hence, a W/P ratio for a steam car powerplant can be calculated only if the sources clearly report a brake horsepower and an engine weight, and it is also clear that the latter includes the boiler (and, if a system element, the condenser).

While these data are generally not available for commercial steam

Part I: Unconventional Power

cars, I have been able to consider some post–World War II designs and prototypes, as detailed in appendix 10.

Even if they do not provide a complete powerplant weight, it is helpful if they at least provide a condenser weight.

Table 2–3 summarizes the data considered on the weight of steam powerplant components.

Table 2–3: Weight and Power of Steam Powerplants and Powerplant Components

Designer, Date, Application	Wt (lb)*	Type	Engine Power (hp)	Total W/P (lb/hp)	Cond W/P (lb/hp)
Giffard 1852 Airship	E (110.20), B (220.50)	NC	3	110	
Henson 1847 Model Airplane	E (12)	NC	0.50		
Henson 1848 Model Airplane	E (9)	NC	0.75		
Moy 1875 Airplane	E (80)	NC	3		
Mozhaiskii 1880s Airplane	E + B (310)	NC	30	10.30	
Ader 1890 Airplane	T (112)	C	20	5.60	
Langley 1897? Airplane	E (5.50)	NC	1.25		
Maxim 1888 Airplane	E (640), B (1,000)	NC	360	4.55	
Groves 1916 Model Airplane	T (1.5)	NC	0.03–0.04	37.50–50	
Besler 1933 Airplane	C (665)	C	150		4.43
Paxton 1953 Car	C (140)	C	150 max 120 cont.		1.16
Fleischer and Zafran 1957 Car	C (187) (Al core)	C	100		1.87
Gibbs, Hosick 1966 Car	E + B (405)	C	60		
Strack 1970 Car	C (130, Cu) C (50, Al)	C	175		1.34 0.28
Lears 1970s	E (110), B (127), C (179), T (727)	C	92.80	7.83	1.93

2. Steam Power

Designer, Date, Application	Wt (lb)*	Type	Engine Power (hp)	Total W/P (lb/hp)	Cond W/P (lb/hp)
Carter 2d gen 1970s	T (359)	C	80	4.49	
SES Preprototype 1970s	T (1147)	C	138 net	8.31	
SES Prototype 1970s	E (419), B (110), C (99), T (853)	C	138 net	6.18	0.72
Besler 1954 Airplane	E (133.70), B (102.80), C (57, Al or 114, Cu), T (372 Al)	C	200	1.86	0.29 0.57
Besler 1958 Airplane	E (134), B (118), C (50), T (417)	C	200	2.09	0.25

*E engine, B boiler, C condenser, T total (may include additional components). Under Type, NC noncondensing, C condensing.

The W/P of Besler's final design (2.09) is only slightly inferior to that of the Lycoming IO-360-C1G6 (1.62), a general aviation gasoline engine. Hence it appears that the W/P disadvantage of steam power has been largely overcome.

But that comes with the caveat that Besler's condenser must be able to handle the heat load expected with the stated power. That in turn depends on the airflow rate over the condenser (which is affected by the airspeed) and the temperature difference between the condenser and the ambient air (which depends on the altitude, latitude, time of year, time of day, and weather). The Besler powerplant was never tested aloft.

Besler's approach to sizing the condenser is suspect because he treated the heat transfer as proportional to the initial temperature difference between the condenser inlet and the ambient cooling air. In fact, while the temperature on the hot side is constant from inlet to outlet (since there is no temperature change during condensation), the temperature of the air at the outlet will be higher than that of the inlet, because the air absorbed heat from the steam.

Strack (1970, 11) used the "conventional log mean rate equation," which sets the heat transfer rate equal to the product of the overall heat transfer coefficient, the corresponding heat transfer area, the log mean temperature difference (LMTD) of the air and water, and a flow configuration correction factor (which happens to be unity for a condenser).[24]

In Fleischer and Zafran's steam car design (1957, 46), the air inlet

Part I: Unconventional Power

temperature was 100°F and the air outlet temperature 146.7°F. Since they condensed at 5 psia, the steam temperature was 162.24°F, and the initial temperature difference was 62.24°F. The LMTD was 33.5°F, so had Fleischer and Zafran followed Besler's example, they would have under designed their condenser by a factor close to two.

Cooling Drag

The aerodynamic drag created by an airplane (or airship) radiator[25] or condenser is the cooling drag. It results from the cooling air being slowed down as it passes over the fins. Parsons (1920, 437) said that "for many of the types of radiator submitted for aeronautic use," the head resistance at 120 mph of one "large enough to cool the engine would absorb from 12 to 15 percent of its power." And a half century later, Katz et al. (1982, 530) said that the "cooling drag for a typical general aviation airplane accounts for as much as 13% of the airplane's total calculated drag."

In general, the expectation is that a drag force is proportional to the square of the airspeed, and consequently, the power to overcome the drag force is proportional to the cube of the airspeed. Airships fly at lower speeds than airplanes, so their cooling drag will be less.

Air-cooled airplane engines may be fan or ram cooled. For the latter, the airflow over the fins is solely a result of the airplane's motion. For the former, a minimum airflow is guaranteed, regardless of airspeed, but there is a power cost when the fan is on (and a weight cost, whether the fan is on or not).

If the airspeed is high, it may be necessary to mask part of the radiator area—otherwise the cooling power of the radiator will be higher than necessary, and an unnecessary price is paid in radiator drag. Controlling the exit area with cowl flaps has been found to be sufficient.

The available data are mainly for airplane (and automotive) radiators, not condensers. However, with similar heat exchanger types, the expectation might be that the drag would be proportional to the air-side heat transfer surface area, which typically is several times higher for condensers than for radiators.

According to Brevoort and Joyner (1941), "the power dissipated in cooling" a gasoline engine varies "from about 70 percent of the indicated horsepower at lower power output to 40 percent at high power output." At the 70% value and 100 hp, the heat rejection rate is about 178,000 Btu/h. However, table 2–2 shows that the Fleischer and Zafran steam powerplant, operating at 100 hp and 70% isentropic efficiency, would need its condenser to handle about 972,000 Btu/h. Hence, it would be expected to have more than fourfold the cooling drag at the same airspeed.

Nonetheless, Besler (1958) expected that the cooling drag would consume about 9.2% of the steam-powered airplane's engine power, comparable to that experienced with an internal combustion engine–driven airplane. Besler did not explain the basis for this optimistic expectation.

Some early auto and airplane radiators were unfinned tube heat exchangers. In the honeycomb (cellular) type, the cold air flowed through horizontal tubes parallel to the direction of vehicle motion, and the engine-heated liquid coolant flowed downward around the tubes from a top tank to a bottom tank (Maybach 1902). This design was still in use during World War II. For data on cooling drag (radiator resistance) for World War I vintage airplanes and various radiator designs, see EDAED (1918) and Loening (1920).

On ducted airplane radiators, to reduce drag, the air fed into the radiator first passes through a diverger, and the air leaving the radiator passes through a converger. The divergence of the air slows it and increases the pressure, and the pressure acts on the walls of the specially shaped diverger to create a forward force, counteracting the drag imposed by the radiator core. The converger increases the air velocity and creates another forward force (Thesee 2024). Thus, jet thrust can be obtained from the waste heat of a ducted radiator if the exit pressure is greater than the freestream air pressure (Meredith effect).

The Meredith effect, proposed in 1935, was exploited in the Messerschmitt Bf 109F and the Mustang P-51D (Piancastelli and Pelligrini 2007). The cooling drag at an airspeed of 100 ft/s was 7 lb (out of 59) for the Spitfire and 8 lb (out of 82) for the Hurricane (Ackroyd 2016, 68). However, the Meredith effect offset this; the combination of heat regeneration and exhaust thrust was 7.5 for the Spitfire and 9 for the Hurricane (Ackroyd 2018, 23).

Since World War II, there has been little study of airplane radiator design (Thesee 2024). However, compact heat exchangers have been developed for automotive use. The cooling drag is related to the pressure drop across the radiator. For some condenser designs, correlations exist for calculating the friction factor and thereby the pressure drop.

3

Alternative External Combustion Power

In the previous chapter, we considered closed Rankine cycle powerplants that burn fuel and use the heat of the combustion gas to turn liquid water into steam. The steam is then supplied to a piston or turbine engine. Here, we examine a few alternative methods of exploiting external combustion.

Analysis—Organic Rankine Cycle Engines

Instead of using water as the working fluid, a closed Rankine cycle engine may use an organic liquid that has a lower boiling point and specific heat capacity than water and therefore requires less heat to evaporate it. Likewise, less heat must be removed from the vapor in order to condense it.

It is also advantageous if the liquid has a lower freezing point than water, as that would facilitate operation in colder environments. (This is even more of an advantage for airplanes and airships than for automobiles.)

The earliest form was the naphtha engine; this used crude oil, or a fraction thereof, as the working fluid. Naphtha engines were used in the late 19th century on small pleasure boats called *vapor launches* or *naphtha launches*.

I am not aware of any use of organic Rankine cycle engines in airplanes or airships. The principal use of such engines has been in the recovery of low-grade heat: waste heat from powerplants and industrial processes, heat from the combustion of biomass, geothermal energy, and solar heat (Tartière and Astolfi 2023). It is possible to use them in airplanes or airships as an adjunct to the conventional internal combustion engine, perhaps to power accessory equipment.

For road use, they do have the advantage of generally lower emissions

3. Alternative External Combustion Power

than internal combustion engines; hence, their utility as the main power system was explored in the 1970s.

Monsanto studied possible working fluids for organic Rankine automobile engines and came up with a mixture of 60% pentafluorobenzene and 40% hexafluorobenzene. This had a slush point of -44°F, an atmospheric boiling point of 172°F, and a corresponding heat of vaporization of 79.1 Btu/lb. Operating between 220°F (condensing pressure 30 psia) and 712°F, it had a theoretical cycle efficiency of 30% (Luchter and Renner 1977, 18).

Several experimental automotive engines have used organic fluids. The Aerojet system used a "mixture of hexafluorobenzene and perfluorotoluene," and the TECO system used "trifluoroethanol with 15 mole% water." System dry weights were 1,501 lb (Aerojet preprototype), 866 lb (Aerojet prototype), and 1,271 lb (TECO preprototype); net power into transmission was 108 hp (Aerojet) and 111 hp (TECO; Luchter and Renner 1977, 3, 34, 61). The corresponding internal combustion engine was 532 lb (31).

The Aerojet system was "intended to fit a 1973 Chevrolet Impala" (Luchter and Renner 1977, 24). Operating between 650°F and 198°F, it had an ideal cycle efficiency of 35% but an estimated actual thermal efficiency of 10.5%. Brake specific fuel consumption was 1.3 lb/hp-h (26). The condenser had a maximum heat load of 1.28×10^6 Btu/h (30).

The TECO system, operating between 625°F and 208°F, had an ideal cycle efficiency of 24.7% at full load and an estimated actual thermal efficiency of 15.5%. Brake specific fuel consumption was 1.26 lb/hp-h (Luchter and Renner 1977, 56).

Sundstrand Aviation built an engine using toluene and installed it in a 25-passenger bus (Luchter and Renner 1977, 6). The Sundstrand powerplant had an overall thermal efficiency of 13.2% (67).

Overall, it appears that the organic Rankine cycle engines have fared worse than their steam counterparts in terms of both fuel efficiency and power-to-weight ratio. It is debatable whether their advantages will outweigh these limitations. However, there remains much room for optimization of organic Rankine cycles, as there are many working fluids to choose from, as well as system parameters to tweak.

Stirling Cycle—Introduction

Since two of the major drawbacks of the Rankine cycle are the energy needed to evaporate the working fluid and the weight of the condenser needed to liquefy it once more, an alternative power cycle that did not include evaporation and condensation steps was considered.

Part I: Unconventional Power

The Stirling engine was invented by Robert Stirling in 1816 (Majeski 2002, 3–1). A Stirling cycle engine, like a steam (Rankine cycle) engine, uses heat to cause a gas to expand and thereby do work. Unlike in a steam engine, the heat is applied to a light gas—a substance that is in the gaseous state at normal sea level temperature and pressure. Thus, air is a light gas, but steam is not. Since a Stirling engine does not change the state of the working fluid, it does not need a boiler or a condenser.

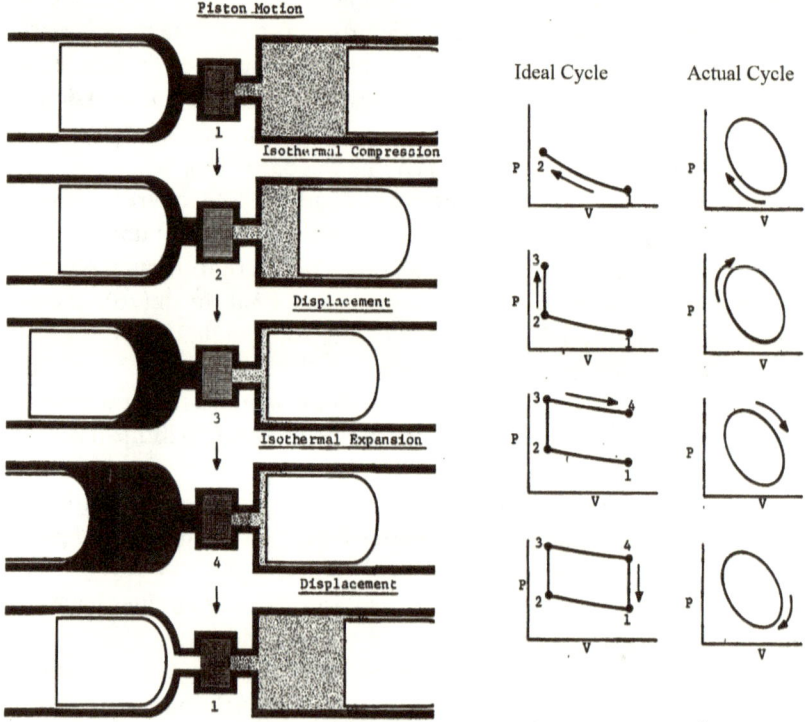

Left column: Piston motion in ideal Stirling cycle (MTI 1979, 2–5). Left is the cold side; right is the hot side. The regenerator is in the fluid path connecting the two cylinders. Four states are shown. The five transitions between states are labeled. *Middle column*: The PV curves show the change in pressure and volume associated with the transitions from each state to the next. The piston movements are steplike, and heat transfer is instantaneous. *Right column*: The PV curves for an actual Stirling cycle (2–7). The piston movements are continuous, heat transfer is not continuous, and "the working gas has a limited capacity to store heat."

3. Alternative External Combustion Power

It is a closed-cycle engine, so the gas is reused. The gas passes through hot and cold zones separated by a heat exchanger, the regenerator. A heater (external heat source) and a cooler (external heat sink) maintain the hot and cold zones, respectively. In this chapter, we consider Stirling engine powerplants in which burning a combustible fuel supplies the required heat. However, the heat source may be solar energy (see chapter 5) or nuclear energy (see chapter 6). The regenerator has a high thermal mass, allowing it to temporarily store heat (Çengel and Boles 2002, 467–468).

Unlike the ideal Rankine cycle, the ideal Stirling cycle has a cycle efficiency equal to that of the Carnot cycle, the thermodynamic limit on all heat engines. Of course, the actual cycle efficiency is less.

History—Stirling Engines

Submarine

Stirling engines have been used on diesel-electric submarines. Normally, such submarines must surface to use their diesel engines to recharge their batteries, as the diesel engines need air. In 1988, a Stirling engine was installed in the Swedish HMS *Näcken*. The gas is heated by burning liquid oxygen or diesel fuel and cooled using seawater. After successful sea trials, the system was installed in Sweden's Gotland-class submarines (Saab 2015; Wertheim 2023).

Swedish submarines are believed to use V4-275R Stirling power modules. The Mark II modules use helium, not air, as the working fluid and have a thermal efficiency of 37%. They have a nominal brake power of 65 kW (87 hp) and a mass of about 700 kg (1,543 lb; Prieto 2000, 457).

Automotive and Airplane

In the 1980s, there was a DOE/NASA experimental study of a Stirling engine in an automobile. The engine weighed 203 kg (447 lb; Beremand 1986, table III). The Mod II SES (standalone engine system configuration) design had a designed maximum power of 62.3 kW (83.5 hp; Ernst and Shaltens 1997, 3–1); its maximum net shaft efficiency was about 38% at 1,500 rpm but declined for higher or lower revolutions per minute (1–11).

Djetel et al. (2019, tables II, III) described a 10 kW (12 kW?) prototype beta engine, operating between 950 K and 300 K, with 39% actual efficiency. (The ideal efficiency would have been 68%.) This was intended for use in a series of hybrid Stirling-battery electric vehicles.

Part I: Unconventional Power

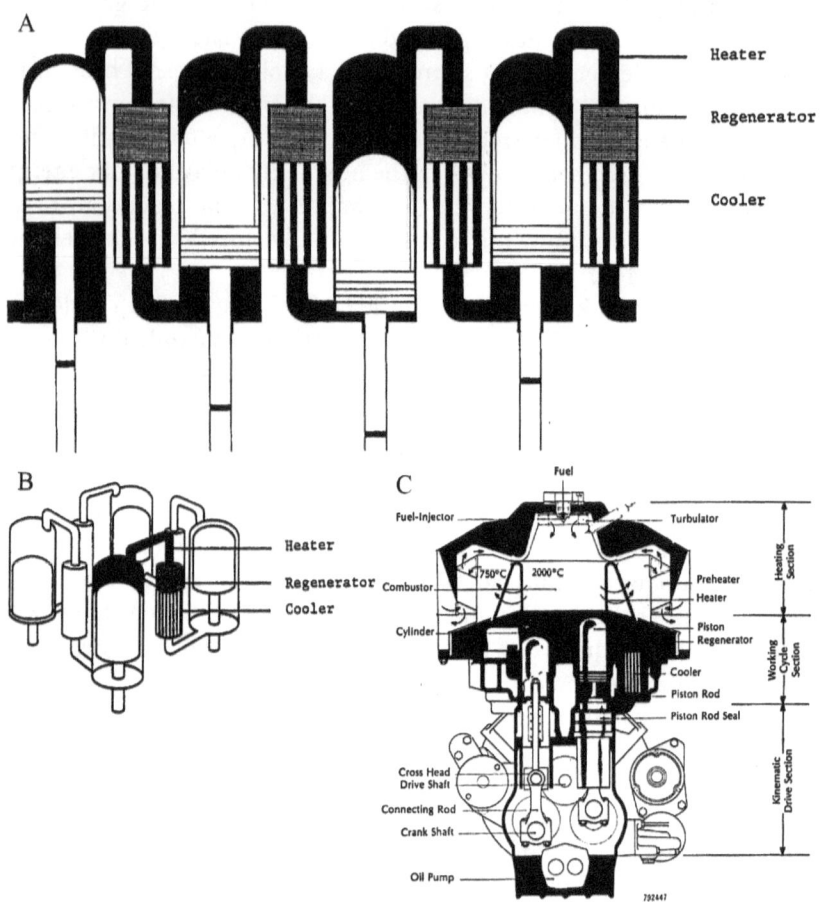

Automotive engines designed in the '70s to operate on Stirling cycle. A. Flat view schematic of a double-acting engine (MTI 1979, 2-3). "In this design, the hot-space of one cylinder is connected to the cold-space of the next cylinder. A single piston stroke then cycles the gas" from one cylinder to the next (2-1). B. Three-dimensional view schematic of same, showing how the last cylinder is connected to the first one (2-1). C. Layout of a P-40 Stirling engine, showing more mechanical details (2-8).

Airplanes

In 1987, Robert McConaghy achieved "marginal flight with a 1.8 meter standard model aircraft glider" powered by a beta-type Stirling engine. This engine weighed 360 grams (g) and produced 20 W. The longest flight

3. Alternative External Combustion Power

was "around 8 minutes of gentle orbiting." McConaghy experienced problems with both "shaft seal leakage" and "torsional vibration" (Hays 2015, 51–52).

In 1996, *Flying Magazine* reported that Darryl Phillips had been working for "20 years ... on development of a Stirling aero engine" (Garrison 102). At the time of publication, he was "working on a 20-hp radially configured four-cylinder engine for an ultralight, with helium at 20 atmospheres as the working fluid" (103).

Airships

Stirling engine–powered airships have been proposed for use on Venus and Titan (see chapter 6).

In 2011, Matthew D. Mitchell received a patent on a "high-altitude long-endurance airship." The airship was to be solar powered during the daytime (see chapter 5). He proposed to use the entire airship as a heat engine at night: "For maximum absorption of heat radiated from the earth by the bottom surface of the airship, that surface is fabricated or coated to approach the absorptivity of a 'black body' at temperatures of the order of 250 to 275 Kelvin. For maximum effectiveness in radiating heat from the upper surface of the airship to space, that upper surface is fabricated or coated to approach the emissivity of a 'black body' at temperatures of the order of 175 to 200 Kelvin."

Two alternative preferred embodiments were disclosed. These resembled "the Stirling cycle in the sense that a confined fluid is alternately compressed when relatively cool and expanded when relatively warm. That is accomplished in the airship, as in a Stirling engine, through use of a displacer that alternately forces the lifting gas into the relatively cool upper part of the airship and into the relatively warm lower part. Both alternate preferred embodiments of the airship differ from a conventional Stirling cycle engine in that they have no explicit regenerators between the warm and cold spaces" (Mitchell 2011).

In the first embodiment, the recovered energy was to be convertible to electrical power and, presumably, used to power the same motors that the solar cells powered during the daytime. In the second embodiment, the variation in net buoyancy would be used to propel the airplane, as described in chapter 8.

Analysis—Stirling Engines

The sine qua non of the Stirling engine is the regenerator, a bidirectional heat exchanger. It is hot when cold working fluid passes through it, thereby warming the fluid, and vice versa. One form of regenerator is just a set of stacked copper screens (Vineeth 2012, 16).

There are three basic Stirling engine configurations. The alpha engine has, in order, a compression piston, a cool zone (surrounded by the cooler), a regenerator, a hot zone (surrounded by the heater), and an expansion piston. The two pistons are in separate, albeit connected, cylinders. The working gas moves back and forth between the zones, passing through the regenerator. The alpha engine "suffers from the disadvantage that both the hot and cold pistons need to have seals to contain the working gas," and mechanisms are needed to ensure "the correct phasing of the two pistons" (Urieli 2020, ch. 2a).

In the beta engine, only one piston and a displacer move within a single cylinder. A displacer is similar to a piston but with a head substantially narrower than the cylinder in which it moves, so while it moves some of the gas, a significant amount will leak around the displacer head. The piston and displacer are linked so that "the gas will compress while it is mainly in the cool compression space and expand while in the hot expansion space" (Urieli 2020, ch. 2b). The gamma engine is similar, but the piston and displacer move in separate cylinders (ch. 2c).

Another design issue relates to how the mechanical power is extracted. In a kinematic engine, the movement of the power piston turns an output shaft. Numerous linkages have been devised for this purpose (Majeski 2002, 2–2 to 2–7). For an airplane or airship, this rotational motion might turn a propeller, or a generator could convert it to electrical power and transmit the current to a motor that turns the propeller.

Beta and gamma engines may be configured as free-piston engines; the power piston oscillates within a magnetic field, forming a linear alternator. The advantage is that the entire engine may be hermetically sealed (Majeski 2002, 2–2, 2–7, 2–8).

While air was the original working fluid, helium, hydrogen and nitrogen have also been used. "The use of hydrogen or helium leads to higher efficiencies than the use of heavier working gases due to the low viscosities and high thermal conductivities of these gases. On the other hand, the high diffusivity of hydrogen and helium molecules makes sealing a more difficult challenge" (Majeski 2002, 2–9). While nitrogen is similar to air in terms of those properties, it is incapable of forming explosive mixtures with lubricants (Planas 2018).

The maximum possible efficiency of a Stirling engine depends on the hot- and cold-end operating temperatures, with the former being easier to manipulate. "Most of the Stirling engines under development have hot-end operating temperatures in the range of 1,200 to 1,400°F." However, higher hot-end operating temperatures increase thermal stress, material degradation, and conduction heat loss. Typical operating pressures are 150–2,200 psi (Majeski 2002, 3-8). Engine speeds vary; lower speeds lead to "lower wear" and "somewhat higher efficiency" (3-9).

While Stirling engines are generally more efficient than steam engines, most are not appreciably more efficient than modern internal combustion airplane engines, and they are significantly heavier and bulkier for a given power.

Like other external combustion engines, Stirling engines can use any fuel. Hence, in theory, it can switch among fuels based on cost. However, solid fuels are awkward to handle, and gaseous fuels have a low energy density. So, as a practical matter, they are likely to use liquid fuels of high specific energy, such as kerosene, gasoline and diesel.

Stirling engines have less noise and vibration, making for a more congenial work environment for the crew. "In aviation applications they have the additional attraction that their performance improves as the ambient temperature drops, and so their output, rather than decline with altitude, can be expected to increase somewhat as an airplane climbs" (Garrison 1996).

A Stirling engine may run on waste heat,[1] and it is possible that one might find a niche as a supplement to a more conventional engine.

Closed Brayton Cycle

The open Brayton cycle is used in jet engines. Air is drawn in and compressed, then mixed with fuel. The fuel-air mixture combusts, and the gases first expand against a turbine and then exhaust as a jet, providing thrust. The turbine powers the compressor. High-speed marine propulsion also uses the open Brayton cycle (Çengel and Boles 2002, 470–472).

A closed Brayton cycle circulates the air through a compressor, a heater, a turbine, and a cooler. The heat is typically generated by burning fuel, and thus, the closed Brayton cycle engine is an external combustion engine, whereas the open cycle engine features internal combustion (Çengel and Boles 2002, 470–472). Thus far, the closed Brayton cycle has been used in stationary powerplants, not in airplanes (or airships).

Hays (2015, 57) has proposed that small, unmanned aerial vehicles could be given a powerplant running on a closed Brayton cycle with regeneration (using the hot gases leaving the turbine to heat the air leaving the

Part I: Unconventional Power

compressor; Çengel and Boles 2002, 477). In Hays's (2015, 137) view, even under the circumstances in which the Rankine cycle provides higher efficiency, the Brayton cycle is superior on safety grounds (avoiding a "BLEVE—boiling liquid expanding vapor explosion").

Closed Brayton cycle engines have also been proposed for use in spacecraft. Between 1968 and 1976, a 65 kg BRU (Brayton Rotating Unit) and a 200 kg BHXU (Brayton Heat Exchanger Unit) were built, with an alternator (AC) power output of 2.25 to 15 kilowatts-electric (kWe). Other prototype systems have been built since then; the expected heat source is a radioisotope or a nuclear reaction (Mason 2023) (see chapter 6).

4

Battery Power

A battery may provide direct current to a motor that turns a propeller. Here, we consider only the airships and airplanes whose batteries are charged by means other than solar power. Using solar power to charge batteries will be addressed in a later chapter.

The batteries may be charged on the ground or in the air by a pedal-driven generator (pedal electric) or by an internal combustion engine–driven generator (hybrid electric).

History

Airships

Battery propulsion of airships enjoyed a brief success. The first steps were taken by Gaston Tissandier (1843–1899), a chemist, meteorologist, and science editor, and his brother Albert (1839–1906), an illustrator and editor. The Tissandier brothers first went aloft in 1868, and in 1870, they escaped the siege of Paris by balloon. In 1875, Gaston ascended in a balloon to 28,200 ft and suffered altitude sickness that rendered him permanently deaf.

In 1881, the Tissandier brothers built a model airship, 3.5 m long and 1.3 m in diameter, with a hydrogen gas volume of 2,200 L and a net lift of 2 kg. Its "petite machine dynamo-electrique" (motor), of the Siemens type, weighed 220 g (Tissandier 1885, 2). The airship attained a speed of about 3 m/s (6). It was powered by lead-acid batteries supplied by Gaston Planté (Desmond 2018, 16).

Tissandier pointed out that the use of battery power "eliminates the danger of fire under a mass of hydrogen." Also, since no fuel was consumed, the weight remained constant, so there would be no need to vent gas to compensate for lightening during flight. Finally, its motor "starts with incomparable ease by the simple touch of a switch." He applied for a

Part I: Unconventional Power

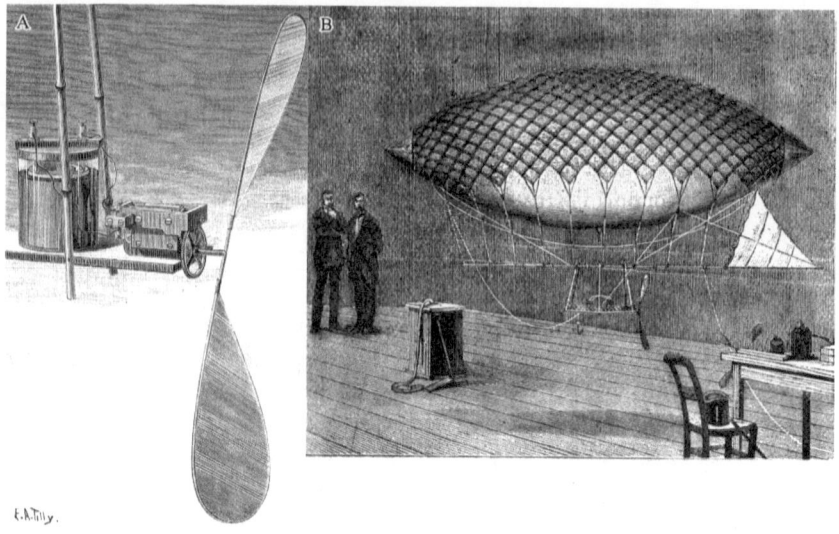

A. The battery, motor and propeller of the small electric aerostat Tissandier exhibited at the 1881 Electricity Exposition (Tissandier 1885, frontispiece). B. The aerostat itself, indoors (fig. 3).

patent on June 9, 1881. In a May 12, 1882, addition, he proposed the use of a potassium dichromate battery (Tissandier 1885, 6).

As constructed in April 1882, this battery had alternating electrodes of carbon and "amalgamated zinc" placed in an ebonite trough (Tissandier 1885, 10). The trough, when full, contained 4 L of a concentrated electrolyte solution of potassium dichromate and sulfuric acid (11–12).[1] With a battery weighing 8 kg, they obtained a current of 110 amperes (A) and 1.68 volts (V; 12).[2]

They referred to their battery as a *flow battery* because they contemplated gravity feeding fresh electrolytes to the trough. However, in modern usage, a flow battery is one with a liquid anode (anolyte) and cathode (catholyte) continuously supplied to the cell.

With an 18-element battery weighing 140 kg, they could provide 1.25–1.5 hp for two to three hours. Tissandier (1885) also refers to a motor weighing 50 kg (12–13).

After an unsuccessful attempt to find funding for building a 3,000 cu m airship and a hangar to house it, he and his brother decided to build one of just 1,000 cu m out of their own financial resources (Tissandier 1885, 15).

The fixed equipment of this airship, as built, was as follows: gas bag and valves (170 kg); suspension and rudder (70 kg); flexible side stretchers

4. Battery Power

(34 kg); "nacelle" (the gondola? 100 kg); batteries with electrolyte, motor and propeller (280 kg); anchor and guide rope (50 kg), totaling 704 kg. The four dichromate batteries, each of six elements with 0.0015 m thick zinc anodes, were thought good for three hours. A mercury bucket switch was arranged so the pilot could choose to pass the current of 6, 12, 18 or all 24 elements. The operating load consisted of two "voyageurs" with instruments (150 kg) and ballast (386 kg), bringing the total weight up to 1,240 kg. The gas volume was actually 1,060 cu m (37,434 cu ft), providing a gross lift force capable of lifting 1,250 kg (Tissandier 1885, 44, 47–48, 51).

Unfortunately, Tissandier does not specify the individual weights of the batteries and motor. If the element here weighed the same as the one in the model airship, then the 24 elements of the four batteries would weigh 112 kg (256.9 lb). However, Chanute (1891) says that the Siemens motor was 99 lb and the batteries 517 lb (12). If so, they total 616 lb (279.4 kg). That is inconsistent with Tissandier's weight data unless the motor includes the propeller.

Nor does Tissandier state the motor power. Values quoted in other literature include 1.5 hp (Chanute, 1891) or 2 hp (D'Orcy 1917, 97). Bailleux (1987, 271) says that the "motor propeller set" required 1.8 kWe to supply "one mechanical kilowatt"—that is, it had a conversion efficiency of 55.5%.

In operation, the propeller was driven at 60–180 rpm, depending on the number of elements in use (Tissandier 1885, 54). Facing into the wind (Chanute [1891] says it was 6.7 mph at 1,600 ft), the airship could at best remain motionless. Attempting to maneuver crosswind, they had problems with rudder control (Tissandier 1885, 55).

We turn next to the endeavors of the French military engineers Charles Renard (1847–1905) and Arthur Constantin Krebs (1850–1935).

Krebs designed a motor that weighed 88 kg and provided 8.6 hp [6.4 kW]. The propeller was 7 m in diameter (Bailleux 1987, 276).

Renard wanted a battery weighing just 65 kg/kW (Bailleux 1987, 272). He ultimately settled on one based on the chlorine-zinc couple. Rather than bringing a large quantity of chlorine gas on board, he decided to produce chlorine in situ by the reaction of hydrochloric acid and chromic acid in aqueous solution (273).

One electrode was pure zinc, and the other was platinum-plated (for corrosion resistance) silver (for high conductivity). The latter was passive; it didn't participate in the reaction; it just conducted electrons. The reaction was between the zinc and the dissolved chlorine. The reaction was energetic enough that there was a danger of the electrolyte boiling off, and consequently, "each stack in the battery was shaped as a vertical tube of small diameter." The outer casing of the tube "acted as a radiator," and

Part I: Unconventional Power

One of the four batteries for Tissandier's 1883 battery-powered airship (Tissandier 1885, fig. 21).

the tubes were spaced sufficiently apart so that they would be adequately cooled by air convection. The voltage was 1.2 V and the current density 0.25 A/cm^2 (15°C; Bailleux 1987, 274–275). Power output was controlled by raising or lowering the zinc electrodes (276).[3]

4. Battery Power

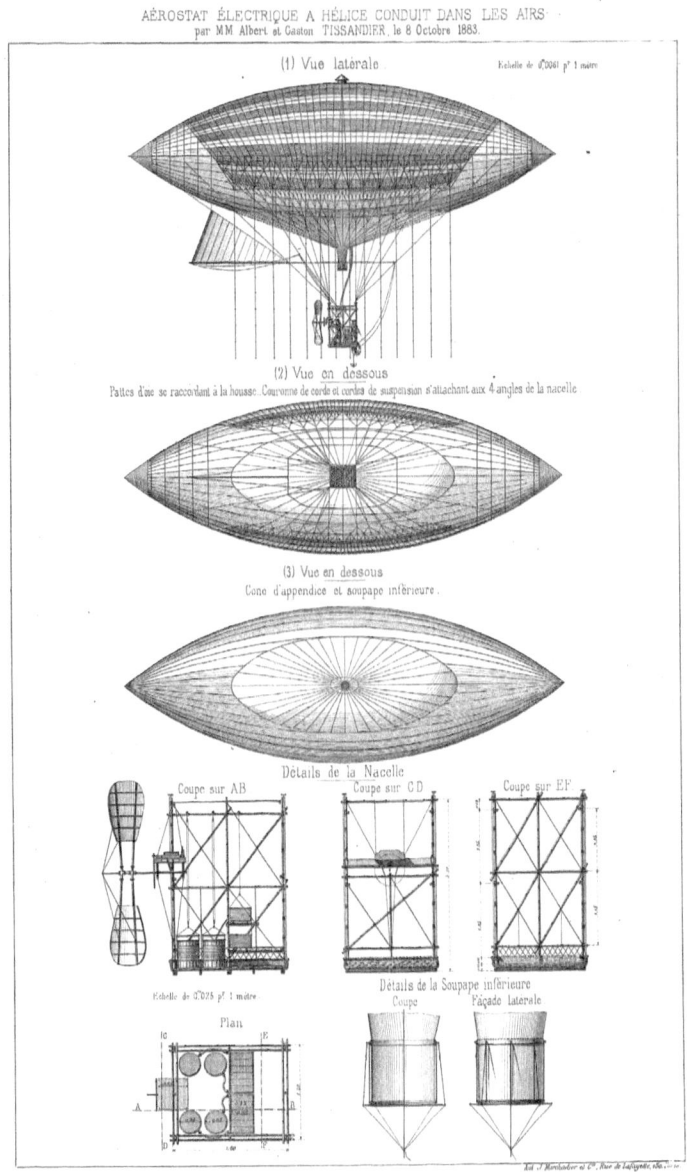

Design drawings for Tissandier's 1883 battery-powered airship. These appear to correspond to figs. 11 and 20 (Tissandier 1885). Reproduction # LC-DIG-ppmsca-02529. Library of Congress Prints and Photographs Division. https://www.loc.gov/pictures/item/2002736617/.

Part I: Unconventional Power

Their *La France* airship was 50.42 m long and 8.4 m in diameter, with a maximum gas volume of 1,864 cu m (65,827 cu ft). Krebs calculated that to achieve a speed of 8–9 m/s, a propulsive power of 5 hp was needed. The engine could output up to 8.5 hp (Tissandier 1885, 80).

The empty weight breakdown for *La France* was as follows: gas bag and valves (369 kg), suspension (127 kg), nacelle (452 kg), rudder (41 kg), propeller (41 kg), "machine" (98 kg), "buildings and gear" (47 kg), engine shaft (30.5 kg), and "battery, apparatus and miscellaneous" (435.5 kg).[4] To this, add the operating load of aeronauts (140 kg) and ballast (214 kg) for a grand total of 2,000 kg (equaling the gross lift of the hydrogen; Tissandier 1885, 83).

On its first flight (August 9, 1884; mapped by Tissandier 1885, fig. 29), *La France* was able to make a U-turn with a turning radius of about 150 m and return to its starting place (85). It had flown for 7.6 kilometers (km) in 23 minutes, for an average speed of 5.5 m/s. The electric power was estimated at 250 kgf-m (13,475 W), but the efficiencies of the motor and propeller were about 70% each, reducing the propulsive power to 123 kgf-m (6,630 W, 8.9 hp; 86). The power usage was 2.5 kW (Bailleux 1987, 277).

On its November 8, 1884, flight, *La France* demonstrated an effective power of 5 hp at 50 propeller rpm. The wind speed was 8 km/h. However, the airship was capable of 23.5 km/h in still air, so even against a direct headwind, it could achieve a ground speed of 15.5 km/h (Tissandier 1885, 96). Overall, "*La France* flew seven times, and returned to its starting point five times" (Bailleux 1987, 277).

Despite the success of *La France*, airship designers turned their attention to internal combustion engines. Over a century passed before the next battery-powered airship was built.

The *Lotte*, an unmanned airship with a hull volume of 109 cu m, was operated from 1993 to 2003. It had a 1.1 kW nickel-cadmium battery and a maximum airspeed of 12.5 m/s, but only 45 minutes of endurance (Dorrington 2007b, 92).

In 1995, in Project Hornbill, G. E. Dorrington used a small battery-powered helium-lift airship to study a tropical rainforest canopy. His two-seater *Dirigible-4* had a hull volume of just 390 cu m (13,773 cu ft) and used a sealed lead-acid battery with a power output of 1.6–1.9 kW (2.15–2.55 hp). It had a maximum airspeed of 5–5.8 m/s (11.2–13.0 mph), which was sufficient for his purpose.

In 2004, Dorrington used a larger airship with more advanced battery technology. The *White Diamond* had a hull volume of 480 cu m and a lithium-ion (lithium-iron-phosphate per Desmond 2018, 111) battery with a power output of 3.2 kW. However, he traded speed for endurance; its maximum speed was only 3–3.5 m/s, but its endurance increased from 60 to 90 minutes.

The *Iris Challenger 2* was a lenticular (oblate spheroid) airship with a gas bag height of 6 m and a diameter of 14 m, holding up to 560 cu m of helium. It was powered by lithium-polymer batteries (four hours autonomy), connected to two electric motors, each 7 kW, turning 1.3 m counter-rotating propellers. The engines and gondola were suspended well below the gas bag, giving it pendulum stability against pitch and roll. Its cruising speed was 15 km/h (9.3 mph). It first flew in 2011, and it successfully crossed the English Channel in 2013 (Lobner 2022d; Desmond 2018, 127).

Battery Electric Airplanes

The purely battery-powered airplanes are more aptly described as motor gliders. They are not capable of sustained powered flight and have high aspect ratio wings suitable for gliding. The battery power is used to climb, and the airplane glides back to the ground.

The Militky-Birditschka MB-E1, which debuted in 1973, was equipped with four nickel-cadmium battery packs (each 25 Ah and 64 lb) and a 10 kW motor (60 kg). Its best performance was climbing 1.5–2 m/s to 360 m and then gliding, with a total air time of 14 minutes (Desmond 2018, 68–69).

The current Lange Antares electric glider uses a 42 kW (57 hp) DC/DC brushless motor and a RED.3 battery system with type 21700 automotive lithium-ion battery cells. A battery block contains 14 (standard block) or 18 (large block) cells, and "36 of these battery blocks are arranged together in one wing, forming a battery chain" (Lange 2024). Lange does not provide the weight of the motor, but the 42 kW EM42 motor had a dry weight of 29.12 kg (64.2 lb; Wikipedia). Lange (2024) says that the large configuration adds 11 kg per battery chain, implying a battery cell weight of 76.39 g[5] and a standard configuration battery chain weight of 38.5 kg.

Hybrid Gas-Electric Airplanes

The use of battery power alone is currently confined to small airplanes and short, powered flights. For regional airplanes, series hybrid, parallel hybrid, or series-parallel hybrid configurations are more likely to

Part I: Unconventional Power

be feasible in the near future. These hybrid technologies were developed previously for hybrid electric automobiles.

In a series hybrid topology, only the electric motor provides mechanical power to the propulsor. "The motor receives electric power from either the battery pack or from a generator run by a gasoline engine."[6] In a parallel hybrid topology, the drivetrain is designed so that either the gasoline engine or the electric motor may provide mechanical power to the propulsor, and indeed, they do so simultaneously. In a series-parallel hybrid technology, while both the engine and the motor may provide mechanical power, it is also possible to use the motor alone (UCS 2018).[7]

The first airplane with a series gas-electric topology was the Diamond DA36 E-Star, a two-seat motor glider, which first flew on June 8, 2011. EADS batteries powered a 70 kW motor. The batteries provided the energy needed for takeoff and climb and were recharged during cruise by a 40 hp (30 kW) Wankel rotary engine running at a constant 30 kW. This approach "decreases fuel consumption and carbon emissions by 25 percent when compared to conventional aircraft" (Diamond Aircraft 2011; Whitfield 2011).

The same year also witnessed the first flight of a series-parallel hybrid gas-electric motor glider, the *Eco Eagle*, built by student engineers at Embry-Riddle Aeronautical University. I classify it as series-parallel because it has a clutch system, which "allows only one of the two power sources to turn the propeller" (Nanda 2011, 27). It had an avgas-burning, air/liquid-cooled, 100 hp (75 hp) Rotax 912ULS four-cylinder engine (134 lb dry weight, 10.5:1 compression ratio, max 5,800 rpm) (7–8, 11) and an air cooled, 40 hp, three-phase AC PMSM (permanent magnet synchronous motors) electric motor (14–15).

A two-blade, 184 cm propeller was employed (Nanda 2011, 24). Since it is more efficient at lower revolutions per minute, the output revolutions per minute to the propeller was reduced by a 2.43:1 gearbox for the engine (10) and a 1.18:1 pulley system (30) for a maximum propeller revolutions per minute under engine power of 2,022. The motor had a maximum output of 7,000 rpm, but this was reduced at the propeller to 1,913 rpm (30).

The *Eco Eagle*'s lithium-iron-phosphate batteries had a nominal capacity of 20 ampere-hours (Ah; 3.2 V), a specific energy of 125 watt-hours per kilogram (Wh/kg), a maximum charging rate of 20 A, and a maximum continuous discharging rate of 40 A. There were two modules in each wing; each module contained 40 cells, and each of the 160 cells weighed 1 lb, 1.92 oz (21, 32). Total battery weight, including control circuitry, was about 200 lb (Sigler 2011).

4. Battery Power

In the *Eco Eagle*'s case, the intent was to cruise on battery power but use the gas engine for takeoff and climb (Nanda 2011, abstract).

Analysis

The problem at the close of the 19th century wasn't that batteries and motors wouldn't work but that their power-to-weight ratio didn't improve as quickly as gasoline internal combustion engines, which eclipsed them.

However, nickel-cadmium, nickel metal hydride and lithium-ion batteries have changed the calculation, at least for smaller craft or short flights.

Batteries and Fuel Cells: Overview

A battery consists of one or more galvanic (voltaic) cells. A galvanic cell is an electrochemical cell (reactor) in which chemical reactions occur spontaneously at two electrodes. One reaction (oxidation) generates electrons, and the other (reduction) absorbs electrons (together, these paired reactions are called a *redox reaction*). The reactions are separated by a non-electron-conductive electrolyte so that the electrons are forced to pass through an electrical wire connecting the electrodes with a device, thereby powering the latter. The battery converts chemical energy directly into electrical energy as direct current.

There are two types of galvanic cells: primary (non-rechargeable) and secondary (rechargeable). Rechargeable batteries are much more difficult to develop because they have a much longer working life (say, over 1,000 charge-discharge cycles) over which they must essentially maintain power output and capacity. That, in turn, means minimizing the side reactions that adversely affect the battery (Dell 1996). Hence, some chemistries exist in practical primary batteries but have not been commercialized in a rechargeable form.

The anode is the electrode at which oxidation occurs, and the cathode is the electrode at which reduction occurs. Since both oxidation and reduction occur at different electrodes, the reactions are called *half-reactions*, and the parts of the cells in which they occur are *half-cells*. In a rechargeable battery, the anode will be negative during discharge and positive during recharge. The opposite is true for the cathode.

An active electrode participates as a reactant in the reaction, and a passive (inert) one just serves as an electrical conductor. In a secondary battery, the active electrode is restored to its original state during recharge.

The electrolyte is a liquid, solid or gel containing mobile ions that render it ionically conductive. Without an electrolyte, the redox reaction would create an ever-increasing charge imbalance that would halt the reaction. With an electrolyte present, negatively and/or positively charged ions can pass through the electrolyte between the anode and the cathode in order to neutralize the charge. In some batteries, the electrolyte is consumed during discharge, and in others, it either doesn't react at all or is (ideally) regenerated by secondary reactions, so there is no net change.

The anode and cathode cannot be in direct contact, as this would short out the cell, and it would produce no power. Since one of the desiderata for batteries is compactness, most commercial batteries are designed to have a nonelectrically conductive separator between and in physical contact with both the anode and cathode. Simple physical separation of anode and cathode is not necessarily sufficient to avoid shorting, as the active material can shed or grow dendrites that reach out toward the other electrode. The separator must be chemically resistant to the electrolyte, ionically conductive, and have a high electron resistance. Wood, cloth, rubber, glass, ceramic and plastic have all been used as separator materials.

A battery may consist of more than one electrochemical cell. If identical cells are connected in series, the voltages are summed, but the maximum current is unchanged. If identical cells are connected in parallel, the maximum currents are summed, and the battery voltage is the same as the cell voltage.

Battery Performance Characteristics

Voltage (V): the voltage difference between cathode and anode, which may be distinguished among the theoretical (nominal) voltage, the practical (rated) voltage, and the cutoff voltage. The voltage declines as the battery discharges, and the cutoff voltage is that at which the battery is fully discharged.

Specific energy (Wh/kg): the total dischargeable energy stored in the battery per unit mass.

Energy density (Wh/L): the total dischargeable energy stored in the battery per unit volume.

Specific power (W/kg): the power (energy/time) a battery can deliver per unit mass.

Power density (W/L): the power a battery can deliver per unit volume.

Cycle life: the number of charge-discharge cycles that a battery can carry out and still satisfy mission requirements, depending on the user's tolerance for reductions in voltage, energy capacity and power.

Charge rate: the time it takes to fully charge the battery. The rate changes as the battery's charge level changes.

4. Battery Power

Self-discharge rate: how quickly a battery loses charge (energy) when not in use. The rate depends on how close the battery is to fully charged and on the temperature.

Operating temperature: the range of temperatures in which the battery can satisfy mission requirements.

The specific energy and energy density affect the endurance of the airship or airplane, which have limited mass and volume to dedicate to the batteries. The specific power and power density affect the maximum speed of the airship or airplane. The cycle life, charge rate and self-discharge rate affect the economics of operation. The operating temperature range potentially affects where and how high they can operate efficiently.

The theoretical (charge) capacity of a battery is the amount of charge (Ampere-hour or milliampere-hour [mAh]) that the battery can deliver at the theoretical voltage. The energy capacity (watt-hours) is the capacity times the voltage.

The theoretical specific charge capacity is the charge capacity divided by the mass of the electroactive components of the anode and cathode, and the theoretical specific energy is similarly defined. The energy or charge density of the battery may be calculated if the proportions and densities of the active materials are known.

In general, the total energy output of a practical cell will be 20%–40% (Pistoia 2005, 7) of the theoretical value. This is due to two factors: 1) the reduction of voltage and thus energy as a result of internal resistance and 2) the impracticality of fully discharging the cell because of various failure modes. (Additionally, the specific capacity and energy density of a practical cell will reflect the mass and volume of the other battery components, such as the electrolyte, separator, current collector, and housing.)

When cells are combined into a battery pack, there may be a further increase in mass (e.g., for cooling systems) and thus a further reduction in specific capacity and energy density.

The effective energy capacity also depends on the discharge rate; more can be pulled out of a battery at a low discharge rate than at maximum power (Dorrington 2007b, 97).

Rechargeable Battery Comparison

Table 4-1 compares the major types of rechargeable batteries. (Even within a single type, the parameter values vary from manufacturer to manufacturer and model to model, because of both differences in construction and differences in testing methods.)

Part I: Unconventional Power

Table 4–1: Performance Characteristics of Selected Commercial Rechargeable Battery Types

Name	Specific Energy Wh/kg	Energy Density Wh/L	Specific Power W/kg	Ref
Lead Acid (cathode is lead dioxide)	30–40 35 (252) 30–50 12–32 30–45	60–75 70	180 330 200	W P A D K
Nickel (Oxide) Cadmium (NiCd)	30 35 (244) 40–50	100 100	150–200 190	W P K
Nickel (Oxide) Metal Hydride (NiMH)	100 75 (240)38–55 50–60	401 240	250–1000 660 180	W P D K
Zinc Silver Oxide	130 70–120 140–220	240 50–415	 100–330	W* C K
Lithium-Ion Batteries				
Lithium Ion (generic)	110–180 150 (410) 120–125 130	400	 87–105 800	A P D K
Lithium Polymer (generic)	100–130			A
Lithium Titanate	60–110	177	3,000–5,100	W
Lithium Cobalt Oxide	195	560		W
Lithium Iron Phosphate	90–160	333	200–1,200	W
Lithium Manganese Oxide	150 150 (1,001)	420 400		W P
Lithium Nickel Cobalt Aluminum Oxide	220	600		W
Lithium Nickel Manganese Cobalt Oxide	205	580		W
Lithium Sulfur (experimental)	400–500	350	550	W*

References: P: Pistoia 2005, table 1.1, practical battery; theoretical values in parentheses; A: Aifantis et al. 2010, table 3.1; D: Dorrington 2007b, table 6; C: Crompton 2000, $5.2. K: Kantor et al. 2001; W: https://en.wikipedia.org/wiki/Comparison_of_commercial_battery_types; W*: https://en.wikipedia.org/wiki/Rechargeable_battery

4. Battery Power

To put these numbers in perspective, gasoline has a specific energy of 12,888.9 W/kg and an energy density of 9,500 W/L (Wikipedia).

Lithium-ion and lithium-polymer batteries are now the dominant types for aerial applications.

The first lithium-ion battery appeared on the market in 1991 (Wu 2015, 3). The appeal of lithium is that it combines a high oxidation potential and a low density. The problem is that it reacts vigorously with water, and most battery electrolytes are aqueous solutions.

In the oldest lithium-ion chemistry, the positive electrode (the cathode when discharging) is initially composed of a cobalt (III) oxide with intercalated lithium ions. When the battery is charged, some lithium ions leave the positive electrode and intercalate themselves into the negative electrode, which is made of graphite. In the process, the cobalt (III) is oxidized to cobalt (IV), and the lithium ion entering the negative electrode is reduced to the neutral state (Wu 2015, 9). The electrolyte was a lithium salt (e.g., hexafluorophosphate) in an organic carbonate ester solvent (Blomgren 2017).

The other lithium-ion chemistries noted in the table also use materials that can intercalate lithium ions.

The lithium-polymer (Li-Po) battery, featuring a polymer electrolyte, was introduced in 1999 (Kumar and Sarakonsri 2010, 18). The earliest Li-Po cells were of rather low power, so their first aerial use was in model airplanes in 2004 (Desmond 2018, 107). However, in 2007, they were used on Ivo Boscarol's *Taurus Electro* microlight two-seat glider. With a 30 kW motor, Boscarol was able to climb to 1,000 m and fly for "20 minutes at speeds of up to 150 kph (90 mph)" (115).

Lithium-sulfur batteries should not be confused with lithium-ion batteries; they use a metallic lithium anode and a sulfur or carbon-sulfur cathode. Lithium-sulfur chemistry provides a "theoretical specific energy in excess of 2700 Wh/kg." Oxis lithium-sulfur batteries (400 Wh/kg) were used in the *Centurion* UAV (Desmond 2018, 128), but they are still considered experimental.

Supercapacitors

Supercapacitors provide a higher specific power (about 10,000 W/kg), a greater cycle life (millions of times), and a faster charge time (a few minutes) than batteries; hence, they may be useful for takeoff on all-battery airplane. However, their specific energy is low (about 5 Wh/kg), their voltage declines linearly as they discharge, and their cost per watt-hour is high (EEPower 2024).

Part I: Unconventional Power

Motors

A battery by itself won't turn a propeller. Motors convert electrical power into mechanical work. Motors may run on AC (alternating current) or DC (direct current) power, but batteries provide the latter.

As with engines, a high power-to-weight ratio is desirable, which generally means that brushless direct current (BLDC) or PMSM are favored.

A brushless motor comprises a rotor and a stator. The stator comprises several fixed coils spaced around the rotor. When an electric current passes through the coils, they generate magnetic fields. The rotor is a permanent magnet that, as its name suggests, rotates. This is accomplished by sensing the rotational position of the rotor and sequentially varying the current passing into the surrounding coils accordingly. The rotor is mounted on a shaft, so when the rotor turns, so does the shaft. The motor housing consists of a cylindrical frame and an end shield.

"The physical construction of the PMSM is similar to a BLDC motor," but the input waves are different (Nanda 2011, 13).

In 2015, Siemens developed a prototype brushless AC electric airplane motor (SP260D-0) weighing 50 kg (110 lb) and providing 260 kW of continuous power at 2,500 rpm. Its end shield has a filigree structure to minimize weight, and the rotor's "permanent magnets are configured into a Hallbach array" (Desmond 2018, 148–149). A Halbach array creates a "one-sided" magnetic field, ideally twice as large on one side and zero on the other. The relatively low motor speed "allows the propeller to be mounted directly on its shaft without the need for an intermediate gearbox," and the motor's "efficiency is 95%" (Ivanov et al. 2022).

The SP260D was used in the Extra 330LE, which set FAI world records for time to climb (3,000 m in 4:22 in 2016) and speed (337.5 km/h in 2017) in its category (Anton 2019, 19). Siemens has also developed the SP260D-A, which weighs only 44 kg and has a specific power of 5.9 kW/kg (17). However, Siemens sold its electric airplane propulsion business to Rolls-Royce in 2019.

H3X (2023) has announced a series of high specific power motors, including the HPDM-250 (200 kW continuous, 18.7 kg); the HPDM-30 (33 kW, 4.1 kg); and (for pre-order) the HPDM-1500, stackable up to 9,000 kW, 760 kg (11.84 kW/kg). These all combine "the electric motor, inverter, and gearbox into a single unit."[8] Cooling is with an ethylene glycol-water mixture (Ivanov et al. 2022).

5

Solar Power

The energy of the sun is free, and it has been used since ancient times to heat buildings. However, its use in airplanes thus far has required finding a means of converting solar (light) energy to electrical energy. The photovoltaic[1] (PV) cell made this possible.

The photovoltaic effect was discovered by Edmond Becquerel in 1839. Charles Fritts made solar cells from selenium in 1883, but they were "less than one percent efficient" at converting sunlight to electricity (GoGreenSolar, 2022). The "first practical silicon solar cell"[2] was demonstrated in 1954; it was "about 6 percent efficient" (APS News, 2009). Solar cells have been much improved since then.

For a complete solar-electric powerplant, the PV cell needs to be combined with an electric motor. And to fly at night or when it is cloudy, an electrical energy storage system is needed that can charge while it is sunny and be drawn from when it is not. Both electric motors and batteries were discussed in the previous chapter.

Using solar energy simply to provide heat for a heat engine has also been proposed but has not been put into practice.

History—Solar-Electric Airplanes

The first solar-powered airplane flight was the remote-controlled *Sunrise I* in 1970. The Sunrise I was equipped with 4,096 wing-mounted Heliotek solar cells having a specific power of 45.4 W/kg and "12 percent efficiency." These "could be set for either series or parallel operation." The craft's wing loading was 0.011 kg/m^2. It made "28 flights ... on solar power alone" (Desmond 2018, 75–77). The *Sunrise II*, which flew in 1975, was given improved Heliotek cells (60.48 W/kg and 14% efficiency) and an improved motor (samarium-cobalt vs. ferrite; 78).

The first manned flight was the *Mauro Solar Riser* (1979). The wings' solar cells (total power 350W) were used on the ground to charge a

Part I: Unconventional Power

nickel-cadmium battery. Its cells were incapable of keeping up with flight power demands: "A charge in bright sunshine for an hour and a half yielded a flight of 3 to 5 minutes." This was "sufficient to reach a gliding altitude." The battery was used during flight to power a 3.5 hp (2.6 kW) motor, which turned a 41 in. propeller via a belt drive (Desmond 2018, 79–80).

The *Gossamer Penguin*, designed originally for human-powered flight, made the first fully solar-powered flight, albeit a short one, in 1980. It weighed "68 pounds without a pilot" and was equipped with 3,921 solar cells with a maximum total output of 541 W Curry 2002). That flight was just 500 ft at an altitude of 5 ft (Desmond 2018, 84). A couple of months later, it made a 1.95 mi, 14-minute, 21-second flight, but there seems to be some uncertainty whether the latter was accomplished solely by solar power (Curry 2002) or "a combination of solar and battery power" (Lee 2010).

The *Solar Challenger* achieved a 163 mi flight on June 7, 1981. Its 16,128 solar cells were mounted on both the wings and the horizontal tailplane. The cells were satellite program rejects, with less than the government-required 14% efficiency. Two 2.75 hp samarium-cobalt motors

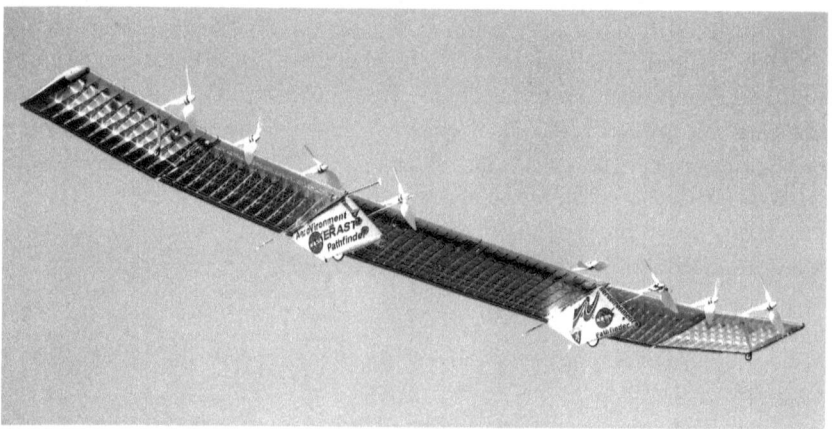

The unmanned *Pathfinder Plus* flies over Hawaii on July 17, 1998. Photo by Jim Ross. Courtesy of the National Aeronautics and Space Administration (Dryden Flight Research Center Photo Collection). NASA Photo EC96-44629-58. The top of the 121 ft flying wing was completely covered by solar cells (a mix of cells of 14% and 19% efficiency), producing 12.5 kW, and these powered eight motors. Control was primarily by autopilot, but also by remote control. It set an unofficial solar-powered aircraft altitude record of 80,201 ft on August 6, 1998, later superseded by *Helios HP01* (Wikipedia). https://web.archive.org/web/20111019000109/http://www.dfrc.nasa.gov/gallery/photo/Pathfinder-Plus/Large/EC98-44629-58.jpg.

"were run in tandem on a common shaft to drive a single ... propeller" (Desmond 2018, 84–91).

The *Sunseeker I* made the first solar-powered crossing of the United States in 1990 (Desmond 2018, 96). The *Sunseeker Duo* (2013) was the first two-seater solar-powered airplane. Its empty weight was 280 kg, and its 1,510 solar cells had 23% efficiency, providing 5 kW (Solar Flight 2024).

In 2012, the *Solar Impulse* flew 4,000 mi round trip (Europe–Africa) in eight legs (Schoeberl 2008; Noth 2008; Wikipedia). *Solar Impulse II*, weighing 2.3 tons (tn; airframe constructed of carbon fiber and an alveolate foam honeycomb) and with a wingspan of 72 m, circumnavigated the Earth from 2015 to 2016 in 16 legs. It cruised at 28,000 ft at an average airspeed of 75 km/h. Its 17,248 monocrystalline silicon solar cells (135 microns thick; 23% efficiency), covering 269.5 sq m of the wings, fuselage and horizontal tailplane, produced a total of 11,655 kilowatt-hours (kWh) over the course of the circumnavigation. It had four brushless motors (each 17 hp), each driving a 4 m diameter propeller. The motor efficiency was variously stated as 94% and 97% (SIF 2023).[3]

History—Solar-Electric Airships[4]

The advantage that a solar-powered airship has over a solar-powered airplane is that it does not need power to generate lift. One disadvantage is that the solar panels must be fitted over a curved envelope.[5] This means that the absorbed power will vary from cell to cell depending on the angle of incidence of the sunlight. Another disadvantage is that because the airship needs to be large in order to have sufficient lift, it is more vulnerable than an airplane to high winds during takeoff and landing.

The first solar-powered airship was the Walden Aerospace XEM-1, which flew, albeit tethered, in 1974. It was 5.5 ft long and weighed 1.8 lb (Lobner 2024).

The *Lotte*, a radio-controlled, solar-powered airship (16 m long, 4 m diameter, 109 cu m volume, 100 kg weight), made its first flight in 1992. It had a 4.8 sq m solar cell array, providing a maximum of 720 W (Lobner 2022a; TAO 2023).

The Lockheed Martin high-altitude, long-endurance demonstrator (*HALE-D*), a remote-controlled airship 240 ft long and 70 ft in diameter, was intended to fly at 60,000 ft. It had a "15 kW thin film array," a "40 kWh Li-Po" battery, and "two 2 kW motors." It was destroyed in a fire after its maiden flight in 2011 (Desmond 2018, 98–99).

Part I: Unconventional Power

Aero Drum Ltd is currently (2023) selling a Solar RC Blimp that is "able to carry a payload of up to 2 kg." It has a length of 10 m, a diameter of 1.9 m, and a volume of 22.5 cu m. The envelope is 125-micron thick polyurethane with a helium permeability of 0.5%–1% total volume daily. It carries three flexible solar cell modules (54 Maxeon GEN III cells, 24% efficiency) on top of its forebody. It has four Li-Po batteries, providing a total of 20,000 mAh for energy storage, and an "intelligent power control" that allocates the solar cell output between the motor and the batteries. It has a "solar autonomy" (ability to operate without sunlight if the batteries are fully charged) of two to three hours. The propeller and main motor are mounted on the bow (Aero Drum 2023).

A much more ambitious project, the manned *Solar Airship One* (Euro Airship 2023), is intended to be capable of circumnavigating the Earth at an altitude of 20,000 ft. It is to be a "rigid" airship with a "double envelope," 151 m long, ellipsoidal in shape, with a "helium expansion volume" of 53,000 cu m in 15 separate gas cells. The artwork shows the solar cells on the upper side of the envelope, not quite reaching its equator and excluding small sections at the bow and stern. The design calls for 4,800 sq m of solar film. The artwork also suggests that it will be driven by four cycloidal propellers, two on each side. Energy will be stored in "fuel cells that produce hydrogen via water electrolysis." (For hydrogen-based power, see chapter 7.)

History—Solar Steam

In 1869, the math teacher Augustin Mouchot displayed a solar boiler that generated 45 psi of steam. In 1878, he won the Paris Exhibition Gold Medal by using a solar engine with a 13 ft diameter mirror and a 21-gallon (gal), 100 psi boiler to power an icemaker. In 1882, his protégé Pifre used solar power to drive a printing press (Collins 2002). Augustin Mouchot, John Ericsson and A. G. Eneas all built solar-powered steam engines (Kalogiru 2023, 26).

In 1876, the publisher Louis Simonin wrote of Mouchot's "solar receiver," "the aeronaut can with its aid propel his airship" (556). In essence, Simonin proposed using solar energy to boil water, then using the expansion of the resulting steam to do work (pushing a piston or turning a turbine). However, no solar-steam propulsion system has ever been built.

5. Solar Power

History—Solar Stirling

Solar heat could be used merely to heat air or other gas, as in a Stirling cycle engine (see chapter 3). Bennett (2007) proposed a solar–Stirling airplane with an internal tracking trough.

In 2011, Laurens Rademakers proposed a solar–Stirling-electric propulsion system for an unmanned airship. The semirigid design featured two spherical, partially transparent balloons linked by a retaining frame with an internal concave solar reflector. Sunlight would pass through the envelope and be concentrated by the reflector on the Stirling engine heat source. The piston movement would be converted to electrical power, which would drive the propeller motor directly or be stored in a battery for later use (Lobner 2022c).

Another solar–Stirling concept was advanced by Melin Kaplan in 2012. This was a semirigid airship with a partially transparent spherical gas bag. Sunlight would be concentrated by a Fresnel lens (rather than a mirror). A two-axis sun-tracking system mounted on the keel would keep the transparent half of the balloons and the Fresnel lens facing the sun. Excess energy would be stored mechanically (rotation of a flywheel) rather than by a battery (Lobner 2022b).

Analysis

Available Solar Power

The power of direct sunlight that would irradiate a surface directly facing the sun is dependent first on the solar constant, the irradiance (1,361 W/m^2) on such a surface at Earth's mean orbital distance (one astronomical unit) but outside Earth's atmosphere. The actual irradiance on such a surface varies seasonally (1,321–1,412 W/m^2) because of the eccentricity of Earth's orbit (Wikipedia).

The irradiance on such a surface, mounted on the ground or on an airship or airplane, further depends on the "path length of clear atmosphere through which the solar radiation penetrates before reaching" that surface. The path length is shortest at a solar altitude of 90°, which depends on the latitude, the time of year, and the time of day. Atmospheric humidity and pollution may reduce the intensity, and the magnitude of the reduction also depends on path length (Khoury 2012, 521–524). On a clear day, the maximum direct irradiance at sea level on a surface facing the sun is about 1,050 W/m^2 (Wikipedia).

Part I: Unconventional Power

For a given solar altitude, the path length is shorter for a solar collector aloft than for one on the ground. However, the relationship between flight altitude and solar irradiance is highly nonlinear.

If the surface does not directly face the sun, then the direct solar radiation is spread over a larger area, and thus the irradiance (energy flux per unit area) will be less. On residential rooftops, fixed-tilt solar panels are tilted from horizontal at an angle close to the local latitude and face south (in the northern hemisphere) to obtain the maximum average total radiation.

Besides direct sunlight, there is also diffuse solar radiation (skylight), the result of the scattering of light by air molecules or particles and solar radiation reflected by clouds and ground surfaces.

The time of year and the latitude also determine the length of the day and thus the total solar energy that can be collected before the airship or airplane must switch over to battery operation.

Photovoltaic Cell Technology

Photovoltaic (solar) cells convert light energy to electrical energy. The latter can then be used to power a motor that turns the propeller. In addition, if excess energy is collected during the daytime, it can be used to charge a battery to power the motor at night.

The critical technology is the solar (PV) cell. The designer must worry about its efficiency, weight, cost and form (thin film or not).

In 2023, the highest confirmed efficiency for a research cell was 47.6% (for a III–V multijunction cell with a concentrator) or 39.46% (without a concentrator). For single-junction gallium-arsenide cells, it was 30.8% (with a concentrator) or 29.1% (without). For crystalline silicon cells, it was 27.1% (NREL 2023).

In 2008, the Alta Devices AnyLight™ gallium-arsenide cells had efficiencies of 28.6% (single junction) or 31.6% (dual junction). "Equipped with AnyLight cells, … an AeroVironment RQ-20 Puma UAV, which normally has an endurance of 2 to 3 hours, flew for" a little over nine hours (Desmond 2018, 104).

The highest efficiency for a thin film technology was 23.6% for an Evolar/UU copper indium gallium diselenide (CIGS) cell (NREL 2023). But "commercial CIGS modules typically have efficiencies between 12% and 14%" (SETO 2023).

Kantor et al. (2011) assumed that an airship would have solar cells of 12.8% efficiency and 1.5 kg/m^2 areal density. Ozoroski et al. (2015) assumed a solar cell efficiency of 25%.

5. Solar Power

Efficiency is adversely affected by high temperatures. Typically, there is a "power loss of about 0.5% for each degree Celsius above 25°C" (Gunther 2024). Solar radiation will tend to heat the PV cells, but they will lose heat by convection and radiation to the exterior and by conduction through the underlying skin to the interior. The greater the airspeed, the greater the heat loss by forced convection. Also, the higher the altitude, the colder the ambient air, which acts as a heat sink. However, the presence of an underlying insulating layer, perhaps to inhibit the superheating or supercooling of the lift gas of an airship, will retard heat loss to the interior and thus reduce PV cell efficiency (Li et al. 2011).

Efficiency is only part of the picture. The specific power (for given sunlight conditions) and the areal power density are also important.[6] In 1979, Marcy and Hockway wrote, "Current technology in solar arrays yields approximately 125 watts/lb for a cell oriented toward the sun; assuming that four times as many cells as this must be used to permit the aerostat heading to be independent of solar direction and latitude reduces the yield to 31 watts/lb, which converts to 23.88 lb/hp" (27). Thirty years later, Law et al. (2009) reported the development by Spectrolab of thin, flexible (50-millimeter [mm] curvature radius) triple-junction cells with an efficiency of 28%, a specific power of 500 W/kg and an aerial power density of 325 W/m². Ultra-thin (12 mm curvature radius) dual-junction cells offered a specific power of 2,067 W/kg and areal power density of 283 W/m², but the efficiency was only 21%.

Bear in mind that specific power also depends on altitude; the higher the altitude, the less atmosphere there is to absorb or scatter sunlight, which is one reason solar-electric power is particularly favored for high-altitude airships.

Cell Placement

Generally, on solar-powered airplanes, the solar cells cover the wings and thus are essentially flat and horizontal during level flight. Therefore, all cells experience the same angle of incidence (in optics, this is the angle between the incident rays and a line perpendicular to the surface).

If an airship has a normal circular cross section, then the solar cells are mounted on a curved surface. The maximum stress on the solar cell as a result of the curvature is inversely proportional to the radius of the curvature. The most flexible solar cells are those with the PV material printed on a thin polymer film. However, a modest degree of flexibility is achieved simply by making the normal PV wafer very thin. That is probably sufficient for airship envelope use, given the large diameter of the typical airship.

A solar-powered airship (*Sunship*) was proposed by Khoury and Mowforth in 1978 (Khoury 2012, 521). They idealized the *Sunship* as a "symmetrical ellipsoid entirely covered by a solar-sensitive skin" (527). They recognized that "the direct rays of the sun would fall on only a portion of the total wetted area at any one time" and the "effective receptive area is the projected area" of the hull in the direction of the sun. They provided a formula for the projected area as a function of the angle between the sun's rays and the airship's major axis. That angle, in turn, depends on the solar altitude and azimuth and the airship heading and pitch (526–529).

Khoury (2012) assumed that the diffuse radiation would fall evenly on the top half and the reflected radiation would fall evenly on the bottom half (530).

Others have proposed solar-powered airships with a more limited distribution of solar cells. Most limit the solar cells to the top half of the airship and exclude the bow and stern. Ozoroski et al. (2015, 30–39) proposed optimizing the array placement for four-season, station-keeping operation in latitudes 30°–50° north by mounting two array strips on either side of the airship at a mounting angle of 65° (a strip on top being at a mounting angle of 90°).

Solar-Electric Airships

A solar-electric powered airship must have a large enough volume that its lift is sufficient to support the weight of the envelope, solar panels, motors, batteries, control car, and crew. And of course, its solar cell array must have a large enough area facing the sun to provide the power it needs (proportional to length squared and speed cubed). But that area is limited by the planform area of the airship. So the airship has both a minimum size and a maximum speed, and the latter is also limited by the solar cell efficiency (see Kantor et al. 2011).

Next, we turn to several more speculative approaches to exploiting solar energy.

Solar Thermoelectric

Instead of converting solar light energy into electricity, solar heat can be converted into energy. Thermoelectric devices exploit the Seebeck effect, the flow of a current between hot and cold regions within a conductor. A thermoelectric material has high electrical conductivity and low thermal conductivity. Different thermoelectric materials have different optimum temperatures.

Choi et al. (2006) proposed using a triple layer of thermoelectric materials on a high-altitude airship. "First, solar flux is concentrated and heats up the first layer which is built with high temperature SiGe. The unused thermal energy from the first layer is subsequently used by the second layer which is built with mid temperature PbTe. Again, the third layer of Bi_2Te_3 uses the unused energy from the second layer." They argued that the thermoelectric system could "harness more broadband energy than photovoltaic cells which are only band structured to capture photons that are resonant with the discrete, allowed transition energies between the valence and conduction bands of the material."

Thermoelectric materials are given a figure of merit (ZT); ZT 1 corresponds to an energy conversion efficiency of 6%. This varies with temperature. Unfortunately, the ZT for modern materials is still rather low. While there has been one report of a material that can reach a ZT of five to six, most have been under three (Science Daily 2019).

The materials specified by Choi et al. (2006 fig. 2) had a ZT (at their optimum temperature) of about 0.8. However, Choi et al. (2006; 2011) proposed incorporating tiny spherical nanovoids into the thermoelectric material in order to scatter phonons and thus reduce thermal conductivity. They hoped that this would increase the effective ZT to 5. I do not know whether this approach was in fact successful.

Solar Steam and Solar Stirling

For solar-steam airships, efficiency is less important than for conventional steam engines, as there is no fuel consumption, but it does affect the size of the solar collector needed. The latter increases weight and thus reduces the power-to-weight ratio, but there would be an overall savings in weight thanks to the elimination of fuel. Since solar–Stirling powerplants do not need to evaporate and condense the working fluid, they have higher efficiency than solar-steam powerplants of equal power and therefore should weigh less.

To convert solar radiation into heat, a collector is needed. The simplest collector is simply a dark, flat plate that absorbs the incident radiation and in turn heats a heat transfer fluid (water, antifreeze) circulating between it and the engine. It may have a transparent cover to reduce heat loss. A lot of surface area is needed to acquire significant energy. And the weight of the collector (especially if it's metallic) and fluid are considerable.

If the airship did not have some way of storing the heat energy or an alternative source of power, it would fly with diminished power on cloudy days and be just a free balloon at night. Heat storage could take the form of a material with a high heat capacity. Water has a high gravimetric and volumetric heat capacity and is needed in any event for steam generation.

The spherical shapes of the solar–Sterling airships proposed by Kaplan and Rademakers are aerodynamically inefficient.

Solar Energy Concentration

A mirror or lens may be used to concentrate sunlight onto a smaller surface called a *receiver*. This can be advantageous if the receiver is an energy collector with a high cost or weight per unit area.

However, such concentration will tend to degrade the performance of a PV cell by raising its temperature. Hence, especially at high concentration ratios, the receiver may be either a thermoelectric device (Choi et al. 2011) or a "heat pipe" containing "a heat transfer working fluid" (Bennett 2007), assuming their efficiency is thus rendered competitive.

Concentration would reduce the weight of the collector, but then the weight of the concentration and tracking system must be considered.

The two basic mirror forms are the trough and the dish. Ideally, these have a parabolic shape to focus the light, but V-shaped or cylindrical troughs or hemispherical dishes have also been used. The dish is more effective than the trough. Lovegrove and Stein (2020, 31–32) calculated the geometric limit on the concentration ratio as 108 for a parabolic trough and 11,600 for a paraboloidal dish.[7] For a spherical dish, the maximum concentration ratio is about 3,000 (Mahdi and Bellel 2014).

The Coolearth solar concentrator is an example of a lightweight terrestrial dish system. It is essentially an 8 ft diameter, air-inflated paraboloidal polyethylene terephthalate (PET) balloon with a transparent upper half and an aluminized lower half. Inside, a strut holds a solar cell at the focal point. The air pressure is managed to maintain the proper concentrator shape.

The most practical lens design would be a Fresnel lens, like those used in lighthouses, as it provides a large aperture and short focal length with relatively small density. The lens is actually built up from prismatic rings.

5. Solar Power

Weight can be reduced further by using transparent plastic (when available) instead of glass.

However, these concentration systems require a sun-tracking mechanism to be fully effective. If the sun is off axis, "the apparent area of the mirror, as seen from the sun, is reduced according to the cosine of the incidence angle" (Lovegrove and Stein 2020, 36). The sun's position in the sky changes in both azimuth and altitude, so ideally this is a two-axis tracking system. The Coolearth concentrator, for example, is mounted on a dual-axis tracking system.

Instead of using a fixed receiver and a tracking dish, the designer may use a tracking receiver and a fixed spherical dish (solar bowl).

Either way, the tracking mechanism adds weight and complexity. If the collector and tracking mechanism stick out of the control car, external aerodynamic drag is increased. At higher speeds, the propulsive power needed to overcome drag may consume an unacceptable fraction of the collected solar power (Lubkowski et al. 2010). If they are inside the airship envelope, the envelope must be transparent so light can reach the collector. This must be a remote-controlled tracking system—since the envelope contains helium, people can't be sent inside to manually adjust the mirror orientations.

Choi et al. (2006; 2011) proposed an airship "2.5 times larger than a Goodyear blimp" with a flattened ellipsoid shape for high-altitude operations. The upper surface of most of the body was to carry "linear parabolic troughs," covered with a transparent membrane, for collecting solar energy. "These troughs were to be formed of an enhanced aluminum coated thin film membrane," rendering them reflective and running parallel to the longitudinal axis of the airship. If need be, the airship would reorient itself according to the sun's position—that is, with its longitudinal axis perpendicular to the solar azimuth. In effect, the entire airship acts as a single-axis tracking system. (However, that would limit it to a station-keeping role.) The contemplated receiver was a thermoelectric generator.

Bennett (2007) proposed a "solar-thermal aircraft" with a "reflective parabolic trough" inside "an optically transparent section of the aircraft body." The trough was to have a single-axis (roll-axis) tracking system. The solar heat was to drive an "improved Stirling engine." Seifert (2018) proposed integrating a Stirling engine into an airplane in such a manner that the external skin of the wing or fuselage "forms a wall of the working chamber" of the engine.

Chessel and Prost (2017) contemplated a stratospheric balloon with

Part I: Unconventional Power

an envelope whose upper half is transparent. In one embodiment, the inner surface of the lower half of the envelope is reflective and shaped to concentrate the light up to fivefold. In another, a separate, internal, reflective surface can be deformed to adjust to the angle of incidence of the solar rays. In both cases, the receiver was a PV cell.

None of the solar-thermal schemes seem practical to this author.

6

Nuclear Power

The great attraction of nuclear power is the extremely high energy density and specific energy (energy/mass) of nuclear fuel. Assuming a reasonable efficiency in converting that energy to useful work (e.g., turning a propeller), the potential endurance of a nuclear-powered vehicle would greatly increase. The 400-pound gorilla in the room is the danger of exposure to radiation, either in normal operation or in the event of a crash.

History—Airplanes

From 1946 to 1961, the United States engaged in the preliminary design and experimental research of nuclear-powered airplanes (James 2000, 162, 180). As part of the research, the Convair NB-36H, a modified B-36 bomber, carried a nuclear reactor aloft to test the effectiveness of its radiation shielding. The NB-36H made 47 flights from 1955 to 1957. According to Gorn and De Chiara (2022), the reactor produced one megawatt (MW; 1,341 hp), and the entire nuclear propulsion system weighed 165,000 lb, including 60,000 lb of reactor shielding, 37,000 lb of crew shielding, a 10,000 lb reactor (see below), and 40,000 lb of "miscellaneous ducting and other equipment" (34). Cousin (2024) offers a similar total figure, "80 tons."

However, there are some uncertainties regarding the numbers. Schwartz (2011, 124) says that the reactor produced 3 MW, not one; Bernier (2025) and Kaplan (2005, 104) say that the reactor weighed 35,000 lb.

Since nuclear power was not actually used for propulsion, the NB-36H also carried conventional airplane engines. These provided over 20,000 hp (Gorn and De Chiara 2022); whether the NB-36H could have actually taken off with just the nuclear system is uncertain.

Insofar as the effectiveness of the radiation shielding was concerned, "the data gathered indicated that the aeroplane would pose no special threat even when flying at low altitude, but that an accident could cause the release of fission products and radioactivity from the reactor" (Kaplan 2005).

In addition, on the ground, a nuclear reactor was used to power a suitably modified General Electric J47 turbojet engine. I assume this was a direct air cycle system, in which a conventional jet engine compressor sent compressed air "through the reactor to heat it before being exhausted through the turbine" (El-Sayed 2016, 54).

History—Airships

In 1954, F. W. Locke, Jr., studied the feasibility of using an atomic reactor to power the gas turbine engines of a rigid, two-million-cubic-foot helium-lift airship. The mission of the airship was to warn against approaching Soviet bombers, and the airship was to be able to "remain on station for 100 hours" (1). Its design speed was 100 knots, and with propellers of 90% efficiency, the estimated shaft power needed was 4,500 hp. The required propulsion system was estimated to weigh 30,000 lb. This was broken down into 22,500 lb for the reactor (5 lb/hp), 2,000 lb for two propellers, 4,000 lb for two modified T-56 gas turbines with special gearing, and 1,500 lb for extra insulation. To this he added 60,000 lb of structural weight, not counting the military load (the radar electronics, the crew, and the ballast; 8).[1]

Locke (1954) observed, "Present day blimps powered with internal combustion engines can have endurances in excess of 100 hours. Their big disadvantage is that the long endurance is performed at such a low speed that the craft is at the mercy of the vagaries of the weather. By raising the cruising speed to 100 knots, the primary difficulty would be almost entirely overcome" (6).

In 1959, Goodyear proposed that it could build a 4.5-million-cubic-foot helium-lift nonrigid airship with nuclear-powered turboprop engines. Goodyear had developed "a new rubberized fabric … capable of withstanding radiation exposures of up to 100 million roentgens" (SNL 1959, 322).

In the 1960s, former Goodyear engineer Francis Morse proposed an atomic airship with a "gross lift of 760,000 pounds." He claimed that it would only need 6,000 hp for propulsion, and therefore the "total weight of nuclear reactor, turbines and shielding would amount to no more than 120,000 pounds" (Geoghegan 2017; Kelly 2006, 141).

Another engineer, Erich von Veress, called and raised Morse, proposing a 14.4-million-cubic-foot helium-lift airship, which advanced as far as Schlichting Shipyard announcing "tentative plans" to construct it (Geoghegan 2017).

In 1972, Clements suggested that the ZRCV (a proposed 9.55-million-cubic-foot airship with a gross lift of 592,000 lb and an empty weight of 200,000 lb, 6,000 total hp) might be equipped with a 5,000 kW reactor that "would weigh about 100,000 lbs and have a volume of 5000 ft^3." While the reactor would reduce its useful load from 341,000 to 253,000 lb, the payload for a 6,500 mi range would increase from 132,000 lb to 253,000 lb (since it would not have to carry liquid fuel), and it could "carry 1,000 men or an equivalent weight of cargo anywhere in the world" (Clements 1972, 18–19).

Likewise, the ZRCCN (a proposed 22-million-cubic-foot airship with a gross lift of 1,360,000 lb and an empty weight of about 400,000 lb, 20,000 total hp) could be equipped with an 18,000 kW reactor, which "would have a volume around 8000 ft^3 and weigh in the neighborhood of 200,000 lb with minimum shielding." The useful load would be reduced from 855,000 lb to 655,000, but the payload for a 6,500 mi range would increase from 326,000 lb to 655,000 (Clements 1972, 21). This was about eight times the payload carried by a C-5A cargo airplane (23).

Clements (1972) urged that "the problems which frustrated attempts to apply nuclear power to heavier-than-air craft appear less challenging to an airship. Reactor size and weight are no barrier, protecting the crew from radiation is simpler, ground crew protection and handling problems no worse than with airplane installation. Further, airship crashes have generally been relatively leisurely affairs, so that there should be less danger to the public" (18).

Unlike Clements, Morse believed that ground handling of airships was problematic. His idea was that the airship "would effectively remain in the air throughout its life," and "heavier-than-air machines would be used to transfer people and supplies to and from the ground" (Khoury 2012, 260).

In 1983, Ph.D. student T. A. Bockrath proposed a semirigid, 250-million-cubic-foot helium-lift airship. Note that this was over 35 times the size of the *Hindenburg*, the largest airship ever built (Geoghegan 2017).

Analysis

If a neutron strikes an atom of uranium-235, it can fission into two atoms (e.g., radioisotopes of barium and krypton), releasing two or three

Part I: Unconventional Power

neutrons in the process. If at least one of those neutrons strikes another uranium-235 atom, the nuclear reaction continues. The fission of a single uranium-235 atom releases 170–200 megaelectron volts (MeV) of energy (WNA 2024b). The "products of the fission process carry the energy away as energy of motion." The released neutrons carry much of the energy, and some will "dissipate their energy in collisions with atoms and molecules within the reactor core." If the core contains water, "while the neutrons are slowed, the water within the core becomes hotter" (Breeze 2005, 254). "A single pound of the uranium isotope U235 could produce the same amount of heat as 1,700,000 pounds of gasoline" (James 2000, 178).

A nuclear propulsion system essentially uses the heat generated by the nuclear reaction in place of heat generated by the combustion of a fuel and thus may be coupled to either a steam (Rankine cycle) engine or a Stirling or Brayton cycle hot gas engine.

While no nuclear-powered airplane or airship has yet gone aloft, nuclear propulsion at sea may be considered conventional, at least for submarines and aircraft carriers. There have also been nuclear-powered cruisers, icebreakers and even a merchant ship (NS *Savannah*, launched 1959; Ragheb 2025).

The first nuclear-powered submarine was the USS *Nautilus* (SSN-571), equipped with a 13,400 hp (10 MW) pressurized water S2W reactor (Global Security 2016). The primary coolant (pressurized water) is heated when it passes through the reactor core. Because of the pressure it is under, it does not boil. The coolant passes into a heat exchanger, the steam generator, where its heat is transferred to the secondary coolant (lower-pressure water), boiling it. The resulting steam then drives a turbine, and a generator converts the mechanical energy into electrical energy. This is transmitted to the motors, which turn the submarine's propeller. The spent steam is routed to a condenser (Duke Energy 2012). In a submarine, the condenser itself would be cooled by seawater.

The efficiency of a heat engine cannot exceed and is usually less than the Carnot efficiency, which is one minus the ratio of the low and high temperatures (in degrees Kelvin) (Çengel and Boles 2002, 275). "The maximum temperature in the fuel was 645°F.... The reactor temperature is limited by the pressure needed to prevent boiling, necessitating high-pressure vessels, piping and heat exchangers" (Ragheb 2025, PDF 13). The low temperature would have been that of ambient seawater.

The reason for the use of two cooling circuits is that the primary coolant "will always contain small amounts of radioactive chemicals produced by the neutrons in the reactor." However, because the secondary coolant does not enter the reactor, "this radioactivity never gets to the steam turbine where it would make it difficult to perform maintenance" (Suppes 2006, 51).

There are reactors with a single reactor coolant loop, in which water passing through the reactor core is boiled, its steam does work (by expansion), and the steam is then condensed to return to the reactor (Duke Energy 2012). However, these boiling water reactors have only been used in stationary nuclear power plants.

In a thermal- or slow-neutron reactor, a moderator is used to slow down the neutrons (so they cause more fission). Water is preferred as it also acts as a coolant. It may be heavy water (deuterium oxide) or light (natural) water. "If graphite or heavy water is used as moderator, it is possible to run a power reactor on natural instead of enriched uranium.... Because the light water absorbs neutrons as well as slowing them, it is less efficient as a moderator than heavy water or graphite" (WNA 2024a).

Woodward (1958, 17) said, "It seems certain that any nuclear reactor for airborne use would have to be of the 'fast fission' type, to eliminate the enormous weight of moderator associated with thermal reactors, and no less important, thereby reduce the area to be shielded." However, de Piolenc (1999, 3) notes that this was the only proposal he could find advocating a fast-fission reactor for airship use, with all others contemplating slow-neutron reactors.

Fast-fission (fast-neutron) reactors use reactor-grade plutonium as fuel (uranium is not as responsive to fast neutrons). While Woodward (1958) envisioned that his airborne nuclear reactor would be cooled by helium gas, using a molten metal (lead, lead-bismuth, or sodium) is more typical (WNA 2021).

The submarine reactor uses highly enriched uranium (HEU) as the nuclear fuel. This allows the reactor to be smaller than if the uranium-235 (the fissionable material) content were low. The smaller the reactor, the less reactor shielding is needed (Naymark 1970). It also allows the use of ordinary (light) water as the coolant.

Natural uranium is 0.72% uranium-235. Low-enriched uranium (LEU) is defined as greater than 0.72% and less than 20%. HEU is defined as at least 20% but less than 90% uranium-235, and weapons-grade HEU is defined as at least 90%. The latter may be used in military propulsion reactors (DoD 2020).

An LEU (4%–7% uranium-235) was used on a mobile high-power plant (a converted Liberty ship) from 1968 to 1977 (DOE 2011).

According to Global Security (2016a), the *Nautilus*'s reactor plant had

Part I: Unconventional Power

a specific mass of 64–66 kg/hp (141–146 lb/hp). A similar figure ("more than 150" lb/hp) is given by James (2000, 163). The *Leninski Konsomol* had two 17,500 hp reactors with a reactor plant-specific mass of 40.6 kg/hp (Global Security 2016a).

In 1960, Jurich assumed "an over-all efficiency of 15 percent ... for the conversion of reactor heat to shaft horsepower" (5).

Van Orden (1957) was more optimistic, assuming 25% efficiency. (Woodward [1958] suggested 26%.) If so, since the *Los Angeles* (2.6-million-cubic-feet helium) "used 2000 hp for a speed of 80 mph," it could have been propelled at the same speed by an 8,000 hp (6 MW) reactor. Even the *Hindenburg* would have needed just a 15.5 MW reactor. "This is considerably less," Van Orden (1957, 10) added, "probably by a factor of 20 to 30, than the power required for a nuclear powered airplane."

Shielding and Reactor Placement

The immediately obvious concern with any airborne nuclear reactor is the adequacy of radiation shielding for the crew. In 1949, W. Winter suggested that a 25,000 hp airplane engine "would require 75 tons of lead shielding" (Snyder 1996, 5–6). (That's 6 lb/hp just for shielding.) Shielding is needed not only for the operating crew but also for the ground handling and maintenance crews. In 1958, Aschenbrenner predicted that the shield system would be "the heaviest single item aboard a nuclear powered aircraft" (Snyder 1996, 163).

The required operating crew shielding depends on the amount of uranium-235 in the reactor core and the distance between the reactor and the crew areas. The former depends on the required propulsive power. As noted by Gordon Vaeth (Senate 1974, 87–88), since airships are supported by buoyancy, "their energy needs are low. Thus, for nuclear propulsion, they need less powerful reactors and less shielding" than would nuclear-powered airplanes.

Shielding is also needed to protect airplane (or airship) components near the reactor. For example, radiation can damage elastomers (in O-rings, insulation, etc.), and the absorption of neutrons could activate structural members of the airplane or its engines, which could then emit radiation themselves, complicating maintenance. This consideration also limits the ability to reduce the reactor shield in favor of the crew shield (Fraas 1954, 17–18). The required combined weight of the reactor and shield increases at a slower-than-linear rate with the reactor power (23–32).

6. Nuclear Power

However, Jurich (1960, 6) pointed out that even the most radiation-sensitive materials have "a threshold of damage, one million times greater than the biological tolerance" and suggested that "no material-selection control needs to be exercised outside a distance 25 to 30 ft from the reactor."

The core volume also affects the amount of shielding required. The larger the core volume, the larger its surface area, and for a given required thickness, the larger the mass of shielding. In this regard, it is helpful if there is a high specific power density (Jurich 1960, 4).

The placement of the reactor also has structural implications. The sectional lift of the airship is greatest amidships and least at bow and stern. If the reactor and engine were at the stern, then this concentrated weight would create local negative net lift there, causing it to sag and thus strain the airframe.

Moreover, this weight would create a pitching movement, causing the stern to sink and the nose to rise. To achieve level trim, ballast would need to be added at the bow or buoyancy at the stern.

The length of Locke's proposed airship was 510 ft. The plan called for "180 feet between the back of the cabin and the front of the reactor.... The distance is so large that the cabin is unshielded and all the necessary shielding is concentrated at the reactor" (Locke 1954, 4).

Locke (1954, 2) had considered stern propulsion, but "this would introduce very serious balance problems unless the reactor were moved forward. Moving the reactor forward would bring about large heat losses between the reactor and powerplant [sic, the gas turbine engines]." Presumably, Locke instead contemplated placing both the reactor and the gas turbine engines amidships.[2]

Goodyear's 1959 proposed blimp was 540 ft long, and the design called for "the reactor to be placed amidship, with the control car near the bow." Thus, the reactor would be "far enough away from the craft's control car to permit personnel to work in an environment comparable to that of an atomic plant" (SNL 1959).

Distance is important because the gamma rays and neutrons will spread out and thus be attenuated by distance according to the inverse-square law. Van Orden (1957, 10–11) also refers to the attenuation properties of helium, which could be improved "by diffusing a few percent of boron trifluoride gas into the helium at the expense of a few percent of lift" (apparently assuming that helium gas cells will be in between the reactor and the crew area, although that does not bode well for anyone having to do maintenance on those cells). This, he says, amounts to

Part I: Unconventional Power

a "radiation intensity reduction factor of 8×10^9 for a distance of 100 feet from the reactor."

That, however, is not enough by itself to reduce human exposure to tolerable levels. Referring again to a *"Los Angeles*–size" 8,000 hp reactor, he argued that the additional shielding needed against neutrons would be 10 in. of boron. That thickness "wrapped entirely around a cylindrical reactor twenty inches in diameter and thirty inches long weighs 2100 lbs" (Van Orden 1957, 10). However, to reduce the intensity of the gamma rays, an additional 6 in. of lead would be needed, "giving a total lead weight of 18,500 lbs" (11). The reactor itself, he thought, would weigh 8,000 lb (11), and the heat it produced would drive a steam turbine (1).

Increasing the separation between the reactor and occupants would, of course, reduce the required shielding weight. With a separation of 300 ft, he thought that 11,000 lb of shielding might be sufficient. The weight of the engines and five days of fuel for the conventionally powered *Los Angeles* was, he said, 120,000 lb (Van Orden 1957, 11).

Woodward (1958, 18–20), for his proposed 12.1 MW fast-fission reactor, calculated a core weight of 266 lb, a reflector weight of 1,050 lb, and a shield weight of 64,000 lb.

A closely related concern is the danger to humans and the environment if the nuclear-powered craft were to crash. Morse was convinced that the airship's "intrinsic buoyancy reduced the inertial forces from an impact to a manageable level." It appears that Morse has not looked at many photographs of airship crash sites. While it is true that if a single one of his airship's 17 gas cells deflated and the airship was sufficiently high above the ground, it could address the sudden loss in buoyancy by dropping ballast and making an emergency but soft landing, it does not allow for the possibility that the airship might be caught in a violent downdraft and be dashed to the ground, breaking into pieces.

Goodyear proposed that "chemical fuel could used for takeoff and landing, with the reactor shut down during these times" (SNL 1959), and Jurich (1960, 7) makes a similar suggestion. However, even if the reactor were shut down, a crash could compromise the shell, leading to the escape of radioactive material into the environment. The seriousness of the risk thus posed would depend on the half-life of those materials.

In 1974, Gordon Vaeth testified to Congress that by virtue of the size of airships, "radioactively 'hot' elements can be effectively isolated and cushioning and shock-absorbing mounting systems provided to safeguard against a nuclear mishap in the event of a crash" (Senate 1974, 88).

I have alluded to the problem of maintenance safety. Van Orden

6. Nuclear Power

(1957) argued that "it appears feasible to locate the grounded airship over an open pit and lower the reactor by itself or the entire powerplant into the pit which can be covered by concrete, or some other door shielding material. The airship can then be moved to a safe location via the mobile mast and allowed to 'cool' before maintenance work commences." A similar procedure was used experimentally with the Aircraft Shield Test Reactor, which was moved from a reactor pit to a B-36 bomb bay and back again (12).

Once the safety issues are addressed comes the familiar weight/power issue. There is, obviously, a tradeoff when it comes to weight. On the one hand, weight is added for the reactor vessel, core, shield, cooling system, power conversion units, and so on. On the other hand, conventional fuel doesn't need to be carried.

In 2002, the W/P for a helium gas–cooled nuclear powerplant for a proposed merchant ship was estimated at 11 kg/kW (18 lb/hp). But it was also estimated that after considering fuel oil and other savings, the propulsion-related weight would still be reduced by 2,590 tn for a ship displacing 30,750 tn (Vergara 2002, table 2).

Van Orden (1957) provided a reasonably detailed calculation for a nuclear airship the size of the *Los Angeles*; with the 100 ft reactor spacing design, the reactor and its shielding came to 3.58 lb/hp, which is higher than that for an airplane engine, but there was still a very substantial reduction in propulsion-related weight once fuel consumption was taken into account.

Much of the allure of nuclear propulsion came from the high energy density of nuclear fuel. However, a solar-powered airship doesn't need any fuel—just solar cells to collect the sunlight and batteries to store power for use when the sunlight is unavailable. Admittedly, the energy thus collected would be substantially less than what a nuclear-powered airship of the same kind could extract from nuclear fuel. But there would also be no need for radiation shielding and no special threat to the environment in the event of a crash. Hence, interest in nuclear propulsion has virtually vanished.

But there is a niche application for nuclear propulsion of an airship. In 2012, Anthony J. Colozza proposed the use of a radioisotope-powered (plutonium-238) Stirling engine in an airship intended to explore the lower atmosphere of Venus. And in 2014, he and Robert L. Cataldo proposed the use of a similar airship to explore the atmosphere of Saturn's largest moon, Titan.

7

Miscellaneous Power Sources

History—Diesel Power

The diesel engine was invented by Rudolf Diesel (1858–1913), the son of a leather goods manufacturer. Diesel engines are internal combustion engines in which the fuel is ignited by compression of the fuel-air mixture. In contrast, in gasoline engines, the fuel is ignited by a spark generated by a spark plug.

Airplanes

The first true airplane diesel (i.e., compression ignition) engine was the five-cylinder FO-3, designed by Hugo Junkers and exhibited in 1926. It "developed 830 hp at 12000 rpm." The first, however, to actually power an airplane was the FO-4 (Jumo 4) in 1929. It produced 720 hp at 1,700 rpm, or in the Jumo 204 variant, 770 hp at 1,800 rpm. In 1935, it was succeeded by the Jumo 205, which provided 880 hp at 3,000 rpm. More variants (Jumo 206, 207) followed. The specific power for the 204 was 1.14 kW/kg; for the 205, 0.87 kW/kg; and for the 207, 1.14 kW/kg (Brouwers 1980, 6).

In 1931, Deutsche Lufthansa installed a 700 hp Jumo 4 in one of its single-engine, six-passenger Junkers F-24 planes. "In 1935, Junkers Jumo 204 diesels were used to replace the gasoline engines in four-engined Junkers G-38 forty-passenger airliners." The more powerful Jumo 205 was used "in three-engined Junkers Ju 42 and two-engined Ju 86 airliners, and in two-engined Dornier DO 18 flying boats." The latter were used for airmail service to South America beginning in 1936. The military variant Ju 86-K, a fighter-bomber, was powered by two Jumo 205-C (600 hp) or 205-D (880 hp) engines, and the Luftwaffe also had diesel-powered DO 18-K and Blohm & Voss BV 138 flying boats (Wilkinson 1940, ch. 5).

"[F]rom 1931 to 1938 Deutsche Lufthansa flew 4,243,895 miles with Diesel-engined civil airplanes," and Wilkinson estimated that "during

7. Miscellaneous Power Sources

A six-cylinder Diesel aircraft engine, designed by Junkers, on a test stand (*AAJ* 1920, 287).

1937 and 1938 the numerous Diesel-engined squadrons of the German Air Force covered 50 per cent more miles than their relatively few civil counterparts." The longest nonstop flights were 3,600 mi over land and 5,125 mi over water (Wilkinson 1940, ch. 5).

The DO-26 carried 700 hp Jumo 205-E engines, which cruised on 560 hp. At cruising speed, the fuel consumption was only 0.36 lb/hp-h (Wilkinson 1940, ch. 5).

In the United States, the Packard DR-980 was used for a cross-country flight in 1929. It developed continuous 225 hp at 1,950 rpm (Wilkinson 1940, ch. 1). It was a four-stroke, air-cooled, nine-cylinder radial engine, weighing 231 kg, with a compression ratio of 16:1 and a power of 174 kW (233 hp) at 2,050 rpm. Specific power was thus 0.75 kW/kg (Brouwers 1980, 6).

The Guiberson A-1020 nine-cylinder, air-cooled, radial diesel engine was used for a 960 mi flight in 1931, consuming "96 gallons of furnace oil." It was rated at 185 hp (1,925 rpm). However, it could achieve a continuous 310 hp at 2,150 rpm. The engine weighed 650 lb, or 2.1 lb/hp, and at that load, its fuel consumption was 0.42 lb/hp-h. At cruising speed, it only used 0.37 l./hp-h (Wilkinson 1940, chs. 1, 3).

The first British aero diesel engine was the Bristol Phoenix 430 hp (2,000 rpm). It was first used to power a plane in 1933 (Wilkinson 1940, ch.

Part I: Unconventional Power

1). In 1934, "it established the world's altitude record for Diesel-engined airplanes," 27,453 ft.

In France, the Clerget 14 F-01, "rated at 940 hp at 2400 rpm, was test-flown to an altitude of 24,115 feet in a Potez 25 observation plane in 1937." And in Italy, the Fiat ANA diesel, with "six in-line, water cooled cylinders and rated at 220 hp at 1700 rpm," was test-flown in 1930. It weighed 4 lb/hp (Wilkinson 1940, ch. 1).

A 1980 study suggested that a 298 kW (max) two-cycle diesel engine for use in a two-engine airplane would be superior to a 280 kW four-cycle GTSIO-520-H gasoline engine in both fuel consumption (37.74 kg/h vs. 49.75 kg/h at cruise) and power-to-weight ratio (cruise power 193.88 kW with dry weight of 207 kg for diesel, 181.76 kW and 262 kg for gasoline; Brouwers 1980).

Among modern diesel engines certified for airplanes, the one with the highest specific power appears to be the RED A03, certified in 2014 (Wikipedia). It offers 1.01 kW/kg (0.61 hp/lb, 1.6 lb/hp). Its brake specific fuel consumption is 210 g/kWh (0.339 lb/hp-h) when running at best economy (176 kW, 240 hp at 3,500 rpm).

Airships

The *Hindenburg* (LZ 129) and *Graf Zeppelin II* (LZ130) each carried four 16-cylinder Daimler-Benz DB602s. The *Hindenburg*'s engines each produced 1,200 hp at 1,600 rpm (Gunston 1998, 51) but could generate 1,300 for five minutes and 850 hp for cruising. They had a dry weight of 4,348 lb (Dick and Robinson 1992, 85). The LZ130 engines achieved 1,320 hp at 1,650 rpm (Gunston 1998).[1] Wilkinson (1940, ch. 5) says that the latter, on "continuous cruise," were 800 hp and at that speed consumed just 0.375 lb/hp-h.

William Beardmore & Co. Ltd. designed an airship diesel, the Tornado. It had eight in-line cylinders and was rated at 585 hp (900 rpm). It had a W/P of 7.8 lb/hp. Five were installed on the ill-fated British R101 airship (Wilkinson 1940, ch. 1).

The Tornado had a compression ratio of 12.25:1 and a dry, uninstalled weight of 2,150 kg (4,733 lb). Its maximum power output was 480 kW (650 hp) at 935 rpm and 350 kW (475 hp) at 825 rpm. Specific fuel consumption was 0.429 or 0.421 lb/hp-h, respectively (Wikipedia).

While the development of airplane diesel (compression ignition) has definitely lagged behind that of airplane gasoline (spark ignition), some recent developments have been of interest. For example, the four-cylinder

7. Miscellaneous Power Sources

DeltaHawk DHK180 compression ignition engine is FAA certified and burns jet fuel. It has a maximum continuous power of 180 hp (134.2 kW) at 2,600 rpm with a corresponding fuel consumption of 10.8 gal/h. Its best economy is 135 hp (100.7 kW) at 2,200 rpm with a fuel consumption of 7.3 gal/h. The dry weight is 335 lb, so W/P is 1.86.

Analysis—Diesel Engines

In 1878, Diesel's mentor, Carl von Linde (known for his work on the liquefaction and fractionation of air), told him that steam engines were only 6%–10% efficient (cp. chapter 2: Steam Power). Beginning in 1889, Diesel sought to develop a more efficient engine, a "rational heat motor." His first truly successful engine was "finished in 1897" (Diesel 1912, 9), and it had an efficiency of 26.2% (Mollenhauer and Tschoeke 2010, 4).

For automotive diesels, brake thermal efficiency increased "from 34% in the 1960s to 44% in the early 2000s" (Folkson and Sapsford 2014, §9.9). In 2020, Weichai announced that it had built a commercial vehicle diesel engine with a brake thermal efficiency of 50.26% (Garrett Motion 2020).

The term *diesel fuel* is potentially misleading, because the early diesel engines ran on a broad range of fuels. In an 1894 monograph, Diesel referred to the use of solid (coal dust; 60), liquid (petroleum; 70) and gaseous (73) combustibles. However, liquid fuels were preferred.[2] This could be crude oil (Diesel 1912, 4) or a "tar or tar oil" (6). Indeed, Diesel demonstrated that vegetable (earthnut, castor or palm oil) or animal oil could be used, and Diesel speculated that such oils could become as important as petroleum-derived oils (7), thus predicting the modern use of biodiesel.

Most compression ignition engines are designed with diesel fuel in mind. Diesel fuel is less volatile than gasoline and has a higher flash point. High compression is needed for it to ignite. Burning gasoline in an ordinary compression ignition engine is problematic. However, experimental gasoline compression ignition engines do exist, and the commercial Mazda SKYACTIV-X engine actually uses a combination of spark and compression ignition (Mazda 2023).

A diesel engine may run on a two-stroke or four-stroke cycle, and it may be air-cooled or liquid cooled. A variety of engine cylinder configurations are possible; 1930s aero diesel engines included flat, opposed, Vee and radial examples (Brouwers 1980, 6).

The principal advantage of the compression ignition (diesel) engine is that it has a higher efficiency than the spark-ignition (gasoline) engine, because of the higher compression ratio. That leads to lower fuel consumption and therefore lower operating costs. Because it can run on fuel oil, which costs less per gallon than avgas (aviation gasoline), there are further savings. And since fuel oil is less volatile than gasoline, there is also less risk of it generating explosive fumes. A diesel engine may also run on kerosene (jet fuel). Finally, with no sparks, there is no interference between the engine ignition system and the airplane's electrical systems (Wilkinson 1940, ch. 6; Brouwers 1980, 4).

The principal disadvantage is a typically lower power-to-weight ratio than equivalent spark-ignition (gasoline) engines. There are some instances of diesel engines with seemingly good power-to-weight ratios, but we don't know whether the weight included "everything necessary to operate the engine." In addition, ULPower (2024), a gasoline engine manufacturer, states that "the diesel engine mount will most probably also be heavier than one needed for a gasoline engine." Other disadvantages include soot in the exhaust, a greater propensity of the fuel to gel in cold weather, and larger torque pulses as a result of the high compression ratio.

Hydrogen Fuel

Hydrogen's advantages as a fuel are its high specific energy and "its ready combustion at the low ambient pressure of high altitude" (Marcy and Hockway 1979, 10). However, there is a considerable volume and weight price to be paid for storing it because of its low energy density.

"Rudolf A. Erres invented the first practical hydrogen engine in the 1920s. He changed 1,000 engines including trucks, buses and torpedoes to hydrogen" (Odougherty 2018, 41).

Early Airship Use

In normal airship operations, gasoline was burned. Since gasoline is heavier than air, the airship's net buoyancy increased as it flew. In order to maintain its altitude, it had to vent gas. In the '20s, hydrogen was the most commonly used lift gas, as it provided greater buoyancy than any alternative.

"In 1920, two British investigators estimated that dirigible range could be increased 20 percent by burning the hydrogen usually vented. They found that an engine could operate on hydrogen as an additive or on hydrogen alone, but in the latter case there was a tendency to knock" (Sloop 1978, 265).

Burning hydrogen was not only an alternative to venting it, but it also reduced net buoyancy by creating water ballast. During the development of the *Hindenburg* (LZ 129), it was found that in a Maybach 250 hp engine, burning "35 to 53 cubic feet of hydrogen ... would yield 2.2 pounds of water." The disadvantage was that "the engine would only develop one-fifth of its rated horsepower with gasoline." Nonetheless, they considered devoting one of the zeppelin's diesel engines to water production; it would reduce the power output to 300 hp but produce 430 lb of water per hour (Dick and Robinson 1992, 102).

While not a major concern at the time, the fact that the combustion of hydrogen produces only water, not any carbon compounds, means that pure hydrogen power is nonpolluting.

Gaseous and Liquid Hydrogen as Fuels

The principal attraction of hydrogen as a fuel was its high specific energy, 120 MJ/kg, compared to 44 MJ/kg for gasoline (EERE 2024a). However, the energy density of hydrogen in its normal gaseous state is low. The density of hydrogen at NTP (normal atmospheric pressure, 20°C) is 0.08375 kg/m^3 (Hydrogen Tools 2024), so its energy density is just 0.003685 MJ/L. The density of gasoline varies, but if it is 740 kg/m^3, then its energy density is 32.56 MJ/L. The situation is improved somewhat if the hydrogen is liquefied (LH2); its energy density is then 8 MJ/L (EERE 2024a), but it is still one-quarter that of gasoline (or jet fuel). So a much larger tank is needed to achieve the same range.

Hydrogen was first liquefied by James Dewar in 1898 (Sloop 1978, 251). To liquefy hydrogen, it must be cooled below its critical temperature, 33.3° K, at which the required pressure is 12.8 atmospheres (250). And for it to be liquid at atmospheric pressure, it must be cooled to 20.35° K (EERE 2024a).

While the tanks also have a "thick layer of insulation," heat from the environment and the engines will cause evaporation and subsequent boil-off unless the tank is equipped with an adequately sized cryocooler to recondense the evaporate. Boil-off limits the time during which liquid hydrogen can be stored, "so the fuel usually needs to be manufactured on site or at a nearby location," and cryogenic equipment to inhibit it adds to the system weight and increases the power load (Colozza 2002, 14).

To minimize heat transfer, the hydrogen fuel tank may—perhaps must—be spherical, or cylindrical with hemispherical ends. But if so, it cannot readily fit into the normal fuel tank location (the wings; Reiman 2009, 20, 52). This is, of course, a general problem with cryogenic fuel, and it also applies to some degree to liquid natural gas or liquid ammonia fuel (see below) (Graham and Glassman 1980, 10).

Since the weight of the tank is proportional to its surface area, the ratio of fuel weight to tank weight increases with tank size (Reiman 2009). So large airplanes have less of a range penalty.

Early Hydrogen-Powered Airplane Engine Testing

"Hydrogen was considered as an aviation fuel by P. Meyer in 1918" (Sloop 1978, 95). In 1937, Hans von Ohain was developing a turbojet engine in Germany and found that it "worked well using hydrogen" (73). Nonetheless, in 1939, Robert Goddard expressed surprise that the National Advisory Committee for Aeronautics was considering liquid hydrogen as a rocket fuel: "I mention this because liquid hydrogen is expensive and difficult to transport and store ... and also because tanks of it have to be surrounded by liquid oxygen or liquid nitrogen" (73).

A few decades later, a new potential niche developed for hydrogen fuel: high-altitude reconnaissance airplanes. "In 1954, current turbojet engines could operate at altitudes of 13,700 meters without serious loss of combustion efficiency." But combustion efficiency declined with altitude, and the choice of fuel mattered. Later that year, experiments showed that "hydrogen burned well in a single turbojet combustor at pressures as low as 1/10 atmosphere; at ¼ atmosphere, combustion efficiency was above 90 percent. These results were within the combustion pressure range for turbojet engines operating at 30,500 meters altitude" (Sloop 1978, 97–98).

To operate "at high altitudes and low speeds, large wings are needed and these call for a proportionately large fuselage.... The large volumes available in the wings and fuselage favored the use of low-density liquid hydrogen, provided lightweight hydrogen tanks proved feasible" (98). "A cigar-shaped 175 m^3 tank, holding 11,300 kg of liquid hydrogen was designed: the estimated tank mass was 10 percent of the fuel mass" (Sloop 1978, 99).[3]

One of the two Curtiss Wright J-65 turbojet engines of a B-57B bomber was modified to operate on either hydrogen or JP-4 (kerosene) fuel. Wind tunnel testing of the engine showed that "with JP-4 the maximum altitude for table combustion was about 20,000 meters and flame-out occurred at 23,000 meters. In contrast, hydrogen was stable to the limit of

7. Miscellaneous Power Sources

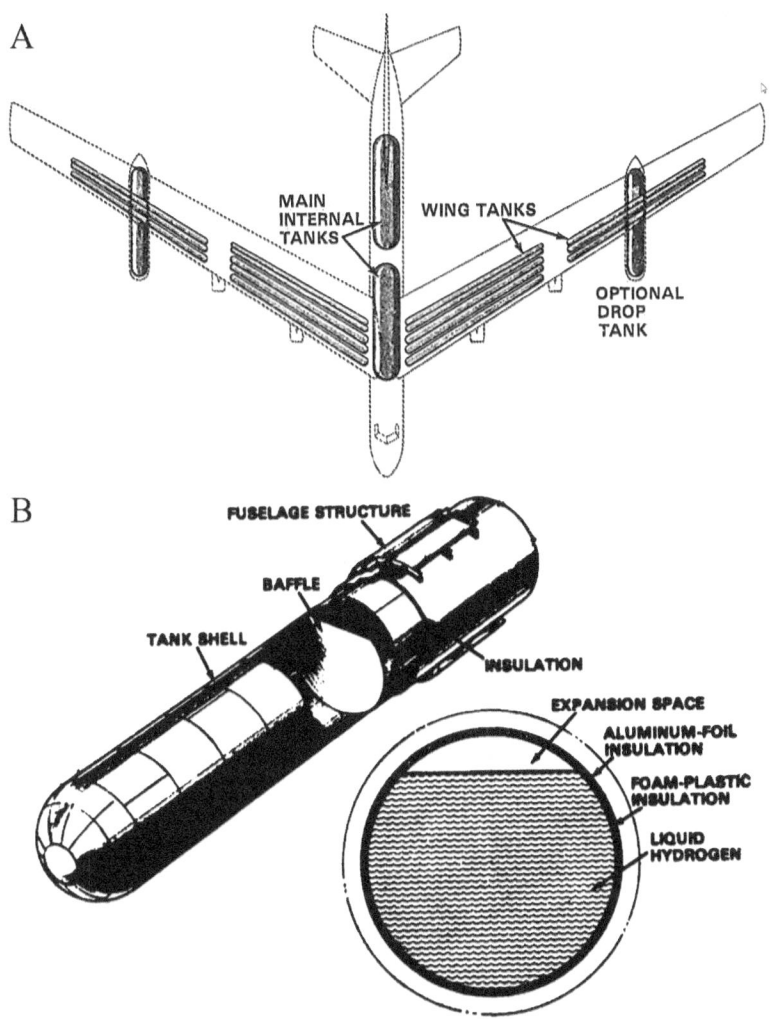

A. Proposed "high-altitude, subsonic reconnaissance aircraft using liquid hydrogen fuel" (Sloop 1978, fig. 20). **B.** Proposed "liquid-hydrogen tank" for use in that aircraft (fig. 19).

the facility at 27,000 meters.... The thrust was 2 to 4 percent higher, and specific fuel consumption was 60 to 70 percent lower, than with JP-4 fuel" (Sloop 1978, 103–106).

The bomber was to climb to 16,400 m and then switch that engine over to hydrogen for testing. In 1957, the first two flights were only partially successful, but three successful ones followed (Sloop 1978, 103–106). Nonetheless, the United States never actually fielded a hydrogen-fueled "spy plane."

Another possible niche for hydrogen fuel was hypersonic flight, which "heats aircraft surfaces and requires cooling for sustained flights." An NACA panel "found that only liquefied methane and hydrogen had significant cooling capacity at flight speeds above Mach 5" (Sloop 1978, 107).

A design for a Mach-4 airplane with hydrogen-fueled turbojet engines offered a range more than 60% greater than its JP-4-fueled counterpart, but both were "outclassed by a hydrogen-fueled ramjet missile" with a great range and Mach-7 capability (Sloop 1978, 110).

In 1988, "retired Pan American pilot Bill Conrad," following in Rudolf Erres's footsteps, "converted a four seater Grumman Cheetah to [liquid] hydrogen." This "became the first airplane to take-off, cruise and land on hydrogen power alone" (Veziroğlu 1995, 5).

Soviet engineers made numerous modifications to a three-engine TU-154 airliner to permit it to use liquid hydrogen fuel. The most obvious, perhaps, was that the 4,000 gal hydrogen tank took up "what would normally be the last eight rows," and "a pressure-tight bulkhead was installed in front of the tank." Pressurizing the passenger cabin therefore would prevent any leaked hydrogen from entering the passenger space. The starboard turbofan engine was modified to use either liquid hydrogen or liquefied natural gas (LNG). The resulting TU-155 made its first flight (21 minutes), burning hydrogen for at least part of the time, on April 15, 1988 (Brewer 2017, 404). However, on most of its flights, it burned LNG (Alverà 2021).

The unmanned X-43A research airplane, with a scramjet[4] engine burning hydrogen, achieved 9.8 Mach in 2004 (Reiman 2009, 31).

Alternatives to Liquid Hydrogen Storage

Hydrogen may also be compressed. Like liquefaction, compression requires energy, but the energy requirement is about one-third that of liquefaction. Moreover, there is no energy requirement to keep the gas compressed; the storage tank must simply be strong enough to withstand the pressure difference. Traditionally, tanks were made of steel, but weight can be reduced at a higher cost by using aluminum and carbon, glass or aramid fiber wraps (Cheng et al. 2024, table 3; cp. Folkson and Sapsford 2022, 6.4.2.1).

One disadvantage is that the density of compressed hydrogen

7. Miscellaneous Power Sources

(23.3 kg/m^3 at 350 bar,[5] 39.3 at 700 bar) is less than that of liquid hydrogen. Also, the walls of a compressed hydrogen tank must be thicker (hence heavier) to withstand the pressure difference. Consequently, to store 1 kg of hydrogen, the ratio of the tank weight to the hydrogen weight is 11.5 for liquid hydrogen but 12.5–25 for compressed hydrogen (Cheng et al. 2024, 270).[6]

Compressed (350 bar) hydrogen gas was used to power a 20 kW (27 hp) PEM (perfluorosulfonic acid polymer electrolyte membrane, see below) fuel cell in 2010 in the ENFICA-FC Rapid 200-FC airplane (Colpan and Kovač 2022, 87). Compressed (350 bar) hydrogen was also used on the Antares DLR-H2; its tank held "up to 4.9 kg hydrogen." The tank powered a 30 kW PEM (Rathke et al. 2013).

A newer approach to hydrogen storage is to take advantage of the ability of some metal hydrides to absorb hydrogen at moderately elevated pressure and moderately reduced temperature and to desorb the hydrogen at lower pressure and moderately high temperature. The advantages of this approach are that it requires less energy to operate than compression or liquefaction and provides a stored hydrogen density rivaling that of liquid hydrogen.

An early example was a metal (iron-manganese-titanium) hydride storage system on board a John Deere Gator utility vehicle. It was charged with hydrogen (2 kg) after 60 minutes at 2,170 kilopascals (kPa; and up to 35°C). The hydrogen was discharged by raising the temperature to 50°C and lowering the pressure to 756 kPa (Heung et al. 2001, 2003).

Unfortunately, the metal hydride storage system weight is currently prohibitive for aerial applications. In the case of the Gator, the storage system weighed 244 kg. Even today, the interstitial hydrides can store only 1%–2% of their own weight. The complex hydride LiBH$_4$ has the greatest known storage capacity (18.5% theoretical, 13.4% reversible) but requires a high desorption temperature (over 300°C) and has poor reversibility (Klopčič et al. 2023).

An airship-only alternative to liquid hydrogen, proposed by HyLight, is to use *uncompressed* hydrogen gas as both the fuel and the lift gas. The airship envelope doubles as both the source of buoyancy and the fuel tank. The HyLighter 35 drone is 10 m long and 2 m in diameter, with an ellipsoidal shape; it has bow and stern vectored thrust engines. As fuel is consumed, the airship loses lift. Vectored thrust engines not only facilitate maneuvering but also allow the drone to compensate for the loss of buoyancy. The drone has a range of 350 km, a payload of 10 kg, and a maximum speed of 10 m/s. Since it is an airship, it can hover easily. HyLight markets it as a tool for pipeline monitoring that is superior to quad drones (more flight time, more payload), plane drones (lower flight speed, so better data), or satellites (more precision; HyLight 2024).

Hydrogen Fuel Cells

Hydrogen may be burned in an internal (or external) combustion engine or a fuel cell. The engines provide mechanical power directly, whereas the fuel cell produces electricity, which drives a motor.

In that respect, a fuel cell is like a battery (galvanic cell). But in a galvanic cell (see chapter 4), all the chemical reactants are present initially in the cell, and the cell provides power until it is consumed. In a fuel cell, the fuel (hydrogen) and oxidant (oxygen/air) are supplied continuously from without[7] (Dell 1996). However, hydrogen-powered fuel cells were not used in airplanes until the 21st century.

"The fuel cell itself requires gaseous hydrogen to function." Hence, if the hydrogen is stored in liquid form, it must be evaporated 1) "at the hydrogen tank," 2) "just before entering the fuel cell," or 3) "in a dedicated element of the fuel system [cell]" (Colpan and Kovač 2022, 88).

The fuel cell, like a battery, also needs an electrolyte. Fuel cells are sometimes classified based on the electrolyte used. The electrolytes considered for vehicular use are typically either alkaline (aqueous potassium hydroxide) or a perfluorosulfonic acid polymer electrolyte membrane (PEM; EERE 2024b). Alkaline fuel cells were the "first type widely used in the space program." Originally, the electrolyte was an aqueous potassium hydroxide solution, but they are now available as an alkaline membrane, too (EERE 2024c).

The unmanned, fuel cell–powered Aerovironment *Global Observer* had its maiden flight in 2005. It had "the capability to climb to 65,000 ft and stay aloft for 24 hours on a full tank of liquid hydrogen." It also demonstrated the feasibility of in-air liquid hydrogen refueling (Reiman 2009, 32).

In 2008, Boeing modified a two-seat Dimona motor glider "to include a Proton Exchange Membrane (PEM) fuel cell/lithium-ion battery hybrid system to power an electric motor coupled to a conventional propeller." The plane climbed to 1,000 m using both power sources and then cruised for 20 minutes on fuel cell power (20 kW) alone (GCG 2008).

The first entirely fuel cell–powered manned airplane was possibly the Antares DLR-H2 (2009), based on the power glider Antares 20E (DLR 2024). The norm, however, is for airplane fuel cells to be integrated into a hybrid hydrogen-battery electric powertrain, and the Antares DLR-H2 was later so modified.

The aforementioned Rapid 200-FC was also equipped with a 20 kW Li-Po battery. Since it had a 40 kW motor and it could "reach a cruising speed of 150–180 km/h (92–112 mph), using hydrogen alone" (GCG 2010), it would appear that this was a series-parallel configuration.

Another DLR airplane, the four-seater, twin-fuselage HY4, made its first flight in 2016. It is based on the Pipistrel Taurus G4. The compressed "hydrogen fuel is stored at a pressure between 4300 and 5800 psi [296–400 bar] in two carbon-fiber tanks, each located in the two fuselages." Besides the fuel cell, there is also a lithium-ion battery with "a storage capacity of approximately 21 kWh at 1°C and continuous power output of 45 kW." The motor maxes out at 80 kW, giving it a maximum speed of about 200 km/h. The "power module"[8] and fuel tank have a combined weight of 400 kg; the rest of the airplane's empty weight is 630 kg (Aerospace Technology 2024).

A ZeroAvia hybrid hydrogen-electric plane based on the six-seat Piper Malibu was flown in 2020. Its ZA250 powertrain comprised a 100 kW hydrogen fuel cell and a 250 kW battery (Colpan and Kovač 87). Later, in 2023, ZeroAvia flew a modified Dornier 228 (a 19-passenger turboprop) with a 600 kW ZA600 powertrain on its left wing (Alcock 2023).

The largest hydrogen fuel cell–battery-electric hybrid to fly at the time of writing was Universal Hydrogen's modified Dash 8-300 (a 40-passenger turboprop), with a fuel cell in one nacelle. Its maiden flight, in 2023, was 15 minutes long (Weitering 2023).

Hydrogen Safety

An obvious concern with hydrogen is safety. The 1937 *Hindenburg* disaster is, of course, one that everyone thinks of when hydrogen vehicles are mentioned (Aggarwal et al. 2024, 270). (In fairness, it should be noted that the *Hindenburg* made 62 successful flights before the one on which she caught fire.) And a substantial number of prior hydrogen-lift airships also met a fiery end.

In 1957, when General Curtis LeMay was briefed on one hydrogen airplane development project (Suntan), he exclaimed, "What, put my pilots up there with a ... bomb?" (Sloop 1978, 164).

However, the risk of hydrogen use can be overstated. Previously, Johnson and Rich had conducted experiments "in which tanks containing liquid hydrogen under pressure were ruptured. In many cases, the hydrogen quickly escaped without ignition." Even when "a small powder charge" was provided "to ignite the escaping hydrogen," the "resulting fireball quickly dissipated because of the rapid flame speed of hydrogen and its low density." That was not the case when a similar experiment was conducted with gasoline. "The gasoline fire was an order of magnitude more severe than the hydrogen fire." They also attempted to "induce hydrogen to explode" but succeeded in only two of 57 attempts; the successes required mixing in liquid oxygen (Sloop 1978, 149). JP-8 aviation fuel has a detonability limit (2%) that is much lower than hydrogen's (20%–60%). It was not possible to ignite liquid hydrogen by impact alone (Reiman 2009, 44–45).

An Arthur D. Little (1982, 6) study concluded that "from a crash fire hazard standpoint, LH2 does not appear to be a significantly more hazardous fuel than conventional jet fuels and LCH4 (liquid methane). In some respects, it offers lesser hazards."

Natural Gas Fuel

In 1865, Haenlein filed a provisional British patent specification disclosing the use of a "gas-engine" to drive the propeller of an "elongated balloon." The "gas required is drawn direct from the balloon," and a ballonet would inflate with air "to compensate for the loss of gas" (i.e., to maintain the shape of the airship; Brewer and Alexander 1893, 33). He received a U.S. patent on the same concept in 1872. The combustible gas (Haenlein is known to have used coal gas, which is primarily methane; Sloop 1978, 265) was mixed with air and burned in a spark-ignition internal combustion engine. He acknowledged that this would result in the reduction of the "ascensive power" of the balloon, but he urged (without specifying the initial gas volume or the engine power) that "the consumption of the gas by the engine is so little that for ten hours' working it amounts to only three per cent of the contents of the balloon."

Liquefied natural gas (LNG) is primarily methane, but the composition varies. It is liquefied by cooling to −160°C or below at near-atmospheric pressure. The specific energy (lower heating value) is 48 to 50 MJ/kg (Rompokos 2020).

The principal attraction of LNG is the expectation that it will be less polluting than normal jet fuel (kerosene), eliminating "sulfur, soot, aromatics" and reducing nitrogen oxides by 80% and carbon dioxide by 25% (Terpitz 2019).

Unfortunately, "LNG fueled aircraft require heavier aircraft systems and larger propellant tankage compared to conventionally fueled aircraft." Although LNG has a higher specific energy than conventional fuel, "the heavier aircraft requires more total energy (+5.6%) for a given flight" (Bradley and Droney 2012, 119).

"The first flights of the Tu-155 on LNG took place in January 1989. Almost 90 test flights were performed. All of them showed that fuel consumption in comparison with kerosene is reduced by almost 15%" (Kretov and Glukhov 2021).

Compressed natural gas (CNG) has been used to power automobiles, trucks, and locomotives. It may also be used in airplanes, although that usage is still limited and experimental. The higher the pressure, the higher the energy density, but also the heavier the fuel tank. Unlike LNG, there is no power drain to keep the natural gas cool, and there is no loss as a result of boil-off. But the energy density (9.5 MJ/L at 3,600 psig) is less than that of LNG (21 MJ/L; Sinor 1992).[9]

The Aviat Husky CNG demonstrator, flown in 2013, has a 3,600 psi (248 bar) CNG belly tank as well as the normal avgas wing tanks. Its 200 hp Lycoming engine can burn either fuel. The all-composite CNG tank weighs 95 lb empty, and when full, its CNG has the same energy content as 9.2 gal of gasoline (GCG 2013).

Blau Gas Fuel

Blau gas was an artificial fuel made by "cracking gas oil in a retort" at a "comparatively low temperature." It was normally liquefied by compression and expanded when ready for use (Navy 1929, 5). Its expanded density was 1.08 times that of air, so burning it did not significantly affect net buoyancy. While propane also has a density similar to air, Blau gas had a complex chemical composition: 51.9% "illuminants," 44.1% methane, 2.7% hydrogen and 1.2% nitrogen (Meade 1918, 192). The rigid airship *Graf Zeppelin* (LZ 127) carried both liquid (gasoline) and Blau gas as fuel, the latter in "fuel bags at a pressure very slightly above atmospheric" (Navy 1929, 5).

Ammonia Fuel

Ammonia (NH_3) may be liquefied at −33°C under atmospheric pressure or at room temperature (25°C) if compressed to about 10 atmospheres. Hence the required cooling power is less than that of LNG (let alone liquid hydrogen). Ammonia has a specific energy of 18.6 MJ/kg and an energy density of 12.29 MJ/L (one atmosphere, −35°C). It is flammable when in a 15%–28% mixture with air (compared to 4.7%–75% for hydrogen; Boretti and Castellato 2022). No cooling is required at altitudes of 25,000 ft or more if it is kept at the outside temperature (Otto et al. 2023).

Because it does not contain carbon, ammonia combustion doesn't produce CO_2. Unfortunately, it does produce nitrogen oxides, which are potent greenhouse gases. In internal combustion engines, this may be addressed by a DeNOx catalyst (Boretti and Castellato 2022). It is also difficult to ignite and therefore may be mixed with hydrogen or other fuels (Tomatore et al. 2022).

Because of its hydrogen content, ammonia is sometimes viewed as a "hydrogen carrier"—it is easier to liquefy and store than hydrogen, but it can be "catalytically cracked to provide H_2 gas before combustion," and the nitrogen that is coproduced inhibits nitrogen oxide formation (Otto et al. 2023).

During World War II, a mixture of liquefied ammonia and coal gas was used as fuel for Belgian buses, diesel fuel being unavailable. The NH_3 Car (a pickup truck) was driven across America in 2007, with its spark-ignition engine running on a mixture of ammonia and gasoline (NH_3 Fuel Association 2024). Another dual-fuel automobile, the AmVeh, was road tested in South Korea in 2013.

Aviation H2 aims to build the "world's first liquid ammonia powered plane." Their intent is to first develop a method of converting a normal turbofan engine for liquid ammonia use and then apply it to an actual airplane. It appears that they intend to "crack" the liquid ammonia, converting it into a mixture of hydrogen, nitrogen and "residual NH_3," and combine the cracked fuel with added NH_3 (Mayer 2022). However, the project is in a very preliminary stage as of 2024.

Piezoelectric and Pyroelectric Power

Here we look at proposals of an even more speculative nature.

The piezoelectric effect is the separation of electric charges (creating a voltage) when certain materials (quartz, topaz, etc.) are mechanically stressed (the effect can also be reversed). Likewise, the pyroelectric effect is the separation of electric charges when certain materials are heated or cooled. Some materials are both piezoelectric and pyroelectric (Dewetron 2022).

7. Miscellaneous Power Sources

Lockheed received two patents (Liggett 2011; Liggett et al. 2013) on the use of a piezoelectric and pyroelectric power–generating laminate for an airship envelope. The idea is that this laminate would "harvest electrical power from the structural and thermal changes of the envelope associated with the operation of the airship."

Lockheed envisions the use of this "free" power to supply electricity. But even if it does not provide power for propulsion directly, it means that none of the power generated by the main engine needs to be diverted to support those electrical systems. Lockheed also argues that if rechargeable batteries would otherwise power those systems, using piezoelectric/pyroelectric power would result in a reduction of the overall weight of the airship, thereby improving its performance. (Less weight would mean that a smaller gas volume envelope is needed, which in turn would mean less drag, and thus a lighter, less powerful main engine for the design airspeed.)

Nonrigid airship envelopes are typically laminates, with one layer providing tensile strength; a second, lift gas impermeability; and a third, protection from ultraviolet radiation and moisture. In the Lockheed design, on top of the gas barrier layer, there is a piezoelectric layer (e.g., polyvinylidene fluoride) sandwiched between two electrically conductive metal layers.

Lockheed acknowledged that piezoelectric and pyroelectric currents are typically transient if the material maintains its new shape or temperature. However, it argued that an airship envelope is subject to a "slow and relatively constant expansion and contraction" and "thermal variations"—that is, there is no equilibration, and the "energy produced by the piezoelectric layer ... is continuous or nearly continuous" (Liggett 2011).

Regrettably, the Lockheed patents don't quantify the expected power production per unit area of laminate.

Riaz et al. (2013) proposed piezoelectric harvesting of the energy associated with flutter, a vibration that occurs when a body moves through a fluid. They proposed placing "piezoelectric cantilevers" on the underside of a solar-powered airship. An isolated piezoelectric harvester, placed in a wind tunnel providing an airspeed of 18.3 m/s, produced 0.00117–0.0025 W in a somewhat cyclic fashion. Riaz et al. thought that a suitable array of harvesters could produce enough power to support "cabin lighting, sensors and controllers."

The size of this harvester was not stated, but Jabbar et al. (2017) disclose one that is 60 mm by 40 mm. If 400 could fit in a square meter, that would bring power output up to, at best, about 0.5 W/m^2. Compare that with the solar power concepts discussed previously!

Part I: Unconventional Power

These piezoelectric concepts do not appear to have advanced beyond the conceptual design stage.

Triboelectric Power

Here is another highly speculative approach. That power can be generated triboelectrically is well established; whether it is a practical source is extremely doubtful.

The triboelectric effect is a transfer of electric charge between objects that touch each other. When such contact occurs, some materials tend to gain electrons (become more negatively charged), and others tend to lose electrons (become more positively charged). Both airships and airplanes, just by passing through the air, experience a triboelectric effect, *triboelectric charging*. (Air contains dust, snow and ice crystals, water droplets, and individual oxygen, nitrogen and water molecules, with densities varying with altitude and location, and parsing out their relative contributions is difficult.)

"The triboelectric effect converts mechanical energy into electrical energy based on the coupling effect of triboelectrification and electrostatic induction and is utilized as the basis for triboelectric generators" (Logothetis et al. 2017).

Most of the triboelectric nanogenerators (TENGs) constructed so far have drawn power from triboelectricity generated by the interaction of solid surfaces, either by vertical contact separation or by linear (horizontal) sliding. However, TENGS have "shown capability to harvest ... mechanical energies from water waves, human motions, vibrations, wind, etc." (Zi and Wang 2017). The last category is the one most relevant here.

Wang et al. (2018) report the use of an airflow-driven triboelectric nanogenerator in a respiratory monitor. It converts the mechanical energy of the breath into electrical output indicative of the exhalation volume. The TENG was a "flexible nanostructured polytetrafluoroethylene (n-PTFE) thin film in an acrylic tube." The nanostructure increases the contact area for charge transfer, and the charge was collected by a very thin copper film. When air flowed into the tube, the film oscillated, producing charge by the contact/separation mode. The airflow rate was 85–216 L/min; at the highest flow rate, the maximum current was 10 milliamperes (mA). The current was used to light one or more LEDs. This current, of course, was minuscule, but so was the TENG (the tube had inner dimensions of $5.5 \times 2 \times 1$ cm).

7. Miscellaneous Power Sources

There have been some attempts to use TENGs to extract energy from breezes, as they are under "the wind velocity threshold of current large wind turbines." There have been a variety of designs, and it's outside the scope of this work to discuss them in detail. However, the "hummingbird TENG," said to be "inspired by the movement of hummingbirds' wings," was able to achieve a "peak power output of 1.5 W/m^2 at winds of 7.5 m/s" (Li et al. 2021). (I wish the *average* power output were reported.) Since the TENG output is variable with time, the energy needs to be stored in a capacitor or battery for future use (Li et al. 2021).

Li (2021) developed a wind speed sensor powered via two TENGs by the wind. The current developed was proportional to the wind speed (Li et al. 2021, fig. 3), and the sensor could "light 50 LEDs at the wind speed of 15 m/s" (abstract). The sensor was a trapezoid with a length of 90 mm and 20 mm and 40 mm sides. The maximum power output was 1.2 mW (milliwatts), at a wind speed of 25 m/s (6–8).

So how does this relate to aerial power and propulsion? Michael Bonikowski proposed (with no quantitative details) the *Eather One*, an airplane running "on electricity generated during the airplane's movement through the air" (Sigler 2020). (This airplane was to use both triboelectric and piezoelectric generators [Bonikowski 2024], but we will concentrate in this section on the former.)

This is, unfortunately, a half-baked idea. If the airplane is propelled by another source of power, then arguably triboelectric generators could be used to recapture some of the energy transferred from the airship to the air as a result of drag. But those generators would presumably increase drag relative to that of a pristine fuselage and wings (Novella 2020). (Novella draws an analogy with regenerative braking in cars.)

More importantly, the magnitude of the triboelectric current is minuscule. The USAF developed a formula for the steady-state current generated via triboelectric charging. It is proportional to both the frontal area of the airplane and the airplane's velocity, but the constant of proportionality is small. For an airship with a frontal area[10] of 1,200 sq m and an airspeed of 50 m/s, the current generated by flying in precipitation would be just 78 mA (Heppe 2014, col. 26), and it would be "substantially less in the absence of precipitation."[11] To put that number in perspective, the USB port on a Windows computer supplies a current of 500 mA.

Part II: Unconventional Propulsion

8

Buoyancy-Driven Propulsion

History

Wingless Airships

Solomon Andrews was the first person to propel a manned airship without an engine by exploiting the action of a net buoyant force (achieved by dropping ballast or venting gas) on an inclined airship. Andrews built and flew two such crafts.

The first (*Aereon I*) had three hulls and was flown on four dates in 1863. It demonstrated the ability to make headway against the wind, although the speed estimates that were made for it are open to question.

Our best source for the geometry of the *Aereon* is his 1864 patent. It had three envelopes, each 80 ft long, 13 ft in diameter, and made of varnished linen. These were cylindrical over the central 48 ft, and the fore- and aftbodies tapered symmetrically to a point. The axes of the three cylindroids were in parallel (like a trimaran). The cylindroids were held together by screwed-together lateral strips and a net of cotton twine, attached to the envelopes by cords.

The net was attached to the control car by 120 cords (four rows of 30 apiece, spaced 20 in. apart), each running to one of four wooden hoops above the car. Another 24 heavier cords passed from these hoops under the car.

The car, suspended 16 ft below the center envelope, was 12 ft long, with a gently curved bottom. Inside this car was an inner car on runners, where the pilot sat and the ballast was placed. The cars weighed 58 lb and the equipment in the cars, about 130 lb. Since the car was attached to the envelopes by a network of cords, the inclination of the car caused the envelopes to pitch.

The airship had a triangular, 17 sq ft rudder made of cambric muslin stretched over a light reed frame. There is no reference to fins of any kind.

There is reference to a flat, 2 in. thick membrane of cambric muslin

Part II: Unconventional Propulsion

bridging the forebodies and aftbodies. Its purpose was to increase the resistance to perpendicular movement. However, this membrane is not apparent in the figure depicting the first *Aereon* in Andrews's book, and it may have been a post-flight afterthought.

The *Aereon* was said to have a total gas volume of 26,000 cu ft and to carry 600 lb (Andrews 1866, 5), which covered the aeronaut, the ballast, and, I believe, the cars and their accoutrements. (I calculated that if it had tangent ogive ends, it would have had a total volume of 26,221 cu ft and, completely filled with pure hydrogen, a total gross lift at ISA sea level of 1,866 lb.)

The *Aereon I* is said to have undergone four trials from June to September 1863. However, the only newspaper account (*NYH*, September 8, 1863) was for its last trial, on September 4, 1863, over Perth Amboy, New Jersey. In this trial, it carried Andrews (172 lb) and 256 lb of ballast.

In seeking government support for his airship, Andrews (1865b, 14–16) presented the testimony of various witnesses. According to one witness (Hamilton Fonda, factory foreman and former ordnance sergeant), it first flew north against the wind, returned and landed. Then it took off again westward, returned, and landed. Witnesses asserted that it was

Selected portion of an 1864 lithograph of the Solomon Andrews airship of 1863. Courtesy New Jersey State Library Digital Jerseyana Collection. https://dspace.njstatelib.org/items/26b1ecb8-62dd-4028-93ef-79628fd733bb. A reproduction of the complete lithograph is available at https://www.loc.gov/resource/cph.3b01438/.

8. Buoyancy-Driven Propulsion

able to make headway against a wind "blowing ... not less than 10 mph" (Fonda) or even "10–15 mph" (architect Ellis White). Four other witnesses (merchant and ex-postmaster John Manning, constable and tax collector N. H. Tyrrell, Justice of the Peace Isaac Ward, and hotelkeeper James Allen) agreed that he had made headway against the wind, but without attempting to guess at the speed.

We don't know what altitudes it favored in this trial, but in the second (July) trial, it didn't ascend above 200 ft (bank cashier S. V. R. Patterson).

After the two manned flights on September 4, it was released unmanned, with a locked rudder and inner car, to spiral upward and destroy itself; its net buoyancy was generated by relieving it of Andrews's weight and "several 7-pound bags of ballast" (Fonda's statement, Andrews 1865b), amounting to "over 200 pounds" (Andrews 1864a). Presumably, the rest of the ballast had already been expended, since the goal was to give it maximum speed. "The *Herald* reporter thought that it reached a speed of not less than 120 mph" (Whitman 1932). Whitman comments, "Lacking experience with high speeds, the reporter may be forgiven for erring on the side of exaggeration." Nonetheless, Andrews, in a subsequent letter to the editor, asserted that it peaked at over 200 mph.[1]

Andrews was not entirely satisfied with this design; on August 26, 1863, he wrote to President Lincoln that she was "too much of the clipper.... She can only be balanced when she is full of gas." Andrews also wanted the ship to be able to ascend to a height "out of reach of bullets" (Whitman 1920).

In 1864, an Indian rubber model of the *Aereon*, with three hollow cylinders (with hemispherical ends) 4 ft long and 8 in. in diameter, was inflated, inclined, and released, rising at an angle of 40°, for the enlightenment of the official commission headed by Joseph Henry (Andrews 1865b, 26). It is clear from their July 22, 1864, report that the commission members never saw the original full-scale airship.

Andrews's 1866 airship (*Aereon II*) was a monohull[2] of at least double the lift. The information concerning the *Aereon II*'s geometry, other than that it was shaped like a "long lemon" (*SciAm* 1866) or a "large fish" (quoted in *Otago Witness* 1866), is hopelessly contradictory.[3]

She was flown twice. On May 25, 1866, she took off with four aeronauts from its base at the corner of Houston and Green Streets in New York City, rising at an angle of "less than 45°," north to Harlem, then was driven by a southwest wind across the East River, passing over part of Blackwell's Island and brought to a standstill by a contrary wind over Hunter's Point. She was then put about and flew slowly toward

Part II: Unconventional Propulsion

Ravenswood, landing near Astoria. Its maximum altitude was 2,000 ft. The rudder was found to be too small to hold the ship head to wind; the car, not long enough to permit the ship to be pitched to the angle desired (*NYT*, May 26, 1866; *SciAm*, May 26, 1866, and June 2, 2024). Total time aloft was 25 minutes (Niagara Falls *Gazette*, December 24, 1928). The *World* estimated its ground speed as at least 20 mph, and the *Tribune*, at 20–25 mph (Whitman 1920).

For its June 5 flight (*NYT*, June 7, 1866), the airship was given a larger rudder. It carried 400 lb of ballast (*The New York Herald*; according to the *Otago Witness*, September 28, 1866, said 450 lb) and two aeronauts. Its initial ascent was too slow relative to its horizontal movement, risking collision with a high building, and the copilot threw out an additional 25 lb of ballast, which allegedly gave the ship an "ascending power of thirty-nine pounds," implying that the original takeoff was effectuated by dropping 14 lb. (Andrews must have also increased the pitch, as otherwise the additional ascending power would just have caused them to collide sooner.)

Further problems ensued. First, the rudder tackle got entangled, and they lost rudder control, moving in circles in the general direction (S or SW toward Canal St.); the wind was blowing. They freed the tackle, threw out more ballast, and returned, heading up against a gentle wind. Then, when they reached an altitude of 1,200–1,500 ft, they lost the ability to control the inclination of the cylindroids as a result of envelope expansion against a control band, and they were at the mercy of the winds, blowing toward the northeast. After 20 minutes, they had risen to 6,000 ft and were over the Long Island Sound.

At this point, the wind was still blowing toward the northeast; they could see clouds below them that were moving south-southwest, and above the airship, the clouds were moving in a third direction.[4]

They vented gas and, dropping to 4,000 ft, regained inclination control. They turned and slowly descended, ascended, and descended again. The wording of the article is ambiguous, but it sounds as though this was 8 mi of controlled flight. If wind direction hadn't changed, then they were probably heading 45°–90° off the wind. They landed by the village of Brookville (ENE of starting point) on Long Island at close to 7 p.m., after a journey of about 30 mi (*NYT*, June 7, 1866). The fact that the *Aereon II* didn't return to its starting point has led some later writers to surmise that it was because it encountered winds it couldn't overcome (McPhee 1973, 105).[5] However, it had already demonstrated some ability to make headway against the wind (Whitman 1932).

8. Buoyancy-Driven Propulsion

While Andrews was the first to actually build and fly an airship with a "buoyancy engine," the basic concept appears in Cayley (1837), Muzzi (1844) and Gage (1859).

Cayley (1837) wrote that in 1815, his friend Evans "tried with success to steer a small Montgolfier balloon by suspending a large oblique surface beneath it, which caused the ascent to be oblique in the direction towards which the upper edge of the plain [sic, plane] was pointed; when the fuel failed, gravitation made its return obliquely to the place from which it set out; had this plaine [plane] been reversed when at the top of its rise, steerage towards the same point of the compass would have been effected in both cases by this sort of vertical tacking." (Muzzi [1844] took an approach similar to that of Evans.)

Cayley (1837) admitted that this approach (with a refinement discussed below) was "simple" and inexpensive, but he considered it "unsatisfactory in being obliged thus to resort to such alternating heights and descents, implying such sudden changes of temperature, to say nothing of the devious and prolonged nature of the track, and the consequent waste of power."

Gage (1859) instead proposed pitching an elongated gas bag (the patent drawing shows a double cone shape), which would have reduced resistance to longitudinal motion and increased resistance to transverse motion while the airship was ascending or descending. While Gage's patent seemingly anticipated several of Andrews's patent claims, the Andrews (1864a) patent asserts that Andrews filed caveats in 1849 and 1850. We do not know their contents, but it seems likely to me that they disclosed the basic concept of the airship having an elongated form, since Andrews implies that the caveats only omitted the disclosure of the longitudinal cavity formed by his multihull.[6]

Figure 8 of the Andrews (1864a) patent depicts a "common balloon" with a 12 ft diameter spherical envelope and a rectangular "plane or sail" suspended below it between the envelope and the control car. The purpose of this plane was to increase resistance to vertical movement and thus ameliorate a weakness of the spherical design. The corresponding text said it had 17 lb of gross lift (that would be correct if the lift gas were illuminating gas, i.e., methane). If the net buoyancy were 3.5 lb, this model airship allegedly could achieve 2 mph.

Despite these prior inventions, a British patent was awarded to Gaggino in 1888 for the combination of an inclined plane with a balloon to "cause it to ascend or descend forward" (Brewer and Alexander 1893, 115).

Part II: Unconventional Propulsion

Winged Airships and their Underwater Kin

After the 1866 flights, Andrews concluded that the *Aereon II* needed a 50 ft car, so he could shift his weight further. In addition, he decided that the airship should be equipped with "two lateral wing-shaped appendages" (*NYT* June 7, 1866).

In the 1960s, Monroe Drew and John Fitzpatrick built an *Aereon III*. This had the triple hull and the approximate size of the first *Aereon* (Johansen 1962), but it was to use helium as the lift gas, and each hull was of rigid construction, with the standard class-C airship hull shape. Also unlike the original *Aereon*, the ends of the hulls were connected by inboard wings (Aereon 2004).

While it may have originally been intended to rely on buoyancy for propulsion, as constructed, the middle hull was equipped with a four-cylinder McCullough drone airplane engine driving a helicopter rotor. In any event, it was wrecked in a 1966 taxi run, and the company switched to deltoid-shaped hybrid lift monohulls, the *Aereon 7* and *Aereon 26*, which owed nothing to Andrews (McPhee 1973, 46ff, 124ff).

The Andrews concept reappeared (without attribution) in a new medium as Farris and Rand's (1964) underwater glider, intended for oceanographic studies. The control means had a depth sensor, and based on the depth, it changed the buoyancy by the intake or expulsion of ballast water. Underwater operation simplified matters, as water ballast was free for the taking. However, to expel the ballast, a gas (usually nitrogen at 1,850 psi) was released from a pressure tank, and thus the endurance was dependent on the supply of gas. The location of the intake and outlet ensured a pitch-down and pitch-up effect, respectively. Unlike the *Aereon*, the Farris and Rand glider had wings. I have not found any evidence that it was actually built.

The Farris and Rand system could be adapted to airship use by employing hydrogen (or helium) as the expelling gas and air as the ballast. However, the buoyancy differential between hydrogen (or helium) and air is much smaller than that between nitrogen gas and water.

In 1989, Henry Stommel's science fiction story "The Slocum Mission" was published in *Oceanography*. It postulated a fleet of autonomous Slocum gliders that glided through the ocean on sawtooth paths by ballast changes and gathered oceanographic data. The next year, he and Webb were awarded a contract to develop a prototype in which a battery drove "a piston type ballast pump and a moving internal mass [the battery pack itself] for pitch and roll," and it was tested in 1991.

8. Buoyancy-Driven Propulsion

By 2000, not only the Slocum but two other glider programs, Seaglider and Spray, had completed 10-day missions. These gliders were all winged (the Slocum's are flat plates) and traveled at speeds of just about half a knot. On the other hand, they had ranges of thousands of kilometers (Graver 2003, 2005). Most underwater gliders have wings, but there are exceptions, such as the ACSA SEAEXPLORER (Khalin and Kizilova 2019).

Flight data from the Slocum underwater glider shows that with a pitch of 23.74°, the attack angle was −2.9°, and with a pitch of −22.77°, the attack angle was 2.7° (Graver 2005, 156).

YouTube videos of underwater gliders in action are available (Kuttenkeuler 2010; Smart Microsystems 2012; Ashraf 2011).

The Krawetz and Celniker (Lockheed) patent (1989) proposed adapting the propulsion system to an aerial reconnaissance vehicle. Like Andrews, Krawetz and Celniker suggested that instead of dropping ballast and venting gas, alternately compressing and expanding the gas cell could vary the buoyancy. They asserted that the gas cell would have a flexible portion to make this possible but did not analyze what this portion might be made of or how thick it must be. The movement of the portion was to be effected by a torsional spring. Krawetz and Celniker conceded that "losses due to friction, hysteresis in the spring, and internal energy losses in the gas due to compression and expansion" would cause the system to wind down if there was no supply of power, but they thought the power demand would be "relatively small." As far as I know, this was strictly a paper patent.

Unlike the *Aereon*, the Krawetz and Celniker craft has wings; these are for generating a lift that opposes the component of the net buoyant force that's perpendicular to the flight path, but particulars aren't given. Necessarily, there is a lift-induced drag that reduces the forward speed along the flight path.

Geery (2001) describes a series of winged, helium-inflated water toys of up to 2 ft long. His preferred model has a guitar pick–shaped body with a bluff nose, a tapered tail, and backswept curved wings. Another model is a long cylinder with conical ends and two pairs of short wings. A third had two saucers, connected in tandem by a cylindrical piece, and reportedly achieved 10 mph with just 8 oz of lift.

Released at an angle underwater, this model can generate enough speed to actually fly out of the pool. Geery (2001) notes that his models "slice through the air" more readily than would the *Aereon*, because of their use of a single hull, the omission of external netting, and (for some embodiments) the higher length-to-diameter ratio of the hull.

Part II: Unconventional Propulsion

This toy was later sold under the name Waterwing or Aqua Glider (possibly filled with air rather than helium), and there are YouTube videos of it in flight underwater (Geery 2006a) and in the air with different wings (Geery 2006b). CargoAirships (2009a, 2009b) has posted videos of similar thermal flyer toys, presumably inflated with warm exhaled air rather than helium.

In early 2000, New Mexico State University's Physical Science Laboratory conducted research and development on an autonomous buoyancy-driven airship. This was to be a swept-winged, nonrigid, helium-lift airship with a volume of 484,000 cu ft and a wingspan of 338 ft, intended for station-keeping recon operations at an altitude of 65,000–75,000 ft (19.8–22.9 km; Purandare 2007, 17–18).

It was contemplated that it would vary its net buoyancy by varying its weight; "ballast" air would be drawn and compressed into or vented from a ballonet (Purandare 2007, 21, 59). When the ballonet filled, the gondola would move forward, pitching the airship nose downward; when it vented, the reverse would happen (119). The initial internal airship superpressure was to be 4.20 kPa; the ballonet air weight, 2.92 kilonewtons (kN); and the gondola weight, 2 kN. The descending airship weight was 9.02 kN; the ascending weight, 6.10 kN (131); that is, the ascending weight corresponded to an empty ballonet.

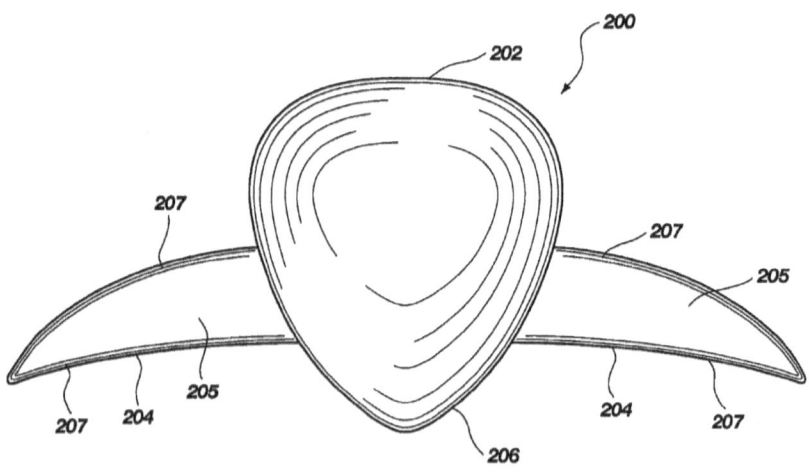

The guitar pick body version of Geery's water toy (Geery 2001, fig 8a). I have a Wahu Aqua Glider (copyright 2006), a 2013 gift from Geery, with the same body shape, but the wings have a shorter span-chord ratio. The wings could also be adjusted to Vee-back.

8. Buoyancy-Driven Propulsion

In August 2004, it demonstrated a one-tenth-scale model that varied its net buoyancy, changed altitude, and generated "a small forward motion" (Purandare 2007, 12–13). I suspect that the 2011 *Vulture II* unmanned airplane program is the outgrowth of this design.

Finally, we have the *Phoenix* remote-controlled, unmanned, teardrop-shaped airship, "15 meters in length, 10.5 meters in wingspan, and when fully loaded weighs 150 kilograms (330 pounds)." It was successfully flown indoors in 2020. It makes itself heavier by "inhaling" air and compressing it and makes itself lighter by reversing the process. The pumps could be powered during the daytime by wing-mounted solar cells and at night by a rechargeable 3 kWh lithium-ion battery (Rae 2020).

The Purandare (2007) dissertation provides two- and limited three-degrees-of-freedom mathematical models of such airships, considering the thermodynamics of different methods of varying net buoyancy (see also Wu et al. 2009; 2010; 2011). Similarly, Graver (2005) modeled the underwater gliders.

Analysis

The Physics of Buoyancy-Driven Propulsion

When a spherical balloon drops ballast or vents gas, it ascends or descends vertically. Andrews's proposal was to give a lighter-than-air craft a "flattened and elongated form" and shift weight (pilot or ballast) to incline it (Andrews 1864a). He predicted that it would then travel in the direction the nose was pointing (this is almost correct), which would be the path of least resistance.

Whitman (1920) suggested a hydrodynamic analogy—a plank forced underwater and released—the buoyant force uplifting it acts vertically, but the resistance offered by the water causes it to follow its path of least resistance and come up endways. "Thus it rises, not vertically, but at an angle, and in so moving covers horizontal distance." I have tried this with a kapla (a miniature pine plank) and found that when released at any angle other than horizontal, it travels end first until it reaches the surface.[7]

In still air, the *Aereon* (or any other buoyancy-driven airship) is acted upon by the following forces: gravity, buoyancy (static lift), aerodynamic lift and aerodynamic drag. Since both gravity and buoyancy act vertically, it's convenient to combine them into net buoyancy (buoyant force minus gravitational force), which may be positive or negative. Aerodynamic lift

Part II: Unconventional Propulsion

is perpendicular to the line of flight, and aerodynamic drag is backward along the line of flight. In steady (constant speed) flight, the forces must be in balance; the vertical components must add up to zero, as must the horizontal ones.

It is simplest to analyze the forces in a frame of reference in which one axis is defined by the line of flight (glide path), and the other is perpendicular to the line of flight and thus is the axis along which lift operates. However, as a check, I also analyze using the more conventional vertical-horizontal frame of reference.

Three angles come into play in a study of buoyancy-driven propulsion. Pitch is the angle that the airship's longitudinal axis makes with the horizontal plane defined by the Earth. The glide path angle is the angle that the airship's line of motion makes with the same plane. The angle of attack is the angle that the airship's longitudinal axis makes with its line of motion. It is evident that any two of these angles determine the value of the third.

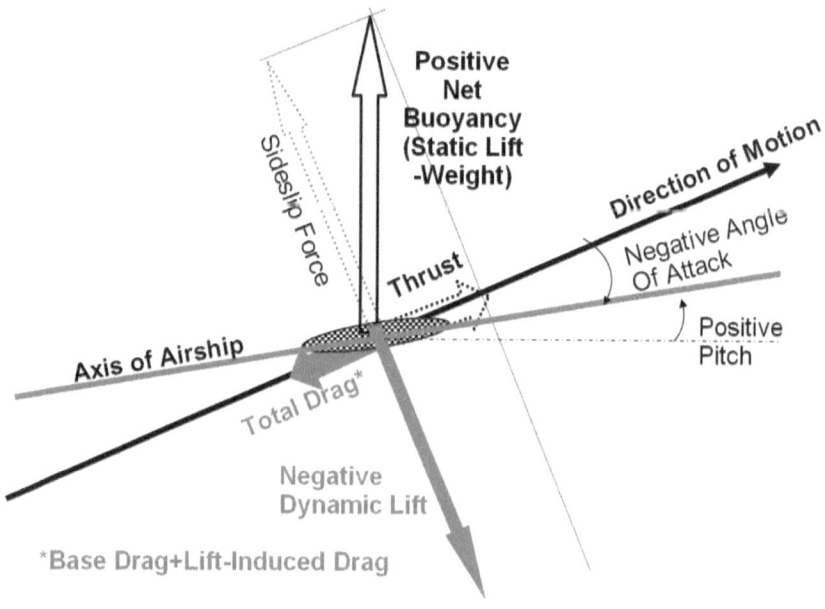

Balance of forces at equilibrium for buoyancy-driven airship during ascent (illustration by author). The vertical component of the dynamic lift is not shown.

8. Buoyancy-Driven Propulsion

Pitch is the only one of these angles directly controlled by the airship pilot. Andrews moved forward and backward inside the gondola, thus shifting the center of mass and achieving a pitch of as much as 15° up or down.

The buoyant force is equal to the lift gas volume times the specific lift (the lift force exerted by a unit volume of the lift gas). The specific lift, in turn, is the difference in density between the lift gas and the ambient air times the gravitational acceleration. Their densities, in turn, are a function of their temperature and pressure. For this analysis, assume that both temperature and pressure decrease with altitude in accordance with the ISA model.

If there is a difference between the internal and external temperatures, heat will flow between them, bringing them closer together. If the internal pressure significantly exceeds the ambient one, automatic valves will open to prevent the pressure difference from rupturing the envelope. Hence, for this analysis, assume that the internal temperature and pressure equal their external counterparts at any given altitude. The density of both the air and the lift gas is proportional to the pressure divided by the temperature, and they, too, decrease with altitude.

An air ballonet is a device used to minimize the changes in buoyant force as an airship changes altitude. As the airship ascends, the density difference and thus the specific lift decrease. However, as long as the lift gas can expand at the expense of the air ballonet—that is, the latter is not fully deflated—the decrease in the specific lift is precisely balanced by the increase in lift gas volume, and the gross lift (buoyant force) remains constant.

By dropping ballast to create positive net buoyancy and bringing the nose up, the *Aereon* glided upward, and by venting gas to create negative net buoyancy and bringing the nose down, the *Aereon* glided downward. The process (a yo-yo) could be repeated as needed; the *Aereon* thus progressed by a cyclic variation in net buoyancy. In still air, the airship would have followed an essentially sawtooth path in the vertical plane.

Roughly speaking, dropping 9 lb of ballast produces 40 N of net buoyant force upward. Venting 126.4 cu ft of pure hydrogen produces the same force downward (this is the result of the loss of buoyancy and thus an unbalanced gravitational force).

The propulsive force provided by the buoyancy engine is the component parallel to the glide path; it is the product of the net buoyancy and the sine of the glide path angle (Krawetz and Celniker 1989). The resulting airspeed is the airspeed along the glide path, which is itself inclined to the

Part II: Unconventional Propulsion

ground. To obtain the horizontal speed, the resulting glide speed must be multiplied by the cosine of the glide path angle.

The glide path angle will be close to but not quite equal to the pitch. Why? The net buoyancy also has a component (net buoyancy × cosine of glide path angle) perpendicular to the glide path, thus altering the direction of motion (contrary to the steady flight assumption) unless some other force opposes it. And plainly, that other force must be aerodynamic lift.

There are essentially two ways of generating aerodynamic lift. First, if a symmetrical airfoil, like the bare hull of an airship or even a flat plate, is inclined to the airflow, giving it a positive or negative angle of attack, it will generate lift (positive or negative, respectively). Second, if there is a camber—an asymmetry between the top and bottom surface—as on a conventional airplane wing, it will generate lift at a zero angle of attack.

The *Aereon* was essentially a vertically symmetrical airfoil. When ascending (positive glide path angle) at a constant speed, it must have had a negative angle of attack, so it generates negative lift—balancing the perpendicular component of the net buoyancy. And to have a negative angle of attack, its pitch must have been a bit less than the glide path angle. The pitch would still be positive, however. The reverse, of course, was true when the *Aereon* was descending at a constant speed.

The pilot determines the net buoyancy (by releasing ballast or venting gas), pitch angle, direction of motion, and airspeed change until the forces are in balance. The drag must equal (cancel out) the propulsive force, and the dynamic lift must equal the perpendicular component of the net buoyancy.

As the glide path angle (for ascent) decreases, the angle of attack becomes more negative, and the pitch angle decreases. A minimum glide path angle is determined by the angle of attack at which the lift-to-total-drag ratio is maximized. Also, there is a limit to how negative (for ascent) or positive (for descent) the angle of attack can be; when it's too far from zero, there is flow separation (stall), and the lift (negative or positive) rapidly returns to zero.

Aereon Performance Prediction

Andrews repeatedly asserted that there was a linear relationship between his ascending power (the net buoyant force created by his ballast drop, which will be proportional to the mass dropped) and the airspeed achieved. Thus, he called for a ballast drop of (a) less than 2 lb for 1 mph, 200 lb for 100 mph (Andrews 1866, 4), or (b) 1 lb for 1 mph, 200 lb for 200 mph (Andrews 1864a).[8]

8. Buoyancy-Driven Propulsion

However, it is well established by experience with airplanes and airships that, depending on various factors, the drag force is proportional to somewhere between $V^{1.5}$ and V^2 for subsonic speeds and higher powers of velocity (V) for transonic flight. For example, the Army Manual *Airship Aerodynamics* suggests $V^{1.85}$. Purandare (2007) assumes that the drag coefficient is constant and thus that the drag force is proportional to V^2. Consequently, the propulsive force must be increased in the same proportion.

I have used my standard airship aerodynamic model (see appendix 1), which is based on standard airship/airplane preliminary design methods, to calculate the performance of the *Aereon* with various combinations of ballast drop and pitch. Appendix 2 compares my modeling of the *Aereon* to Purandare's (2007) modeling of a hypothetical buoyancy-driven airship. Appendix 3 discusses the sensitivity of the predicted performance to the assumptions made by the model.

The force balance is arrived at by an iterative process in which the angle of attack and airspeed are adjusted until the sum of the forces on both axes is tolerably close to zero. The nonlinear solver built into Microsoft Excel can carry out a thousand iterations in a fraction of a second, and I have found it generally produces more exact solutions than I can achieve manually (and much faster).

The *Aereon* was equipped with bags containing 7 lb of ballast apiece. Assuming the *Aereon* is at sea level, fully inflated with pure hydrogen, and that it drops 28 lb of ballast and assumes a nose-up pitch of 15°, I arrive at the following force balance[9] using my standard aerodynamic model (see table 8–1):

Table 8–1: Force Balance, *Aereon*, 28 lb drop, sea level, 15° pitch

Forces (in Newtons)	Glide Path Frame of Reference		Earth Frame of Reference	
	Parallel GP	Perpendicular GP	Horizontal	Vertical
Buoyancy Weight	43.2892	116.7853	0.0000	124.5502
Total Drag Force	−43.2892	0	−40.5904	15.0458
Zero-Lift Drag	−35.5020	0	−34.2263	−12.6868
Lift-Induced Drag	−6.7872	0	−6.3641	−2.23590
Dynamic Lift	0	−116.7854	40.5904	−109.5045
Grand Total	0.0000	−0.0001	0.0000	−0.0001

Part II: Unconventional Propulsion

This force balance is achieved by setting the airspeed to about 6.799 mph and the angle of attack to about −5.34°. The glide path angle is about 20.34°, and hence the horizontal speed is about 6.38 mph. The airspeed is rather low, considering the eyewitness testimony.

But we know that the change in weight for the unmanned flight was 200 lb or close to it. So I propose the following scenario: On each manned flight, Andrews dropped 16 ballast bags (112 lb). If he started with 256 lb of ballast, that left him with 32 lb, which is not evenly divisible by seven, the alleged weight of a single ballast bag. So I suggest that he actually had 252 lb initially, leaving him with 28 lb (four bags could be considered several). And since he weighed 172 lb, the unmanned flight was propelled by removing 200 lb. And for all flights, I assume the maximum pitch of 15°. Table 8–2 shows the results:

	Table 8–2: Aerodynamic Model Predictions for *Aereon I* Final Flights					
Ballast Drop (lb)	Glide Path deg	AoA deg	Airspeed mph	Horiz Air Spd mph	Vert Air Spd mph	RMS %Dev
112	20.03	−5.0267	14.0274	13.1792	4.8038	6.821E-07
200	19.87	−4.8734	19.0467	17.9124	6.4748	8.3917E-07

Note that quadrupling the ballast drop (from 28 lb to 112 lb) approximately doubled the airspeed, which is exactly as expected.

I did not attempt to model the *Aereon II*, given the uncertainties regarding its dimensions.

Plausibility of Andrews's Speed Claims

I have considered the consistency of my performance calculations with the reports of those who witnessed the *Aereon I* flights and the reliability of the witness statements.

For the manned flights, the consistency depends on the ballast drop assumed. According to my model predictions, a 28 lb drop resulted in a horizontal speed of 6.38 mph, whereas one of 112 lb was 13.18 mph.

The witnesses testified that the *Aereon* made headway against the wind, and consequently, their wind speed estimates (and the reliability thereof) are relevant. One witness thought the wind speed was 10 mph; another, 10–15 mph; the others didn't say. These wind speed estimates are of doubtful reliability for the reasons detailed in appendix 4.

8. Buoyancy-Driven Propulsion

I am sure they could tell whether there was a surface wind. If they actually felt the wind, that would imply that it was at least a light breeze (4–7 mph), and if they merely saw smoke drifting, that it was at least a light air (1–3 mph).

The witnesses agreed that the *Aereon* was able to make headway against the wind. But there is nothing to indicate that the *Aereon* was flying directly upwind. The *Aereon* would need less propulsive force to make headway against a 10 mph wind that was coming from 45° off its bow than one blowing directly against it.

None of the witnesses stated the ground speed of the *Aereon*, but it is conceivable that they estimated the wind speed based on the apparent ground speed. If so, it is not likely that they were able to accurately estimate the ground speed of the *Aereon* (see appendix 5).

Andrews did not claim that the *Aereon* flew a set course before observers trained and prepared to estimate its speed. Rather, it seems that the witnesses were simply curious about whether Andrews would manage to fly, and they weren't questioned about the *Aereon*'s performance until a month after the flight was observed. This plainly reduces the reliability of the estimates (of both wind and airship speed) even further.

Given the limitations of the eyewitness testimony, the predictions here seem reasonably consistent with the eyewitness reports.

We come next to the unmanned flight, where the *Aereon* was set loose. When given "over two hundred pounds ascending power" (Andrews 1864a), it flew with a "streamer thirty feet long on the tail ... [that] stood out in a straight line behind her" (Fonda's testimony, Andrews 1865b). This ascending power was the result of it being relieved of Andrews's own weight (172 lb; *NYH* 1863) and "several 7 pound bags of ballast."

The wind speed needed to cause a flag to fly straight out depends on the weight of the flag, but the "modern" (1906) version of the Beaufort scale says that force 3, gentle breeze, results in light flags extended and corresponds to a wind speed of 8–12 mph. (For a longer, heavier flag, it could be somewhat more.)

By my calculation, starting from sea level with a 15° pitch, if four bags had been tossed (with Andrews disembarked, yielding a total net buoyancy of 200 lb), the airspeed would have been about 19 mph (on the low end of Beaufort force 5). That seems consistent with the reported streamer behavior, which is the only objective (albeit ambiguous) evidence of the *Aereon*'s speed.

Now, the *Herald* reporter claimed that the airship spiraled up at 120 mph, and in a letter to the editor, Andrews claimed that its true speed was over 200 mph.[10] Those estimates are absurd.

Part II: Unconventional Propulsion

If a flag is flown on a vehicle that is being driven at "highway speed" (55–65 mph) for 10 minutes, "you have put your flag through a 'Severe Cyclonic Storm.' That kind of wear is devastating for flags" (Cavalari 2023). The Flagpole Company says that normal size flags can be flown in force 6 winds (25–31 mph) but should be replaced with storm flags (one-third normal size) in force 7 (32–38 mph) and taken down entirely in force 9 (47–54 mph).

At the speeds estimated by Andrews and the reporter, the streamer would have done much more than fly straight out. They would have behaved as if they were caught in a hurricane or tornado and been torn off or destroyed. (Hurricanes have winds over 73 mph; category 3 is 111–129 mph; category 5 is over 157 mph; for tornadoes, EF2 is 111–135 mph; EF4 is 166–200 mph.)

The fastest airspeed ever recorded for an airship was the USS *Macon*'s 140.3 km/h (87.2 mph; Camplin 2020, 15).

Musings on the Buoyancy Engine

Initial Altitude Effects

An airship relying on buoyancy-driven propulsion, by definition, is not engaging in level flight. Rather, it pitches nose up and drops ballast (or otherwise increases buoyancy) and zigs upward; it pitches nose down and vents gas (or otherwise decreases buoyancy) and zags downward.

For obvious reasons, the airship will not zigzag between sea level (or other takeoff site altitude) and some higher altitude. Rather, it will first climb to a lower cruising altitude and then zigzag between that altitude and a higher cruising altitude until it is ready to land.

Now, suppose the *Aereon* first rose vertically to 1,000 ft. To take off, it had to drop a little ballast. Since it took off fully inflated, as it ascends, it vents gas, thus losing some of its buoyancy. It stops at 1,000 ft because that is when its reduced buoyancy equals its reduced weight.

At 1,000 ft, it begins the yo-yo with the same 200 lb ballast drop and the same 15° pitch angle assumed previously. Because it is at a higher altitude, the air density, and thus the aerodynamic forces (lift and drag), are reduced (the air density is 97.11% that at sea level). If these forces were exactly proportional to the square of the airspeed, a speed increase is expected by a factor (1.0148) equal to the reciprocal of the square root of the relative air density.

According to my aerodynamic model, which assumes a more complex dependency on airspeed, the airspeed increases from 19.0467 to 19.3185 mph (1.014-fold).[11]

8. Buoyancy-Driven Propulsion

TRAJECTORY: THE YO-YO

An important limitation on the length of a "zig" is that the higher the upper cruising altitude, the less payload the airship can carry. If it is fully inflated on takeoff, then as it first ascends to the upper cruising altitude, the lift gas will expand, and it will vent gas to avoid excessive strain on the envelope. The airship's gross lift, and hence its weight-carrying capability, will decline as it does so.

It was not unusual for hydrogen-lift airships to take off fully inflated. Helium is rather precious, and consequently, rather than vent helium on the ascent to cruising altitude, helium-lift airships took off only partially inflated with helium, the remainder of the airship's hull volume being occupied by an inflated air ballonet. That, too, of course, reduces the gross lift, but at least it doesn't waste helium. Ideally, the ballonet volume at takeoff, as a percentage of hull volume, would correspond to the air density at the intended upper cruising altitude as a percentage of the air density at the takeoff altitude.

The smaller the glide path angle, the longer it takes for the airship to ascend to its upper cruising altitude and thus the greater its range.

Each time the airship vents lift gas—as it will do when it is ready to begin the descent—it increases its *pressure height*, the altitude it can climb to without venting lift gas, thus reducing its gross lift. Hence, the pilot could, rather than flying a yo-yo between two fixed altitudes, increase the upper cruising altitude for each successive cycle.

SPEED CHANGES DURING THE YO-YO

Assuming that the airship has a ballonet and is not fully inflated with lift gas until it reaches the top of the yo-yo, the gross lift, and therefore the net buoyancy (gross lift weight), is positive and constant during the ascent (ignoring the time it takes to drop the ballast). Likewise, the net buoyancy will be negative and constant during the descent (ignoring the time it takes to vent the lift gas). If so, then the only effect is the changing air density on the aerodynamic forces.

A reduction in air density with altitude will reduce all aerodynamic forces, both lift and drag. However, because the change in air density with altitude is slow (air at 100 ft is 99.71% the density at sea level), and the vertical speed of the airship is also slow, the airship behavior can be modeled as a quasi-steady state, as if it reached an equilibrium of forces at each altitude considered (Purandare 2007, 56).

The net result is that the speed will increase slightly during the ascent and decrease slightly during the descent.

Part II: Unconventional Propulsion

Purandare's Proposed Airship

Purandare (2007) assumes that the lift gas volume of his hypothetical airship is constant, regardless of altitude. If this were the case, the superpressure (internal–external pressure) of the airship would increase as it ascended, and the envelope would need to be strong enough to resist the superpressure generated at the upper cruising altitude.

With a constant lift gas volume, the gross lift would decrease with altitude, and since the positive net lift (gross lift minus weight) provides the propulsive force, the speed would also decrease as the airship ascended (Purandare 2007, 58). Likewise, the descent is powered by negative net lift, and the increase in gross lift with decreasing altitude would cause the speed to also decrease as the airship descended (58). This would be on top of the effect on aerodynamic forces already discussed. But I must emphasize that a constant volume, variable superpressure airship is not a typical airship design.

Pitch Angle Effects

For the *Aereon* dropping 200 lb of ballast at sea level, the use of a 5° pitch reduces the airspeed to 13.56 mph and the horizontal component to 13.01 mph. So it appears that the use of a small pitch is not advantageous. Geery (2001) comments that the shallower the angle of pitch, "the trickier the balancing of forces involved."

A pitch of 15° was the highest one Andrews recommended in his patent, and the relative dimensions of his car and envelopes suggest that it was the maximum achievable by the *Aereon I*.

If the *Aereon* could assume a 30° pitch, the glide path angle would increase to 32.38°, and the airspeed would increase to 25.82 mph (horizontal component 21.81 mph).

The Andrews method of pitch control wouldn't scale up very well; a larger ship would either need movable ballast and a pulley system for hauling it forward or aft (as Andrews suggested), or if the ballast were water, it could be pumped between a forward tank and an aft tank. Or the trimming could be carried out in the envelope directly by inflation or deflation of a fore or aft internal airbag (ballonet).

Buoyancy-driven airships, of course, can be designed to permit a greater pitch and therefore a greater glide path angle (and speed). Future airships of this type, if any, are likely to be unmanned. But if they were manned, a closed control car would be advisable if higher pitch operations are contemplated. Airships can be designed to fly at high pitch safely; the FAA requires that an airship be able to recover from 30° nose down or nose up (FAA 1995, 2.15).

8. Buoyancy-Driven Propulsion

Range Limitations

The range and endurance of a buoyancy-propelled airship are limited by 1) the glide path angle it can achieve, 2) the maximum upper cruising altitude it can accept, 3) the amount of ballast it carries, and 4) the winds it expects to encounter.

The higher the glide path angle, the less horizontal distance it will cover before reaching its upper cruising altitude. The achievable glide path angle depends on the airship's lift-to-drag ratio (Graver et al. 2003).

The higher the upper cruising altitude, the less the airship's gross lift (at takeoff or after its first climb to that altitude). The gross lift must, at a minimum, be sufficient to support the sum of the empty weight, the weight of the crew, and the weight of the ballast. The smaller the gross lift, the smaller the amount of ballast that can be carried. The less ballast carried, the lower the airspeed achievable, or the fewer yo-yo cycles the airship can fly before exhausting its supply of ballast. Of course, a practical airship would also have sufficient gross lift to carry an economically sustainable or militarily useful payload.

If the winds are expected to be unfavorable, then the faster the wind, the greater the amount of ballast that must be dropped to make headway.

The basic problem with the *Aereon*'s buoyancy engine was that to go forward, Andrews had to repeatedly drop ballast and then vent gas. He had only a finite supply of each, so the endurance of the craft was limited. The Andrews (1864a) patent admits this.

If the *Aereon* were completely inflated with pure hydrogen at sea level, its gross lift would be 1,866 lb. However, if it were to yo-yo between 1,000 and 5,000 ft, then on its first ascent to 5,000 ft, its gross lift would be reduced to 1,583 lb.

If the *Aereon* had an empty weight of 933 lb (50% of its maximum gross lift at ISA sea level) and a pilot weighing 172 lb (Andrews's weight), it could carry only 761 lb of combined ballast and payload.

If its glide path angle was 35°, then in ascending 4,000 ft, it would travel 5,713 ft horizontally. It would then have to vent gas. Just to halt the ascent, it would have to vent enough to reduce the net buoyancy to zero. To descend, it would have to vent additional gas. If the descending glide path angle were −35°, it would then travel another 5,713 ft, completing one cycle. To halt the descent, it would need to drop enough ballast to increase the net buoyancy to zero.

The amount of ballast consumed per cycle would depend on the

Part II: Unconventional Propulsion

airspeed that was deemed required, but doubling the airspeed would require roughly quadrupling the ballast drop.

Andrews's proposed solution was to compress the lift gas rather than venting it to reduce buoyancy. If at neutral (zero net) buoyancy, some of the gas is compressed, then expanding that gas creates positive net buoyancy, and recompressing it creates negative net buoyancy. However, this is easier said than done (Cooper 2025). It is quite implausible that it could have been done with mid-19th-century materials and compressor technology.

The *Phoenix* has apparently accomplished this feat recently (Rae 2020). However, compression is not free; energy is needed to do the work of compression, and that energy would presumably come from burning fuel. While it is certainly better to consume gasoline than to vent helium, that still means that the airship's range is limited by its supply of fuel.

Temperature Control of Buoyancy

A different approach to varying the net lift between positive and negative was proposed by Cayley (1837, 10–11): The airship could receive lift equal to two-thirds of its weight from a hydrogen gas balloon and *equal* lift from a "fire" (hot-air) balloon. Thus, it would initially have a net positive lift equal to one-third of its weight, which would permit a rapid ascent, "and when at the highest point of elevation the heated air is let off by the valve, and the plain [plane] reversed, one-third of the whole gravitation would give it an equally effective oblique descent." (With a modern hot-air balloon, intermittent bursts of heat from a propane burner provide the heat, and leaving the burner off long enough that the total net lift becomes negative would trigger a descent.)

The use of separate hydrogen and hot-air balloons for lift was pioneered by Jean-François Pilâtre de Rozière (1754–1785), but his balloon caught fire and crashed, killing him and his companion. Cayley (1837) sought to avoid this sort of tragedy by positioning the hydrogen balloon "50 to 100 yards" above the fire balloon and the latter "immediately above the car." However, modern Rozière designs use helium instead of hydrogen. Because they need less fuel to remain aloft than would a hot-air balloon of equal size, they have achieved distance and endurance records, including the circumnavigation of the Earth in the *Breitling Orbiter 3* in 1999 (flight time almost 478 hours). The hot air component allows them to adjust for changes in the buoyancy of the helium as a result of diurnal changes in ambient temperature.

While the Rozière approach avoids the need to drop ballast and vent

8. Buoyancy-Driven Propulsion

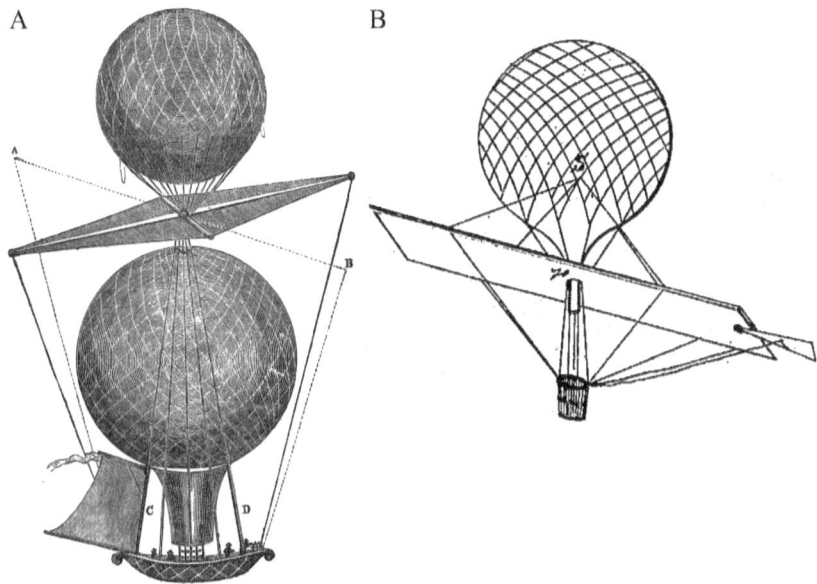

A. Cayley's Rozière-type buoyancy-propelled machine (Cayley 1837, plate 1). B. Andrews's (1864a, fig. 8) "common balloon with an oblong plane or sail attached below," ascending. Andrews noted that the spherical balloon was the worst possible shape for buoyancy propulsion, but its performance was somewhat improved by the obliquely oriented plane, as that increased the resistance to vertical movement.

lift gas, fuel is needed to heat the air, so there is still a finite limit to the endurance and range of the airship. But there is a very definite advantage to conserving precious helium.

Triple Hull versus Monohull

Frictional drag is roughly proportional to exposed surface area, and the total hull surface area of the triple-hulled *Aereon* (10,185 sq ft) is considerably greater than that of a monohull of the same volume (26,221 cu ft).

If the *Aereon* is replaced with a monohull (AereonTOgMono) having the same shape as one of the *Aereon*'s cylindroids but with length and diameter increased (115.38 × 18.75 ft) to keep the volume the same, the surface area is decreased to 7,062 square ft.

A ballast drop of 200 lb at sea level with a 15° pitch results in a glide path angle of 26.12°, an airspeed of 25.41 mph, and a horizontal airspeed of 22.81 mph. This is a substantial speed improvement! The angle of attack becomes more extreme (–11.12°) but not enough to pose a risk of stall (see appendix 1).

My standard aerodynamic model does not consider interference drag—that is, the drag created by the interaction between components of the airship, except to the extent it is encompassed by the rigging factor (see appendix 1).

Nonetheless, I have considered the possibility that the use of the triple hulls would reduce drag (negative interference) because of the way the air would tunnel between the hulls.

Burgess (1927, 290) wrote, "Innumerable inventors have proposed to reduce the resistance of both air and water craft by providing ducts or channels to permit some of the air or water to flow from the bow to the stern by a more direct passage through the ship ... tests have proved that such channels actually increase the resistance."

The more recent experience in the airplane industry is that interference is usually positive (bad). The closest aerial analogy to the Andrews multihull is the combination of a fuselage and an engine nacelle—they are parallel, streamlined bodies. According to Boeing, interference drag ranged from 14% at a spacing of half-nacelle diameter to about 1% at a spacing of about four diameters (Kroo 2016). There was no evidence of negative interference.

Another analogy would be to a pair of parallel, streamlined struts. The peak interference drag in a wind tunnel was at a spacing of about one-quarter the strut diameter, but it was never negative (Hoerner 1965, 8–3). The only example I found of negative interference was with two parallel cylinders; there was a dip when the spacing was 0.9 diameters (8–2). And the dip was tiny, perhaps 18%.

Geery (2001) flatly rejected Andrews's contention that the multihull design was beneficial, arguing that it didn't increase vertical resistance (over a monohull of the same planform area) but did contribute unnecessarily to drag when the vessel was moving toward the nose.

SHAPE

Reducing the surface area further is possible by using an ellipsoid (prolate spheroid) 123.78 ft long and 20.114 ft in diameter (same length-to-diameter ratio as the *Aereon*'s cylindroids) (Aereon EMono); the volume remains the same, but the surface area is reduced to 6,214 sq ft.

A ballast drop of 200 lb at sea level with a 15° pitch results in a glide path angle of 23.92°, an airspeed of 26.69 mph, and a horizontal airspeed

8. Buoyancy-Driven Propulsion

of 24.39 mph. This is a modest further improvement. The angle of attack is less extreme (−8.92°).

Airship Size

Of course, the *Aereon* is a rather small airship. In general, bigger is better. If the envelope volume is increased, keeping the shape the same, the gross lift increases. The structural mass also increases, but that should be proportional to the envelope surface area for a nonrigid airship unless it increases less rapidly. Thus, the useful lift is increased. With more useful lift, the airship can carry more ballast, and with more gross lift, it can vent more gas as needed. Thus, endurance (more cycles) or propulsive force per cycle is increased.

The larger airship will experience more drag, but the frictional drag will scale with the surface area, whereas the propulsive force available scales with the volume. So the achievable speed will be greater. Double the length and diameter, and the airship has eight times the volume and four times the surface area; octuple the ballast drop, and it should get about 41.4% more airspeed.

I doubled all dimensions of the Aereon EMono. The hull volume of the new hypothetical airship (Aereon EMonoVx8) increased to 209,765 cu ft and the surface area to 24,858 cu ft. With a 1,600 lb ballast drop at sea level and a 15° pitch, the glide path angle was 22.93°, the airspeed was 40.20 mph, and the horizontal airspeed was 37.02 mph. The angle of attack was −7.93°. The speed increase was actually 50.6%.

Winged *Aereon*

What about wings? The advantage of wings is that they provide a much better lift-to-drag ratio than a highly elongated body, which means a lower minimum glide path angle. That's good for endurance but not for speed. All the commonly used underwater gliders and the aerial designs of Krawetz and Celniker (1989), Purandare (2007), and Wu (2011) had wings. The developed aerodynamic lift is proportional to the speed squared.

If I equip my hypothetical Aereon EMono with trapezoidal wings of 90 ft span, 10 ft chord at root, and 5 ft at tip, 20% thick (NACA 0020 airfoil), aspect ratio 12, and have it drop 200 lb at sea level, 15° pitch, the glide path angle is reduced to 16.73°, the airspeed is only 24.15 mph, but the horizontal airspeed is 23.13 mph! Adding wings therefore made it possible to substantially reduce the glide path angle, so more of the airspeed was translatable into range. The angle of attack was merely −1.73°.

The two basic choices for wings are a monohull with outboard

Part II: Unconventional Propulsion

wings and a multihull with inboard (between the hulls) wings. A few twin-fuselage airplanes with a partially inboard wing have been built, notably the F-82 Twin Mustang.

If the disadvantages of a second hull are acceptable (higher surface-area-to-volume ratio, higher construction cost and more zero-lift drag), the inboard wing has both structural and aerodynamic advantages. Structurally, since the wing is suspended between two hulls, there is less bending moment for a given span, and the wing may be more lightly built than if it were cantilevered out from a single fuselage. Also, the fuselages are presumably half as long, so they have greater stiffness.

My aerodynamic model does not consider interactions, favorable or otherwise, between the airship (fuselage) body (bodies) and the wing(s). Wind tunnel experiments suggest that wing tip tanks on conventional airplanes increase effective aspect ratio slightly and thus reduce lift-induced drag if they are attached to increase the span (Hoerner 1965, 7–7). Some preliminary model testing has shown that the addition of airship-like bodies to a low aspect ratio wing (forming, in effect, a catamaran airship) eliminates spanwise flow over the wing, increasing its lifting efficiency by about 20% and reducing lift-induced drag (Spearman 2003; Orr 2000). (*Low* is relative; Orr's wing was aspect ratio (AR) 2, whereas the effective AR of the *Aereon* was 0.56, and with two hulls, it would have been lower.) On the other hand, data show that for catamaran airplanes, the twin hulls reduce lift relative to the lift from the wings alone (Maimun et al. 2010).

Lifting Body Shape

The one advantage that the touching triple hulls conferred is that they increased the effective aspect ratio from 0.19 (for a single cylindroid) to 0.56:1. (The aspect ratio for the AereonMonoEl was 0.05:1.) The lift-induced drag coefficient is inversely proportional to the aspect ratio, so if the aspect ratio could be increased without changing anything else, there would be an increase in the lift-to-drag ratio and therefore an increase in airspeed.

The conventional way of doing that is by providing wings with a high ratio of span to chord. The wing postulated in the previous section had an aspect ratio of 12:1.

However, building a wingless airship is also possible with a flattened (noncircular) cross section. If the volume were kept the same, the planform area and aspect ratio would be increased.

If, for example, a general ellipsoid were defined with the same total volume as the *Aereon* (26,221 cu ft) and the proportions 80 L:39 H:13 V, it

8. Buoyancy-Driven Propulsion

would be 85.824 ft long, 41.839 ft in horizontal diameter, and 13.946 ft in vertical diameter, for a surface area of 6,452 sq ft and a planform area of 2,820 sq ft. The aspect ratio would be 0.62 and the length-to-diameter ratio 2.05:1.

However, I have not attempted to calculate the aerodynamic performance of such an airship, as the shape factor used in my model was derived for bodies of circular cross section.

Emergency Use

It's worth noting that an airship doesn't need any special equipment in order to use buoyancy-driven propulsion. Thus, if a conventionally powered airship runs low on fuel, and there's no or little wind, it might crawl to its destination by this method—if the pilot knows about it and has enough ballast and lift gas. Even if a conventional military airship is not low on fuel, it might want to use buoyancy-driven propulsion to close silently on a target when the air is still or moving in the wrong direction so it can't free balloon. Of course, the ballast drop must be in due proportion to the gross lift of the vessel.

Conclusion

At the time of its invention—the American Civil War—Andrews's airship could have made a significant military contribution. Andrews's buoyancy engine gave the *Aereon* significant advantages for battlefield surveillance over an ordinary observation balloon, which would have been completely at the mercy of the wind. Especially if the air was still. And for short-range stealth missions, it had the advantage of complete silence.

However, it seems that nowadays, with helium being the customary lift gas, venting the lift gas for propulsive purposes is undesirable. And rather than carry ballast for propulsive purposes, greater speed and range would be achieved by devoting that weight to engines and fuel.

9

Wind Propulsion

History

The Jesuit priest Francesco Lana de Terzi (1631–1687), a mathematician and naturalist, proposed a buoyant flying ship with a single square sail. This was the first of many similar proposals.

Unfortunately, sails don't enable an ordinary unpowered airship to sail in any direction other than downwind; it acts just like a free balloon. Why? Well, to sail in any other direction, the airship must be moving relative to the medium in which it's traveling, the air. And if wind (air motion) is the only force acting on the airship, that's impossible. An unpowered submarine with the hull underwater and only underwater sails would have the analogous problem; it could only travel in the direction of the water current.

Sailing ships can travel in a direction other than downwind because they are traveling simultaneously in two media: the sails and superstructure in the air and the hull and keel in the water. The force of an oblique wind acts both to drive the ship forward and to push it sideways (leeway). However, the sidewise push is met by the resistance of the water (which is greater for sideways than for forward motion of the hull and keel), and the ship's motion results from the combined aerodynamic and hydrodynamic forces and thus is not directly downwind.

If somehow the sail could be separated from the hull but kept connected by some kind of strong tether, the resulting contraption would still feel both aerodynamic forces on the sails and hydrodynamic forces on the keel, so it could still travel in directions other than downwind.

The preacher George Pocock (1774–1843) used a train of kites to tow a yacht in the Bristol Channel during a three-week cruise (Pocock 1851, 47–49). The top (pilot) kite could be raised, lowered or braced to either side (10–11). A modern cargo ship, the M/V *Beluga Skysails*, uses a kite flying at 100–300 m as a supplemental propulsion system, and it can operate on "courses up to 50° to the wind" (Konrad 2009).

9. Wind Propulsion

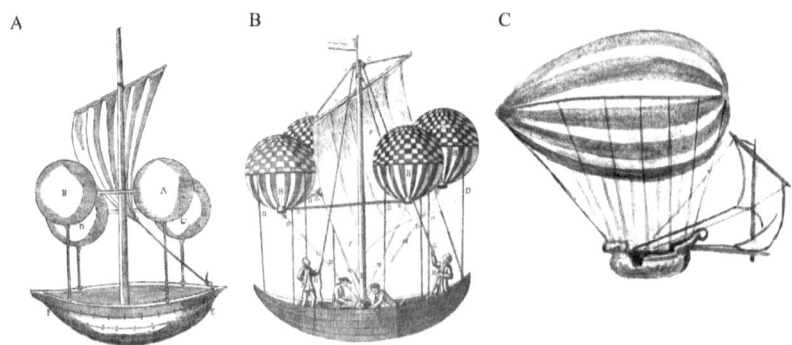

A. The aerial ship of de Terzi (Lana 1910, 14, with inset drawings removed). B. A 1784 reprint of de Terzi's *Prodromo* suggested replacing the vacuum-containing copper globes with hydrogen gas balloons (plate after 22, with inscriptions removed). C. A sailing balloon design by Guyot (1784), as depicted by A. Molynk in a postcard found in a 1909 scrapbook (SHI 2024). Note that this is a kite sail—there is no mast—and the balloon has been given a streamlined shape.

In these cases, the watercraft was manned, and the aerial one was not. In 1971, Hagedoorn argued that it was theoretically possible to reverse this using an inflated buoyant kite.[1] However, this proved difficult to achieve in practice (Schmidt 2001). Kites cannot operate under low-wind conditions, and they can be difficult to control.

Syroco, a 2019 startup, had the most recent proposal involving a kite. Its Moonshot project aims to reach a speed of 150 km/h. Instead of the pilot standing on a board tethered to a kite, as in kiteboarding, the pilot would be in an aerodynamically shaped aerial capsule interposed between the board and the kite. The kite provides the driving force but also provides an undesirable upward and leeward force. The board's purpose is to provide opposing downward and windward forces (Syroco 2024). In this respect, it differs from the normal purpose of a hydrofoil, which is to lift a watercraft out of the water. The plane of the board is perpendicular to a strut extending obliquely downward from the capsule (Syroco 2020).

A video (Syroco 2022a, 2022b) purports to show the flight of a remote-controlled, one-third-scale prototype in December 2021. However, there is only a brief, rather unsatisfactory, simultaneous view of all three components in motion.

In 1939, Burgess proposed that airships could use a tethered, floating hull with a submerged, near-vertical hydrovane to tack against the wind.

Part II: Unconventional Propulsion

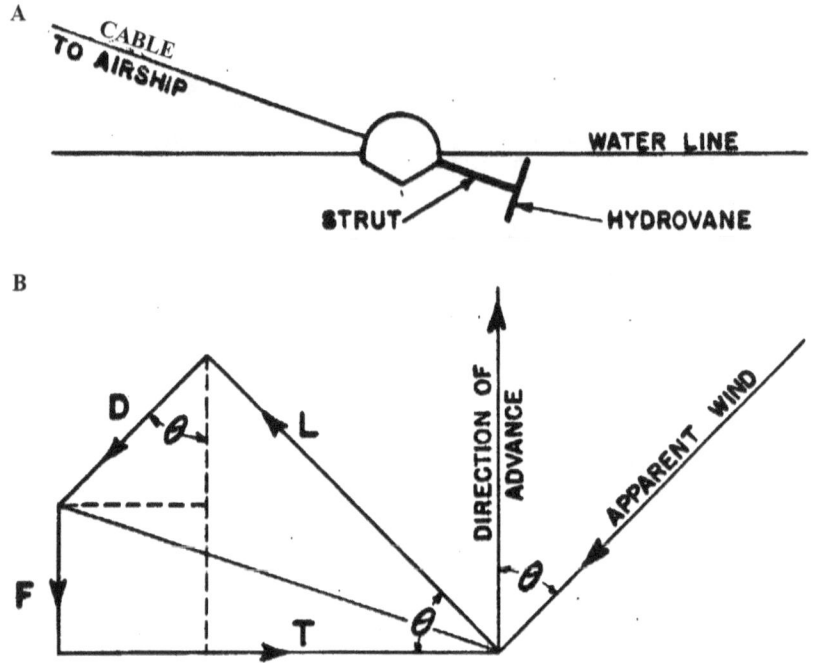

A. Schematic rear view of the boat with strut and hydrovane for a sailing airship (Burgess 1939, fig. 1). B. Schematic of horizontal forces acting on the sailing airship (fig. 2). The apparent wind acting on a yawed airship results in a drag force (D) parallel to the apparent wind and a horizontal lift force (L) perpendicular to it. The vector combination of D and L (the hypotenuse of the triangle they form) creates a tension on the tether that (at equilibrium) results in an equal and opposite hydrodynamic force on the boat. The latter force is the vector sum of the drag force (F) opposing the direction of advance and the lift (hydrodynamic side) force (T) perpendicular to the direction of advance. The angle ? between the direction of advance (course made good) and the apparent wind is determined by the values of the ratios L/D and T/F.

In 1993, Costes filed a French patent application that described an airship tethered to a *chien de mer*, a float with a curved wing and an anti-pitching tail. In 2000, he filed another application with a somewhat different *chien de mer* design.

Stephane Rousson received sponsorship from Theolia for a project to build a 900 cu m, two-seater, sailing airship and attempt to cross the Atlantic with it. He attached a *chien de mer* of a new design to the pedal-powered, one-seater *Mademoiselle Louise* (160 cu m) he had built

9. Wind Propulsion

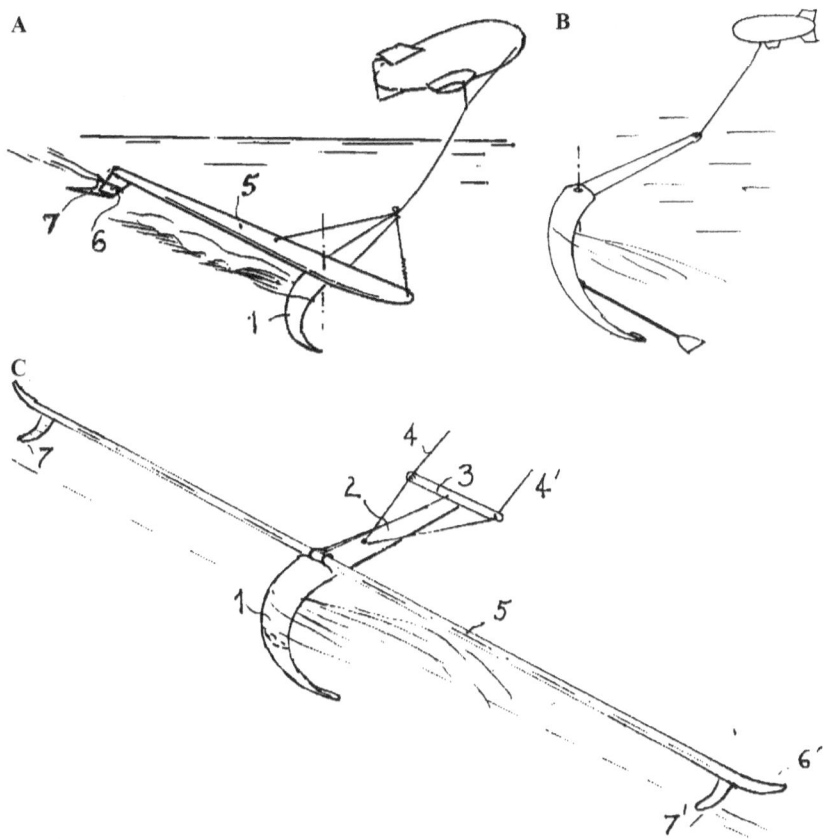

A. Cover figure from Costes (1993), showing *chien de mer* tethered to airship. B. Costes (2000) figure 2, showing improved *chien de mer*, likewise. C. Close-up of the improved *chien de mer* (fig. 5).

and piloted previously (July 2006) and used it as a subscale prototype. The sponsor renamed it *WINDREAM ONE*, and the concept was tested on June 14, 2007. However, the sponsor withdrew support for unrelated reasons (Rousson, private communication).

In 2010, he built a new airship, the *Aerosail* (19 m long, 4.72 m diameter, 189 cu m). It was completely reliant on the wind for propulsion. The *Aerosail* was intended to sail at a height not more than 50 m above the water surface. The pilot could adjust the pitch by shifting weight forward or backward, and the rudder could control the yaw. The hydrofoil (seaglider) was 5 kg and connected to the airframe by two Dyneema cables, 6 mm in diameter, with a breaking strength of 12 kN.[2] The incidence of the

Part II: Unconventional Propulsion

The *WINDREAM ONE* with the *chien de mer* deployed. Image courtesy of Stephane Belgrand Rousson. Note the diagonal running cable from the airship gondola to the *chien de mer*. The vertical line running from the nose of the airship is the front rope of the airship and is not involved in the sailing process.

hydrofoil could be adjusted by these cables. At a speed of 10 knots, the tension on the cables was 0.5 kN (Rousson 2014a). Rousson later chose to use 10 mm cables, as they provided a more comfortable fit for his hand (private communication).

Rousson intended to attempt a Mediterranean crossing with this airship, but this has not yet come to pass. Some news reports refer to the airship as the *Zeppy-3* (Ridden 2010).[3]

In 2018, Bousquet et al. reported the tethered flight of the *UNAV*, a "wind-powered UAV." The airframe component was a glider with a 3.4 m span and an 18 cm chord wing (aspect ratio 17); the wing profile was NACA 0009. The active part of the keel (NACA 0014) had a 2 cm chord and a 10 cm immersed span. The *UNAV* was "designed to fly at a height ... 40 cm above the water surface." The inclusion of a "vertical wing sail" was contemplated, but it is not shown in the photos. Bousquet et al. assert that with a weight of 3 kg, it "could stay airborne in winds as low as 2.8 m/s (5.5 knots), and travel several times faster than the wind speed."

9. Wind Propulsion

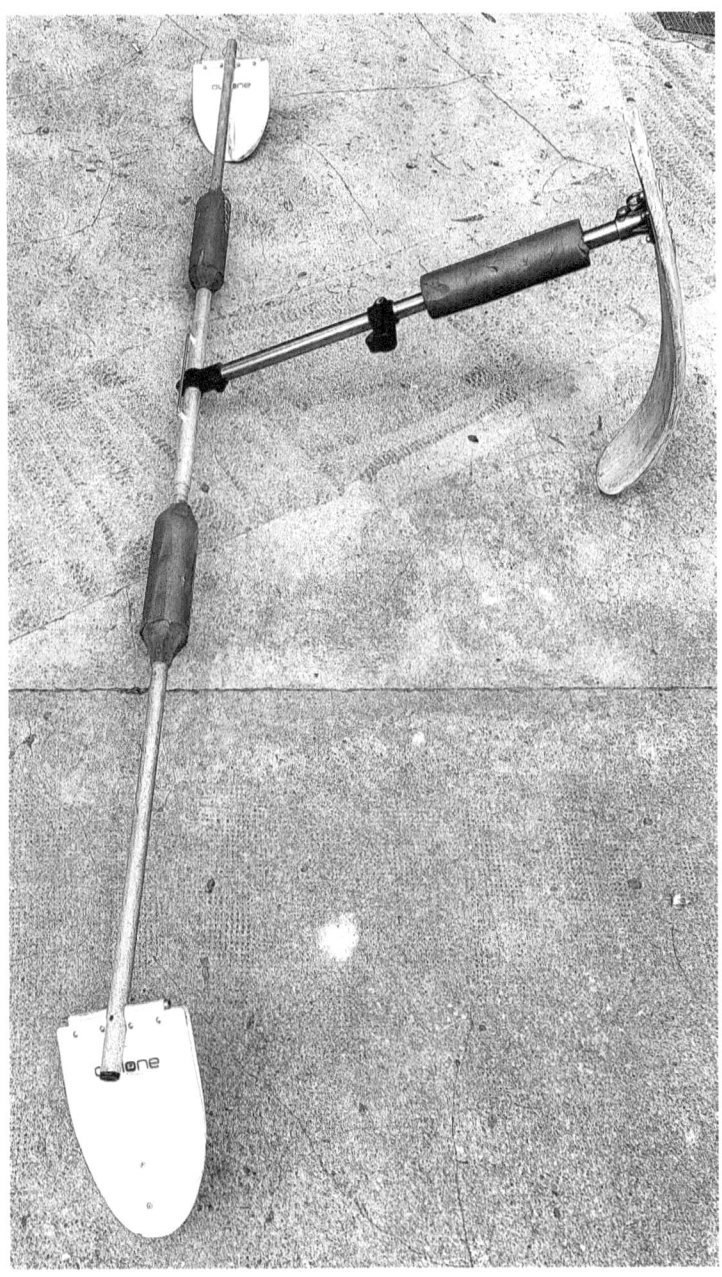

The *chien de mer* of the *Aerosail*, laid out on a floor. Photograph by and courtesy of Stephane Belgrand Rousson.

Part II: Unconventional Propulsion

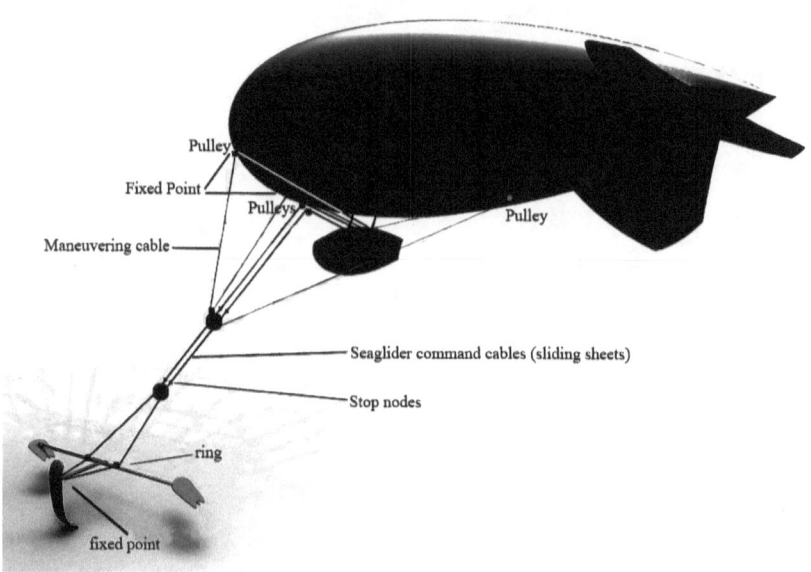

Schematic side view of the *Aerosail* and the seaglider (hydrofoil). Image courtesy of Stephane Belgrand Rousson, and modified by author per instructions of Rousson.

Following page: Schematic overhead view of the *Aerosail*'s airship hull and seaglider; author's modification of the image, provided courtesy of Stephane Belgrand Rousson. Here, the *Aerosail* is sailing upwind. Three triangles are depicted. The top triangle is the velocity vector triangle. This shows that the true wind velocity is the vector sum of the apparent wind velocity and the ship velocity. Hence, the apparent wind velocity is the true wind velocity minus the ship velocity. Next is the aerodynamic force triangle. The aerodynamic forces are created by the apparent wind. The aerodynamic drag force vector points in the same direction as the apparent wind. The airship is yawed (its nose points offwind), creating a nonzero angle of attack and generating an aerodynamic lift force that acts horizontally and perpendicularly to the apparent wind. The total aerodynamic force is the sum of the aerodynamic lift and drag forces. This total aerodynamic force creates a tension on the cable, which in turn imposes a force on the seaglider, causing it to move with the airship. At equilibrium, this force is balanced by a hydrodynamic force created by the movement of the seaglider through the water as a result of the pull of the cable. This may be resolved (hydrodynamic force triangle) into two components, one parallel to the ship velocity vector (motion), and opposing it (hydrodynamic drag) and the other perpendicular to the ship's motion (hydrodynamic lift).

9. Wind Propulsion

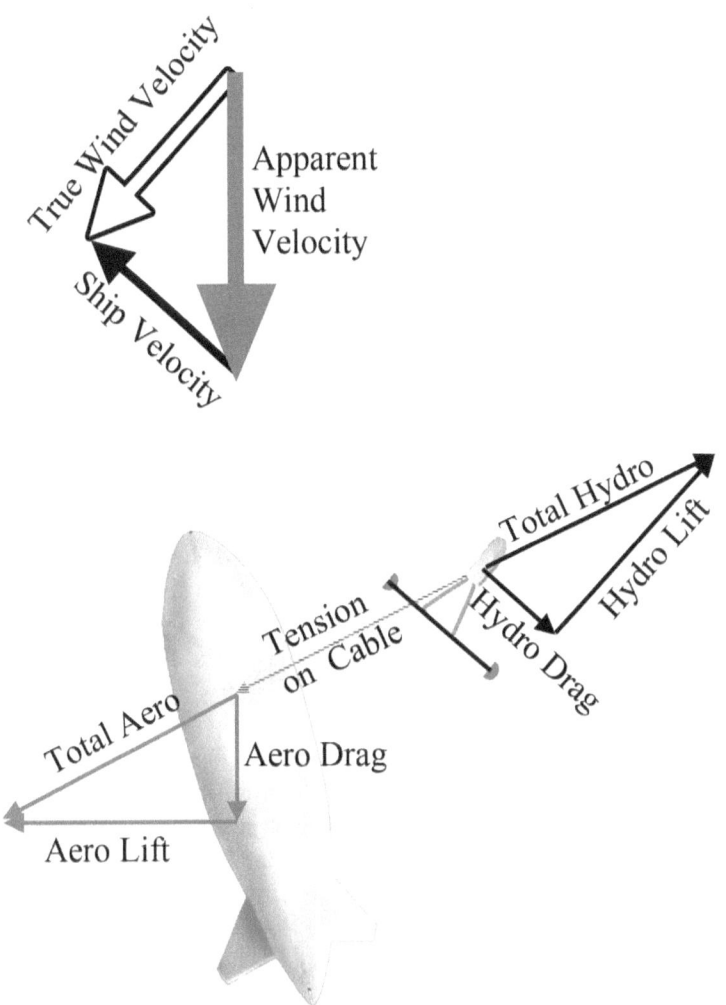

Analysis

Burgess (1939) conducted a serious analysis of the possible flight characteristics. He visualized a small, double-ended boat in the water, "heavy enough to avoid jumping out of the water" and with "enough reserve buoyancy to prevent being towed under." He proposed attaching an underwater hydrovane via a strut obliquely mounted on the windward side of

Part II: Unconventional Propulsion

the boat hull (like a proa); the strut would be in line with the cable to the airship and the hydrovane perpendicular to the strut. Since water is 900 times denser than air, he reasoned that the area of the hydrovane should be 1/900th of the volumetric area (volume$^{2/3}$) of the airship; that's just 6 sq ft for a 400,000 cu ft airship, and he figured that the corresponding boat would be 16 ft long, with an empty weight of 200 lb, and carrying up to 1,000 lb of water ballast if fighting strong winds.

To facilitate the control of the "angle of attack of the airship to the apparent wind," he proposed "attaching two cables from the boat to a single point on the airship at about a quarter of the length from the bow, and controlling the rudders in accordance with an angle of yaw indicator." The cables would be adjusted to make the forward cable shorter; as a result, the airship would float forward or abeam of the boat. This lead angle is important because it determines the direction that the cable pulls the boat, and thus the hydrodynamic forces on the boat and how they relate to the boat's heading.

In terms of aerodynamics, Burgess (1939) pointed out that the cable can be positioned so the wind force transmitted through the cable acts through the boat's center of lateral resistance, thus eliminating the heeling moment. Therefore, speed doesn't have to be limited in strong wind to keep from heeling over. However, the airship is a less efficient airfoil (lower lift-to-drag ratio) than a sail.

So how does this work? Imagine this sailing airship with the wind calm. If there's no other propulsion system, then both the airship and the boat are floating. If the wind picks up, the airship will accelerate. As it picks up speed, the apparent wind on it decreases, decreasing the wind force. If the airship weren't tethered to the boat, it would eventually reach wind speed, and there would be no horizontal force on the airship; it would "free balloon."

However, at some point, the airship travels far enough downwind that the cable is taut. At this point, a component of the wind force on the airship is parallel to and pulling on the cable. This exerts a force on the boat. As it starts to move, it encounters a resistive force from the water it is trying to push aside.

Now, the airship has its rudder adjusted so that instead of pointing directly into or away from the apparent wind, it is yawed (turned left or right) at a positive angle of attack—if yaw has the same effect as pitch on the lift-to-drag ratio, then an angle of 9°–15° is ideal. This angle of attack of the airship to the apparent wind determines its lift-to-drag ratio. The airship feels a drag force downwind and a lift force perpendicular to the wind

9. Wind Propulsion

flow. Since the ship is yawed not pitched, this lift force is horizontal and oblique in the desired direction of motion. Thus, the aerodynamic force produces not only some forward motion along the airship heading but also some leeway (actual course off heading).

The resistive hydrodynamic force on the boat has a component perpendicular to the advance and a component opposing it. "Because of leeway, these directions will not be quite perpendicular and parallel to the longitudinal axis of the boat" (Burgess 1939).

Burgess (1939) estimated that the lift-to-drag ratio for the airship and cables would be 2:1 (based on data for the airship USS *Akron* for pitch angles of 0°–20° and rudder angles of –20° to +20°) and that for the boat and hydrovane would be 3:1 (a wild guess). With these assumptions, the airship could sail (nominally, see below) within 45° of the apparent wind. With the true wind on its beam, the airship can sail at the speed of the wind. Its best speed overall is 141% of true wind speed, which is achieved with the true wind 135° off the bow.

Its best speed to windward is with the true wind 67.5° off the bow, and the ship's speed is then 21% of the true wind speed.[4] But that still means that the airship can tack upwind without the use of engine power!

So how does the airship control the boat? Burgess (1939) envisioned that this would be through cable adjustment. If the airship is turned into the wind, it would drop behind the boat, which would slacken the stern line and pull the boat bow to leeward, making the boat fall away from the wind. And if the airship falls away from the wind, the boat comes into it.

Tacking is a little tricky since the hydrovane is on the windward side of the boat. The "lengths of the two towing cables must be interchanged" (Burgess 1939), and the prow of the boat becomes its stern (hence the double-ended design).

What happens if the ship runs into a gale? If a sailing ship has a sail or spar carried away by the wind, it mounts up a spare. But the airship isn't likely to have a spare hydrovane boat if that gets torn away. That implies the cables have to be sized for heavy weather, and hoisting the boat up to the airship must be an option if a storm is coming.

Another reason for making it possible to hoist up the boat is that, presumably, the wind propulsion would be an auxiliary propulsion system used only to economize on fuel for a long passage. Hence, avoid suffering the drag penalty of the boat and cable when they aren't needed. The logical questions would be, what would it add to the weight and cost of the airship, and how long would it take to recover the cost through fuel savings? The answers, in turn, depend on many factors, including the price of

Part II: Unconventional Propulsion

airship fuel, the wind-driven performance of the sailing airship, and the expected wind patterns over the route the airship is expected to sail.

The tension on the cable would depend on the apparent wind force felt by the airship and the cables, the weight of the cables, and the geometry (the position of the airship relative to the boat).

Burgess (1939) estimated, without explanation, that "in a 30 knot [15.4 m/s apparent] wind, the cable tension would be from 3500 to 4000 lbs [15.6–17.8 kN]." I assume that was the estimate for each cable, not the total for both. In his day, the strongest cable was wire rope, but it is very heavy for its length. Nylon has a higher strength-to-weight ratio but is stretchy. And Manila is light but weak. Assuming a safety factor of five, a 24 mm diameter nylon (355 g/m), 1-⅝ in. of Manila (1,060 g/m), or ½ in. of wire rope (630 g/m) would be needed.

There are better materials available nowadays. Rope strength is roughly proportional to the square of the diameter. With a typical safety factor of five, the safe working load would be one-fifth the breaking load stated in table 9–1.

Table 9-1: Rope Minimum Breaking Load and Linear Density vs. Rope Diameter

Rope	Minimum Breaking Load (kN)		Linear Density (g/m)	
	6 mm	12 mm	6 mm	12 mm
12-strand Dyneema D12 with PU coating	26.28	104.6	19.30	58.20
12-strand Vectran V12 with PU coating	30.22	107.82	27.80	86.40
3-strand aramid core with high-tenacity polyester cover	11.87	54.25	31	116
3-strand polyester core with 16-plait polyester cover	8.93	35.90	30	100
3-strand nylon	7.36	29.43	23	89
3-strand staple-spun polypropylene	5.89	21.68	17	65
12-strand polyester core with 24-plait polyester cover	11.92	37.96	28	116
	¼"	½"	¼"	½"
6 strand × 19 wire plow steel wire rope	24.40	95.20	160	630
3-strand Manila	2.40	10.60	27	104
Sources: wire rope and Manila, ETB 2009; others, Marlow Ropes 2023.				

9. Wind Propulsion

There are standard methods for calculating the tension on a single tether for a balloon tethered to a fixed point on the ground.[5] For such a balloon, the apparent wind equals the true wind. For an airship (engines off) or a balloon tethered to an underwater keel, the apparent wind will be less than the true wind because the airship-keel system moves somewhat with the latter.

There have been (at least) two recent analyses of the physics of kiteboarding, by Armant (1990) and van der Vlugt (2009). While a kite is likely to have a higher lift-to-drag ratio than an airship, these analyses are still helpful. I will focus on the latter reference, as Armant (1990) is in French.

Van der Vlugt (2009) analyzes the two-dimensional (horizontal) force balance on the kite and board and deduces that the angle β between the course achieved and the apparent wind is the sum of the aerodynamic and hydrodynamic glide angles. These, in turn, are the arc tangents of the respective drag-to-lift ratios. The ratio of the ship speed to the true wind speed is then $\sin(\gamma - \beta)/\sin(\beta)$, where γ is the angle between the course and the true wind.

It follows that the ship cannot make headway on a course that is β degrees or less off the true wind. As a practical matter, the course will need to significantly exceed β.

If the aerodynamic and hydrodynamic lift-to-drag ratios are constant, so β is constant, then the highest speed is achieved when the angle between true and apparent wind is 90° and the course is 90 + β degrees from the true wind. And the ratio of the ship speed to the true wind speed then equals $1/\sin(\beta)$.

Burgess (1939) assumed an airship lift-to-drag ratio of two and a hydrovane lift-to-drag ratio of three, for which β is 45°. At 60° relative to the true wind, the ship speed would be (by Vlugt's formulae) 36.6% of the true wind.

It has been asserted that for an airship tethered to a *chien de mer*, it is reasonable to assume a lift-to-drag ratio (in French, "finesse") of 4 for the airship (Rousson 2014b)[6] and 9 (Rousson 2014b) or 10 (Costes 2000) for the *chien de mer*. Assuming a constant 4 and 10, respectively, then β would be 19.75° and the fastest speed would be 2.96 times the true wind speed. The ship could sail at 25° off the true wind at a speed of 27% of the true wind speed.

Unfortunately, these calculations do not provide a complete picture of the physics of a tethered airship or kite. It is likely that both the aerodynamic and the hydrodynamic lift-to-drag ratios will vary with the course sailed and/or the speed. But they do suggest that a sailing airship, tethered

Part II: Unconventional Propulsion

to a *chien de mer* or equivalent, can sail upwind at least as well as a premodern sailing ship and perhaps as well as a modern racing yacht.

Wind-Differential Propulsion

The traditional method of trajectory control in free ballooning is to ascend to the altitude at which the wind is blowing in the direction the balloon pilot wishes to travel. Winds change in both speed and direction with altitude because of two factors: friction from the surface slows the movement of air, with the effect diminishing as the balloon ascends, and the rotation of the Earth deflects the winds, with the deflection proportional to the wind speed.

Albuquerque is a popular locale for ballooning because of the "Albuquerque box": "At low elevations the winds tend to be southerly (from the south), but at higher elevations they tend to be northerly" (Weatherbug 2020). By judicious exploitation of this wind pattern, the balloonist can return the balloon close to its starting point.

The normal balloon only experiences the wind at essentially a single altitude; a large balloon might have a vertical extent of perhaps 100 ft, and the change of speed and direction over that distance is minor.

Suppose, however, it was possible to give the craft a much larger vertical extent so that it was simultaneously feeling the wind at two quite different altitudes. Since winds change in strength and direction as the craft ascends into the atmosphere, it is possible to take advantage of the difference in wind direction at two different heights in order to sail in an intermediate direction. The first engineering problem is giving the craft a sufficient vertical extension so its ends feel a significant wind difference, and the second is controlling the extension.

The goal for some designs has not been dirigibility but station keeping, the ability to hover at a fixed point without being driven off by the wind. But that implies the capacity to sail upwind.

Balloon-Drag or Lift Device

The craft described in this section are unmanned balloons, but conceivably, they could be scaled up to envelope sizes that would allow them to carry a pilot.

In 1969, Bourke proposed that a drag device (e.g., a parachute) could be deployed well below a balloon to facilitate station keeping. The wind at the parachute altitude exercises a force on the parachute that is transmitted through a tether to the balloon. As a result, the balloon can be drawn in a direction other than the one the wind is blowing at the balloon altitude.

If the balloon is equipped with a winch, then the altitude of the drag device can be adjusted to take advantage of various wind conditions and speeds. The range of directions that the balloon can move in is limited by the difference in wind direction at the balloon and drag device altitudes. That difference will depend on the length of the tether, and it can be winched in and out to find the best drag condition. If the variation of wind with altitude is not known before the balloon is launched, then some experimentation may be needed to find the optimum drag device altitude.

Given that the drag device is at a lower altitude than the balloon, it is likely to experience a smaller wind force and hence may not be able to completely negate the perturbing effect of the stronger wind higher up. The result may be that the drag device merely slows down the departure from the desired station.

Aaron et al. (2000) and Aaron (2002) increase the potential arc of movement somewhat. In essence, a lift device (a vertical wing or sail) hangs by a tether far below the balloon. By changing the angle of attack of the wing versus the wind at the lower altitude, the magnitude and direction of the lift the wing generates can be changed. The combination of lift and drag on the wing exerts a force on the balloon through tension in the tether, allowing it to move in a direction other than the one the upper altitude wind is blowing toward.

The tether contemplated by Aaron et al. (2000) and Aaron (2002) is extremely long—15 km. The air at the wing altitude is perhaps tenfold denser than at the balloon altitude; "this allows the wing area to be significantly smaller than the balloon cross-sectional area." In 1999, a one-fourth scale model of the Stratosail® trajectory control system was tested; the model was suspended 60 m below a blimp floating 70 m above the ground (the latter 1,000 m above sea level).

Obviously, the tether must be very strong, and because of its length, it is likely to experience considerable drag force.

Dual Airship

Heppe (2014) proposed tethering two airships together, one above the other, in opposing wind currents to facilitate station keeping. Winds aloft data showed winds tending to be in opposite directions in the upper

Part II: Unconventional Propulsion

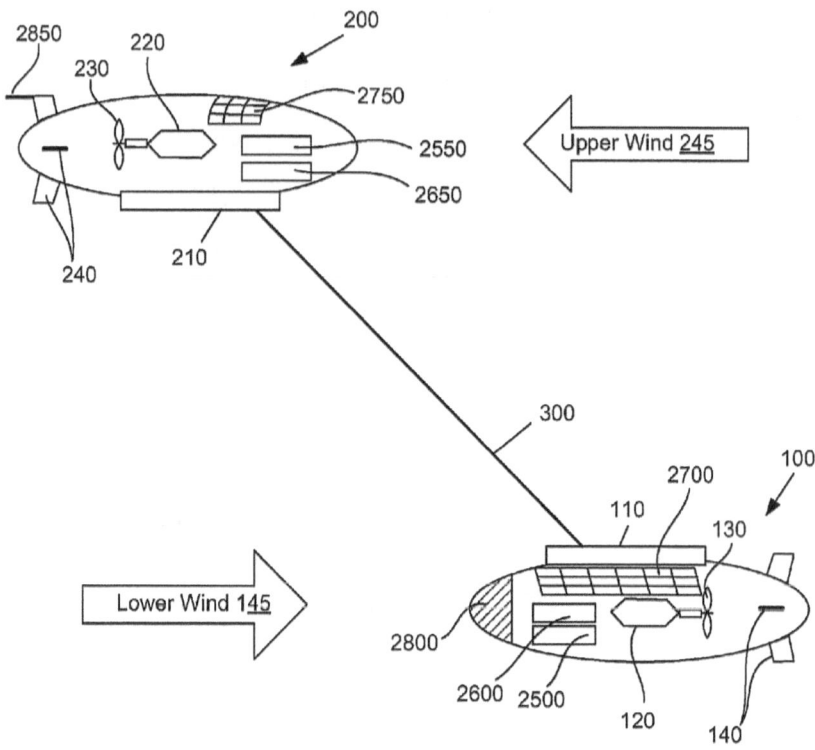

Figure 1 from Heppe (2014).

stratosphere (near 40 km altitude) relative to the lower stratosphere (near 20 km) and, to a lesser degree, near 20 km versus 10–15 km. The upper airship must carry the weight of the tether as well as its own weight. Proposed tether materials included Kevlar (Spectra 2000) and quartz fibers.

Dual Airplanes, Gliders or Kites

Miller (1967, 115) asserts that Alois Wolfmüller experimented with two kites at different altitudes in 1909 and that he replicated this experiment, but neither statement could be confirmed (Lippincott 2022).

Engblom (2015) patented a Dual-Aircraft Atmospheric Platform. The DAAP is a pair of unmanned, autonomous winged airplane connected by an adjustable tether with a maximum length of 0.5–8 km (2 km preferred). The preferred high specific strength tether materials include "para-aramid synthetic fiber, carbon fiber, [and] a material formed with nano-tubes." At

9. Wind Propulsion

least one of these "glider-like" airplanes "includes a docking mechanism configured to attach and release said aircraft from a deployment vehicle," as well as "internal propulsion" and "a wind turbine and generator." There may be "batteries for energy storage."

The intent is for the DAAP to take advantage of a "natural wind differential" to maintain its station. The specification (Engblom 2015) notes that wind gradients are strongest in the tropopause (11–17 km), but "to avoid commercial air traffic … a minimum cruise altitude of 18 kilometers (60,000 feet) is also advantageous." Deployment could be by means of a "balloon, helicopter, or fixed wing aircraft." The purpose of the "onboard propulsion" appears to be to "change tether length."

Engblom (2015) figure 1 depicts an airplane with a single pair of rectangular main wings and a single pair of small canards. Engblom's student, McKee (2012), instead proposed a tandem wing (40) with a high aspect ratio.

Akimov and Polivanov (2019) have derived the requirements for "steady horizontal flight." The ratio of the wind shear (speed difference) to the intended horizontal flight speed must attain a minimum value, and that value depends on the lift-to-drag ratio of the two identical gliders and the ratio of the lift on the lower glider to the lift on the upper one. The higher the lift-to-drag ratio, the lower the required wind shear.

The methods of calculating the required tether strength for an airship underwater keel system apply mutatis mutandis to a wind-differential system. The lower airship simply serves in place of the underwater keel. The required tether strength and weight will be much higher since the tether length is much longer.

An obvious question with all wind-differential systems is how the pilot (human or computer) knows which altitudes are best. While meteorological data could be radioed from the ground, Lippincott (2022) suggests that the craft could carry the Ball Aerospace optical autocovariance wind lidar (OAWL). "OAWL uses green (532 nm) and/or UV (355 nm) lasers to track the movement of water vapor and particles to infer wind speed."

10

Oars, Paddle Wheels and Cycloidal Propellers

History—Rowing with Oars

We begin with a highly dubious form of aerial propulsion: oars. Oars and paddles have been used for centuries to propel boats across the water. The oar acts as a lever, with an oarlock or thole as the fulcrum, potentially providing a mechanical advantage that the paddle lacks. Rowers face backward; paddlers, forward. In either case, after the power stroke, the blade is lifted from the water, lest it push the boat backward during the recovery.

Even before the first attempt at the use of oars to convert a balloon into a dirigible, Joseph-Michel Montgolfier warned his brother Etienne, "Calculate well before you employ oars. Oars must either be great or small; if great, they will be heavy; if small, it will be necessary to move them with great rapidity" (Branson 2011).

The physics of rowing is complex, but the simplest way to look at rowing is as a process of momentum transfer; momentum transfers from the oar to the water, and then conservation of momentum applies: "You move water one way with your oar, the boat moves the other way" (Dudhia 2007; Pulman 2004). The same is true of paddling.

Momentum is mass times velocity. At sea level, the density of air is about 1/800th that of water, and that suggests that to move an aerial vehicle with the mass of a rowboat at a typical rowboat speed, it would either need to move a volume of air 800 times the volume of water that was moved, or it would need to move the same volume 800 times as fast (cp. Rose 2021, 28).

In addition, rowing in air has no analog to releasing the blade from the water; at best, one may feather the flat blade of the oar (turn it 90°) so that the recovery stroke experiences as little air resistance as possible. Nonetheless, several late 18th-century writers thought that rowing a balloon through the air was feasible.

10. Oars, Paddle Wheels and Cycloidal Propellers

In 1784, Jean Baptiste Meusnier (1754–1793) presented a paper to the Academy of Lyon arguing that an oar pulling against air would be three times as effective as the same oar in water, "since the ratio of the weight of the vessel to that of the oars was much less in aircraft [*sic*, balloons]" (Gillispie 2014, 89).

Etienne Montgolfier also analyzed the ability of a pair of oars to move a balloon. By his analysis, the velocity of the balloon was proportional to the square root of the "quantity of action" (the product of the force exerted by the rowers on each stroke and the stroke rate) and to the "sixth root of the combined surface of the blades" (Gillispie 2014, 89–90). Further, he thought that "a rower moving the handle of an oar at two-and-a-half feet per second makes an effort equivalent to lifting twenty pounds." He further assumed a stroke 3 ft long (allowing 25 strokes a minute), a blade of 100 sq ft, and "a shaft twenty-two feet long pivoted four feet from the handle," and predicted that a pair of these oars would drive a balloon 70 ft in diameter at 2,000 yd an hour (1.14 mph). And a balloon of 26 ft in diameter, propelled by two oars, each with 49 sq ft in blade surface, could achieve, he calculated, 2.6 mph (91).

Now, let's set dubious theoretical predictions aside. The brothers Nicolas-Louis and Anne-Jean Robert had a "melon-shaped" silk balloon, "fifty-two feet long by thirty-two feet in diameter," suspending a wooden car. The Roberts were students of the physicist Jacques Charles, and they followed his advice to inflate the balloon with hydrogen rather than hot air. On July 15, 1784, they made their ascent, together with the Duc de Chartres, from St. Cloud (Darnton 2023). Their means of propulsion were "three pairs of oars with blades made like a racquet-frame, covered with silk" (Walters 1917, 14). With this rather unprepossessing propulsion apparatus, they allegedly were able to achieve "a curve of one kilometer radius, thus deviating 22° from the feeble wind then prevailing" (Walters, 1917, 14; Zahm 1911, 81–83).[1] A circle of that radius would have a perimeter of 3.1416 km, and a 22° circular arc thereon would have an arc length of 0.19 km (0.12 mi).

Also in 1784, Jean-Pierre Blanchard (1753–1809) and Vincenzo Lunardi (1754–1806) used oars with no evidence that they altered their course from that of the free balloon.

Wright (1803) declared that "according to the present mode of rowing balloons from the car," the deviation they provided was "scarcely half a point from the wind"—that is, not more than 5.6°. "For oars to produce their full effect they should be not less than twenty feet long, and three in width at their extremities…. The oars recommended (being made of only varnished linen stretched over netting fixed to arms of pliable wood)

Part II: Unconventional Propulsion

might be easily worked, if a projecting staff of wood were attached to each lateral par [sic], so as to form at its extremity a fulcrum whereon to rest the oar at eight or ten feet distance from the rower" (26).

In 1852, Auguste Lanteigne proposed the use of "a continuous belt of sails to achieve propulsion." Each sail may be equated with an oar. From Lanteigne's figure 5 (LOC 2024b), it appears that the sails moved aftward on four longitudinal cables engaging their corners. This would be the power stroke. When they reached the aft end of the system, they were drawn around two cylinders and returned forward, edge on. This is the equivalent of feathering an oar on its return stroke. When they reached the forward end of the system, they were raised to repeat the power stroke. A much simpler way of accomplishing the same result is with a feathered paddle wheel, as discussed in the next chapter. There is no evidence that Lanteigne's belt of sails was ever built.

Even at the end of the 19th century, there were those who thought rowing an airship was a viable proposition. In 1897, Graybill disclosed an airship with a pair of wings. The wings were mounted on "lever arms" driven by a gasoline engine. According to his claim 2, "the wings are caused to move similar to an oar in rowing." Myers's 1897 patent shows an airship equipped

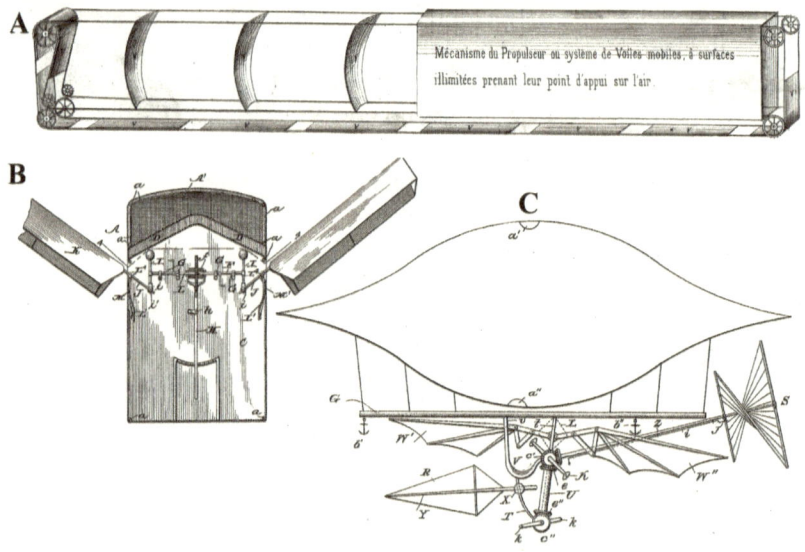

A. Lanteigne's 1852 "belt of sails" mechanism (LOC 2024b, fig. 5). B. Patent illustration of Graybill airship (1897, fig. 3). Patent illustration of Myers airship (1897b, fig. 1).

10. Oars, Paddle Wheels and Cycloidal Propellers

with bat-like "wings"; the "wing-shaft may be rotated like a crank or operated like a feathering-oar or simply move backward and forward or up and down." Reed's 1897 patent described a "hand and foot" powered airship equipped with side paddle wheels and a puller propeller as well as "lateral paddles." The latter were feathered by a double crank mechanism.

In 1905, Alva Reynolds flew in the *Man-Angel*, a 2,500 cu ft airship equipped with a pair of oars with which he claimed to achieve a speed of 4–6 mph (Wade 2022, 151; Royal 1905; Reynolds 1906).

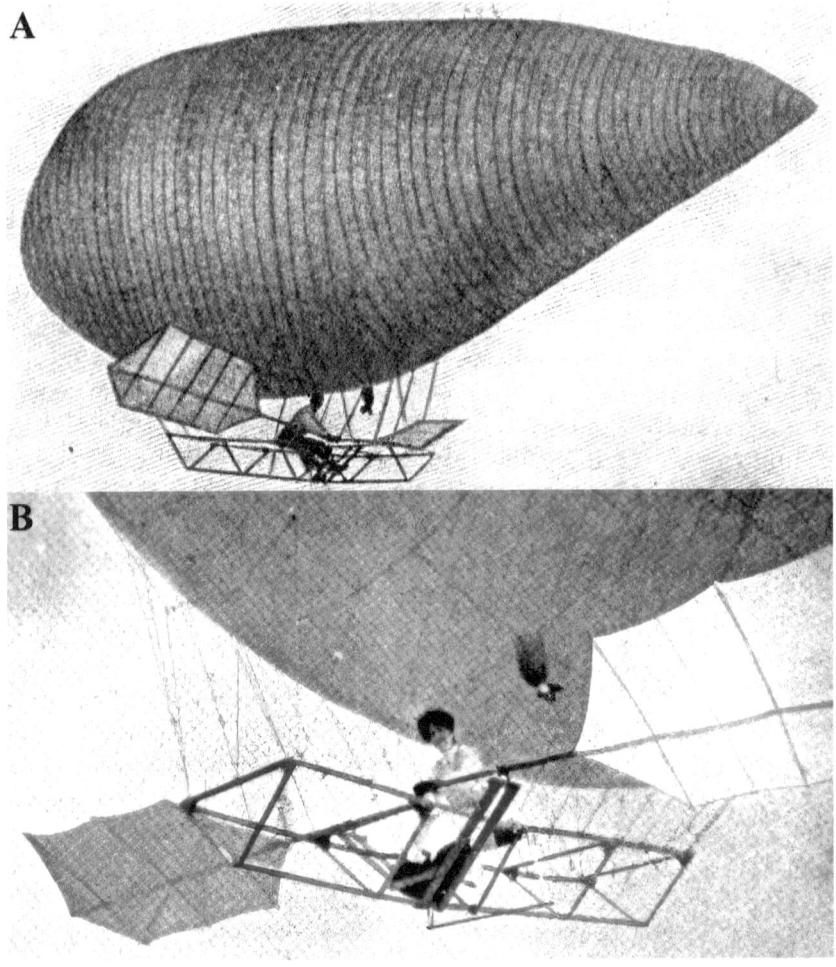

A. Reynolds airship (Reynolds 1906). *B*. Close-up of Alva Reynolds and her oar (*Royal* 1905).

Part II: Unconventional Propulsion

A human-powered airship that would cruise on rowing power alone but be equipped for hand cranking for takeoff, landing, and navigation was proposed in 2014 by a student group at the University of Technology of Belfort-Montbéliard (UTBM; Dreno 2014).

Analysis—Rowing

In chapter 1, we reviewed the literature on human power output, but our emphasis was on the power generated by pedaling. Here, we look briefly at rowing per se. As for pedaling, different sources report different values.

According to Hagerman and Hagerman (2020), "Rowers performing 2000 m competitive efforts generated average power outputs of between 250 and 500 watts depending on whether they were heavyweights or lightweights, male or female." To put this in perspective, "It takes five to eight minutes to row 2000 m." Wilson (2004, 44) cites a 1998 report of about 550 W over six minutes.

Rowing Level (2024a) provides standards[2] for rowing times and the equivalent power by age and ability. For males, the best-performing age group was 30–34, with power ranging from 194 (beginner) to 589 (world record contender). For females, it was age 25–29, running from 100 to 405.

Veteran rowers in a 6,000 m indoor rowing test produced an average of 325 W in a little over 20 minutes (Almeidia-Neto et al. 2023). This seems low; Wilson (2004, 44) presents a data point from 1998 of about 450 W for a 20-minute effort.

However, a relay of rowers, each rowing for 3–30 minutes, generated 12.4 kWh of electrical energy in 24 hours, for an average of 517 W (Thome 2012).

Rowing Level (2024b) provides standards for marathon (42.195 km) rowing. The best finish time (2:22:09) was for a man in the 25–29 age group and corresponded to a power of 339 W. In the same age group, the male power output ranged from 113 W (beginner) up; for females, 72 to 208 W. However, the best female performance (210 W; 02:46:53) was in the 30–35 age group.

Rodgers suggested that on an ancient war galley, "an oarsman could provide 140 watts of output for ten hours, 170 watts for four hours and 200 watts for one hour" (Williams 2014, 95).[3] However, that was extremely speculative.

In modern rowing, work is done not just by the arms but also by the legs and back; a total of 70% of human muscle mass is utilized (Crockford 2017). That might not, however, be the case with the rowing setups used by the airship pilots discussed in the preceding section.

History—Paddle Wheels

The traditional paddle wheel found on early 19th-century steamships had radial blades revolving about a lateral axis. They can be thought of as a series of oars used sequentially for propulsion.

Some proposed using a paddle wheel to propel an airship or even an airplane. Between 1899 and 1902, Count Zeppelin "had his co-worker Heinrich Rüb design a 'paddlewheel aircraft,' which, however, did not go into operation" (Hirschel et al. 2012, 27). Unfortunately, I have not been able to uncover any details of the design.

On steamships, the rotation of the wheel lifted the paddle out of the water, so it didn't push the wrong way. This is analogous to lifting an oar out of the water to commence the recovery stroke.

However, for an airship or airplane, the blade is in the air all the time. An obvious problem with using paddle wheels for aerial propulsion is that only the blades pushing the air backward would propel the airplane forward; those pushing the air forward would have the reverse effect.

An 1859 French patent drawing shows fore-and-aft pairs of paddle wheels flanking an airplane fuselage. It appears that the French inventor F. Ducroz addressed the pushback issue by placing a spiral cowl, somewhat like that on a centrifugal pump, over the wheels so that all the air would be pushed backward (LOC 2024a). An 1880 American airship patent (Sullivan) merely covers the top half of the paddle wheels with a hood, not very different from the paddle boxes used on paddle steamers to prevent splashing. See also Emsley (1883), Gabrielli (1893), Reed (1897), and Crowley (1919).

In 1828, the rocket pioneer William Congreve proposed a human-powered "aerial carriage." This was to be equipped with "four ... paddle-wheels, furnished each with eight vanes of silk." He argued that for these to produce a net thrust, they should be constructed so that "their planes may be always parallel to each other as they revolve." Moreover, he proposed that "the plane of their common parallelism [be] adjustable at pleasure." With the paddle wheel hand cranked on a horizontal axis, "the angle of flight may be regulated from the perpendicular direction to the horizontal, or to any angle above or below" (Liberatore 1954, 8).

Part II: Unconventional Propulsion

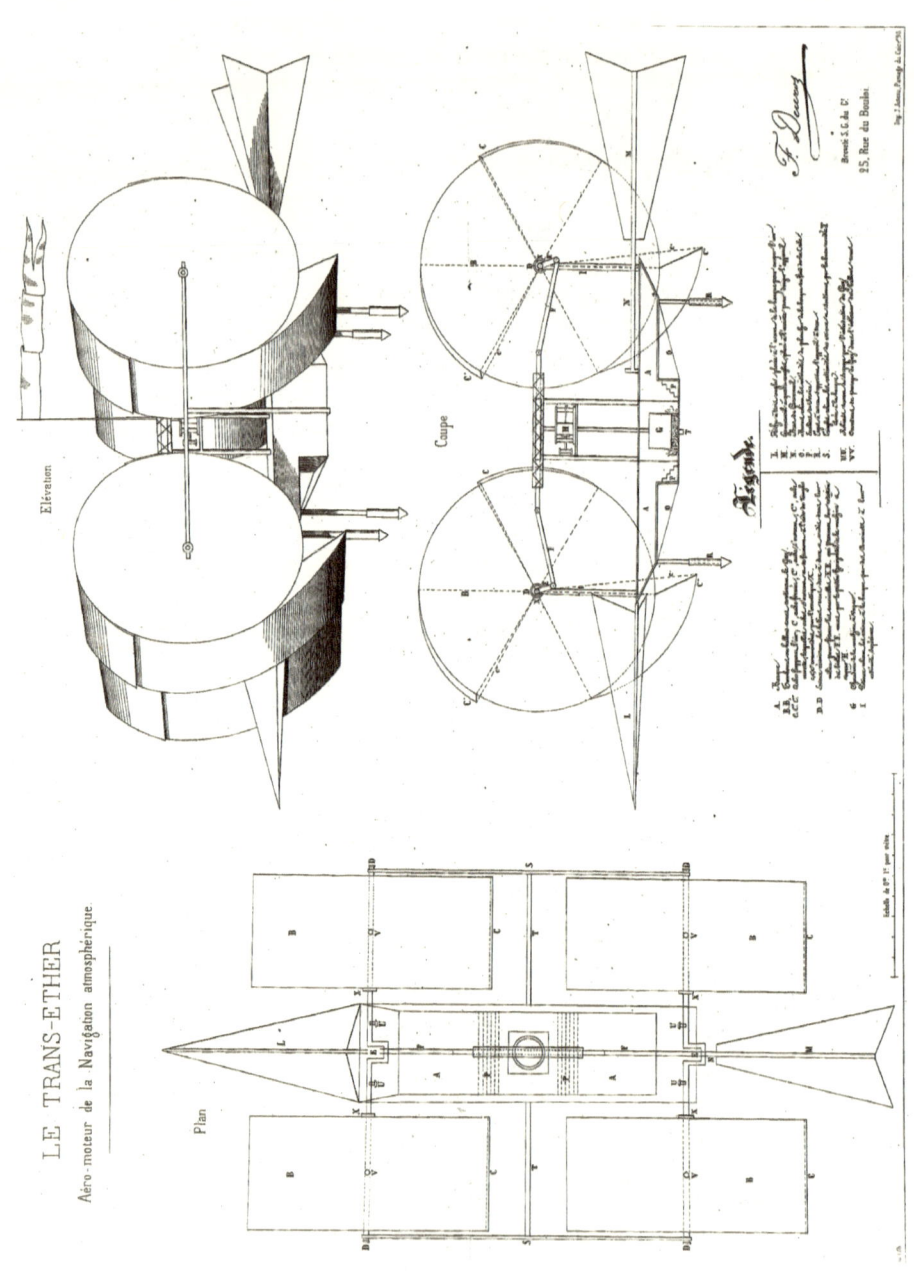

10. Oars, Paddle Wheels and Cycloidal Propellers

The vanes of Congreve's paddle wheel were to be equipped with flaps that, when opened, would allow air to pass through. Hence, the vanes moving in the wrong direction to produce the desired force would have minimal effect.

In the case of steamships, a further improvement in propulsive efficiency was obtained by feathering the paddle wheel blades. *Feathering* refers to the ability to rotate the paddle wheel blade around its own axis to assume various angles relative to the tangent to the paddle wheel circumference. One possible aim was "presenting knife edges to the water when entering and rising, but offering resistance to the water when in the optimal position to push the vessel forward" (NMAH 2024). Another was to keep the blade parallel to its direction of motion when traveling through the air to minimize air resistance.[4] The latter had potential applicability to aerial paddle wheels.

In 1853, Johnson obtained a British patent on an "elongated balloon" with a steam engine driving "two pairs of paddle-wheels and parachute propellers. The paddle-wheels are made to act on the air during half their revolutions, the blades being feathered during the return motion" (Brewer and Alexander 1893, 9). (The term *parachute propeller* refers to a propulsor that moves air by expanding and collapsing.) Cameron received an American patent disclosing (but not claiming) an airship with feathered paddle wheels in 1878 (see also Riddle 1892).

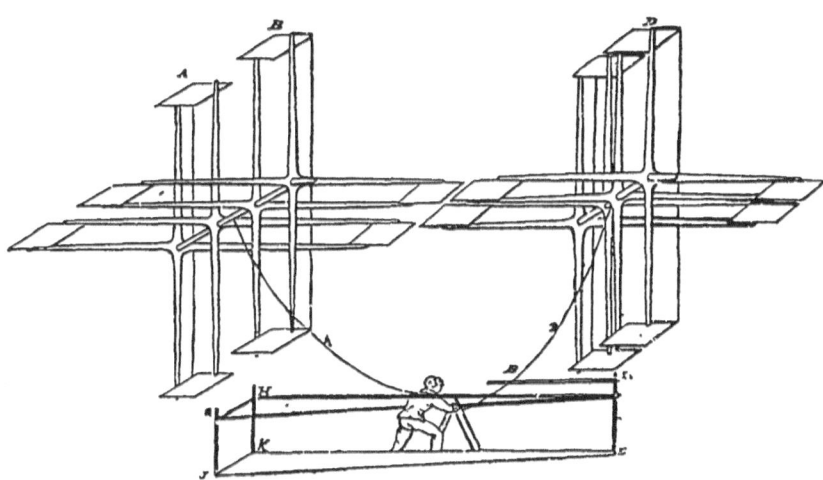

Congreve's "aerial carriage," from the cover of the March 22, 1828, issue of the *Mechanics' Magazine* (reprinted in Foshag and Boehler 1969, 84).

Opposite: The 1859 Ducroz steam paddle-wheel airplane (LOC 2024a).

Part II: Unconventional Propulsion

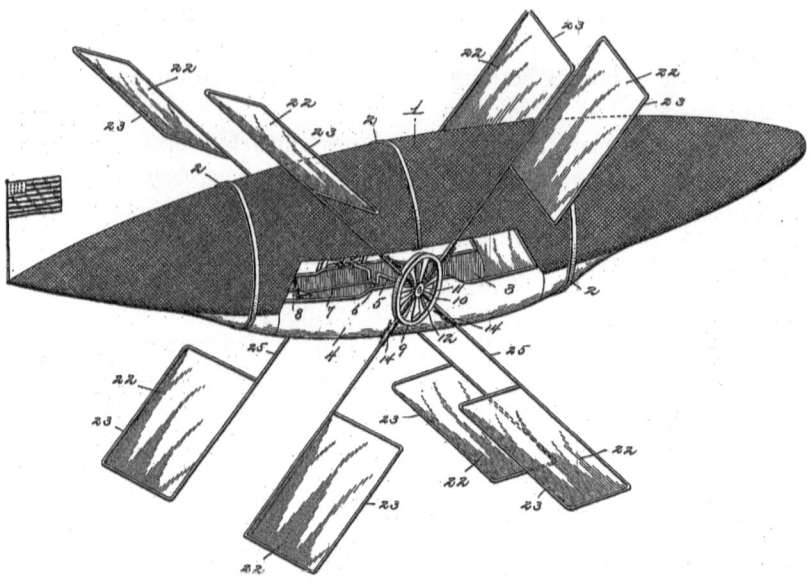

Figure 1 from Frederick R. Merritt's 1898 patent for an airship with windmill sails on either side. It included feathering means. There is no evidence that it was ever built.

In 1878, Haddan[5] received a British patent on an airship propelled by paddle wheels. As the paddles are rotated, a projection on the paddle "comes in contact with a bar, which turns the paddle at right angles." They are edge on to the wind save when held in position by the bar. This is a simple feathering design, but Haddan stated that "the paddles may be made to act in any direction by adjusting the bar, and thus the balloon may be propelled up or down, or in any other direction" (Brewer and Alexander 1893, 75).

Analysis—Paddle Wheels

A few modern analyses of feathering paddle wheels for marine propulsion have concluded that (1) they can propel a surface craft at a speed greater than 30 knots (Harte et al. 2011), and (2) at some ship speeds, they are more efficient than a propeller providing the same thrust (Olis 2017).

At sea, a problem for the paddle wheel was that the lower paddles didn't remain completely submerged at their design depth. If the ship heeled to one side, then the paddle wheel on that side might be lifted clear of the water. And as the ship consumed fuel or unloaded cargo, its draft was reduced. Paddle wheels also lost effectiveness in waves, as the paddles would sometimes hang in the trough (Contact Patch 2021). An aerial paddle wheel doesn't have these problems, because it always pushes against the same fluid, air.

However, I think it is likely that a paddle wheel will be heavier than a propeller of equal thrust. A propeller is essentially a spinning, twisted wing, and the entire blade generates thrust. The only passive component is the hub. In contrast, on a paddle wheel, the spokes and the hub are passive weights that do not directly generate thrust.

History—Cycloidal Propellers[6]

Strictly speaking, even with a conventional paddle wheel, the motion of an individual paddle in space follows a cycloid curve as a result of the combination of the revolution of the paddle wheel and the forward motion of the ship (and thus the wheel).

However, the term *cycloidal propeller* is usually applied to a paddle wheel in which the feathering of the blades is synchronized with the rotation of the paddle wheel in such a way that a net force may be generated that is in any desired direction perpendicular to the wheel's axis of rotation.[7] Thus, with a lateral axis, the force may propel the craft up, down, forward, backward, or in any intermediate direction.

An individual blade will generate a lift force if it is at a nonzero angle of attack (the angle its chord makes to the direction of fluid flow around it). The direction of fluid flow is opposite the direction of movement of the blade in space. Initially, the direction of fluid flow encountered by each blade is tangent to the blade circle. But once the ship is moving, the blades move on a cycloidal path (hence the name), and thus the direction of fluid flow becomes tangent to this path (Jürgens 2006, 5). The lift force on the blade is perpendicular to the direction of local fluid flow, and the drag force is parallel to it.

With the conventional feathered paddle wheel, at any one time, half the blades provided no thrust whatsoever and indeed were rotated to a zero-pitch position so they would not provide thrust opposite the desired direction of movement. In contrast, with a true cycloidal propeller, the blades oscillate between a positive and negative pitch (relative to their individual direction of motion), so all the blades contribute simultaneously to the thrust.

Also, in general, with the conventional paddle wheel, the resistance of the medium to the paddle blade's movement creates a drag force, which

Part II: Unconventional Propulsion

propels the craft. The paddle blade moves in a direction perpendicular to its face, so it does not also generate a lift force. In contrast, with cycloidal propellers, while drag forces are created, the blades move through the medium at a nonzero angle of attack, creating lift forces, too.

It is, unfortunately, often difficult to discern whether a feathered paddle wheel disclosed in a patent is intended merely to minimize air resistance on the recovery or to permit the orientation of the net force in any direction perpendicular to the wheel axis. And the motion of the paddle wheel blade in space is cycloidal, whether or not the blades are properly oscillated for the latter effect. Hence, in the remainder of this section, I use the terms *paddle wheel* and *cycloidal propeller* interchangeably.

A multibladed feathering rotor intended for use as a rotating, lift-providing wing for airplanes has been called a *cyclorotor*, and the

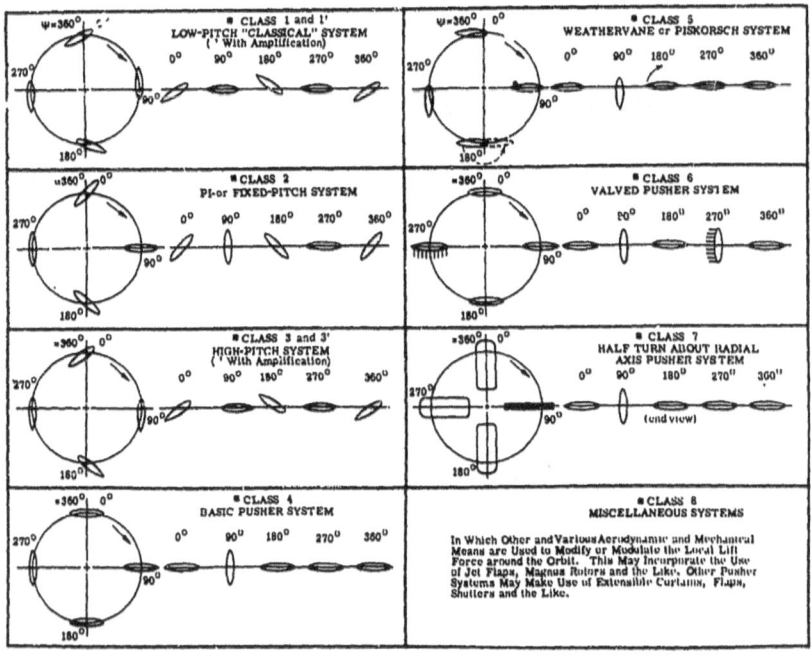

"Classification of Cyclogiro Feathering Systems by Blade Motion and Position Relative to Rotor Axis of Rotation" (Foshag and Boehler 1969, 123). The blade settings shown are for hovering flight; the direction of thrust is upward. The true cycloidal propellers are classes 1–3. The original simply feathered paddle wheel is class 4. Foshag and Boehler's appendix 2 provides the classifications of the cyclogiros of numerous publications, with much additional information.

10. Oars, Paddle Wheels and Cycloidal Propellers

airplane so equipped, a *cyclogiro*. I found that these are very broadly defined, as seen from the classification systems proposed by Liberatore (1954, 2–5) and Foshag and Boehler (1969, 122–131).

Cycloidal propellers have been used thus far only for marine propulsion, and even for this use, it took some time for them to gain acceptance.

The Fowler Wheel, patented in 1870 (King 1878, 111), was an early form of cycloidal marine propulsor. Unlike a conventional paddle wheel, it turned on a vertical axis—that is, in the horizontal plane.

According to the patent, "these blades oscillate on their pivots, as the propeller revolves, in such a manner that they exert a propelling force throughout their entire circuit except when passing two points or centers, when they are neutral. This oscillating motion is produced by an eccentric with which each blades is connected, and the propelling force is exerted in the direction in which the short radius of the eccentric extends. By suitable connections between the eccentric and the helm the steersman is enabled to turn the eccentric, and thereby cast the propelling force to any point of the compass" (Fowler 1870).

A four-bladed Fowler Wheel was installed experimentally on the torpedo boat *Alarm*. Unfortunately, the "wheel required about three times the power needed by an ordinary screw to achieve the same speed" (Caiella 2019).[8]

The Kirsten-Boeing propeller (KBP) resulted from a collaboration between Frederick Kirsten, an engineering professor at the University of Washington, and the aviator and airplane manufacturer William Boeing. In 1921, they founded the Kirsten-Boeing Engineering Company to promote and manufacture this propeller, and Kirsten obtained several patents (1922, 1929, 1936, 1937).

The propeller was inspired by bird flight; Kirsten had realized that the "trajectory of the tip of a bird's wing as it flew through the air" was "a cycloid" (Lee and Bruckner 2017).

With the Kirsten-Boeing cycloidal propeller, "all the blades work simultaneously in the fluid medium" (air or water; Sachse 1926, 1). To accomplish this, the individual blades were rotated "in a direction … opposite to the direction of rotation of the system as a whole and, in fact, at half the angular velocity." On each blade, the tangential component of the fluid flow exerts a pure drag force, and the radial component is resolvable into a "'thrust component' and a lateral force." However, "the lateral forces of the different blades counteract one another. The sum of the thrust components is then the total propeller thrust" (1–2).

Part II: Unconventional Propulsion

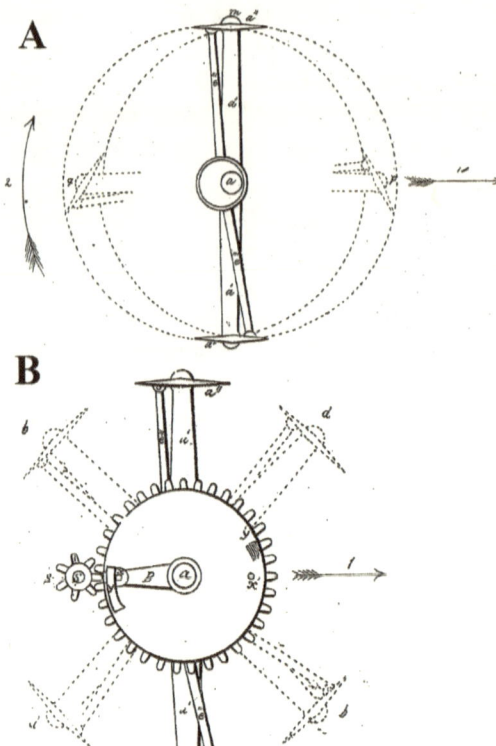

Sachse (1926) pointed out the advantages for an airship of either a lateral axis propeller (to combine propulsion with net lift control) or a vertical axis propeller (to permit movement in any horizontal direction; 3).

Kirsten-Boeing constructed an experimental airship propeller with "24 blades 4 ft. 9.1 in. long and 23 in. wide, the diameter of the whole propeller being about 15 ft. 1.1 in." The intent was to drive this with "a 400 hp Wright airplane engine," using a reduction gear to turn "the propeller at only 225 rpm." The thrust was "about 212 pounds" (Sachse 1926, 3–4).

A. Figure 3 from the Fowler patent (1870) shows the basic operation of a two-blade propeller. The blades (a') are attached to arms (a'), which are turned by a vertical shaft (a). The blades can pivot on their own centers, and the angle of the blade, relative to the tangent of the blade circle, is controlled by the eccentric (e)—an arm attached to a hub mounted eccentrically on the shaft (a). The solid lines show the blades in their neutral positions (m, n), parallel to the tangent of the circle. Since the blades have a symmetric (uncambered) shape, in this position, the water flow past them creates no lift force but minimum drag force. The dashed lines show them in a position where they reach their maximum angle relative to the tangent. Consider first the blade shown at three o'clock (if the *m* position is twelve o'clock). Since the wheel is turning clockwise, the blade is moving down the page, so the local flow is up the page. The leading edge of the blade is lifted above the flow, so there is a positive angle of attack. A lift force is generated, pointing to the right of the page (forward motion of the ship), which an arrow shows is the intended direction of motion. Now look at the opposite blade position (nine o'clock). Here the leading edge of the blade is turned inward. The blade is moving toward the top of the page, so the flow is toward the bottom of the page, and the angle

10. Oars, Paddle Wheels and Cycloidal Propellers

The intent was to equip the airship USS *Shenandoah* with six main propellers of this type, "with their axes at an angle of 30° to the horizontal plane,"[9] and two stern propellers on near-vertical axes[10] to "replace the customary rudders" (Sachse 1926, 4–5). The main propellers "were designed for a thrust of about 1800 pounds each" (6). However, "the plan was not carried out, due to the destruction of the airship" in 1925, and the Navy turned to experimenting with the propeller (turning on a vertical axis) for possible use on boats (7).

A model of Kirsten's proposed cycloplane was placed in a wind tunnel at the University of Washington, which appears to be the closest to an actual test that it had. The construction of the wind tunnel was completed in 1936, but because of commercial and military demands, Kirsten's model was not tested until 1942. Based on a photograph, it had two three-bladed, lateral axis paddle wheels and no wings (Bruckner et al. 2021). The results of the wind tunnel testing do not appear to have been publicly disclosed. From 1943 to 1945, Kirsten equipped two Navy test vessels with cycloidal propellers, and they performed well, but the project petered out after World War II (Levinson 1992, 23).

The Voith-Schneider propeller (VSP) was designed by Ernst Schneider for use in a hydroelectric turbine; the flowing water would turn its blades, and power would be generated. A Voith employee saw the potential for using the propeller in reverse, with an engine causing the propeller to turn and thereby act on the water either as a pump or as a combined propeller and rudder, and around 1928, a VSP was successfully used on the experimental boat *Torqueo* (Sockel 2013, 370–372). The VSP has been used on minesweepers, tugs and ferries (Ficken and Dickerson 1969, 2).

In the VSP, the individual blades make one complete rotation for each complete rotation of the propeller. The associated mechanical linkages allow for control of the average pitch of the blades, and thus their average angle of attack relative to the local fluid flow, and thereby the magnitude of the generated lift forces (and total thrust).

---

of attack is negative. Thus, the lift force is again toward the right of the page. B. Figure 4 from the Fowler patent. This shows the different positions that can be set as the neutral position by means of the displayed mechanism. The solid lines show the neutral position as being the same as in figure 2, so the ship moves to the right of the page. The dashed lines show two alternative positions. If that of b, the ship will move diagonally to the top and right of the page (forward and port motion), and if that of d, to the bottom and right of the page (forward and starboard motion).

Part II: Unconventional Propulsion

If the blades are oscillating, then at any given moment, each blade will be at a different angle relative to the blade circle, and thus the lift force on the blades will differ. However, since the blades are arranged symmetrically around the rotor, for a given phase setting, there will be a favored direction of thrust; the transverse force components on the symmetrically opposite blades will cancel each other out (Jürgens 2006, 5–7; see generally Fork and Jürgens 2002).

On the VSP, the "amplitude and phase of the blades' motion," and thus the magnitude and direction of the net thrust, are controlled by the position of a mechanical "steering center." When this is at the "center of the rotor casing," the blades remain tangent to the blade circle for the entire revolution. There is thus a zero angle of attack, zero lift force, and zero thrust. When it is moved away from that center to an "eccentric" position, the blades oscillate, creating lift and thus thrust. The degree of displacement determines the magnitude of thrust and the direction of displacement, the direction of thrust (Jürgens 2006, 3, 7).

One advantage of the VSP over the KBP was this variable pitch, allowing total thrust control. The KBP only offered a fixed pitch (Ficken and Dickerson 1969, 2), and consequently, thrust had to be controlled by varying the revolutions per minute of the propeller.

Lateral (Pitch) Axis Designs

The lateral axis cycloidal propeller was potentially attractive to airplane designers, as it offered vertical takeoff and landing capability as well as forward propulsion if the generated force was great enough.

In 1930, San Franciscan E. A. Schroeder unveiled his *S1* cyclogyro. While this had two lateral axis cycloidal propellers, they were mounted ahead of the wing (Bowers 1990, 234). Self (2018) suggests that Schroeder thought of it as a substitute for the conventional screw propeller. It is not believed ever to have been flown.

Despite the lack of any proof of concept, there was continued interest in cycloidal propulsion, as evidenced by occasional patent filings. For example, in Boyea's 1945 airplane patent, the "laterally extending" paddle wheels take the form of "auxiliary wings disposed beneath" the normal fixed wings. However, there were no new prototypes until the 1980s.

Unmanned Airships

The renewed interest was mostly in small, unmanned aerial vehicles. *ACROSTAT*, a small (1.5 m × 1 m) acrobatic airship, was flown at least as early as 1989 and was described by Onda and Morikawa (1991). They reported that this model airship "can ascend and descend vertically, and can perform somersaults, spiral flights, and rotate around its C.G."

In 1998, Bosch Aerospace tested a lateral axis curtate cycloid[11] propeller. This had six blades (NACA 0012 airfoil) with a one-foot chord and a 4 ft orbit diameter. Generating 350 lb of lift required a rotational speed of 650 rpm (Boschma 1998, PDF 5, 26). The goal was to determine whether this could be used to propel a ship-launched UAV. The results were quite favorable: "Thrust levels demonstrated were substantially higher than achievable by the best screw-type propellers, and approximately equal to those of high-end helicopters. Vectoring of thrust through a 360° arc, and low-noise characteristics throughout the RPM range were demonstrated. Also accomplished was identification of efficiency gain techniques that may increase the overall thrust by approximately 30%" (5, 26).

Two different mounting configurations were considered: cantilever (blades supported at one end) and center (blades supported in the middle; Boschma 1998, fig. 2). A test airship was built, but the project lost funding, and the airship never flew (Lobner 2023).

Thrust tests on an experimental 600 cu m, dual lateral axis, cyclorotor airship, 20 m long and 7 m in diameter, were reported in 2007 (Nozaki et al. 2007), and an indoor flight test was carried out in 2008. Each 2 m diameter cycloidal propeller had three blades with NACA 0012 profiles. The maximum thrust achieved was 500 N at 6 rps (revolutions per second). The expected maximum vehicle speed was 14–30 m/s. The flight test reportedly showed that the "cycloidal propeller equipped airship [was] much [more] maneuverable than vehicles equipped with conventional fan-type thrusters" (Nozaki et al. 2009).

UNMANNED AIRPLANES

IAT (Innovative Aeronautics Technologies) built a 1.2 m cyclogyro rotor (L3 rotor) in 2005 and subjected it to wind tunnel tests in early 2006. It provided 2,000 N of thrust at 70 kW and 1,000 rpm power (Schwaiger and Wills 2006).

IAT's first flight of "an untethered 100% cyclogyro driven aircraft was on 13th June 2006." This was an electric-powered model airplane with four L1 rotors ("rotor diameter 230 mm, span-length 230 mm, weight around 16 kg"). Each provided 40 N of thrust at 4,000 rpm. A 2014 redesign of the rotor increased its thrust to 75 N without changing its size or power consumption (Schwaiger and Wills 2006).

In 2012, a larger cyclocopter (L2 rotor: "rotor diameter 600 mm,

Part II: Unconventional Propulsion

span-length 00 mm, piston engine powered, weight around 175 kg"), the *D–Dalus*, was flown indoors (Schwaiger and Wills 2006).

IAT contemplated incorporating the four rotors into a "wing-body" with upturned wingtips. The rotors are partially recessed into this body (Schwaiger and Wills 2006, fig. 5). The wing-body would permit *D–Dalus* to "create lift in forward flight," as a conventional airplane does.

One surprising finding was that the rotor thrust efficiency increased with forward flight speed. "The reason for this appears to lie in the 'Virtual Chamber' effect generated within the rotor space" (Schwaiger and Wills 2006, fig. 5). Unfortunately, this effect was not further explained.

Unmanned cyclogyros have also been built by other groups, including those at the National University of Singapore (SNU) and the University of Maryland. SNU achieved a tethered hover in 2007. A video is available that shows the untethered 2011 indoor and outdoor test flights of SNU's dual propeller Fire Wheel. The takeoff weight was 130 g, and the maximum thrust was 2,200 g (huyu0711, 2011).

Free flight was also achieved by the University of Maryland's twin-rotor "cyclocopter micro air vehicle" in 2011 (Benedict et al. 2011). Benedict et al. (2012) comment that "one of the biggest disadvantages of a cyclocopter is that rotor weight forms a significant fraction of the empty weight of the vehicle. The rotor weight is directly related to the blade weight because it governs the centrifugal force, which is the predominant structural load on a cyclorotor." They reported having halved the blade weight and simplified the blade pitching mechanism relative to the previous design.

Habibnia et al. (2020) envisioned the combination of front and rear lateral axis cycloidal propellers with rectangular biplane wings in between them. The intent was to "guide a portion of downwash jet from the front cyclorotor toward the pair-wing vane" and thereby increase thrust. The wing, in turn, "guides the flow toward the rear cyclorotor."

They also placed dielectric barrier discharge plasma actuators on the trailing surface of the lower wings. These ionize the air and then accelerate the ionized air molecules. The intent is to reduce flow separation and thus improve the flow to the rear cyclorotor.

The cyclorotor-wing combination was studied only by computational fluid dynamics (CFD) simulation, but there was an experimental test of the effect of the plasma actuators.

Katnur et al. (2024) reported a small experimental aerial drone with two counter-rotating lateral axis cycloidal propellers, each with six blades. It was able to get 20 cm off the ground.

10. Oars, Paddle Wheels and Cycloidal Propellers

MANNED AIRSHIP

Onda et al. (2003) proposed a human-powered airship, 9 m long and 6 m in diameter (volume 170 cu m), with lateral axis, three-bladed, 2 m diameter cycloidal propellers. The expected airspeed was 3–5 m/s, and at 3 m/s, the expected required power at 3 m/s was less than 100 W.

Vertical (Yaw) Axis Designs

In 1935, Voith-Schneider published a concept design for an airplane with *vertical* axis cycloidal propellers in front of each of its conventional wings (Schwaiger and Wills 2016). These would not provide lift directly (if they increased forward speed, they would indirectly increase lift from the wings), but they would make it easy for the plane to jink to one side or another.

An unusual vertical axis design was created by SunPlower (2022). Normally, on cycloidal propellers, the blade pivot axis is parallel to the propeller axis. On the SunPlower propeller, the blade pivot axes are splayed outward. In addition, while the blade pitching schedule is the same as on the KBP, the SunPlower propeller has a relatively small, conical hub. The blade movements are controlled by a complex gearing system (cp. Chennupati 2021).

Longitudinal (Roll) Axis Designs

In 1937, Jonathan Caldwell mounted two three-bladed paddle wheels on either side of an airplane fuselage. Photos (of uncertain provenance) show that the paddle wheels turned on a *longitudinal* axis. Moreover, it appears that each paddle could rotate around its own axis—that is, they could be feathered (Aerofiles 2024). There is no evidence that this craft ever flew.[12]

A paddle wheel mounted on a longitudinal axis (i.e., parallel to the long dimension of the aerial vehicle) could provide lift but not propulsion. However, the Thompson and Niegenfind airplane patent (1925) contemplated that the frames of such wheels could be tilted "so that they will act as propellers for driving the ship forwardly or rearwardly according to the direction for tilt." The paddles themselves were feathered as the wheel rotated for the reasons previously discussed (see also Darbyson 1933; Stewart 1944).

Multi-Axis Combined Systems

In 2001, Boschma expressed an intent "to install a three-axis propulsion system on a 26-meter unmanned airship by Spring 2002." In 2007, Sullivan received a patent (assigned to Boschma Research) describing a "tri-cycloidal" airship equipped with three cycloidal propellers: a

Part II: Unconventional Propulsion

longitudinal axis propeller on the nose, a vertical axis propeller on top and amidships, and at least one lateral axis propeller on the side and in the same midships plane as the vertical axis propeller.

Analysis—Cycloidal Propeller

We have already seen that one important characteristic of the cycloidal propeller is the orientation of its axis of revolution, as this determines the potential directions of thrust.

Another important characteristic is the type of cycloid curve that is traced by the blades as a result of the combination of their revolution around the propeller axis and the ship's motion. The pitch ratio is the ratio of the theoretical advance (distance traveled by the propeller axis) during one complete revolution to the diameter of the blade circle. Three types of cycloids can be distinguished: curtate (ratio $< \pi$), simple (ratio $= \pi$), and prolate (ratio $> \pi$).

Imagine that for each possible blade position during the revolution, a line is drawn through the pivot point (P) of the blade and perpendicular to the chord of the

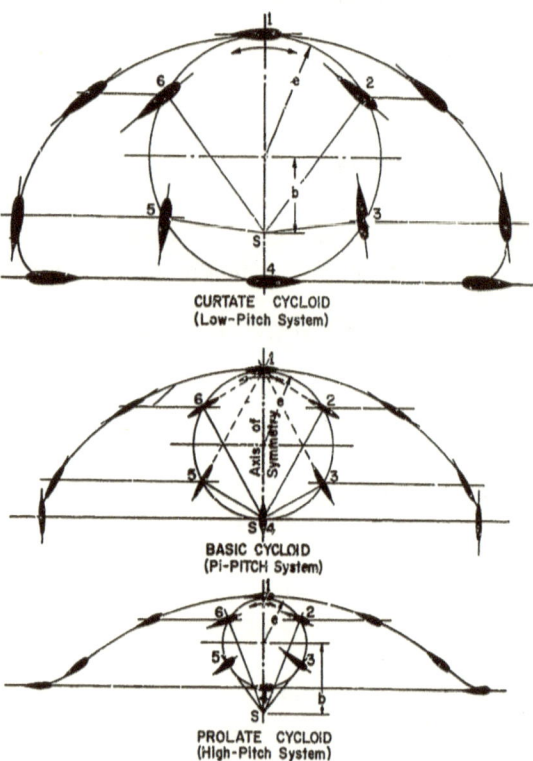

Figure 88 from Foshag and Boehler (1969) showing the "ideal path trajectories of cyclogiro rotor blade" for the three different pitch ratio systems. In each of the three views, see the blade pitches referenced to the blade circle and referenced to the cycloid path of the blade. The S marks the location of the control point.

10. Oars, Paddle Wheels and Cycloidal Propellers

blade. If the blades are following true cycloid motion, they are pitched so all these lines intersect at a single point, the control point (S). If this control point lies on the blade circle, it is a simple cycloid (π-pitch system); if inside it, a curtate cycloid (low-pitch system); if outside it, a prolate cycloid (high-pitch system). The eccentricity is the ratio of the radial position of the control position to the radius of the blade circle, and the pitch ratio is thus π times eccentricity.

The cycloidal propeller for Onda et al.'s (2003) proposed human-powered airship is intended to operate with an eccentricity of 0.3.

The magnitude of the total thrust is determined by the location of the control point; the further radially outward it is from the propeller axis, the greater the thrust. And the direction of the thrust is determined by the circumferential position of the control point (Henry 1959, 11–12).

The pitch ratio is a function of the internal geometry of the propeller. The advance ratio is the ratio of the airspeed of the vehicle to the circumferential speed of the blade. The latter, in turn, is the product of π, the blade circle diameter, and the rotational speed of the propeller (Foshag and Boehler 1969, 109).

When the advance ratio equals the pitch ratio, then throughout their revolution, the blades are continuously pitched so their chords are tangent to their cycloidal path, and the cycloidal propeller therefore does not develop any thrust (Jürgens 2006, 6).

The airspeed is affected not merely by the thrust of the cycloidal propeller but by that of any other propellers carried by the craft. The rotational speed is adjustable by the pilot. Hence, the advance ratio can be made to assume a value that is not equal to the pitch ratio.

For a propeller with a pitch ratio of π, the blades follow a simple cycloid path, with a cusp on each propeller revolution. When the blades pass through the cusp, the leading edge becomes the trailing edge, and vice versa (Henry 1959, fig. 1). It is therefore necessary to use a "doubly symmetric" (head/tail, top/bottom) blade profile. This unfortunately has a "poor lift-drag" ratio compared with a more streamlined profile (13).

Low-pitch systems work best "at hover and low advance ratios" (Foshag and Boehler 1969, 124). The "π-pitch system has a good aerodynamic efficiency only at moderate advance ratios. It stands to reason, therefore, that the high-pitch system is well suited for high-speed aircraft configurations" (126).

The KBP had a fixed pitch ratio (π), whereas the pitch ratio for the VSP is variable. Its pitch ratio is controlled by moving a steering center that, by mechanical linkages, corresponds to the aforementioned control

Part II: Unconventional Propulsion

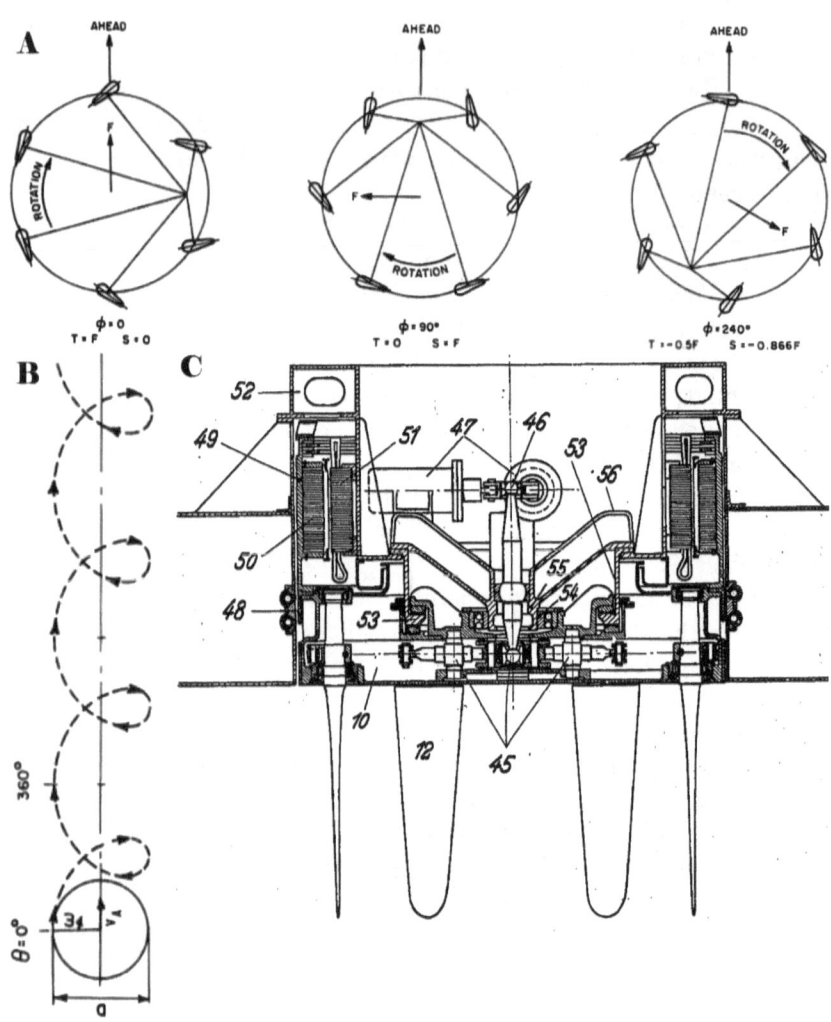

A. Schematic showing how the displacement of the control center of a cycloidal propeller changes the blade orientations and the direction of the resultant force (shown by arrow labeled F) relative to the ahead (bow) direction (Ficken and Dickerson 1969, 17). B. Schematic showing the cycloidal path of one blade of such a propeller (15). C. The Voith-Schneider propeller, vertical cross section. Servomotors 47 act on lever 46 (top end of the control rod), the lower end of which acts on the blade shifting mechanism 45. The blades 12 are mounted on the blade wheel 10 (Ehrhart 1935, fig. 7).

10. Oars, Paddle Wheels and Cycloidal Propellers

point in terms of how the pitch of the blades changes (Jürgens 2006, 5). However, its pitch ratio cannot exceed 0.8π (Esmailian et al. 2014).

A full-feathering (universal pitch) system can vary its pitch from less than to greater than π. This was first proposed by Rohrbach in 1932 (Foshag and Boehler 1969, 129), and mechanisms have been proposed by Kirsten in 1950 and Eastman in 1951. Foshag and Boehler deemed these too complex and delicate (132); for more recent developments, see Benedict et al. (2013).

If the pitch progressions were such that the aforementioned lines did not all intersect at a single point, the blade motion would not be a true cycloid. However, this might be necessitated by other considerations. Henry (1959, 12) reported that "the pitch ratio of cycloidal propellers having true cycloidal blade motion is limited to about 0.62π due to the large angular accelerations involved in the blade motion near theta 0°. As a result, this type of propeller cannot obtain the high efficiencies associated with propeller operation at high pitch ratios."

The solution was what Henry (1959, 13) called "amplified" cycloidal motion; "the blade angle at each position θ is multiplied by a constant k." While the motion is no longer truly cycloidal, and there is no longer a simple control point,[13] this permitted an increase in the pitch ratio. In 1959, 0.73π was achievable, the new limit being "due to acceleration stresses. All of the Voith-Schneider propellers have used amplified cycloidal motion except the first few which used true cycloidal motion."

The mechanisms needed to achieve either true or amplified cycloidal motion were complex. A sinusoidal variation in blade pitch could be achieved more simply. Again, the motion is not a true cycloid, and "the efficiency of a cycloidal propeller with sinusoidal blade motion does not compare favorably with other types" (Henry 1959, 14). In water tests, the discrepancy increased with increasing pitch ratio (Nakonechny 1961, 6). Nonetheless, Boschma (1998, PDF 28) chose a sine curve. Andrisani et al. (2016) have argued that the sinusoidal pitching profile is optimal for hovering flight but not otherwise.

Brockett (1991) presents a plot of the blade pitch angle against the blade angle of revolution for sinusoidal, cycloidal, amplified cycloidal and compensated amplified cycloidal motion.[14]

Sunplower (2022) presents an illustration showing the difference in blade movement between the Voith-Schneider propeller and the Kirsten-Boeing propeller. Sunplower points out that the VSP requires an abrupt blade angle change at a phase angle of about 90°, whereas the blade angle changes on the KBP are smooth.

Part II: Unconventional Propulsion

Next, consider the nature of the linkage mechanism used to accomplish that pitch profile. Gerhardt (1993) criticized the blade pitch control mechanisms of prior cycloidal propeller lift/propulsion systems: "far too complicated to render them practical, have limited or no flexibility to adapt to differing flight conditions, and the extent of control achieved is minimal." He claimed the use of "variable stroke linear actuators" in place of the prior art rotary actuators (cams and gears). The control system for these actuators was only shown schematically.

For the Boschma propeller, the mechanism was a "four bar linkage" (Boschma 1998, PDF 31), and for the NSU's 2007 cyclorotor, a five bar one (Benedict 2010, 54). Benedict et al. (2013) describe a 3D cam-based mechanism capable of producing curtate, simple and prolate cycloidal motion (a circular cam would produce sinusoidal motion; see also Adams 2016).

The propeller parameters include the number of blades, the diameter of the blade circle, the chord and span length of the blades, and the airfoil shape of the blade. There were experimental studies of the effect of these parameters on the performance of vertical axis cyclorotors used for marine propulsion (Foshag and Boehler 1969; Li 1991). And a CFD parametric analysis for a lateral axis cyclorotor intended for hovering in air is available (Xisto et al. 2016).

The cycloidal propeller proposed by Gabriel Babillot in 1909 had scoop-like (thin and highly cambered) blades. Self (2018) comments, "This matches early aerofoils on conventional aeroplanes that were also thin and highly cambered. This is because such shapes are more effective than thicker ones at the very low Reynolds numbers where the initial studies were done. As engine power and hence speed increased, aerofoils became thicker." However, while airplane wings remained cambered, uncambered blades are the norm for cycloidal propellers. The blades used by Onda et al. (2003) have the NACA 0012 profile.[15]

Aerodynamic modeling of a cycloidal propeller generally requires consideration of unsteady flow aerodynamics. Boschma (1998) states, "The reason we need to use unsteady aerodynamics is it takes a finite amount of time to develop lift. Steady aerodynamics does not take this into account. The blades are moving and the rotating fast enough to make steady aerodynamics a bad assumption." In the case of the Boschma propeller, the maximum angle of attack needed to produce 350 lb of lift/thrust according to steady aerodynamics was 20°, whereas unsteady aerodynamics warned that 25.36° was needed (PDF 31–32).

Referring to experiments conducted by Wheatley (1933), whose results did not agree with theoretical predictions, Boirum and Post (2009) comment, "The drag inducing effects of an oscillating airfoil were not understood at the time of this experiment, and as the rotor's rotational speed was increased, the drag coefficient of the blade profile increased dramatically. This created the net effect of reducing the predicted performances substantially and requiring far more power than anticipated to achieve higher rotational speeds. A comparison between a cycloidal propeller and a typical airplane propeller showed that at a 100 ft/sec tip speed, the maximum lift per horsepower is 23.8 lb/hp for the cycloidal propeller and 50 lb/hp for a 10 degree pitch airplane propeller." And in the conclusion, Boirum and Post add, "When an airfoil's angle of attack is oscillating at a high enough frequency, with a high enough amplitude, it causes boundary layer separation bubbles to form on the trailing surface of the wing. The formation of these bubbles is still difficult to predict, and requires detailed experimentation and numerical analysis."

Further review of the development of the aerodynamic theory for cycloidal propellers is in Foshag and Boehler (1969), McNabb (2001) and Benedict (2010).

Conclusion

The high maneuverability afforded by the cycloidal propeller would seem to be most useful in unmanned aerial vehicles used for reconnaissance. For larger airships and airplanes, the question is whether it will be competitive with swiveling conventional propellers. But it should be noted that a tail-mounted cycloidal propeller can turn an airship or airplane on a dime, whereas a conventional rudder is ineffectual if there is no craft motion.

11

Biomimetic Propulsion (Flapping and Undulating)

The word *ornithopter* comes from the Greek words for *bird* and for *wing*, and ornithopter designers originally tried to imitate the wing flapping of birds. However, flight has evolved at least four times in Earth's history: in insects, pterosaurs, birds and bats. While our ability to study pterosaurs is limited, insects and bats also can serve as models for flying machines.

An ornithopter may be manned or unmanned. Manned ornithopters may be muscle or engine powered. Unmanned ones, depending on size, may be engine, battery, or even rubber band powered.

Birds versus Humans

In attempting to emulate birds, humans run into the problem of lacking birds' anatomical and physiological adaptations for flapping flight. These include the following:

1. thin-walled, air-filled, hollow bones (high strength-to-weight ratio) and reduction in the number of bones in the wing (Shipman 1998, 55, 59);
2. airfoil shape of wing built up from overlapping layers of feathers (low weight-to-volume ratio; 55, 59);
3. feathers capable of rotation in place (57);
4. mechanical linkage of the elbow and wrist joints, so one muscle extends both (60);
5. a high ratio of flight muscle mass to total mass (63);
6. an enlarged sternum (*carina*) to provide additional flight muscle attachment points (61);
7. "the bones and muscles of the wing are arranged so that a wing flip [for takeoff] is possible" (62–63);
8. the *alula* (winglet)—the "thumb," bearing small flight feathers—may be moved to create a slot on the wing's leading edge; this allows the

11. Biomimetic Propulsion (Flapping and Undulating)

wing to assume a higher angle of attack, creating additional lift without stalling (Norberg 2006, 121); and

9. the ability to twist the wing "to attain an optimal angle of attack along the entire wing" (124).

As a result of the first two adaptations, birds have low wing loading. As noted in chapter 1, *wing loading* is the ratio between airplane (bird) mass (or weight) and wing planform area. Wing loading in modern birds "ranges from about 17 N/m² in small hummingbirds (2.3 g) to 230 N/m² in the Whooper Swan (10 kg)." The higher the wing loading, the faster the bird must fly to generate sufficient lift (Norberg 2006, 139).

Elaborating on point 5, "the stronger flying birds have flight muscles that amount to about 15 to 25% of their total weight.... Our much lower relative muscular weight cannot compare to theirs" (Wegener 2012, 124). Human arm muscle mass has been estimated to be 3.8% of body mass (Fuller et al. 1992).

The hummingbird, with a mass of about 5 g (30% of which is breast muscle), has a high specific power (power-to-body weight). In hovering flight, its power output is 16 W/kg; at 14 km/h, 12 W/kg; and at 50 km/h, 32 W/kg. "Good athletes who can pedal for four to six hours sustain a power of about 3 to 3.5" W/kg (Wilson 2004, 124–5).

Flapping is not straight up and down. For albatrosses, the wing tip path is an inclined oval, and for pigeons, an inclined figure eight (Shyy et al. 2013, 27). Because of the rotation of the wing at the shoulder joint, the flapping of wings has been compared to the turning of a helicopter rotor (26).

To avoid creating negative lift on the upstroke, "birds use one of two strategies. Some birds slightly fold and flex the wings on the upstroke, effectively reducing the area of the airfoil.... Other birds keep their wings outspread but tilt their wings differently in different segments of the wingbeat, thus adjusting the effective surface area" (Shipman 1998, 56).

A further difference between upstroke and downstroke arises passively. Flight feathers have a *rachis* (quill) dividing "each feather into two asymmetrical vanes, with the forward or leading edge being narrower. During the downstroke, the pressure on the underside of the feather causes it to twist" so "the trailing edge vane is pressed upward, making the entire wing a broad structure.... In the upstroke, the opposite occurs.... This movement separates adjacent feathers from each other slightly, forming a tiny slot through which air can pass" (Shipman 1998, 57).

Part II: Unconventional Propulsion

History

Human-Powered LTA Ornithopter

The Viennese clockmaker Jakob Degen built "an ornithopter with a wing area of 12 m^2," suspended from a "small hydrogen balloon," and allegedly achieved a short ascent in 1812 (Reay 1977, 34). This likely resulted from buoyant lift rather than dynamic lift generated by the wings.

Konstantin Danilewsky built at least two airships that, when carrying the pilot, had a small negative net buoyancy, small enough so that the pilot could generate sufficient dynamic lift by flapping wings to maintain level flight (Akimov and Welker 2019, 27). This, of course, allowed him to explore the capabilities of human muscle power without having to depend on the wings completely to get (and stay) aloft.

His first airship, the *Embryo* (1897), was about 36 ft long and 12 ft in diameter. It was essentially cylindrical. Based on a photo in Danilewsky's 1900 book, reproduced, with translation, in Akimov and Welker 2019 (25) it had a flat bow and a slightly rounded stern—not exactly an aerodynamic shape. It made about 25 ascents.

In figure 11 of Danilewsky's (1897) Russian patent (Akimov and Welker 2019, 32), the pilot is almost prone, with his arms bent at the elbows, resting on a transverse spar to which the wings are attached, and his feet engage on a sort of treadle from which ropes extend to the wings. The wings are also pitched, so they are in a vertical plane. This, presumably, is the position for maximum forward motion. In figure 12 (Akimov and Welker 2019, 32), the pilot is upright. I assume this is the position for maximum lift (32).

It appears that when the pilot presses down on a treadle, the corresponding wing flaps in the same direction. There is no obvious mechanical coordination between the two wings, and the point of attachment of the line from the treadle seems rather close to the wing root (Akimov and Welker 2019, 32).

In his 1900 book, he commented, "The wings were very cumbersome, heavy, slowly opened when struck by air" (Akimov and Welker 2019, 292).

His second airship, the *Pilstrom* (1898), was about 43 ft long and 14.5 ft in diameter. It had a sharply pointed bow and a rounded stern. It made perhaps 150 ascents (Akimov and Welker 2019, 34). Based on available photos (36–37), it was flapped (or rowed) using the arms alone. It had "lighter, smaller" wings (292).

Danilewsky's 1900 book refers cryptically to the *Pilstrom*'s wing being

11. Biomimetic Propulsion (Flapping and Undulating)

equipped with shutters (Akimov and Welker 2019, 242). He also says that "(1) the aeronaut's work on the wings during ascent was tedious; (2) oscillatory movements of wings resulted in unproductive loss of time when 'recovering' (i.e., moving them upward); and (3) when wings were 'catching' the air, some additional force was spent to stretch the springs which would subsequently lift (i.e., recover) the wings" (244).

It is unknown whether Danilewsky's third airship relied on flapping wings; his fourth airship definitely did not.

There is a U.S. patent on an airship with multiple pairs of flapping wings (Schweers 1905).

Human-Powered HTA Ornithopters

Unsuccessful attempts to achieve flapping flight are legion, and insofar as human-powered flight is concerned, the successes are of a qualified nature because the launch was assisted by towing or other means. I only discuss a few of these here.

Alexander Lippisch made a noteworthy attempt in 1929, but it remains controversial whether his pilot was able to sustain flight or merely glided for 300 m (Reay 1977, 88). Adalbert Schmid's ornithopter flew 900 m after a towed launch in 1942 (Chronister 2008, 5), but he then turned his attention to engine-powered craft.

In 2010, the University of Toronto's *Snowbird*, piloted by Todd Reichert, achieved a sustained flight of 19.3 seconds after a towed launch. The *Snowbird* weighed 94 lb and had a wingspan of 105 ft (Toronto 2010). The drive was based on a Thys rowing bike, designed so the pilot simultaneously presses forward with their feet and pulls back on the handles. A wire was attached to the foot slider and ran to a 2:1 block to increase the force. From the block, drive wires ran to the wings. It was "primarily the outboard section of the wing that is flapping" (Aerovelo 2016b).

Engine-Powered Manned Ornithopters

Adalbert Schmid also experimented with engine-powered ornithopters. After installing a "3 hp Sachs motorcycle engine" in his previous (1942) human-powered ornithopter and "adding wheels," the airplane was able "to take off unassisted at the very first test flight which lasted 15 minutes [and] averaged 60 km/h. Fuel consumption was low at 1.5 liters per 100 km." Later, "installing a 6 hp engine ... increased speed to 80 km/h" (Arndt 2024).

Part II: Unconventional Propulsion

This ornithopter had a bent drive shaft, so the wing tips described a circular motion in the vertical plane rather than a simple flapping motion (Chronister 2018).

In 1947, Schmid converted a Grunau Baby IIa sailplane into a two-seat ornithopter with a 10 hp engine. The wings were not hinged at the wing roots; only the outer sections flapped. Its speed was allegedly 100–120 km/h (Arndt 2024).

Engine- or Motor-Powered Unmanned Ornithopters

The first successful engine-powered, remote-controlled ornithopter was the Spencer Orniplane (1961). It had a biplane configuration with opposing flappers to minimize bouncing motion that might damage the remote control relays. The flappers were energized by a 0.35 hp two-stroke engine. The plane weighed 7.5 lb and had a lower wingspan of 90.7 in. (Stilley 1999).

Later, there were radio-controlled ornithopter flights in Russia (by Valentin Kiselev, 1984), Germany (by Horst Raebiger, 1990), and Canada (by Jeremy Harris and James DeLaurier, in 1991; Chronister 2008, 7). In 1998, a radio-controlled ornithopter, the Skybird, became commercially available.

One ornithopter of particular interest is the remote-controlled AeroVironment Nano Hummingbird (wingspan 16 cm, weight 19 g). It looks like a real hummingbird, and by 2011, it had demonstrated that it could hover, "climb and descend vertically ... fly sideways to both left and right," and move forward (10 m/s maximum) and backward (AFT 2013).

Pterosaur-Inspired Unmanned Ornithopters

In 1986, a half-size model (QN) of the giant pterosaur *Quetzalcoatlus northropi* was flown with a combination of autonomous and remote control (Chronister 2008, 8). This pterosaur had a wingspan of 11 m (making it "the largest natural flyer known") and an estimated wing loading of 8 kg/m^2. On the replica, the wing flapping was driven by "two one-horsepower samarium-cobalt DC motors ... through a gear box and ball screw drive," and these were powered by "six lbs. of nickel-cadmium batteries." The flapping mechanism controlled not only flapping but also wing twist and wing sweep (MacCready 1985). The head was used as "a steerable forward fin" and "the three small finger digits as drag devices" (Zakaria et al. 2015).

11. Biomimetic Propulsion (Flapping and Undulating)

Bat-Inspired Unmanned Ornithopters

Bats are highly maneuverable flyers with the ability to hover. They have a "metamorphic musculoskeletal system that has over 40 Degrees of Freedom (DoF)" (Ramezani et al. 2016).

Pornsin-Sirirak et al. (2000) developed a palm-sized Microbat. The first prototype (7.5 g), powered by supercapacitors, flew for nine seconds in 1998. The second prototype (10.5 g), relying on a NiCd battery, flew for 22 seconds. The third, with radio control (12.5 g), was able to fly for 45 seconds. Unlike real wings, the Microbat wings did not have a 3-D shape (Pornsin-Sirirak et al. 2000). Also, they only flapped in a vertical plane, and they did not actively change shape (Bunget 2010, 5). I would consider it a bat mimetic in name only.

Bunget (2010) fabricated a flight platform (BATMAV) that attempted to duplicate the kinematics of a bat's wing, including movement at the shoulder (with a simplification), elbow, and wrist joints that allowed the wing to fold. Shape memory alloy wires were used to "replicate joints and muscles." Flapping tests were conducted, but the model was not flown.

Ramezani et al. (2016) built *Bat Bot* (B2), a "flapping machine with 5 degrees of actuation," loosely based on *Rousettus aegyptiacus* (the Egyptian fruit bat). The 93 g model had a flight speed of 4 m/s in untethered indoor flight, flapping 10 times a second.

Festo (2018) produced a 580 g semi-autonomous BionicFlyingFox capable of flight. Bie et al. (2021) designed and flew a Li-Po-powered UAV (289 g) modeled on the large flying fox; it flew outdoors for five minutes at 6.8 m/s. For a recent review of bat-inspired UAVs, see Bie et al. (2022).

Insect-Inspired Unmanned Ornithopters

The motivation to create insect-inspired unmanned ornithopters has come from two quite different directions. The first is from the intelligence, military, law enforcement and rescue communities, which saw a need for small, highly maneuverable reconnaissance vehicles (Ansari 2004). The second is from biologists who wish to use "mechanical models to study insect flight" (Sane 2003).

In the 1970s, the CIA developed the Insectothopter. It looked very much like a dragonfly, weighed just 1 g, and had a 9 cm wingspan and a 6 cm body length. It contained a listening device. A laser beam acted to guide it and as a data link. The wings were flapped by a "miniature fluidic oscillator," driven by a "propellant-produced gas." (The vented gas also provided supplemental jet propulsion.) It could "fly 200 meters in 60

Part II: Unconventional Propulsion

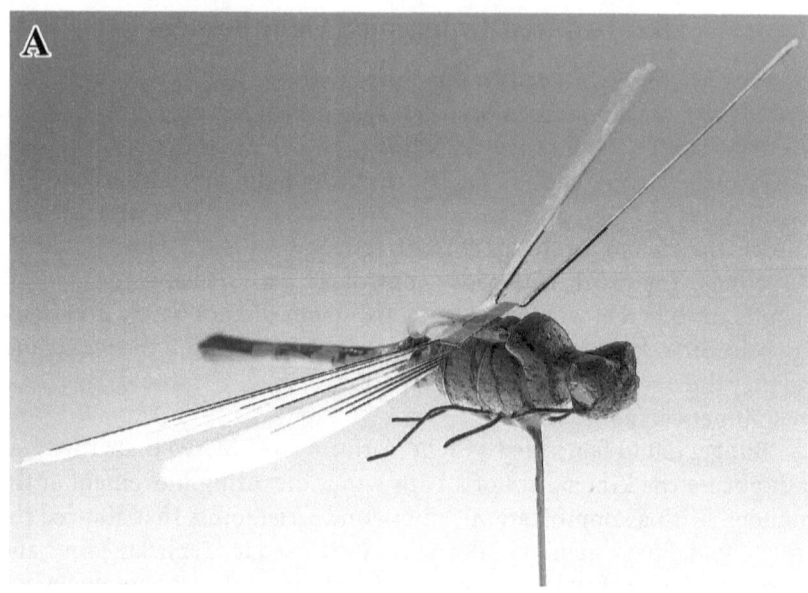

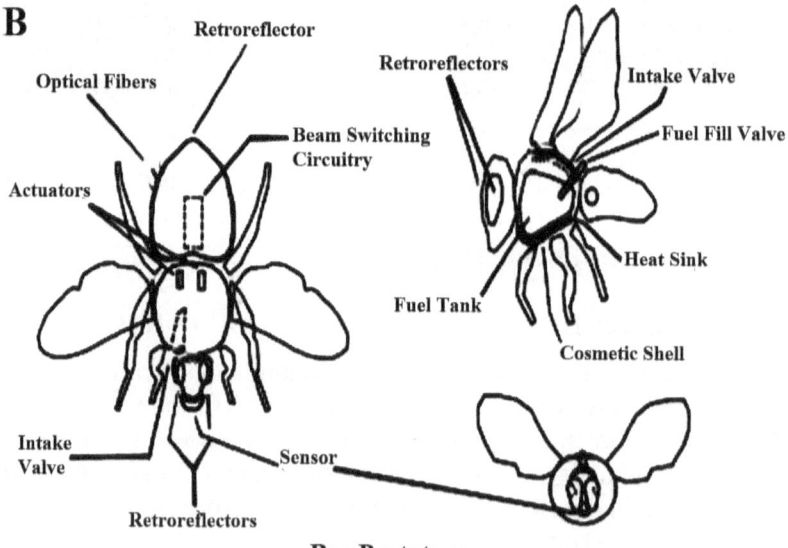

Bee Prototype

A. The dragonfly insectothopter, mounted on a pin (CIA 2024a). *B.* The first concept for an insectoid listening device was based on the bumblebee, but it was abandoned because (1) bumblebees fly erratically, and a straight-line flight by the spy device would be suspicious, and (2) bumblebees sting, and the device might be swatted. Image is frame capture from CIA 2024b, 0:19/1:15.

11. Biomimetic Propulsion (Flapping and Undulating)

seconds." Unfortunately, it could not cope with a crosswind over 5 mph (Central Intelligence Agency 2024a, 2024b).

The Li-Po battery-powered DelFly (21 g, 2005), DelFly II (16 g, 2007), DelFly Micro (3 g, 10 cm wingspan, 2008), and DelFly Explorer (20 g, autonomous flight, 2013) were small, had flapping wings, and were capable of both hovering and forward flight (MAVLab 2024). All were tailed designs; nonetheless, the designers declared "that DelFly employs at least two of the high-lift mechanisms that are found in insect flight. First, we think that DelFly creates a stable leading edge vortex.... Second, we think DelFly benefits from the clap and fling mechanism of aero-elastic wings." The DelFly wings were "based on the forewing of a dragonfly (Sympetrum vulgatum)" (Lentink et al. 2010).

The first tailless model in this series was the DelFly Nimble (29 g, 33 cm wingspan, 2018). Its top speed is 7 m/s, and it can travel a kilometer at its cruising speed of 3 m/s. It can hover for five minutes, flapping its wings

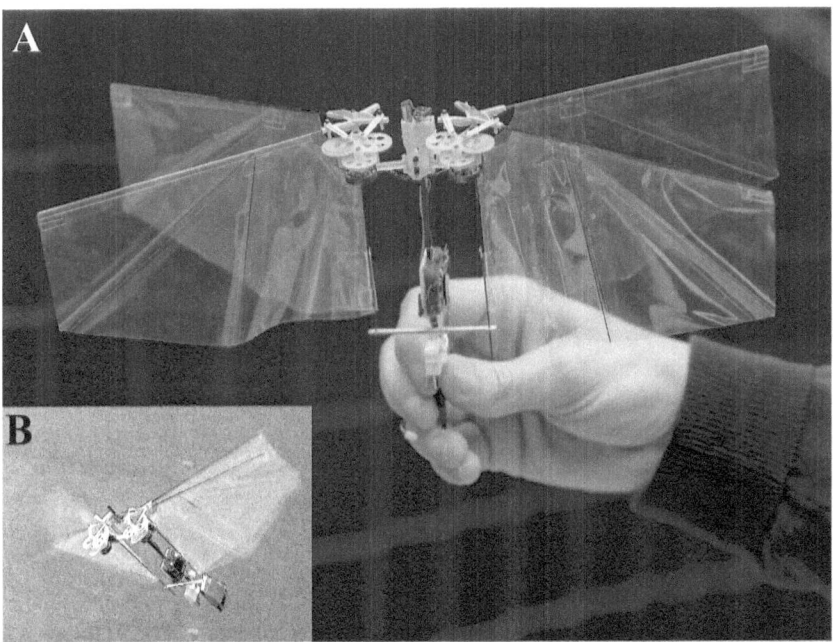

A. DelFly Nimble held in hand, note the two pairs of wings (Delfly image 20180124-IMG_4986.jpg). *B.* DelFly Nimble in flight (Delfly image dsc_0483-2.jpg.). Both CC BY SA 4.0 licenses, courtesy of the Technical University of Delft. Both images have been cropped. https://surfdrive.surf.nl/files/index.php/s/q9uo1na7ldYlVzv#/files_mediaviewer/dsc_0483-2.jpg.

17 times a second, and fly sidewise. Its two pairs of wings can flap at different frequencies to make a banked turn (MAVLab 2024; Karasek et al. 2018).

Robobees are even smaller (80 mg, 3 cm wingspan) than the DelFly Micro, but they are incapable of free flight as they require a power tether. Despite the name, they are modeled (loosely) on flies, not bees. (The name was given because another research goal was to use them in cooperative swarms.) Their wings use dual piezoelectric actuators; they are capable of flapping (120 hertz [Hz]) as well as passive pitch rotation (Ma et al. 2013).

KUBeetle-S examined the ability of the rhinoceros beetle (*Allomyrina dichotoma*) to survive a midair collision. The beetle has two pairs of wings, but only the hind wings are used for flying. The latter have "an origami-type construction that folds up when resting and expands when needed during flight." This "can partially fold during collisions, acting as a sort of shock absorber. After the collision, the wing then snaps back automatically to the wing shape to allow the beetle to resume flying" (Yirka 2020).

The robotic beetle has only one pair of wings, but they can passively fold and unfold. "The tests show that the folding mechanism enables the robot to maintain stable flight after wing-tip collision. In the absence of the folding mechanism, the robot tumbles" (Phan et al. 2020b).

The robot was Li-Po powered (160 mAh) and weighed 15.8 g, with a wing loading of 37.5 N/m^2. It could hover for 8.8 minutes (flapping at 18 Hz), fly forward, backward or sideways at 2.5 m/s, and it could fly outdoors if the wind speed was less than 1 m/s (Phan et al. 2020a).

Ray-Inspired Unmanned Ornithopter

The Festo AG Air_ray winged airship mimicked the underwater movement of a manta ray: "The propulsion is effected by a flapping-wing mechanism. The wing module, which can be moved up and down by a servo drive unit, has a structure like that of the tail fins of many fish. This structure consists of two alternating pressure and tension flanks flexibly connected by ribs. When one flank is subjected to pressure, the geometrical structure automatically bends in the direction opposed to the force applied. This concept, named Fin Ray Effect®, was developed by Leif Kniese. In Air_ray it serves as an active structure. A servo drive unit pulls on the two flanks longitudinally in alternation, thus moving the wing module up and down." The power supply was two 8-volt Li-Po cells, each 1,500 mAh. The airship had a length of 2.8 m, a wingspan of 4.2 m, and a weight of 1.60 kg (Festo 2009).

11. Biomimetic Propulsion (Flapping and Undulating)

Analysis

Fixed-wing aircraft cannot fly at speeds below their stall speed. While rotary-wing aircraft (helicopters) are capable of low forward speeds and even hover, they have been predicted to be less energy efficient than flapping-wing aircraft at low speeds, at least in the case of micro air vehicles (Ansari 2004, 11).

How Insects Fly

The smallest flyers are insects, and designers seeking to miniaturize UAVs have looked to insects for inspiration. The smallest flying insect is the *Kikiki huna*, a fairyfly wasp, with a body length of about 158 microns (Huber and Noyes 2013); human hair has a diameter of 17/181 microns (Wikipedia).

Some butterflies and moths are large enough to have wing kinematics similar to those of birds. Indeed, the largest modern flying insect is the Queen Alexandra's Birdwing butterfly, with a 12.5 in. wingspan (Page and Jenkins 2005). On the other hand, hummingbirds have wingspans less than 5 in. and, like many insects and unlike other birds, are capable of sustained hover.

The Reynolds number (Re) indicates the relative importance of inertial and viscous forces in determining the airflow around a flying object. The higher the Re, the less important viscous forces are. "Large birds have a wing chord Re larger than 15000 but still within 1×10^5 range, small birds to large insects having Re between 1000 and 15000, and small insects having Re between 100 and 1000" (Abas et al. 2016). "Even at a Reynolds number of 10, inertial forces are roughly an order of magnitude larger than viscous forces," but the viscous forces at low Re cannot be ignored (Sane 2003).

Schirber (2020) wrote: "Bird-like flapping—up and down at a low angle of attack—would only generate enough lift for a centimeter-sized insect if it flapped its wings extremely fast." But insects can't flap their wings fast enough. "Rather than flapping up and down like a bird, insects move their wings forward and backward. During the forward stroke, the wings are tilted at roughly 45° with respect to the horizontal, thus pushing down on the air, which exerts an upward force, or lift, on the insect. During the backward stroke, the wings are flipped over to 135° so that they continue to push down on the air and generate lift."

However, that isn't quite right, either. Flapping, sweeping, and wing rotation **all** occur. In, say, a dragonfly, the "wing tip traces a figure-8

Part II: Unconventional Propulsion

pattern with respect to the wing root" (Abas et al. 2016). The axis of symmetry of the pattern may be inclined (pitched) or horizontal.

"The wing stroke of an insect consists of two translational phases, the downstroke and upstroke, separated by two rotational phases, pronation and supination." As the wing accelerates into the downstroke (or upstroke), it carries some of the surrounding air with it. This is called *added* or *virtual mass* by aerodynamicists, and it increases the forces acting on the wing. In the middle of the stroke, leading-edge vortices (LEVs) form; these remain attached to the wing and prevent stall.[1] Consequently, the wings may meet the air at a relatively high angle of attack, which increases lift. When the insect rotates its wing, it "generates circulation in the surrounding air" (Kramer effect). If the wing flip occurs before the stroke is reversed, it increases lift. It creates negative (downward-directed) lift if it occurs after stroke reversal (Chin and Link 2016).

Insects (and birds) may occasionally enhance lift further by a mechanism known as "clap and fling. After the upstroke, the leading edges of the wings may meet during the 'clap.' This causes the opposing air circulations on each wing to cancel one another out, reducing the vorticity ... shed from the trailing edge during the next stroke. Consequently, the wings can generate circulation at a faster rate and extend the period of lift generation during the following downstroke." During the fling, the "leading edges separate first," creating a "region of lower pressure between the wings [that] sucks in fluid," thereby increasing circulation (Chin and Link 2016).

Modeling of Insect Flight

In order to predict the behavior of insect-inspired ornithopters, we might reasonably look at the available models of insect flight. However, this is something of a quagmire.

In 1934, the eminent entomologist Antoine Magnan wrote, "First prompted by what is done in aviation, I applied the laws of air resistance to insects, and I arrived, with M. Sainte-Laguë, at the conclusion that their flight is impossible" (8).[2] This passage is often quoted out of context.

In the very next paragraph, Magnan (1934) acknowledged that insects in fact generate enough lift to support their own weight and enough propulsive force to fly. "However, there is no reason to be surprised that the results provided by the calculation do not agree with reality." Magnan was inclined to blame this discrepancy on lack of knowledge of the "aerodynamic qualities of an insect wing." However, the problem was likely more pervasive.

11. Biomimetic Propulsion (Flapping and Undulating)

We do not know precisely how Magnan and Saint-Laguë analyzed insect flight. The analysis of Hoff (1919) "was based on the forward flight of insects and did not account for the flapping motion of their wings" (Ansari 2004, 15). Vance (2009, 4) opines that Magnan and Saint-Laguë likewise "applied simple, fixed-wing aerodynamic theory."

There was in fact some early theoretical work by Knoller (1909) and Betz (1912) on flapping-wing aerodynamics, but the first major analysis was by Garrick (1936), and his predictions were not verified experimentally until 1939 (Goodheart 2011). Garrick found that the efficiency of propulsion was "50% for infinitely rapid oscillations and 100% for infinitely slow flapping" (7).

For a fixed-wing flyer, a steady-state model may be used. A steady-state model assumes that "the aerodynamic forces acting on wings remain constant." Steady-state models of animal flight have been based on actuator disk theory (applied by Hoff to insects in hovering flight) and lifting line theory (applied by Philips to birds in 1981; Xuan et al. 2020).

The next level of sophistication is a quasi-steady (QS) state analytic model. In essence, this dissects a flapping motion into a series of discrete views, like frames from a film, and in each view, steady-state analysis is applied to the wing-flapping velocity, position and shape at that moment. The lift and drag forces are then added up over the entire flapping cycle. Osborne (1951) "was probably the first to use a QS model to predict flapping wing aerodynamic forces," and he applied it to insects (Xuan et al. 2020).

The catch is that a QS model has no memory; what the wing did in one moment doesn't affect the flow of air about it in the next moment. Thus, it cannot address the *Wagner effect*; the circulation and lift do not immediately attain steady-state values (Dudley and Ellington 1990).

Whether the quasi-steady flow assumption is valid depends on the "value of the reduced frequency parameter." This is the "ratio of the flapping velocity of the wings to the forward flight velocity."[3] When this is small, steady flow dominates. "Hovering flight presents the extreme condition where the flight velocity is zero and the reduced frequency becomes infinite" (Ellington 1984, 3).

In 1990, Dudley and Ellington reported that in bumblebees, "quasi-steady aerodynamic mechanisms are inadequate to explain even fast forward flight."

One solution to the problem was to add corrections based on experimental data, thus creating a semiempirical QS model. The problem with such models is that their range of applicability is uncertain (Xuan et al. 2020).

Part II: Unconventional Propulsion

A second solution is to use an unsteady-state analytic model. These address "the unsteady phenomena related to vortices.... Compared with steady-state models, unsteady models can provide more details of the flow field, but the computational cost is higher." Unsteady "models for flapping flight are relatively new" and "have limitations" (Xuan et al. 2020).

The third solution is computational fluid dynamics. It potentially can come closer to capturing reality than any analytic model, but it requires "large computational resources" and "empirical data both for validation and relevant kinematic input" (Sane 2003).

Wings

An ornithopter may have one, two or three pairs of flappable wings. In the two-pair case, they may be mounted forward and back (tandem) rather than stacked vertically. The ornithopter may also have fixed lifting surfaces, which only provide lift if there is forward motion.

Most insects have two pairs of wings. In *Odonata* (dragonflies and damselflies), the four wings are controlled independently. However, in *Diptera* (true flies) and *Coleoptera* (beetles), only one pair is used to fly. In *Hymenoptera* (ants, bees, wasps), the forewings and hind wings are attached. However, the "abdomen of butterflies moves in an anti-phase manner with its flapping wing motion" (Abas et al. 2016).

Insect wings have a variety of sophisticated nuances that are generally lacking in robotic imitations.

A flexible wing "allows the wing to passively change its relative angles of attack and camber during flapping" (Abas et al. 2016). Insect wings are veined membranes, and consequently, the spanwise and chordwise stiffness may differ. Some natural fliers can actively change the shape of the wing.

Insect wings exhibit a variety of textures and forms that have aerodynamic effects. Dragonflies have corrugated wings (Abas et al. 2016), and "the smallest flying insects often have bristled wings resembling feathers or combs" (Lin et al. 2023).

Transmission

The transmission converts the human, motor or engine output into a flapping motion of the wing. A "four-bar crank rocker mechanism is commonly used to transform the rotational motion of an electric motor into a harmonic flapping motion." An alternative is a slider crank mechanism (Abas et al. 2016).

11. Biomimetic Propulsion (Flapping and Undulating)

For micro air vehicles, robotic artificial muscles may be considered. These take a variety of forms, including piezoelectric, electroactive polymer, shape memory alloy, shape memory polymer, pneumatic, twisted string, and super-coiled polymer actuators (Zhang et al. 2019).

In piezoelectric actuation, an electric field is applied, which causes the piezoelectric material to be deformed by about 0.1%. This displacement may be amplified, perhaps tenfold (Abas et al. 2016).

Electroactive polymers are activated by applying an electric field. In the DEA (dielectric elastomer) type, the polymer is compressed in one direction as a result of Coulomb charge attraction, so it expands in other directions. There is also the IPMC (ionic polymer-metal composite) type, in which the electric field causes bending deformation (Zhang et al. 2019).

The flapping rates achieved by insects are higher than those for birds. Two different flapping actuation modes are known. In some (*Lepidoptera, Orthoptera, Odonata*), the muscles are activated "synchronously with each wingstroke," and a flapping rate of 100 Hz (flaps./s) is achievable. In others (*Diptera, Hymenoptera, Coleoptera*), the "flight power muscles possess a delayed stretch activation response2, which causes wing oscillations to self-excite without the need for regular timing from the nervous system" (Gau et al. 2023). The mosquito can flap at 800 Hz (Ramos 2023).

Lynch et al. (2022) reported building an asynchronously flapping, insect-scale flapping wing (not a complete flying robot) using a piezoelectric "PZT bimorph bending actuator"; Mingjing et al. (2023) used electrostatic actuation.

Undulation

Michel et al. (2008) proposed a bionic airship that mimics a fish's body motion by deforming (a) the envelope of the rear lifting body and (b) flapping an aft tail. This was realized in a 3 m long, 910 g blimp using dielectric elastomers, with two actuators at the base of the tail and two a little aft of amidships. Thus, there were two bending body segments. The blimp caudal (tail) fin was modeled on that of a rainbow trout, whereas the body shape was penguin-like. There were passive dorsal and ventral fins. The maximum speed achieved was 1.55 m/s, with a flapping frequency of 84 flaps a minute.

In a dielectric elastomer, "a passive elastomer film is sandwiched between two compliant electrodes," forming a capacitor. Applying a voltage across the electrodes squeezes the film, and since it is "essentially incompressible," reducing the thickness of the film causes it to

Part II: Unconventional Propulsion

spread out. "As soon as the voltage is switched off and the electrodes are short-circuited the capacitor contracts back to its original shape" (Michel et al. 2008).

A later design by the same research group (Jordi et al. 2010, fig. 11) was 9 m long, featured three bending points (two amidships and one at the base of the tail), and omitted the passive fins. With an undulating frequency of 0.2 Hz (12/min), the speed was about 0.27 m/s if only the fin was undulated and about 0.42 if the body also participated (fig. 13). The efficiency of the actuator system is low (about 6%; 8).

12

Miscellaneous Propulsion Methods

Rocket Propulsion

Both rockets and jets propel themselves forward by ejecting a high-velocity stream of combustion gas. However, a jet engine inhales the oxygen needed for combustion from the atmosphere, while a rocket engine has an internal supply of oxygen in the form of an oxidizer.

Rocket engines are essential (and conventional) for spacecraft, which must travel in a vacuum. They are also conventional for unmanned explosive-carrying projectiles; the advantage of a rocket over an artillery shell is that it carries its own propulsion system.

However, rockets are not conventional for manned airplanes, and those are the focus of this section.

History

Boulton (1868), in a patent generally relating to jet propulsion, proposed that "mixtures of inflammable gases may be ignited ... and thus produce the required jet by its escape through a suitable orifice" (Brewer and Alexander 1893, 46). The same year, Hunter received a patent disclosing both stern rockets and rocket-tipped propellers (51). Johnson, in 1887, proposed propelling an airship by the expulsion of the combustion products of ammonium nitrate, petroleum and charcoal (112).

Alexander Lippisch's Ente was essentially a sailplane modified experimentally for rocket propulsion. It made its first successful flight in 1928, using two sequentially fired black powder rockets of 44 lb thrust apiece. On its next flight, the pilot attempted to fire both rockets simultaneously, and one exploded (Boyne 2004).

Opel, in the meantime, had been developing rocket cars for racing.

Part II: Unconventional Propulsion

Julius Hatry designed a plane for him, which Opel equipped with 16 black powder rockets, with a total thrust of 800 lb. Its first (and only successful) flight was a little over a minute long and reached a speed of 90 mph. Unfortunately, it crashed on landing (Boyne 2004).

The Heinkel HE 176, which made its first powered flight in 1939, used a liquid propellant (hydrogen peroxide; Sutton 2006, 11).

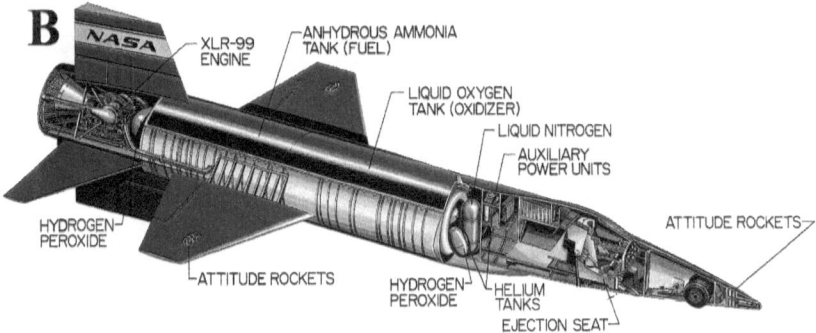

A. NASA photograph (June 23, 1967) of the X-15A-2 (EC67–1776) just after it received "a full-scale ablative coating to protect the craft from the high temperatures associated with hypersonic flight" and a "white sealant coat." B. NASA cutaway drawing (Jan. 20, 1962) of the X-15 (courtesy NASA).

12. Miscellaneous Propulsion Methods

While the above were all experimental airplanes, in 1944, Germany introduced the Messerschmitt ME 163 Komet interceptor. In the production version (163B), the fuel was a mixture of hydrazine hydrate and methyl alcohol, and the oxidizer was hydrogen peroxide. This provided 1,700 kg of thrust, giving it a climb rate of 3,600 m/min and a maximum speed of 960 km/h, but it had a tendency to overshoot its target (Bishop 2002, 324).

The most famous rocket-propelled airplane was probably the Bell X-1, the first airplane to exceed the speed of sound (Mach 1; Gorn and De Chiara 2022, 7). The Bell X-15 was the first hypersonic (Mach 5) airplane (it reached Mach 6.7) and flew high enough to qualify its crew as astronauts (ix, 71).

There have been some experimental rocket-jet hybrids, such as the Republic XF-91 Thunderceptor (flight tested, 1949). It had a Reaction Motors XLR11 rocket engine (4,000 lb of thrust) and a General Electric J47 turbojet (5,000 lb of thrust). Only two were built, and the rocket engine on one of them exploded (Yenne 2001, 112–114).

An unusual application of rocket propulsion was to helicopters. The Swisscopter Dragonfly DF1 "has peroxide-powered rocket engines on the tips of its main blades, with a mechanical take-off to drive the tail-rotor. An 18.5 gallon tank of concentrated peroxide provides up to 50 minutes of flight at 40 mph"; the empty weight is 234 lb, and the takeoff weight is 500 lb (Ragan 2010; Quick 2010). It had its "origins in a 1950/60s U.S. military project to help downed airmen escape from enemy territory by parachuting a foldable helicopter that could be assembled and then flown to safety" (Helicopter Museum 2017). It is quite similar to the Rotorcraft RH-1 (1954), but that was "designed to carry one fully armed soldier short distances" and had a cruising speed of 70 mph (Bowers 1990, 86).

Analysis

The theory of rocket flight was first developed by the Russian school-teacher Konstantin Eduardovich Tsiolkovskiy (1857–1935). Despite his humble background, he was "unanimously elected a member of the [Petersburg Physico-Chemical] Society" (Sloop 1978, 252–253). He showed that the rocket velocity is linearly and "directly proportional to the rocket exhaust jet velocity."

He also recognized that the exhaust jet velocity would depend in part on the "heat that could be generated per kilogram of burning propellants." In 1903, he proposed the use of liquid oxygen and liquid hydrogen for propulsion (even though "some heat would be expended in converting" them "to their gaseous states"; Sloop 1978, 254–255). The oxygen is the oxidizer, and the hydrogen is the fuel, and together they form the propellant.

The principal disadvantage of liquid hydrogen, other than the difficulty of producing it, was its low density. In 1934, he therefore proposed benzene and ethylene as alternative fuels. "Among oxidizers, he considered ozone, oxygen, nitrous oxide, nitrogen dioxide, and nitrogen tetroxide" (Sloop 1978, 257).

Tsiolkovskiy rejected solid propellants "on the basis of their low energy and the danger of unexpected explosion" (Sloop 1978, 257). In 1909, Robert Hutchings Goddard (1882–1945) calculated that it would take "nearly 50 times as much gunpowder as hydrogen-oxygen for the same mission" (Sloop 1978, 258).

The first use of liquid propellant was probably by Goddard in 1920: ether initially and later gasoline. He used liquid oxygen as the oxidizer (Sloop 1978, 258–259, 263). However, Goddard never actually experimented with hydrogen-oxygen.

Liquid rocket propellants include hydrogen, hydrazine and ammonia (Sloop 1978, 76). Diborane was considered in the late 1940s but proved problematic (75).

Oxygen, despite its name, is not the most effective oxidizer; that distinction goes to fluorine. The combination of liquid hydrogen and liquid fluorine was tested from 1950 to 1951, albeit for use in unmanned rockets (Sloop 1978, 26–28). Other oxidizers that have been considered for rocket use include hydrogen peroxide and chlorine trifluoride.

In sufficiently concentrated form, hydrogen peroxide will decompose in the presence of a catalyst such as metallic silver or manganese dioxide. On the Dragonfly DF1, inert gas is used to pressurize concentrated hydrogen peroxide,[1] and it is forced through "a nozzle with a silver-coated screen" (Ragan 2010). The decomposition produces steam, which is what actually propels the blade tip.

Ramjet Propulsion

The ramjet was invented by René Lorin (1877–1933). In a conventional turbojet engine, intake air passes into a compressor prior to mixing with the fuel. A ramjet has no compressor; the air is compressed because it is forced into the engine inlet by the airplane's forward motion, usually at least supersonic. Thus, a ramjet is necessarily a supplemental

12. Miscellaneous Propulsion Methods

propulsion system, albeit a self-sustaining one. Its advantage is its high thrust-to-weight ratio.

Ramjet designs have been used primarily in missiles. However, there have been a few airplane designs. Focke-Wulf proposed several ramjet interceptors near the end of World War II. The Lockheed *X-7* (first flight 1951) was an unmanned ramjet airplane with a rocket booster; it evolved into the Lockheed AQM-60 Kingfisher target drone.

Hermeus (2024) has proposed a hypersonic (Mach 5) airplane with a hybrid (turboramjet) engine. It begins operation in turbojet mode, and when it reaches a high enough speed (Mach 3), "Chimera bypasses the incoming air around the turbojet and the ramjet takes over completely." Hermeus demonstrated a successful bench test transition in November 2022.

Magnus Effect Devices

A rotating cylinder, placed in an airflow with its axis perpendicular to the flow direction, develops a lift force (the Magnus force) that is perpendicular to both. In the 1920s, Flettner proposed to use vertical axis cylinders to propel a water ship. If, by way of example, the cylinders are rotating counterclockwise (as viewed from above) and the wind is from the east, the lift force will move the ship northward (Borg 1986, I:18). The wind may be natural or artificial wind generated by also propelling the ship more conventionally.[2]

Flettner conducted experiments and "concluded that a rotor could produce 8 to 10 times the driving force of conventional sails having the same projected area" (Borg 1986, 6). He retrofitted the barkentine *Buckau* (renamed the *Baden-Baden*) as a rotor ship, with rotatable cylinders fore and aft. It crossed the Atlantic in both directions. Not only could the rotor ship "be sailed much closer to the wind than was possible with the conventional sail plan," but it "was also possible to steer the vessel by changing the rotational speed of the rotor sails and even to sail in reverse" (Borg 1986, I:8).

There were several proposals to use rotating cylinders with airplanes. However, the goal there was normally to use them as high-lift devices, and for that purpose, they were usually mounted on a fixed lateral (or occasionally, longitudinal) axis.

In 1934, La Fon received a patent on an airplane equipped with "a lifting element mounted for rotation about a horizontal axis." The necessary

Part II: Unconventional Propulsion

wind was to be generated by a movable "centrifugal blower" positioned "for impelling a continuous blast of air in a horizontal direction against its surface for one side." While figure 1 depicts fore and aft elements rotating on axes parallel to the airplane's lateral axis, figure 2 shows both elements with axes in the airplane's sagittal plane and tilted from the horizontal "to produce a component of movement in a forward direction." (This would require a corresponding shift in the position and orientation of the blower.[3])

A cylinder of circular cross section is not capable of autorotation—that is, if placed in a wind, it will not start turning; it must be driven by an engine or motor (Seifert 2012). However, other shapes can exhibit a Magnus effect that does experience autorotation. La Fon (1934) proposed lifting elements with curved vanes, which would autorotate, as well as corrugated cylinders, which would not.

Seifert (2013) proposed a hybrid rotor in which a cycloidal propeller (transverse flow rotor) is mounted concentrically around a Magnus cylinder. These are to be mounted parallel to the transverse axis of the airplane. The cycloidal propeller not only provides forward propulsion, but it also generates the airflow about the Magnus cylinder necessary for the latter to provide lift.

Electrokinetic Propulsion

The term *electrokinetic propulsion* is a rather vague one, encompassing several propulsion mechanisms reliant in some way on an electric field.

Ion thrusters work by first ionizing gas molecules and then accelerating them. In an electrostatic thruster, they are accelerated by an electric field. In an electromagnetic thruster, they are accelerated by the combined action of electric and magnetic fields. The "characteristics of ion thruster are small thrust and high specific impulse." Consequently, they are best suited for vacuum or near-vacuum flight, where air resistance is minimal (Zheng et al. 2020).

In general, they have been used in spacecraft that carried the propellant (e.g., xenon) into space with them and ionized it. However, it has been proposed that "atmosphere-breathing electric propulsion" could be used in low or very low Earth orbit (LEO; VLEO). Using air molecules as propellant would permit obvious weight savings (Zheng et al. 2020).

Spektor and Jones (2021) warn that it "can only work in the sliver of altitudes where air molecules exist in sufficient abundance to provide propellant for the thruster but where the density of these molecules does not cause excessive vehicle drag to exceed the thrust produced by the vehicle."

12. Miscellaneous Propulsion Methods

The required orbital velocity in VLEO is about 8,000 m/s, but "a modern EP device can typically produce exhaust velocity around 20,000 m/s." The system would scoop up the air, ionize the air molecules, and accelerate them in the exhaust. For LEO and VLEO, the field generator would be solar powered.

Spacecraft, per se, are outside the scope of this work. However, in 1974, Walden Aerospace built the XEM-1, a "subscale proof-of-concept demonstrator for a solar-powered airship with … an ionic airflow electro-kinetic (IAF/EK) propulsion system." There was a tethered flight demonstration in 1977. In this propulsion system, "the flow of ions from emitter to collector imparts momentum to neutral air molecules, creating usable thrust for propulsion" (Lobner 2024).

The EK-1 was "a remotely controlled, self-powered, subscale model of a lenticular airship with a skin-integrated EK drive installed on the outer surface of the hull" built by Walden Aerospace in 2003. A photograph shows an indoor flight test conducted the same year (Lobner 2024).

It exploited the Biesfeld-Brown effect, "a device with two asymmetric electrodes is connected to a few kV voltage. A force is obtained [by] pushing the device towards the small electrode, regardless of the voltage polarity. Levitation can easily be obtained without any moving parts" (Einat and Kalderon 2014).

The Biesfeld-Brown effect is only poorly understood (and it didn't help matters that Brown considered it a form of antigravity), but it has been characterized as an ionic wind effect. Wilson (2009) was pessimistic about its prospects for airplane propulsion.

In 2018, MIT researchers claimed to have achieved the first steady-level flight of a fixed-wing airplane powered by an ion drive. The flight was indoors, and the remote-controlled airplane had a 5 m wingspan. They commented, "We show that conventionally accepted limitations in thrust-to-power ratio and thrust density, which were previously thought to make electroaerodynamics unfeasible as a method of aeroplane propulsion, are surmountable" (Xu et al. 2018; for flight video, Baker 2018). The airplane uses thin wires in front and thick wires in back, creating an asymmetric capacitor, and this was charged up to 20 kV. Energy efficiency was low, just 2.6% (Bogalsky 2018).

A Touch of Levity

For the reader's amusement, I close this chapter with a discussion of one of the odder concepts I have found in the patent literature.

Part II: Unconventional Propulsion

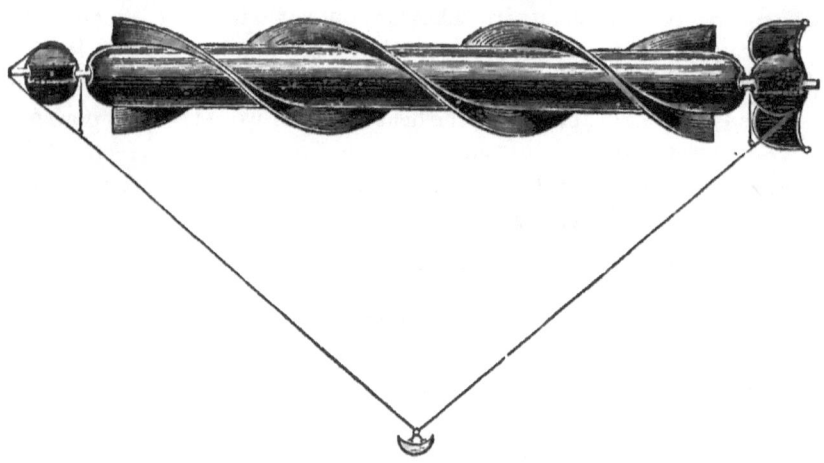

Lassie's navigable balloon. The structure suspended below the hull is an adjustable weight to control the pitch of the airship.

Lassie (1856), a mechanical engineer, proposed a cylindrical "navigable balloon" with a rigid hull "made of iron, copper or aluminum." This hull was to have "a projecting helical screw on its outer surface"—yes, the hull was to serve as its own propeller! The hull was to have an inner cylinder "in which ... the crew walk round in a similar manner to convicts in a treadmill." This fanciful aerostat was to be 900 ft long and have a crew of "three hundred..., half ... on duty at a time" (Brewer and Alexander 1893, 16).

Conclusion

The judgment of what is conventional and what is unconventional changes with time. A century and a half ago, all aerial vehicles were experimental. Steam power was conventional for ships and locomotives, but Giffard's steam-powered airship (1852) could only fly in still air. Andrews's *Aereon* (1863) could fly in light winds but failed to usher in an era of buoyancy-driven aerial propulsion. The internal combustion engine, while known since 1860, was not used in a vehicle until the 1880s and not in an airplane until the Wright Flyer (1903).

The traditional reason to experiment with unconventional fuels, engines and propulsion systems was to fly faster, longer or higher than the competition. In the last half century, other considerations have come into play: diminishing reliance on the ever-diminishing supply of fossil fuel and reducing air pollution.

Both solar-electric power and hydrogen fuel technologies have been positioned as environmentally friendly. The adoption of solar-electric has been slowed by the relatively low energy-to-weight ratio of the batteries and the adoption of hydrogen by the low energy density of even liquid hydrogen. Nonetheless, at the time of writing, solar-electric power appears to be on the cusp of finding several commercial niches: unmanned, long-endurance surveillance and communication airships and short-hop general aviation airplanes. The Pipistrel Velis Electro two-seater is intended primarily for pilot training.

I find it difficult to envision any future for steam propulsion, except perhaps for hobbyists. (There are still a few steam cars on the road.) While a steam engine can burn biofuel, the same is true, to a limited degree, of internal combustion engines, and they cannot compete with the latter on a thermal efficiency basis. Stirling engine development has been the darling of shady, fly-by-night promoters, and decades have been spent trying to get an airplane Stirling engine to work. Nuclear propulsion, despite its potential fuel savings, seems a nonstarter.

Diesel engine technology, of course, is well developed for its current

Part II: Unconventional Propulsion

truck and marine applications. The big advantage of diesel is its high thermal efficiency, and I would expect that the power-to-weight ratio of the diesel engine could be improved if the necessary research and development commitment were made. However, even if biodiesel were used, I would not call it a green technology.

Human-powered airplanes are likely to remain the domain of elite athletes attempting to test the limits of human potential. I see somewhat more of a market for human-powered airships; while they are unlikely to ever be a mainstream mode of personal transportation, the fact that the pilot may rest periodically without falling from the sky does expand both who can pilot them and how long they may stay in the air.

Buoyancy-driven propulsion and aerosail or wind-differential propulsion are most suitable for use as fuel-saving supplemental propulsion means for short-hop conventionally powered airships—for example, sightseeing or pleasure flights.

Motor-powered ornithopters, especially very small ones inspired by insects, are likely to be a growth area. Their development has been helped by advances in materials technology and hindered by uncertainties regarding flapping-wing aerodynamics.

It will be interesting to see how the definition of conventional aerial power and propulsion changes over the next decade.

APPENDICES

Appendix 1
Author's Airship Aerodynamics Standard Model

The performance data for many of the airships discussed in this book are limited, and the data for one airship might not be readily comparable to that for another.

However, the author's airship dynamics standard model may be used to make predictions of how they would have performed under the same conditions. It is certainly not perfect, but it is better than nothing.

The information required to predict drag, at a minimum, is the airship hull's volume and fineness (length-to-maximum diameter) ratio.

Aerodynamic Forces

The dynamic pressure is $0.5\,\rho v^2$, where ρ is the air density and v the airspeed. The air density is calculated for a given altitude according to the International Standard Atmosphere model.

Drag

Drag is the sum of the zero-lift drag and the lift-induced drag. The zero-lift drag force is the product of the dynamic pressure, the zero-lift drag coefficient, and the reference area for which the drag coefficient is defined.

For a wingless airship of the typical vertically symmetric hull profile, dynamic lift (and therefore lift-induced drag) is generated only if the airship is flying inclined (creating a nonzero angle of attack). Such is the natural state of affairs for airships using buoyancy-driven propulsion.

I calculate the zero-lift drag coefficient for a wingless airship as the product of the frictional drag coefficient, a shape factor, and a rigging factor. The shape factor is the ratio of the total drag on the bare airship hull to the frictional drag on that hull. The rigging factor is the ratio of the total

Appendices

drag on the fully rigged airship (hull and suspended cars) to the total drag on the bare airship hull.

Frictional Drag Coefficient (Cf)

This reflects the zero-lift drag on a flat plate parallel to the airflow. I use the Prandtl-Schlichting transitional flow formula for a critical Reynolds number of 5e5. The equation is then $Cf = 0.455 \times (\text{Log}[ReL])^{2.58} - (1{,}700/ReL)$, where ReL is the Reynolds number referenced to the length of the hull. It is valid for ReL $10^7 - 10^9$ (Balachandran 2011, 293). The Reynolds number (ReL) is the airspeed times the length times the ratio of the air's density to its dynamic viscosity (dependent on temperature).

Reference Area

I prefer to use the actual surface area as the reference area; airships with the same length and diameter may have different surface areas (and volumes) depending on their exact shape. For this purpose, I usually model the airship as having a forebody, an aftbody, and, optionally, a cylindrical midbody. The forebody and aftbody shapes I can calculate surface areas for are hemispheres, hemiellipsoids (prolate spheroids), cones, and the surface of revolution for a tangent ogive.

If this appears unsuitable, I use the volumetric area—the two-thirds power of the volume.

Shape Factor (SF)

I use Hoerner's (1965, 6–17) equations:

$SF = 1 + 1.5\,(D/L)^{1.5} + 7(D/L)^3$ (referenced to surface area) (equation 28); or

$SF = 4(L/D)^{1/3} + 6(D/L)^{1.2} + 24(D/L)^{2.7}$ (referenced to volumetric area) (equation 36).

Rigging Factor

I assumed that the rigging factor is two. (For rigid airships, Arnstein and Klemperer [1936, 77] reported that bare hull drag was 47% of total drag for the *Bodensee*, 53.2% for *Los Angeles*, and 57.1% for *Macon*.) The rigging factor was probably higher for early airships with external suspensions and nonaerodynamic cars. The War Department (1941, 29) recommended a rigging factor of 2.86 for "small nonrigids with open cars."

Appendix 1

Dorrington (2007a, 92) recommends the speed-dependent rigging factor 2.55 − (ReL/4.65e8). For the *Aereon*, this would have been 2.52–2.53 for speeds of 10–20 mph.

Lift

I used the standard equation for the lift force, which is analogous to the one for the zero-lift drag force, except that it uses a lift coefficient (C_L) referenced to planform area.

A 2D lift coefficient assumes that the span of the airfoil is infinite. Thin airfoil theory suggests a 2D lift coefficient (for wings) of $2\pi\alpha$, where α is the angle of attack in radians. The factor 2π is sometimes referred to as the lift curve slope. Thin airfoil theory is not entirely suitable for airships, which have a greater relative thickness than wings. My 2D lift coefficient, referenced to planform area, is taken from Sadraey's (2013, 178) empirical equation for airplane fuselages:

$1.8\pi(1 + 0.8/\text{LDRatio})\alpha$

This converges to $2\pi\alpha$ for an LD ratio of about 7:1.

Since airfoils are of finite span, the lift slope is multiplied by the Helmbold correction (Anderson 2017, 474), an empirical blend of the formulae for low and high aspect ratio (AR) airfoils intended to cover moderate aspect ratios, to obtain the necessary 3D lift coefficient.

For a wing, the aspect ratio is the square of the wingspan divided by the wing planform area. (Any part of the fuselage included between two wings is included in calculating both.) For an airship hull, the aspect ratio is the square of the maximum diameter divided by the hull planform area.

Lift-Induced Drag

I use the standard equation for the lift-induced drag force, which is analogous to the one for the zero-lift drag force, except that it uses a lift-induced drag coefficient (C_{Di}) referenced to planform area. That coefficient is calculated by the standard equation

$C_{Di} = C_L^2 / (\pi \times \text{Oswald efficiency} \times \text{AR})$

with the Oswald efficiency taken to be 0.8 (0.7–0.9 is typical for airplane wings). Note that since the lift coefficient is proportional to the angle of attack, the lift-induced drag must be proportional to the squared angle.

Stall

An important limitation of my standard aerodynamic model is that it does not adjust the lift calculation to reflect that an airfoil stalls (loses

Appendices

dynamic lift) at an extreme angle of attack (positive or negative) as a result of flow separation. There is no easy method of calculating, for an airship, either the critical angle of attack at which stall occurs or the lift lost at a particular angle beyond the stall angle. These are likely to be quantified, if at all, by wind tunnel studies or three-dimensional computational fluid dynamics.

When a stall occurs, the lift does not drop to zero. With the NACA 0012 airfoil (an idealized wing of infinite span), which is symmetric (like an airship), the XFOIL program predicts a critical stall angle of about $-18°$ and a lift coefficient of about -1.6 at $-20°$, as opposed to one of about -2 according to thin airfoil theory (Scott 2006). Indeed, Lambert (2002, 58) suggests that for a low-aspect airfoil like an airship, once the critical stall angle is exceeded, the lift coefficient becomes constant. However, that begs the question of what that critical stall angle is.

Appendix 2
Aerodynamic Modeling of Buoyancy-Driven Propulsion

In this appendix, I compare my modeling of the *Aereon* to Purandare's (2007) modeling of a hypothetical buoyancy-driven airship.

If the drag coefficient and lift coefficient are independent of the airspeed, then the angle of attack is independent of the airspeed and can be calculated from the glide path angle (or vice versa). Given the angle of attack, the total drag may be calculated and, from that, the steady-state airspeed. In other words, with speed-independent lift and drag coefficients, the pitch of the airship determines the glide path angle and angle of attack, and the amount of ballast dropped determines the airspeed for a given angle of attack (Purandare 2007, 43; Graver 2005, 94).

In the drag and lift formulae used by Graver (2005) for underwater gliders and Purandare (2007) for buoyancy-propelled airships, those coefficients are indeed independent of airspeed and also have a particular dependence on the angle of attack. If I used drag and lift formulae with the same properties, I could use the supplemental equations they provided (Graver 2005, 4.24) to quite quickly calculate the angle of attack and airspeed for a given glide path (or pitch) angle and ballast drop.

With my present drag model, that is not possible, as my coefficients are airspeed dependent. However, the Graver/Purandare equations can be used to guess trial values of the angle of attack and airspeed, and I can keep refining those guesses until the forces are essentially in balance.

Purandare proposed an airship with a 130 ft long main hull having the shape of a rotated NACA 0050 airfoil (a teardrop with a fineness ratio of 2:1) and swept wings having the cross section of a NACA 0020 airfoil, a wingspan of 338 ft and an aspect ratio of 3.77.

Appendices

Purandare predicted zero-lift drag forces separately for the hull and wing and added them together. Since the *Aereon* lacks a wing, I could ignore wing forces.

Purandare derived a zero-lift drag coefficient for the hull by quadratic fit to Young's data for turbulent flow over airship hulls of different fineness ratios (2007, 32). For the NACA 0050, this resulted in a drag coefficient of 0.0374, referenced to the volumetric area. This results in a higher drag than the formula I used.

The total bare hull drag for the *Aereon* is, of course, the drag per hull times the number of hulls. The individual hulls of the *Aereon* have a fineness ratio of 6.15. However, the hulls are touching, and so the *Aereon* might experience pressure drag more like a single hull with a fineness ratio of one-third that (2.05), or at least that of one with the diameter yielding the same cross-sectional area as the combined cross-sectional area of the three hulls. Nonetheless, for the purpose of further calculations, I decided to use the shape factor for a fineness ratio of 6.15, which is more favorable to the *Aereon*.

I multiply the total bare hull drag by a rigging factor of two to account for drag by the rudder, the control car, and the cables suspending it. In calculating drag, Purandare ignored the gondola and its cables.

Purandare chose to ignore the lift (and lift-induced drag) generated by his body, which he expected to be small compared to that of his large wing. I, of course, couldn't do this, since the *Aereon* is wingless.

Since the *Aereon*'s hulls are touching, I treated the three hulls as a single airfoil for lift calculation purposes. That is, I calculated the aspect ratio assuming the effective span to be the sum of the diameters of the three hulls rather than the diameter of a single hull. The aspect ratio for the *Aereon* is thus 0.53:1 rather than 0.17:1. This gave the *Aereon* a higher lift-to-drag ratio than would otherwise have been the case.

For his wing, Purandare analyzed 2D lift using XFOIL and fitted the data with a linear function of the angle of attack. (Note that the Sadraey equation is, too.) His lift slope was 6.30, whereas mine (for a different airfoil, of course) was 6.40. XFOIL predicted that the wing's lift curve became nonlinear at a 12° angle of attack and maxed out at 19°, so Purandare (2007, 25) decided that his airship should operate in the −4° to +4° range.

To correct to 3D, Purandare used a standard empirical equation for swept wings. Obviously, that doesn't apply for the *Aereon*, and XFOIL can't be used to analyze a solid of revolution like an airship hull.

Purandare looked at lift-induced drag for the wing, not the body; his wing's aspect ratio was 3.77, and he decided to set the Oswald efficiency to 1.

Appendix 2

It is possible to make some generalizations about performance if a simple aerodynamic model is used (Graver 2005; Purandare 2007). Both treated the zero-lift drag coefficient as constant (thus, independent of airspeed) and the lift coefficient as proportional to the angle of attack (per thin airfoil theory). Thus, the lift-induced drag coefficient was proportional to the squared angle of attack. The total drag coefficient would be the sum of the zero-lift and lift-induced drag coefficients independent of airspeed.

According to Purandare's (2007) analysis, the horizontal airspeed is proportional to the square root of the net buoyancy (equation 3.16). Also, the tangent of the glide path angle equals the reciprocal of the lift-to-drag ratio (equation 3.21), which means that it depends on the angle of attack alone (43).

Graver concluded that both the airspeed and the horizontal airspeed would be proportional to the square root of the net buoyancy (equations 7.1, 7.2). And Graver (2005, 158) agreed with Purandare regarding the glide path angle.

Some additional relationships of interest are shown by Purandare (2007, equation 3.16) and Graver (2005, equation 7.2).

Please remember that the assumptions underlying these conclusions do not apply to my standard aerodynamic model.

Appendix 3
Sensitivity of Aereon *Predictions to Modeling Method*

Given the length of the *Aereon* (80 ft), its Reynolds number (based on length) at 10 mph is 7.464e6. The transition between laminar and turbulent flow tends to occur at a Reynolds number between 3e5 and 3e6, depending on, for example, surface roughness. Hence, at 10 mph, I would expect the flow over the *Aereon* to be turbulent.

The Prandtl-Schlichting transitional flow formula I used assumes a critical Reynolds number of 5e5 and yields a frictional drag coefficient of 0.00292. A different critical Reynolds number would result in a somewhat different frictional drag coefficient. For the hulls of *Aereon* (taken individually), I used Hoerner's (1965) formula and calculated a shape factor of 1.128 based on its length-to-diameter ratio of 6.15. Other authorities suggest slightly different shape factors: Young (1939) 1.107; Dorrington (2007a), equation 8) 1.186; Torenbeek (1982) 1.160; Shevell (cited by Gur 2010, equation 11) 1.183; Boeing-Vertol (cited by Dorrington 2007a, equation 5) 1.267; and Jobe (1984) 1.273.

Insofar as the rigging factor is concerned, I assumed a value of two. Dorrington (2007a) suggested a formula that would have given the *Aereon* a rigging factor of 2.53 at 10 mph.

I also constructed a geometric and aerodynamic model of the 120 cords used in the *Aereon*'s suspension system and modeled each cord as a cylinder. The angles of attack of a horizontal wind would depend on whether the cord was running from the bow or amidships. The angles of attack of the cords were 40.9°–84.2°, putting them in the range in which Hoerner's (1965) analysis for inclined cylinders is valid. I used Abney's equation to calculate the drag coefficient. This varied from cord to cord, the average being 0.6267, and at 10 mph, the total drag on the 120 cords was 28.51 N. At that speed, the bare hull drag is 13 N/hull, or 39 N for the trihull.

Appendix 3

On top of the drag from the 120 envelope cords, add the drag from the control car, the 24 cords under the bag, and Andrews (open cockpit). So the assumed rigging factor of two seems quite optimistic.

So, in general, my standard model was rather kind to the *Aereon*.

Appendix 4
Reliability of Wind Speed Estimates by the Aereon Flight Eyewitnesses

The scientific instrument used to measure wind speed is the anemometer. The first anemometer was one in which the wind caused a hinged, hanging plate to be deflected from the vertical; Leon Battista Alberti described this in 1450 (Huler 2004, 189). The more practical cup anemometer was invented by Robinson in 1846 (191).

In 1849, the Smithsonian supplied weather instruments to telegraph companies, which reported back to the Smithsonian, and by 1860, 500 stations were furnishing daily telegraphic weather reports to the *Washington Evening Star*. Class 1 observers received a barometer, thermometer, wind vane, rain gauge, and sometimes a hygrometer—note, no anemometer—class 2 observers lacked the barometer, and class 3 had no instruments (Dipigny-Giroux and Mock 2009, 179).

The observers nonetheless estimated wind speed. The winds were reported on an arbitrary 0–10 scale (Doty 2004), and it is not known to me what guidance was given regarding the use of that scale. Likewise, in 1861, the U.S. Naval Observatory merely stated wind speed on an arbitrary 0–10 scale. It didn't obtain an anemometer until 1886 (Grice 2005a). Wind force was similarly recorded at the Smithsonian Institution, although it may well have had an anemometer (Grice 2005b).

The Civil War essentially disrupted the reporting; "urgent public business forced weather information off the telegraph lines" (Millikan 2007). It therefore seems safe to assume that wind speeds were not reported in the local newspaper (even NYC papers) for the day of the flight.

The version of the Beaufort wind scale that the Royal Navy adopted in 1838 only specified wind speeds for light (1–2 knots), gentle (3–4 knots) and moderate (5–6 knots) breezes; all stronger winds were defined by their

Appendix 4

effect on what sail a ship could carry. It was not otherwise correlated with wind speeds until the early 20th century (NMLA 2018).

Nor was it correlated with land effects (smoke, trees) until after the *Aereon* flight. In 1870, the Smithsonian developed a "direction for observations" for meteorological observers without anemometers, which provided a 0–4 wind scale that referred to land effects. Its points 1–4 corresponded to Beaufort forces 1, 4, 8 and 11 (Huler 2004, 195).

A formula correlating wind speeds to Beaufort number was proposed in 1903 (NMLA 2018), and there was a follow-up publication in 1906. The latter also proposed land observation equivalents for each Beaufort force (Huler 2004, 76ff). But these refinements, likewise, were after the *Aereon*'s ascent.

It has been suggested to me that one or more of the witnesses would have remembered what the apparent wind generated by riding a horse felt like. According to Heney (2021), the walk is about 4 mph; the trot, 8–12 mph; the canter, 12–15 mph; and the gallop, 25–35 mph. However, quite different speeds are specified for cavalry; the "maneuvering gallop" is 12 mph, and the "full gallop" is 16 mph (War 1898, 199).

Whether the witness would have known which gait corresponded to which speed seems questionable. And it is debatable whether the witness would accurately remember the tactile sensation and be able to use it to calibrate the wind felt on the day of the flight.

The modern Beaufort scale assumes only that the observer can tactilely distinguish between a wind strong enough to be felt on exposed skin (force 2, light breeze, 4–7 mph) and one that requires effort to walk against (force 7, near gale, 31–38 mph).

Appendix 5

Reliability of Estimates of the Ground Speed of the *Aereon*

Loftus (1996, 29) comments, "Many investigators produced evidence of marked inaccuracies in the reporting of details such as time, speed, and distance. The judgment of speed is especially difficult, and practically every automobile accident results in huge variations from one witness to another as to how fast a vehicle was actually traveling (Gardner 1933). In one test administered to air force personnel who knew in advance that they would be questioned about the speed of a moving automobile, estimates ranged from ten to fifty miles per hour. The car they watched was actually going only twelve miles per hour (Marshall 1966/1969, p. 12)."

Guzy et al. (1991) report their study, again with individuals "prepared to estimate speed as the event occurred." When the actual speed of the auto on an oval track was 15 mph, the estimates ranged from 3 to 20 mph (mean 11.2).

Vehicle speed estimates have been found to be more accurate when the vehicle was traveling away from the witness than when traveling toward the witness or on an offset course (Mazer et al. 1994). This was probably a combination of sound cues and extended viewing time. Sound cues would have been missing for the *Aereon*.

Karas (1959) commented, "Anything which gives the impression of speed results in a higher guess of actual velocity." It is conceivable that the very fact that the *Aereon* was flying would result in its speed being overestimated. (On the other hand, the absence of sound could have the reverse effect.)

Estimating speed, if it is to be done with any consistency, requires making conjoint estimates of distance and time. Distance is typically judged relative to a familiar measurement, such as (in modern America)

Appendix 5

the length of a football field. That doesn't mean that the witness has an undistorted recollection of that distance, however.

People also have a sense of the length of a second and a minute. But Mazer et al. (1994) said that "as a whole, witness estimates of time are even less reliable than the judgment of distance."

While the courts tend to accept that police officers can be trained to make good visual estimates of vehicle speed, the officers are sometimes tripped up by making inconsistent distance and time estimates about the incident in deposition or trial testimony.

In *United States v. Sowards* (2012), the Fourth Circuit Court of Appeals agreed with defendant that "the police lacked probable cause to initiate a traffic stop based exclusively on an officer's visual estimate—uncorroborated by radar or pacing and unsupported by any other indicia of reliability—that Sowards's vehicle was traveling 75 miles per hour ('mph') in a 70-mph zone." This was, the court noted, a "speed differential difficult for the naked eye to discern," and the court observed that "one cannot discern a speed of a vehicle measured in miles-per-hour without discerning both the increment of distance traveled and the increment of time passed."

There have been a few published studies of the accuracy of ground observers in recognizing an airplane and estimating its range (without which estimating speed is not possible). Wright's study (1966) was conducted in flat desert terrain, and the observer was given a warning that the airplane was inbound and the clock direction from which it was coming. The observers were given one week of training in airplane recognition and range estimation; the aircraft included jets (400 knots), props (100 knots) and copters (75 knots), with the planes flying at 100–300 ft and the copters under 100 ft. The ranges were underestimated for the distance where positive recognition occurred, and for observers without binoculars, the mean actual range was 2,350 m, and the mean estimated range was 1,430 m. The observers did best if they were at a 650 m offset from the airplane course, but their estimates were 28% short even then. Nothing indicates that Andrews's eyewitnesses expected to be asked to make written speed estimates. Hence, there was no reason for them to prepare themselves by, for example, determining the distances to various landmarks along the expected flight route, equipping themselves with a chronograph, or training themselves to estimate the speed of a distant vehicle.

Moreover, they were not asked to estimate the speed immediately after the flight; Andrews solicited the statements a month later, when Lincoln asked him for witness statements to corroborate his assertions. It's

Appendices

therefore unlikely that by then, they remembered the underlying judgments of time, range and angular movement that might have rationalized the estimate. Moreover, there was plenty of time for the witnesses' recollections to be "clouded or distorted by interaction with other witnesses" (Mazer et al. 1994, 193).

Nor do we know precisely how Andrews couched his request. Loftus and Palmer (1974) demonstrated that students who were first shown a film clip of a traffic accident and then asked to estimate the vehicle speeds were influenced by whether the question used a word suggestive of great speed or not (*smashed*, 40.8 mph vs. *contacted*, 31.8 mph).

Furthermore, Andrews was an authority figure in Perth Amboy—Andrews was mayor of Perth Amboy in 1849, 1853 and 1855 (History of Middlesex County)—and if he questioned a figure he thought too low, he might well have persuaded the witness to give Andrews the benefit of the doubt.

Finally, selection bias was likely. The witnesses were selected by Andrews. It is unlikely he would have sent Lincoln an unfavorable eyewitness report if there were any.

Appendix 6

*Analysis of Steam (Rankine)
Cycle Thermodynamics*

With certain basic information about a steam powerplant (engine inlet pressure and temperature, isentropic efficiency of expansion, condenser inlet pressure, condenser outlet pressure), the theoretical overall thermal efficiency of its Rankine cycle and the heat removed by the condenser per unit mass of steam can be calculated.

I implemented the model in Microsoft Excel. Steam thermodynamic data were obtained by calls to XSteam for Excel functions, which implement the International Association for Properties of Water and Steam Industrial Formulation 1997 (IAPWD IF97) standard formulation. Pressures may range up to 100,000 kPa and temperatures up to 2,000°C. For water, the critical pressure is 22,064 kPa.

The model was validated by entering data from examples in various thermodynamics textbooks and comparing the model's predictions to the textbook answers. The model allows for reheating and/or regeneration (with a single open feedwater heater).

Appendices

Table App 6–1: Thermodynamic Model Validation

Reference Example	BP kPa	BT °C	CP kPa	RHP kPa	OFW Bleed kPa	Comp Isen Eff	Exp Isen Eff	Ref Eff	My Eff
Çengel and Boles 9.1	3,000	350	75			100	100	26.00	26.02
Çengel and Boles 9.3(a)	3,000	350	10			100	100	33.50	33.44
Çengel and Boles 9.3(b)	3,000	600	10			100	100	37.30	37.26
Çengel and Boles 9.3(c)	15,000	600	10			100	100	43.00	43.03
Çengel and Boles 9.4	15,000	600	10	4		100	100	45.00	45.00
Çengel and Boles 9.5	15,000	600	10		1,200	100	100	46.30	46.32
Demirel 4.14	9,000	550	10	4,350		95	80	33.90	34.26
Demirel 4.15	8,200	500	20		350	100	100	39.80	39.86
Demirel 4.16	11,000	500	10		475	95	75	32.60	32.61
Demirel 4.17	9,000	500	10	850	850	100	100	42.80	42.72
Demirel 4.18 corrected*	11,000	500	10	2,000	475	100	80	34.00 *36.2	36.58

*Demirel (2007) gives two different values for H6 and for H8. If the H6 value set forth in the state table is used in his equation for Qin, the calculated efficiency changes to 36.2.

228

Appendix 7
Thermal Efficiency of Historical and Proposed Steam Locomotives

"At optimum performance, the modern steam locomotive can theoretically produce a maximum of 12 percent thermal efficiency, but 6 to 8 percent is the maximum achievable in actual operation" (Solomon 1998, 120). Or slightly more optimistically, "During the nineteenth century, the best steam engines operated at about 6 percent thermal efficiency, a figure that climbed to 10 to 12 percent by the end of the steam era" (Solomon 2000, 13). Unfortunately, Solomon doesn't clarify what losses he is considering in the calculation of thermal efficiency.

Usually, steam locomotive efficiency is quoted as overall drawbar efficiency. That's the product of 1–6 below. (Hudson [2011] comments, "It is generally accepted that American steam locomotives achieved thermal efficiencies of around 6% at the drawbar.") However, some sources will use overall wheel rim efficiency, which is the product of 1–5 below.

Table App 7–1: Efficiency Definitions	
Efficiencies	Definition
1) Boiler Combustion	(a) heat in combustion gas in firebox/heat content of fuel fired
2) Boiler Absorption	(b) heat in steam leaving boilers/(a)
3) Auxiliary	(c) heat in steam to cylinders/(b)
4) Cylinder (Cycle)	(d) piston work/(c)
5) Transmission	(e) wheel rim work/(d)
6) Drawbar	drawbar work/(e)

The following table states the thermal efficiency components for selected historic steam locomotives and estimated values (by Wardale

Appendices

1998) for proposed modifications of them (SGS is second-generation steam; TGS is third-generation steam):

Table App 7–2: Actual Efficiency Breakdown for Selected Steam Locomotives and Estimates for Proposed Modified Locomotives

	C&O 4-8-4 (1946) J-3 (3)	SAR 4-8-2 19D (4)	SAR 25NC (5)		China QJ 2-10-2 (1964–1988) (1)		Wardale (2)
Type	Std	Std	Std	Mod SGS	Std	Mod SGS	TGS
Boiler Pressure (kPa)	1,724	1,380	1,550	1,550	1,471	1,600	
Steam Temperature °C	405	331	366	450	400	460	
Efficiency							
1) Boiler Combustion	?	86	47	81	78%	87	95
2) Boiler Absorption	?	86	81	80	78.20	80	90
3) Auxiliary	93.60	?	10.50	96	93.10	94	96
4) Cylinder	10.20	11		14.40	16.40	19.05	22
5) Transmission	84.90	91	80.40	79	89	93	94
6) Drawbar		?			94	95	96
Overall Boiler (1)*(2)	45	74	38	65	61	67	85.50
Overall Pre-Transmission Product (1)–(4)	4.30	?	4.10	9.00	9.30	12.40	18.10
Overall Wheel Rim Product (1)–(5)	?	7.4	?	?	8.30	11.60	17.00
Overall Drawbar Product (1)–(6)	3.65	<6	3.30	7.80	7.80	11.00	16.30

Wardale (1998): (1) tables 71, 78; (2) 501; 1978 estimate of maximum values to be expected from conventional, noncondensing, coal-fired steam locomotive; (3) 397; (4) 51; typical steaming conditions; (5) 151, 184.

Appendix 7

The numbers above present only part of the picture, as we do not know the circumstances under which efficiency was measured. It can vary depending on the feedwater temperature, the fuel, the firing rate, the actual (vs. design) boiler pressure, and the moment in the piston stroke at which the inlet valve is closed (cutoff; Hudson 2011).

Steam proponents are quick to urge that the actual locomotive numbers can be bettered. Porta envisioned second-generation steam (SGS) as featuring 290–362 psi pressure, 450°C steam, double expansion, a gas producer combustion system, feedwater treatment to minimize scaling, corrosion, et cetera, feedwater and combustion air preheating, and an advanced (Lempor) exhaust system; Porta prophesied that this could achieve 14% efficiency. His concept of third generation steam (TGS) added higher pressure (870 psi) and temperature (550°C), triple expansion, and multistage feedwater and combustion air heating, hopefully achieving 21% efficiency, or even 27% if a condenser were provided (Rhodes 2024). But I am not inclined to put much faith in efficiency figures for hypothetical engines, and Wardale's (1998) claims for his own hypothetical SGS and TGS modifications were more conservative (highest pre-transmission efficiency was 18.1%).

Appendix 8
Methods of Improving Theoretical Cycle Efficiency of Steam Powerplants

Increasing Boiler Pressure

To safely increase the boiler pressure, a higher tensile strength structural metal (steel is superior to wrought iron), a greater metal thickness (thus, a heavier boiler), or a smaller diameter boiler is needed. "In practice, for locomotives there is an optimum in the range 200–300 psig" (Semmens and Goldfinch 2000, 152ff).

Steam locomotives were occasionally constructed with pressures above 350 psi, but none were particularly successful. Scale and corrosion problems increased, and distilled water had to be used in a closed circuit like the Schmidt system. The increased acquisition and maintenance costs were not justified by the efficiency gain (HPSLT 2018).

Superheating

Heating water beyond its boiling point not only increases efficiency but also decreases moisture content, rendering the steam less corrosive. However, higher temperatures can weaken or even melt the steam containment structure. For carbon steel, the highest allowable temperature is 950°F (Ganapathy 2001). Superheating may also dictate the use of high-temperature lubricants.

Using exhaust steam or combustion gases in the flue, temperatures can increase perhaps 24°F–40°F, which is sufficient to dry the steam. For a greater effect, the superheater must be exposed to hotter temperatures. In an integral superheater, the superheater is inside the firebox, preferably in a zone with temperatures of at least 1,000°F (the higher the temperature and the greater the superheater surface, the greater the heating effect).

Appendix 8

Or the superheater may be separately fired; it was found that the superheater could use a cheaper grade of coal. In early 20th-century stationary plants, integral superheaters could achieve up to 300°F and separately fired ones at least 500°F (but the efficiency of the separate superheater was only 25%; Ennis 1915, 428; Jude 1906, 252). At roughly the same time, typically up to 270°F superheat was used on locomotives (Marks and Baumeister 1916, 1215).

Feedwater Heating

Exhaust steam may be used to preheat the feedwater for the boiler. Preheating to 150°F theoretically increases cycle efficiency by 0.7% in a 105 psi boiler and 1% in a 285 psi boiler (Lamb 2003, 38). Exhaust steam, at best, increases the feedwater temperature to the atmospheric boiling point (212°F; Ennis 1915, 429); that is, it causes a noncondensing engine (open cycle) to have the efficiency of an atmospheric condensing (closed cycle) one.

A second option, used in the economizer, employs the waste gas from the furnace. This can achieve a feedwater temperature of 300°F or more (Ennis 1915).

Steam may be deliberately bled off at an intermediate expansion state to heat the feedwater (regenerative heating) instead of being used to do work. While less work is done, the heat is used more efficiently. Stationary powerplants may have a series of feedwater heaters at different bleed points.

In an open feedwater heater, the steam is mixed directly with the feedwater (or condenser water), and in a closed one, heat transfer is permitted without physical mixing. For the former, the feedwater temperature achievable is limited by the saturation temperature corresponding to the pressure of the hot water pump, whereas the latter requires scaling up the heat exchanger tubes (Wardale 1998, 157). Also, the former captures lubrication oil from the cylinder and mixes it into the boiler feedwater, whereas the additional piping of the latter is prone to leaks.

Both types were used on locomotives; the Worthington was open, and the Elesco and Coffin were closed (Barris 2018). The weight of a feedwater heater was perhaps 1 ton for a 200 ton locomotive, and it increased sustained boiler capacity by 15% (closed) or 17% (open; Wardale 1998, 156). While the feedwater heater was invented earlier, only three units were sold in the United States before 1919. "By 1936 heaters were in use on perhaps a fourth of all steam locomotives in services, and were built into all new steam locomotives" (Hultgren 1948, 224).

Appendices

Reheating

At an intermediate stage of expansion, the steam can be reheated by passing it in fire tubes back through the boiler, thus restoring it to the inlet temperature. This dries out the steam, improves its quality, and may also increase efficiency. Reheat was first used in a stationary powerplant in the 1920s. Reheat was used in the SNCF 160 A-1 (1940) compound expansion locomotive; the reheater was essentially a Schmidt superheater.

For a single reheat, the optimum extraction pressure from an efficiency standpoint is usually at about 20%–25% of the boiler pressure (Srinivas 2007). Ideally, the steam is extracted when it is no longer superheated but still of high quality (low moisture). Consequently, a second reheat stage is typically used only in plants operated at very high (supercritical) pressures (3,500 psia). The efficiency improvement from a second stage will likely be about half that of the first stage (Logan and Joy 2003, 382).

Appendix 9
Improving Actual Cycle Efficiency of Steam Powerplants

There are several expedients for mitigating the irreversibilities that reduce cycle efficiency.

Jacketing

When steam enters the cylinder, it meets a relatively cold surface, and condensation can occur, speeding heat loss and increasing corrosion. Hot air or steam may be introduced into an annular casing surrounding the cylinder to warm the cylinder walls and prevent this. The net reduction in steam consumption is on the order of 2%–15% (Ennis 1915, 307); in terms of efficiency ratio, the increase is 3–5 percentage points (399).

Compound Expansion

In compounding, the steam is expanded in a series of cylinders. In double expansion, the exhaust of the high-pressure cylinder is fed into the inlet of the low-pressure cylinder. Triple and quadruple expansion engines are analogously defined.

Compounding does not affect the theoretical efficiency but does increase the real-life efficiency by reducing heat losses through the cylinder wall (Ennis 1915, 319). Ennis reported that for saturated steam, the efficiency ratio increased from 40% (simple) to 50% (double); for noncondensing engines, 60% (triple); and for condensing ones, from 60% (simple) to 65% (compound) and 80% (triple) (399). Unfortunately, compound engines are larger than their simple counterparts (Semmens and Goldfinch 2000, 162).

In stationary plants, compounding is often combined with reheating for increased efficiency.

Appendices

Superheating also reduces condensation, and a simple engine using superheated steam could be as economical as a compound with saturated steam (Ennis 1915, 402). Superheating also obviates the need for jacketing (405).

Uniflow

In a normal steam engine, steam enters the cylinder at one end and, expanding, leaves at the other, and then the direction of steam expansion is reversed. In a uniflow system, steam always enters the cylinder at an end but is exhausted from the center. This means that the ends always stay hot and the center cold, so heat losses are reduced. Unfortunately, the fact that the center remains cool means that the piston can seize up there, among other mechanical problems. Abner Doble declared that it was "unsuited for use in a motor vehicle" (SCCGB 2024).

It must be emphasized that **all** of these modifications for increasing efficiency also increase the initial cost and often the maintenance costs, and these must be weighed against the fuel cost savings.

Appendix 10
Steam Car Data

The prototype 1953 Paxton steam car has contradictory specifications: steam pressure is said to be 2,000 psi at the boiler and 1,560 psig at the engine; engine temperature, 900°F and 1,200°F max; maximum continuous steaming rate, 900 lb/h or 750 lb/h. Engine power was a maximum of 150 bhp, with a continuous 120 bhp; the expected average water rate was 9 lb/bhp-h. The condenser with fans and housings weighed 140 lb (Senate 1968, 216–217).

The prototype Williams steam car had a 1,000 psi, 1,000°F boiler, four single-acting cylinders with a 23.5" bore × 2.75" stroke, consuming steam at a rate of 6 lb/hp-h, discharging to 3–9 psi and 230°F–300°F. The required condenser size was 250 sq ft; I assume that's surface area (SACA 1965). Its maximum continuous power output was 150 hp (VSCM 2015).

In 1957, MIT students designed a powerplant for a steam-powered sports car (Fleischer and Zafran 1957). The engine (660°F, 1,100 psia inlet) exhausted (after expansion at 70% isentropic efficiency) to a subatmospheric (5 psia) air-cooled condenser. At 100 hp, the steam rate is 1,280 lb/h.

The designers assumed a plate-fin exchanger of 75% effectiveness. The exchanger was sized to handle 2,000 lb of steam/hour; the necessary heat rejection rate was estimated as 2,000,000 Btu/h. The condenser temperature was a constant 162.24°F; a 100°F outside air inlet temperature was assumed; outlet air was calculated as 146.7°F.

The designed condenser of aluminum construction had a frontal area of 7.63 sq ft and a depth of 1.175 ft. A 5 hp fan provided an airflow of 4,000 cu ft/min. On the steam side, plate separation was ⅛ in., and between plates, there were five plain fins/inch. On the air side, the surface was Kays and London (1998) 17.8-3/8w: plate separation 0.413 in., 17.8 wavy fins/in., wavelength ⅜ in. The plates were 0.012 in. thick and the fins 0.006 in.

Appendices

Weight was not reported. However, the fin surface area is 89.2% of the total area. The air-side area is 3,390 sq ft, and the steam-side-to-air-side ratio is 0.192. The total area is thus 4,040.88. Treating the fins and plates as two-sided (edges ignored), calculate:

fin metal volume: $0.892 \times 4,040.88 \times 0.006/12/2 = 0.901$ cu ft
plate metal volume: $0.108 \times 4,040.88 \times 0.012/12/2 = 0.218$ cu ft
total: 1.119 cu ft
core weight (aluminum density 167): 186.93 lb

Thus, the W/P, if the power were increased to correspond to a steam rate of 2,000 lb of steam per hour, is 1.2 lb/hp just for the radiator core.

Gibbs and Hosick designed a steam powerplant, the Elliptocline, with a monotube boiler, a uniflow steam engine (with a rotating cylinder block!), and a condenser. The engine weight was 60 lb, and the steam generator weight was 325 lb; the condenser weight was not stated. The engine ran on 2,000 psi, 850°F steam, and could provide 60 hp at 2,470 rpm. The water consumption rate was 12 lb/hp-h (Miner 1966).

Strack (1970), in a NASA study, noted that since a steam car condenser must handle more of the waste heat load than an automobile radiator, it can be expected to be larger than the latter. He proposed a powerplant with a boiler outlet of temperature 1,000°F and pressure 2,000 psia (13), with a maximum shaft horsepower of 175 hp (said to be equivalent, in view of avoided parasitic losses, to an IC engine of 290 hp). The expansion isentropic efficiency was assumed to be 70% (8). He matched it with an air-cooled atmospheric condenser that used flat vertical brass tubes for the condensing side and plain horizontal copper fins on the air side, with copper headers. The condenser was sized with the expectation that the air inlet temperature would be 80°F. The total weight for a condenser with a core volume of 3 cu ft and a heat transfer rate of 1,425,000 Btu/h was 130 lb (table I). He predicted that with aluminum parts, the condenser weight would be just 50 lb (13).

Lears Motor Corporation built a prototype automobile steam turbine powerplant in the early 1970s. The maximum net brake horsepower was 92.8 (with four nozzles), and the system dry weight was 727 lb, of which 127 lb was the generator-burner; 110 lb, the turbine gearbox; and 179 lb, the condenser fan. Its plate-fin condenser subsystem had a heat rejection capability of 1.16×10^6 Btu/h (Luchter and Renner 1977, 40–41). BSFC (brake specific fuel consumption) was 0.89 lb/hp-h with four nozzles and 1.89 with one. The best overall net thermal efficiency was 15.5% (43).

The second-generation Carter engine, at 2,000 psia and 1,000°F, "delivered approximately 80 net hp, with a system weight of 359 lb"; the

Appendix 10

"overall thermal efficiency" was 20%. The best BSFC was 0.68 lb/hp-h (Luchter and Renner 1977, 70, 73).

Later that decade, Scientific Energy Systems Corp. developed a piston unit (1,000 psia, 1,000°F). The gross power was 158, but the net of auxiliaries was 138 hp at 1,500 rpm. The ideal cycle efficiency was 30.7%, the estimated maximum actual thermal efficiency was 19.4%, and the BSFC was 0.71 lb/-hp-h. The condenser was rated at 1.27×10^6 Btu/h (Luchter and Renner 1977, 46–48). The total dry weight was 1,147 lb (preprototype) or 853 lb (proposed prototype). For the latter, the component weights included expander (419 lb), evaporator-burner (110 lb), and condenser fans (99 lb; 53).

There was also speculation that for a compact car, the engine could be downsized to 90 gross hp at 4,000 rpm, with component weights including expander (225 lb in cast iron or 175 lb in aluminum alloys), evaporator (52 lb), and condenser (60 lb). The projected wet weight was 479 lb (versus a wet weight of 904 lb for the larger car's proposed prototype; Luchter and Renner 1977, 53).

Appendix 11
Condenser Pressure

The condensers discussed in chapter 2 were all atmospheric condensers—that is, the steam entering the condenser was at atmospheric pressure.

The thermodynamic efficiency (work output/energy input) of a steam powerplant is increased if the condenser operates at a partial vacuum. This occurs if the coolant fluid is cool enough that the temperature of the working fluid is reduced below its saturation temperature at atmospheric pressure. At the lower temperature, the vapor pressure of the working fluid is subatmospheric. Such operation is common for condensers in stationary steam powerplants.

Lowering the condenser pressure (and thus temperature) does have some drawbacks. The subatmospheric condenser is more expensive to construct (it has to resist collapse from air pressure), and the temperature difference between it and the coolant fluid is reduced, so the heat transfer rate is less. That's especially a concern for an air-cooled condenser.

The condenser pressure cannot be lower than "the saturation pressure corresponding to the saturation temperature of the cooling medium" and, because of heat flow considerations, will need to be higher. For example, a stationary plant using water cooling might condense to a pressure for which the saturation temperature is 10°C higher than the water temperature (Çengel and Boles 2002, 522).

Alternatively, the steam can exhaust at substantially higher than atmospheric pressure. This would increase the driving temperature difference; the heat transfer rate could be the same with less cooling surface and thus less weight. The disadvantages are a lower developed power and thermodynamic efficiency and a higher heat load on the condenser.

While it is advantageous from an efficiency standpoint for the condensate to be as hot as possible (to reduce the amount of heating needed when it returns to the boiler), a few degrees of subcooling

Appendix 11

is advantageous to prevent cavitation (vapor bubble formation) in the pump returning the condensate. It also assures a liquid seal at the bottom of the condenser so any noncondensable gases can't enter the liquid line. A typical subcooling is 2°F–5°F (Blank et al. 2005, 169) or 5°F–10°F (Lindeburg 2010).

Chapter Notes

Introduction

1. 1) air intake stroke, 2) isentropic compression stroke, 3) constant volume combustion (heat addition) stroke, and 4) exhaust (isentropic expansion) stroke.
2. These run on the Brayton cycle. They run best when working at near-maximum power; the specific fuel consumption is high at low power settings. This makes them unsuitable for station-keeping airships. They also have a high rotation speed and thus require a more extreme and therefore heavier speed reduction scheme in the transmission "to match the engine to the propeller" (Marcy and Hockway 1979, 15).
3. In the 1950s, Wilkie observed a linear relationship between the power of aircraft engines and their weight, about 1 kW/kg (Reay 1977, 148).
4. Wikipedia says 6.08:1.
5. Wikipedia says that the engine rating of 245 hp was at an altitude of 1,800 m and that, while this would "theoretically correspond to rating of about 300 hp at sea level," it was not designed to withstand a power level higher than 245 hp, so at lower altitudes it would need to be throttled down.
6. Wikipedia says 881 lb dry weight for the original version and 859 lb for the "later variant with aluminum pistons."
7. Horsepower is a measurement of work, i.e., force times distance. Pounds of thrust is a pure force measurement; they are apples and oranges. "A jet engine that is static fired is not moving through any distance and is therefore doing no work, nor is it developing any horsepower." Pounds thrust can be converted to a thrust horsepower by multiplying by the speed of the aircraft (mph) and dividing by 375 (USAF 1964, 61).
8. The combustion gases are larger molecules than the nitrogen and oxygen or air and thus have a lower specific heat ratio (e.g., 1.2 for carbon dioxide). If this were taken into account, the calculated efficiency would be less.

Chapter 1

1. The fabric was a composite of silk taffeta, nansouk, and rubber, with a total weight prior to coating of 240 g per square meter (De Lôme 16). The coatings added 100 g per square meter (19).
2. Ten pounds thrust is 44.48 N, and 6 mph is 2.68 m/s, so that implies a propulsive power of 119.2 W.
3. Khoury (2012, 624) says 11.6 mph.
4. "*Zeppy-1* was designed and built in 1985 by ... Luc Geieser." Geiser lost his life in a diving accident, and the attempt to fly *Zeppy-1* across the English Channel was not made until 2008, with Rousson as the pilot. Geiser also designed and built the *Zeppy-2* in 1992, a winged, pedal-powered, two-seater airship (820 cu m) designed to cross the Atlantic, but it was "driven into the sea by a gust of wind after a 500 km flight" (Khoury 2012, 622).
5. ReL 5.399e6; Cf 0.00301; SF 1.8805; RF 2; surface area 1,852 sq m; air density 1.190 kg/m3. De Lôme calculated the surface area as 1,225 sq m (De Lôme 22).
6. If the forebody were a hemisphere, it would have been 17.7% of the length and the envelope volume, 6,131 cu ft.
7. Wilson took the 1964 version of NASA SP-3006, added some data points

Chapter Notes

for champion athletes in the 1970s through 1990s, and drew a best fit curve through the latter.

8. Reay (1977) gives data on maximum power output in the units kg-m/s. Strictly speaking, that is a unit of momentum, not power. However, if kgf (kilograms-force) was intended, it would be a unit of power. One kgf is 9.80665 N, and so 1 kgf-m/s is 9.80665 W.

9. Strictly speaking, weight is a gravitational force, usually measured in newtons (N). However, it is often quoted as the corresponding mass (lb or kg) of the aircraft; the force is the mass times the gravitational acceleration.

Chapter 2

1. The quotations are from the Google Translate translations of Ernouf's book, and I apologize in advance for any inaccuracies.

2. I calculated it as 29.96%.

3. The proposal also suggested 1,028 lb for water recovery and preheater, but that is not strictly required. It also listed 700 lb of water (part of the wet weight), 2,400 lb for outriggers and transmission (the outriggers would be part of the installed weight), and 3,920 lb for the propeller (the transmission and propeller would be part of the propulsion system weight, but not, by my definitions, the powerplant weight).

4. This was based on Besler's experience in 1931. That engine was run at 785°F and 890 psi.

5. This was a good estimate. Testing showed a slight decline in efficiency from a little over 80% at a fuel rate of 70 lb/h to about 75% at a burn rate of 180 lb/h (Besler 1958, 9).

6. The engine was subsequently built and tested but at a lower steam temperature. At, for example, 720°F, its actual thermal efficiency was 9%, which was 70% of its theoretical (Rankine) efficiency (Besler 1958, 7).

7. Per page 9. The illustration on page 10 and the caption to the graph on page 13 state a depth of 3% in. It is possible that the page 9 value includes the header.

8. The weight of the core alone was 6 lb per square foot of face area (9).

9. According to pages 10 and 13. Page 9 said that there were 10 fins per inch.

10. I assume the pressures in the 1958 report were given as psia, consistent with the 1954 report.

11. Ground-supplied steam was actually used previously by Emmanuel Dieuaide in 1877 (USCoFC 2024).

12. The cycle efficiency was called the cylinder efficiency because almost all steam locomotives had reciprocating engines in which the piston moved within a cylinder. The term cycle efficiency is preferred because a steam powerplant may be a turbine type.

13. Marcy and Hockway (1979, 11) assert that the low pressure at high altitude will also increase the efficiency of the Rankine cycle. That would be true for an open cycle, where the spent steam is exhausted to the atmosphere. But this assumes a closed cycle.

14. This means *constant entropy*. An isentropic process is one that is reversible and adiabatic (no heat gained from or lost to the surroundings).

15. The isentropic efficiency of compression affects the actual cycle efficiency, but not the condenser load.

16. The effect on cycle efficiency can vary. For example, with an engine operating at 2,000 psig/1,000°F, with 100% isentropic efficiency, extraction for reheat at 410.25 psig increases steam quality to 100% and cycle efficiency to 36.53%. But extraction at less than about 128.9 psig decreases cycle efficiency.

17. Balmer (2010, 520) calculated the cycle efficiency as 20.7% at 70% isentropic efficiency.

18. Besler's 1933 engine is said to be 1,200 psi. I have assumed it to be 1,200 psia since that is what was given for Besler 1954.

19. Besler (1954) calculated 30.70% for the theoretical cycle efficiency. But Besler assumed that the condenser inlet pressure was 2 psig, not atmospheric (0 psig). That should have reduced the theoretical efficiency to 30.29%.

Despite assuming a slightly higher isentropic efficiency (72%), Besler predicted a

Chapter Notes

higher condenser load and heat rejection rate than I do: 966 Btu/lb steam/cycle or 1,932,000 Btu/h, respectively. If I set isentropic efficiency to 72% and condenser inlet pressure to 2 psig, I get a condenser load of 921.35 and a heat rejection rate of 1,809,077.

20. Gibbs's pressure was 2,000 psi; I assumed psia was intended.

21. Strack (1970, 12) states a thermal efficiency of 24% if the isentropic efficiency of expansion is 70% and pump (compression) efficiency is 50%. My result is then 22.37%.

22. Luchter and Renner (1977) reported the ideal efficiency as 30.7%.

23. In comparing the P/W or W/P ratios of engines, an implicit assumption is made that the weight is linearly proportional to the power. However, Marcy (1979, 14) teaches that at least "with high-altitude turbocharger and starting system," the correlation is that engine weight (lb) = 27.6 × (HP)$^{0.468}$.

24. I am not going to trouble the reader with the formula for the LMTD (See, e.g., Das 2005, 112), but I will note that one of the independent variables is the air outlet temperature, which is not initially known. A trial value is assumed, and various heat transfer calculations are made. These ultimately yield a value for the air outlet temperature, and if it differs too much from the assumed value, it becomes the new trial value, and the process is repeated. Strack says that "normally, three to six iterations are sufficient to produce an accuracy of 0.01 percent" (1970, 44).

Another approach is the exchanger effectiveness method described by Kays and London (1998, 16–27) and shown by them to be equivalent to the LMTD method. Both methods are used by Fleischer and Zafran (1957, 46).

25. There is also cooling drag from the cylinder head fins of a piston engine.

Chapter 3

1. Even as small a temperature differential as 6°C (Vineeth 2011, 6).

Chapter 4

1. The acidification of the dichromate forms chromic acid, which acts as a depolarizer—it inhibits hydrogen gas bubble formation. The amalgamation of the zinc (with mercury) increased its shelf life.

2. If those were maintained, it would imply a delivered power of 184.8 W (0.25 hp). However, as shown below, 18 of these units only supplied 1.25–1.5 hp, so that suggests that a single unit was 0.07–0.08 hp.

3. Some authors (UPSBC 2022; Desmond 2018, 23) refer to this battery, inaccurately, as a *flow battery*. A flow battery is one in which **both** electrochemically active components are in solutions circulated on opposite sides of an ion-selective membrane (IFBF 2024). Renard's zinc is not provided in liquid form; the chlorine is in solution, but it is not circulated (no flow!), and there is no membrane. However, it can be considered a hybrid between a normal battery and a flow battery.

It is possible to implement a zinc-chlorine battery chemistry as a flow cell. The electrolyte would be a zinc chloride solution. During charging, "metallic zinc is plated on the dense graphite electrode [anode] while chlorine is evolved at the porous graphite electrode [cathode]," and "mixed with water and cooled to form ... chlorine hydrate." To discharge, "the stored chlorine hydrate is heated to release chlorine," which is mixed with zinc chloride solution "and pumped through the porous electrode." The zinc is oxidized, and the chlorine is reduced to chloride ion. Both electrodes are passive electrodes (Ohajianya et al. 2020).

4. Boyne (2005, 2) says that the batteries weighed 1,500 lb (680.4 kg), which is substantially greater than the figure provided by Tissandier.

5. A more typical weight for a 21,700 cell is about 70 g.

6. Since a generator provides AC power and a battery, DC power, one or the other must be converted to the form that the motor demands.

7. Some older literature subsumes series-parallel in parallel.

8. On the HPDM-250, the built-in

245

Chapter Notes

gearbox offers a 6.7:1 reduction, and the final output is 2,985 rpm at maximum continuous power. That implies that the motor output was 20,000 rpm, consistent with Ivanov et al. (2022).

Chapter 5

1. In the photoelectric effect, a metal atom absorbs a light photon (typically blue or ultraviolet light), and this provides enough energy for one of its electrons to "escape completely from the surface." In the photovoltaic effect, the absorption of the light energy raises the electron to a higher energy state, but not enough for escape. In a PV cell, the cell construction is such that the excited electron is removed before it can "relax" back to its ground state, and the electron is directed into an internal circuit (Nelson 2003, 1–2).

2. Any light source can be used (a laser has been used to activate PV cells on a model airplane; Desmond 2018, 132), but the sun is the normal source, hence the term *solar cell*.

3. The discussion of *Solar Impulse* and *Solar Impulse II* is taken from my book on airships, also published by McFarland.

4. This discussion is primarily copied from my book on airships, also published by McFarland.

5. Or on the horizontal fins, but that's a much smaller surface than the airship hull.

6. The areal power density is the specific power (power/mass) times the areal density (mass/surface area).

7. There is also a thermodynamic limit of 215 for linear focus concentrators (parabolic trough) and 46,250 for point-focus concentrators (paraboloidal dish; Lovegrove and Stein 2020, 28).

Chapter 6

1. These estimates were not entirely consistent with the graph at the end of Locke's (1954) report. This showed that the basic empty weight (empty weight less powerplant and electronics) of a two-million-cubic-foot airship should be slightly more than 50,000 lb, not 60,000.

Also, in the body of the report, Locke estimated that the static lift would be 110,000 lb, with another 10,000 lb lift provided dynamically, like an aircraft. But the graph shows the static lift to be 120,000 lb. It is not clear how Locke calculated that the required propulsive power at 100 knots would be 4,000 hp. (Ninety percent of 4.500 is 4,050.)

2. Locke (1954) refers to BuPlan 54A119B1, Nuclear Powered AEW Airship, but I have not located a copy.

Chapter 7

1. Other sources give somewhat different values. Maximum power, maximum continuous power, and cruising power may all be different, of course. So, too, is power at sea level and power at cruising altitude.

2. Diesel had abandoned coal dust in accordance with a contract he signed with a manufacturer in early 1893. The first fuel he used was gasoline (Mollenhauer and Tschoeke 2010, 4).

3. Surprisingly, two decades later, Marcy and Hockway (1979, 10) estimated that the tankage weight for liquid hydrogen was "approximately equal to the weight of the hydrogen stored." The difference may be attributable, at least in part, to differences in the assumed temperature and pressure. Also, there may be economies of scale, since tank weight should be proportional to surface area and hydrogen weight to tank volume.

4. A scramjet is a supersonic combustion ramjet.

5. Earth's atmosphere at sea level has an average pressure of 1.013 bar.

6. I do not know whether this weight calculation took into account the weight of the cryogenic equipment for liquefied hydrogen tanks.

7. There are some in-between designs in which the oxidant is external and the anode is conventional (metal-air batteries) or the consumed anode is an externally supplied fluid and the cathode is conventional (hydrogen-nickel oxide batteries).

8. I do not know whether this includes the motor.

9. The reference misplaced the decimal point by three places in its conversion of imperial to SI units; my text gives the correct values.
10. The *Hindenburg* had a frontal area of 1,333 sq m (diameter 41.2 m).
11. The power generated would depend on the voltage (power equals voltage times current) and therefore on altitude. The voltage gradient in the atmosphere declines exponentially from about 100 V/m near the Earth's surface to about 0.2 V/m at 31 km altitude (col. 15). At 5 km, it is at least 10 V/m (Ogawa and Tanaka 1967, fig. 6). For the potential at different altitudes, see Volland (2013, 7).

Chapter 8

1. It is not clear how he arrived at that number. The reporter said that the initial circumference of its upward spiral was 1.5 mi, and Andrews, that the diameter was 0.5 mi; these are reasonably consistent. In his letter to the editor, Andrews said that the initial, more rapid movement was 11 revolutions in seven minutes and a few seconds. Later, the *Aereon* allegedly made three revolutions in 3.5 minutes. And overall, he says that it made 20 revolutions in 14.5 minutes, upon which it was lost in the upper strata of clouds. He believed that the circles got larger as the *Aereon* ascended, which suggests that the rope used to secure the rudder in position stretched. If so, it becomes impossible to calculate the speed.
2. Some sources (Whitman 1920) describe it as having a double hull, and this was probably a misunderstanding; it was equipped with a longitudinal leather strap that, if tightened, would create a lengthwise depression, dividing the hull into two lobes (*The Nation*, 619, May 15, 1866). The purpose of the strap was not to alter the aerodynamics but to limit the volume of the envelope when it was filled with gas at sea level; the strap would be relaxed at altitude to allow for gas expansion (Andrews 1866, 11–12). However, the Andrews (1864a) patent did disclose a double hull embodiment (fig. 7).
3. Whitman (1932, 124) said that the ship was 86 ft long, 50 ft wide, and 36 ft high, but remember that he thought it was a catamaran, so the implication is that the individual hulls were 25 ft wide and 36 ft high. The *Country Gentleman*, 28: 24, July 5, 1866, said that the hull diameter was 42 ft, and the same dimension is given in *Alden's Illustrated Family Miscellany* (August 1866).

The *Aereon II* was made by combining the envelopes of the government balloons *Union* and *Intrepid*. These each had a 32,000 cu ft gas capacity according to Haydon (1941, 238), but there are other published values.

Sci. Am. (1866) says that the *Aereon II* contained 40,000 cu ft of gas and provided 2 tn of lift. Andrews (1866, 14) agrees. However, it would take 51,681 cu ft of hydrogen to provide 2 tn of lift. Whitman (1920) ascribes to it a volume of 70,000 cu ft Whitman (1932) says that the volume was 60,000 cu ft, with which Allen agrees (and says the lift was 1,800 lb), and *The Nation* (May 15, 1866) reported that the *Aereon II*'s volume was 66,000 cu ft.

4. The wind typically changes both direction and strength with altitude. While winds aloft tend to be stronger, the rate of increase with altitude is very slow. Moreover, what appears to be a headwind to a ground observer probably won't be so aloft, as the wind also changes direction with altitude (Ekman spiral).
5. Whitman (1932) suggested that the problem with the Aereon II was that its hull was rounded top and bottom, whereas the Aereon I had a 60% cylindrical midbody. He therefore thought that the Aereon II didn't offer enough resistance to vertical (perpendicular to longitudinal axis) movement. However, with conventional airships, it became customary to eschew the cylindrical midbody (which reduced construction costs) and move to a teardrop shape for reduced air resistance.
6. A caveat was a filed invention disclosure that was not examined for patentability. It expired after one year unless renewed. Its purpose was to provoke a patent interference (to determine priority of invention) if another inventor filed an application claiming the same invention while the caveat was still in force.

Chapter Notes

7. The article "Aerial Navigation" in the *NYT* (9/29/1865) stated that an ordinary spherical balloon rises perpendicularly, a cylindroid at 45°, and with two or three cylindroids together, this can be reduced to 15°.

8. It is possible that there was some data point at which the relationship was apparently linear, and Andrews just extrapolated from that.

9. The root-mean-square deviation of the balanced forces in the glide path frame of reference, expressed as a percentage of the net buoyant force (buoyancy weight), was 8.5345E-07.

10. I find it curious that Andrews's estimated speed was 200 mph, precisely following his linear drag law given the over 200 lb of ascending power he gave to the abandoned Aereon.

11. The angle of attack and the glide path angle change slightly to −4.8782 and 19.88, respectively.

Chapter 9

1. Hagedoorn called this a *Hapa*, short for Hagedoorn paravane. However, *hapa* is a Hawaiian word meaning half, usually used in the context of *hapa haole* (half-European). So I prefer to avoid its use.

2. By modern standards, this is rather low strength for Dyneema. Marlow's eight-strand 6 mm Dyneema rope is 16.7 kN.

3. The *Zeppy-1* and *Zeppy-2* were pedal-powered; see chapter 1.

4. According to Burgess (1939). Using the formulae of van der Vlugt (2009), it is 54% of the true wind speed.

5. Modern software (e.g., Elliott et al. 1965) sets the balloon at the desired float altitude and calculates the wind force upon it. It also divides the tether into small cylindrical elements and calculates the tension and angle for each, starting at the balloon end and working its way down to the ground. This procedure permits consideration of the weight and wind drag of the tether and input of an arbitrary wind profile rather than a single wind speed. "Failure of the system is indicated by an increase in tension beyond the specified breaking strength of the tether or an increase in the tether [zenith] angle beyond the horizontal (in which case, of course, the tether cannot reach the ground)" (Elliott et al. 1965, 3, 17–18). The calculated tether is curved, and its length and weight should be calculated and compared to the net lift.

The formula on step 14 of Elliot's calculation procedure is in error. If there were no tether wind drag D1, T1 would equal T0 for all heights. Whereas, as noted by many authors, with a catenary, the tension decreases from the top end to the bottom end. The first sine should be of theta 0, not theta 1.

6. The tether connecting the airship to the *chien de mer* is a pure drag element. It is unclear whether Costes included its effect in positing the lift-to-drag ratio for the airship.

Chapter 10

1. What was measured, if this weren't simply a guess, was probably the deviation of the track of the balloon from the surface wind direction. But the wind changes in both direction and speed as one changes altitude.

2. Rowing Level says that these standards are "based on well-known formulas and data sources available freely online" but doesn't provide any citations.

3. Rodgers (1937, 32) said that it "may be learned from any good handbook that a man working for 8 hours a day can only develop about one-fourth horsepower." He further asserted that "a man working on his own oar for a watch of 4 hours can develop little more than 3.5 percent of a horsepower" (cp. 208).

4. Simplistically, it could be kept horizontal for the top half of the wheel rotation. But that would minimize air resistance in level flight only when the spoke holding the blade was vertical. One could keep it perpendicular to the spoke, but that ignores the fact that the blade's motion through space is cycloidal, the combination of the blade's revolution around the wheel axis and the forward motion of the wheel axis. So the minimum

Chapter Notes

air resistance would occur if it were kept tangent to the cycloid.

5. Haddan was a British patent agent. The patent was granted in his name, but the actual inventors were Richard William Cowan and Charles Page.

6. Portions of this section are copied or adapted from my book *Work at Sea: The Evolution of Seafaring Technology* (McFarland 2025).

7. Henry (1959) defines a cycloidal propeller both as "a combined propulsion and steering device that produces a useful thrust (which may be controlled in magnitude and direction)" and as "a propulsion device in which the blades rotate and revolve in a manner similar to the motions of a planet relative to the sun" (1).

8. Caiella (2019) describes its operation differently, and I don't know whether Caiella was simply mistaken or if a simpler mechanism was used in this test than the one described in the patent. "To move forward, all the paddles would be feathered—pointed in the direction of travel—except as they approached the starboard beam position. There the paddles were rotated perpendicularly to the ship, providing forward thrust. Similarly, reverse thrust could be provided immediately by adjusting the cam to allow only the paddle on the port beam to provide thrust. The cam could be adjusted to accommodate any point of the compass." Thus, in Caiella's interpretation, the blades exert a propelling force only when they reach a single position in the revolution.

9. The reason for the oblique axis of the main propellers is that they were to be mounted on the hull of the *Shenandoah*, in three port and starboard pairs, near the keel, rather than in separate engine cars (Sachse 1926, fig. 9 and fig. 10). They were thus essentially lateral axis mounts, the tilt being a concession to the shape of the hull.

10. The stern propellers were mounted on the top and bottom of the stern, respectively. However, because of the slope of the top and bottom of the stern, their axes were not quite vertical (Sachse 1926, fig. 9).

11. A *curtate cycloid* is a curve described by a point lying on the radius, but not the perimeter, of a rolling circle (Weisstein 2025).

12. Caldwell had obtained an aircraft cyclogyro patent in 1927, but it depicted the more familiar lateral axis paddle wheel with feathering blades. It is doubtful that he contemplated its use for propulsion, as he sets forth its purpose as "elevating and supporting the vehicle," and the patent also alludes to a "propeller shaft."

13. Henry (1959) defined what I will call a secondary control point (S') as being the intersection of a line drawn perpendicular to the radial line OP connecting the center of the circle to the blade pivot point and the line SP. As the blade revolves around the center O, S' will trace out a control path. Henry, figure 2 shows the control paths for three different blade motions in the case of forward thrust: true cycloidal, amplified cycloidal, and sinusoidal; the latter is associated with a circular control path.

14. The maximum pitch amplitude generally corresponds to the maximum angle of attack and thus the maximum lift force generated by an individual blade. It is related to the pitch ratio.

15. The first digit indicates the maximum camber as a percentage of the chord.

Chapter 11

1. Even spinning maple seeds create LEVs, thus generating lift. See
https://www.popsci.com/military-aviation-amp-space/article/2009-06/inspired-spinning-maple-seeds-tested-robofly/ .

2. He and Magnan had previously coauthored *Sur la Distribution en Vol des Vitesses Aérodynamiques Autour d'un Avion en Vol* (1932) [On the In-Flight Distribution of Aerodynamic Speeds Around an Aircraft in Flight].

3. The Strouhal number can also be used. It equals the product of the flapping frequency and the flapping amplitude, divided by the flight speed. The Strouhal number is 2 pi times the reduced frequency. And the reduced frequency is the reciprocal of the advance ratio (Norberg 2006, 123).

Chapter Notes

Chapter 12

1. Quick (2010) says it is 70% concentration; Ragan (2010), 85%.

2. The first two paragraphs of this section are taken from my book *Work at Sea: The Evolution of Shipboard Technology* (McFarland 2025).

3. La Fon (1934), figure 2 shows the two lifting elements (corrugated cylinders) allegedly oriented to provide propulsion as well as lift. The drawing appears to be a bit distorted; the lifting elements are drawn as if Veed to one side, but that is not disclosed in the patent text. Moreover, I believe that they are tilted the wrong way (fore end up); the Magnus force must be perpendicular to the axis of rotation; with the tilt shown, it must either be down and forward or up and backward. Neither of these is desirable if both positive lift and forward propulsion are wanted.

Bibliography

Abbreviations List

AAJ   Aviation and Aircraft Journal
ABMA   American Boiler Manufacturers Association
AENews   Alternative Energy News
AFT   AirForce Technology
AHME   CAmerican Helicopter Museum & Education Center
CAM   Combat Air Museum
CIA   Central Intelligence Agency
DLR   Deutsches Zentrum fur Luft- und Raumfahrt (German Aerospace Center)
DOD   Defense, U.S. Department of
DOE   Energy, U.S. Department of
EASA   European Aviation Space Agency
EDAED   Experimental Department of Airplane Engineering Division (Bureau of Aircraft Production, U.S. War Dept.)
EERE   Energy Efficiency & Renewable Energy
EMMS   English Mechanic and Mirror of Science
ETB   Engineering Toolbox, The
FAA   Federal Aviation Administration (U.S.)
FAI   Fédération Aéronautique Internationale
FKP   Flying Kettle Project
GCG   Green Car Congress
HPSLT   High Pressure Steam Locomotive Technology
LOC   Library of Congress
MAVLab   Micro Air Vehicles Laboratory (Delft University of Technology)
MTI   Mechanical Technology Incorporated
NASM   National Air and Space Museum (Smithsonian Institution)
NMAH   National Museum of American History (Smithsonian Institution)
NMLA   National Meteorological Library and Archive (U.K.)
NREL   National Renewable Energy Laboratory
NYH   New York Herald
NYT   New York Times
SACA   Steam Automobile Club of America, Inc.
SCCGB   Steam Car Club of Great Britain
SCDSA   Steam Car Developments & Steam Aviation
SciAm   *Scientific American*
SETO   Solar Energy Technologies Office
SHI   Science History Institute
SIF   Solar Impulse Foundation
SNL   Science News-Letter
SPCN   Steam Power Club News
T&T   Time and Tide
TWM   *Technical World Magazine*
UCS   Union of Concerned Scientists
UPSBC   UPSBatteryCenter
USAF   United States Air Force
USCoFC   United States Centennial of Flight Commission
USSS   United States Submarine School
VSCM   Virtual Steam Car Museum
WNA   World Nuclear Association

Journal Abbreviations

Bull   Bulletin
J   Journal
Int   International
Soc'y   Society

Bibliography

References

Aaron, Kim Maynard. 2002, June 11 (issue date). "Balloon Trajectory Control System," U.S. Patent 6,402,090 (application filed June 29, 1998).

Aaron, Kim Maynard, et al. 2000, July 13 (PDF last modified date). "A Method for Balloon Trajectory Control," http://www.gaerospace.com/projects/ULBDStratoSail/pdfs_docs/COSPAR2000StratoSail.pdf.

Abas, Mohd Firdous Bin, et al. 2016, October. "Flapping Wing Micro-Aerial-Vehicle: Kinematics, Membranes, and Flapping Mechanisms of Ornithopter and Insect Flight," *Chinese J. Aeronautics*, 29(5): 1159–77. https://www.sciencedirect.com/science/article/pii/S1000936116300978.

Ackroyd, J. A. 2016 (Draft 2). "The Aerodynamics of the Spitfire," *J. Aeronautical History*, Paper 2016/03, 59–86.

Ackroyd, J. A. 2018. "Aerodynamics as the Basis of Aviation: How Well Did It Do?," *J. Aeronautical History*, Paper 2018/01, 1–62.

Adams, Zachary H. 2016, May 24 (issue date). "Ring Cam and Ring Cam Assembly for Dynamically Controlling Pitch of Cycloidal Rotor Blades," U.S. patent 9,346,535 (application filed Feb. 12, 2013).

Adler, Cyrus. 1907. *Samuel Pierpont Langley*. Philosophical Society of Washington.

Aereon Corporation. 2004, Feb. 19. "Aereon III," https://aereoncorp.com/.pages/aereon3.html.

Aero Drum Ltd. 2023. "Solar RC Blimps Designed and Made by Aero Drum Ltd," https://www.rc-zeppelin.com/solar-blimp.html.

Aerofiles. 2024, May 14 (access date). "The Fantastically Flighty Gray Goose," http://www.aerofiles.com/graygoose.html, and the following photos: near frontal view: http://www.impdb.org/images/5/56/Frhlichezukunft006thegrls3.jpg; rear view: http://www.aerofiles.com/-graygoose-cyclogyro.jpg.

Aerospace Technology. 2024, May 12 (access date). "HY4 Aircraft," https://www.aerospace-technology.com/projects/hy4-aircraft/.

Aerovelo. 2016a. "Atlas Technical Information," http://www.aerovelo.com/atlas-technical-info.

Aerovelo. 2016b. "Snowbird: Technical Information," http://www.aerovelo.com/snowbird-technical-info.

Aggarwal, Avinash Kumar, et al. 2024. *Ammonia and Hydrogen for Green Energy Transition*. Springer Nature Singapore.

Aifantis, Katerina E, et al. 2010. *High Energy Density Lithium Batteries: Materials, Engineering, Applications*. Wiley.

Airboyd (username). 2012, Dec. 15. "The Besler Steam Driven Plane (1933)," https://www.youtube.com/watch?v=2TtHOkgwrk8.

AirForce Technology. 2013, August 7. "Hummingbird Nano Air Vehicle (NAV)," https://www.airforce-technology.com/projects/hummingbird-nano-air-vehicle/?cf-view&cf-closed.

Akimov, Alexander B., and William J. Welker. 2019. "Air Bike ... 1897," https://airbike.welweb.org/AirBike_1897%20(1st%20Ed%2020190410a).pdf.

Akimov, A. M., and P. A. Polivanov. 2019. "Study of the Possibility of Steady Horizontal Flight of the Dual Aircraft Platform with the Wind Shear," *J. Physics: Conference Series*, 1404: 012075. https://iopscience.iop.org/article/10.1088/1742-6596/1404/1/012075/meta.

Alcock, Charles. 2023, Jan. 19. "ZeroAvia Achieves First Flight with Hydrogen-powered Regional Airliner," https://www.ainonline.com/news-article/2023-01-19/zeroavia-achieves-first-flight-hydrogen-powered-regional-airliner.

Allen, Bill. 1977, July. "Big Boom in Gas Bags," *Popular Mechanics*, 148(1): 67 et al.

Allen, Hunter, et al. 2019 (3rd ed.). *Training + Racing with a Power Meter*. Velopress.

Almeida-Neto, Paulo Francisco de, et al. 2023, June 7. "Physiological Mechanisms of Muscle Strength and Power Are Dependent on the Years Post Obtaining Peak Height Velocity in Elite Juniors Rowers: a Cross-Sectional Study," *PLoS One*. 18(6): e0286687. https://www.ncbi.nlm.nih.gov/pmc/articles/PMC10246840/.

Alternative Energy News. 2008,

Bibliography

November. "Pedal Powered Electricity Generator from Windstream," https://www.alternative-energy-news.info/pedal-powered-electricity-generator-windstream/.

Alverà, Marco. 2021. *The Hydrogen Revolution: A Blueprint for the Future of Clean Energy*. Basic Books.

American Boiler Manufacturers Association. 2015, Nov. 9 (PDF last modified date). "Boiler Horsepower: History of Definitions in the Firetube Boiler Industry."

American Helicopter Museum & Education Center. 2022. "Aerovelo Atlas," https://americanhelicopter.museum/exhibits/aerovelo-atlas/.

Anderson, John David. 2002. *The Airplane, a History of its Technology*. AIAA.

Anderson, John D., Jr. 2017 (6th ed.). *Fundamentals of Aerodynamics*. McGraw-Hill.

Andrews, Solomon. 1848. *Aerial Navigation*. Self-published. 4 pp. (Library of Congress [LOC] Call # T6639 A7, in Rare Book Room).

Andrews, Solomon. 1863, Sept. 9. "Aerial Navigation" (Sept. 6 letter to the editor). *New York Herald*, Sept. 9, 1863, p. 4. https://www.loc.gov/resource/sn83030313/1863-09-09/ed-1/?sp=4&r=0.578,0.967,0.301,0.176,0.

Andrews, Solomon. 1864a, July 5 (issue date). "Aerostat," U.S. Patent 43,449.

Andrews, Solomon. 1864b. *The Aereon*. ("A protest, addressed to the Senate and House of Representatives, by the inventor of a war aerostat, complaining of the conduct of the War Department in regard to the matter.") (LOC # TL 654 A6 A27, in Rare Book Room).

Andrews, Solomon. 1865a. *Aerial Navigation and a Proposal to Form an Aerial Navigation Company*. J. F. Trow. 32 pp. (LOC # TL 654 A6 A33, in Rare Book Room).

Andrews, Solomon. 1865b. *The Art of Flying*. J. F. Trow. 32 pp. (LOC # TL 654 A6 A35, in Rare Book Room).

Andrews, Solomon. 1866. *The Aereon: or Flying Ship, Invented by Solomon Andrews*. J. F. Trow. 15 pp. (LOC # TL 654 A6 A3, in Rare Book Room).

Andrisani, Andrea, et al. 2016, August. "Optimal Pitching Schedules for a Cycloidal Rotor in Hovering," *Aircraft Engineering & Aerospace Technology*, 88(5): 623–635. https://www.researchgate.net/publication/306468978.

Ansari, Salman Ahmad. 2004, September. "A Nonlinear, Unsteady, Aerodynamic Model for Insect-Like Flapping Wings in the Hover with Micro Air Vehicle Applications" (Ph.D., Department of Aerospace, Power and Sensors, Cranfield University).

Anton, Frank. 2019, Sept. 10. "eAircraft: Hybrid-elektrische Antriebe für Luftfahrzeuge," https://www.bbaa.de/fileadmin/user_upload/02-preis/02-02-preistraeger/newsletter-2019/02-2019-09/02_Siemens_Anton.pdf.

APS News. 2009, April 1. "April 25, 1954: Bell Labs Demonstrates the First Practical Silicon Solar Cell," https://www.aps.org/apsnews/2009/04/bell-labs-silicon-solar-cell.

Armant, Luc. 1990. L'Aile d'Eau: Réflexion pour un Voilier sans Masse" (The Water Wing: Reflection for a Massless Sailboat), https://www.augredelair.fr/wp-content/uploads/2015/01/luc_armant_ailedeau.pdf.

Army Air Corps, United States. 1938, May 15. "Towards the Steam-Driven Aeroplane," *Technical Data Digest of Current Publications*, 4(1): 38.

Arndt, Rob. 2024, May 21 (access date). "Adalbert Schmid Ornithopter SC-28 Wolke (1942)," http://discaircraft.greyfalcon.us/Adalbert%20Schmid%20Ornithopter.htm.

Arnstein, K., and W. Klemperer. 1936. "Performance of Airships," in Durand, William Frederick., *Aerodynamic Theory*, vol. VI. Julius Springer.

Arthur D. Little, Inc. 1982, Feb. "An Assessment of the Crash Fire Hazard of Liquid Hydrogen Fueled Aircraft," National Aeronautics & Space Administration. https://ntrs.nasa.gov/api/citations/19820011322/downloads/19820011322.pdf.

Ashraf, Intesaaf. 2011, Nov. 21. "SHWAS: Underwater Glider Developed at IIT Bombay," http://www.youtube.com/watch?v=q0N2ZevF6no.

Bibliography

Aviation and Aircraft Journal. 1920, Nov. 15. "A German Diesel Airplane Engine," *Aviation & Aircraft J.*, 9(9): 287–8.

Bailleux, C. 1987. "When Electrochemistry Paved the Way to the Sky," in *Proceedings of the Symposium on History of Battery Technology*, proceedings vol. 87–14, pp. 268–278, edited by Alvin J. Salkind. Electrochemical Society, Inc.

Baker, Noah. 2018, Nov. 21. "Watch: Plane with No Moving Parts Takes First Flight," https://www.nature.com/articles/d41586-018-07485-9.

Balachandran, P. 2011. *Engineering Fluid Mechanics*. PHI Learning.

Balmer, Robert. 2010. *Modern Engineering Thermodynamics*. Academic Press.

Barris, Wes. 2018, Aug. 24 (Wayback Machine Archive Date). "Steam Locomotive Feedwater Heaters," https://web.archive.org/web/20180824093759/http://www.steamlocomotive.com/appliances/feedwaterheaters.php.

Bassett, Preston R. 1963, October. "Carl E. Myers of the Balloon Farm," *New York History*, 44(4): 365–390.

Bell, Hugh. 1848, Nov. 23. "Certain Improvements in Aerial Machines and Machinery in Connection with the Buoyant Power Produced by Gaseous Matter," British Patent 12,337. https://babel.hathitrust.org/cgi/pt?id=nyp.33433011666124&view=1up&seq=153.

Bender, Asher, et al. 2008, January. "Analysis of an Autonomous Underwater Glider," Australasian Conference on Robotics and Automation. https://www.researchgate.net/publication/230642957_Analysis_of_an_autonomous_underwater_glider.

Benedict, Moble. 2010. "Fundamental Understanding of the Cycloidal-Rotor Concept for Micro Air Vehicle Applications" (Ph.D., University of Maryland, College Park). UMI Number: 3443488.

Benedict, Moble, et al. 2011, May 3–5. "Design, Development and Flight Testing of a Twin-Rotor Cyclocopter Micro Air Vehicle," *Proceedings 67th Annual National Forum, American Helicopter Society*, Virginia Beach, VA.

Benedict, Moble, et al. 2013, June. "Design and Development of a Small-Scale Cyclogyro UAV Utilizing a Novel Cam-Based Passive Blade Pitching Mechanism," *Int. J. Micro Air Vehicles*, 5(2): 145–162.

Benedict, Moble, et al. 2014, March–April. "Development of a Micro Twin-Rotor Cyclocopter Capable of Autonomous Hover," *J. Aircraft*, 51(2): 672–6. https://www.researchgate.net/publication/288791455.

Bennett, Charles L. 2007, Sept. 18 (issue date). "Solar Thermal Aircraft," U.S. Patent 7,270,295 (application filed April 30, 2004).

Bents, D. J. 2011. "Long-Duration Low- to Medium-Altitude Solar Electric Airship Concept," https://ntrs.nasa.gov/citations/20110020831.

Beremand, Donald G., and Richard K. Shaltens. 1986, Jan. 1. "NASA/DOE Automotive Stirling Engine Project: Overview 1986" (USDOE), https://ntrs.nasa.gov/citations/19860020259.

Bernier, Michael. 2025, March 20. "The World Wasn't Ready for Nuclear-Powered Bombers," https://airandspace.si.edu/air-and-space-quarterly/issue-14/nuclear-bomber.

Besler, William J., and Stanley J. Whitlock. 1954, Sept. "A Steam Powerplant for an Airplane Equipped with Boundary-Layer Control and Appendices A–C," Engineering Study 157 (Besler Engineering Report No. 551). For the Office of Naval Research, Contract No. Nonr-201(01).

Besler Corporation. 1958, Dec. 19. "Final Report on Design, Construction and Test of an Aircraft Steam Powerplant for the Office of Naval Research," Contract Nonr 1843(00).

Bie, Dawei, et al. 2021, May. "Design, Aerodynamic Analysis and Test Flight of a Bat-Inspired Tailless Flapping Wing Unmanned Aerial Vehicle," *Aerospace Sci. & Technology*, 112: 106557. https://www.sciencedirect.com/science/article/abs/pii/S1270963821000687.

Bie, Dawei, et al. 2022, March 18 (first online). "Research Progress in Bat-Inspired Flapping Wing Aerial Vehicle," *Proceedings of 2021 International Conference on Autonomous Unmanned Systems* (ICAUS 2021). https://link.springer.com/chapter/10.1007/978-981-16-9492-9_148.

Bibliography

Bishop, Chris. 2002. *The Encyclopedia of Weapons of World War II*. MetroBooks.

Blank, David A., et al. 2005 (2nd ed.). *Introduction to Naval Engineering*. Naval Institute Press.

Blomgren, George F. 2017. "The Development and Future of Lithium Ion Batteries," *J. Electrochemical Soc'y*, 164(1): A5019–25.

Bluffield, Robert. 2014. *Over Empires and Oceans: Pioneers, Aviators and Adventurers—Forging the International Air Routes 1918–1939*. Tattered Flag.

Bogalsky, Jeremy. 2018, Nov. 30. "First Test of Aircraft with an Ion Drive Points to a Radically Different Future for Aviation," https://www.forbes.com/sites/jeremybogaisky/2018/11/30/-ion-engine-mit-solid-state-aircraft/?sh=4f2f0b09468d.

Boirum, Curtis G., and Scott L. Post. 2009, Aug. 2–5. "Review of Historic and Modern Cyclogyro Design," AIAA 2009–5023. 45th AIAA/ASME/SAE/ASEE Joint Propulsion Conference & Exhibit, Denver, CO. https://www.semanticscholar.org/paper/Review-of-Historic-and-Modern-Cyclogyro-Design-Boirum-Post/d36d90de96f3dd248af535fb0d586c04a2bff03b.

Bonikowski, Michael. 2024. "Eather One," https://www.bonikowski.eu/work/eatherone.

Bonnevie-Svendsen, Martin. 2022, Oct. 12. "A Giant Study on Power Records in 144 Professional Cyclists," https://www.wattkg.com/power-records/.

Boretti, Alberto, and Stefania Castellato. 2022, July 13. "NH3 Prospects in Combustion Engines and Fuel Cells for Commercial Aviation by 2030," *ACS Energy Letters*, 7(8): 2557–64. https://doi.org/10.1021/acsenergylett.2c00994.

Borg, John E. 1986, March 28 (DTIC date stamp). "Magnus Effect—an Overview of Its Past and Future Practical Applications," 2 volumes. Contract N00024–83-C-5350. Naval Sea Systems Command.

Boschma, James. 1998, Nov. 15. "Cycloidal Propulsion for UAV VTOL Applications" (Final Report). Contract N68335–98-C-0120/Item 0001AF. Naval Air Warfare Center—Aircraft Division.

Boschma, James J. 2001. "Modern Aviation Applications for Cycloidal Propulsion," AIAA 2001–5267, https://arc.aiaa.org/doi/abs/10.2514/6.2001-5267.

Bourke, E. R. II. 1969. "Unique Approach to Balloon Station Keeping," Raytheon report R69–4041A. Raytheon Corporation.

Bousquet, Gabriel D., et al. 2018, May. "The UNAV, a Wind-Powered UAV for Ocean Monitoring: Performance, Control and Validation," 2018 IEEE International Conference on Robotics and Automation (ICRA), Brisbane, Queensland, Australia. https://dspace.mit.edu/bitstream/handle/1721.1/123685/icra_2018_with_reviews.pdf?sequence=1&isAllowed=y.

Bowers, Peter M. 1990 (2nd ed.). *Unconventional Aircraft*. TAB Books.

Boyea, Ovila W. 1945, July 10 (issue date). "Airplane," U.S. Patent 2,379,875 (application filed Sept. 14, 1943).

Boyne, Walter J. 2004, Sept. "Rocket Men," *Air Force Magazine*, 87: 107–110.

Boyne, Walter J. 2005. *The Influence of Air Power Upon History*. Pen & Sword Books Limited.

Bradley, Marty K., and Christopher K. Droney. 2012, May 1. "Subsonic Ultra Green Aircraft Research Phase II: N+4 Advanced Concept Development," National Aeronautics and Space Administration. https://ntrs.nasa.gov/api/citations/20120009038/downloads/20120009038.pdf.

Branson, Richard. 2011. *Reach for the Skies: Ballooning, Birdmen, and Blasting into Space*. Penguin Publishing Group.

Breeze, Paul. 2005. *Power Generation Technologies* (Elsevier).

Brevoort, M. J., and U. T. Joyner. 1941. "The Problem of Cooling an Air-Cooled Cylinder on an Aircraft Engine," NACA Report 719. National Advisory Committee for Aeronautics.

Brewer, G. Daniel. 2017 (1991). *Hydrogen Aircraft Technology*. CRC Press.

Brewer, Griffith, and Patrick Y. Alexander. 1893. *Aeronautics: An Abridgment of Aeronautical Specifications Filed at the Patent Office from A.D. 1815 to A.D. 1892*. Taylor and Francis.

Brockett, Terry. 1991, Sept. 17–18. "Hydrodynamic Analysis of Cycloidal

255

Bibliography

Propellers," Propeller/Shafting '91 Symposium, Virginia Beach, VA. Society of Naval Architects and Marine Engineers. https://repository.tudelft.nl/islandora/object/uuid:4884991d-071b-4fc5-9732-9edd4b8a2734/datastream/OBJ/download&ved=2ahUKEwjngs6V6uWGAxVeD1kFHY1pCuUQFnoECC0QAQ&usg=AOvVaw1D_ONKQfLbj3r8pOi2_ma0.

Brouwers, Alex P. 1980. "150 and 300 kW Lightweight Diesel Aircraft Engine Design Study," Contract NAS3–20830. National Air and Space Administration.

Brown, Trevor. 2013, June 20. "The AmVeh—an Ammonia Fueled Car from South Korea," https://nh3fuelassociation.org/2013/06/20/the-amveh-an-ammonia-fueled-car-from-south-korea/.

Bruckner, Adam, et al. 2021, January. "The Kirsten Wind Tunnel at the University of Washington," Conference: AIAA Scitech 2021 Forum. https://doi.org/10.2514/6.2021-0518.

Bunget, Gheorghe. 2010. "BATMAV—a Bio-Inspired Micro-Aerial Vehicle for Flapping Flight" (Ph.D., Mechanical Engineering, North Carolina State University). https://repository.lib.ncsu.edu/bitstream/handle/1840.16/6465/etd.pdf.

Burgess, Charles. 1927. *Airship Design* (Ronald Press Co.).

Burgess, Charles. 1932, April. "Steam Power Plant for Airships, Proposed by the Great Lakes Aircraft Corp.," NACA Design Memo. 120.

Burgess, Charles. 1939, July. Sailing Airships at Sea, U.S. Navy Bureau Aeronautics Design Memo. 322.

Bussolari, Steven R., and Ethan R. Nadel. 1989, Summer. "The Physiological Limits of Long-Duration Human Power Production—Lessons Learned from the Daedalus Project," *Human Power: Technical J. IHPVA*, 7(4): 1, 8–10.

Caiella, J. M. 2019, August. "Technological Dead End," *Naval History Magazine*, 33(4): xx. https://www.usni.org/magazines/naval-history-magazine/2019/august/technological-dead-end.

Caldwell, Jonathan E. 1927, August 30 (issue date). "Aeroplane," U.S. Patent 1,640,645 (application filed Feb. 8, 1923).

CAM. 2018. "Pratt & Whitney R-4360-59B Wasp Major," https://combatairmuseum.org/engines/prattwaspmajor.html.

Cameron, John F. 1878, Nov. 26 (issue date). "Improvement in Air-Ships," U.S. Patent 210,238 (application filed Aug. 28, 1878).

Campbell, Joseph K. 1990. *Dibble Sticks, Donkeys, and Diesels: Machines in Crop Production*. International Rice Research Institute.

Camplin, Giles. 2020, Summer. "Breaking Records," *Dirigible: Journal of the Airship Heritage Trust*. 90: (whole issue).

CargoAirships. 2009a, June 28. "Thermal Flyer Outdoors 001," http://www.youtube.com/watch?v=VRV0FdYFewI&feature=plcp.

CargoAirships. 2009b, June 28. "Thermal Flyer Prototype 009," http://www.youtube.com/watch?v=_ncCz3V4ewU.

Cavalari, Al. 2023. "Flags on Vehicles," http://www.flagguys.com/howto.html#vechicles.

Cayley, Sir George. 1816, May. "LXIV. On Aerial Navigation," *The Philosophical Magazine* (Alexander Tilloch), 47(217): 321–329.

Cayley, Sir George. 1837. *Practical Remarks on Aerial Navigation*. Cunningham and Salmon.

Çengel, Yunus A., and Michael A. Boles. 2002 (4th ed.). *Thermodynamics: An Engineering Approach*. McGraw-Hill.

Central Intelligence Agency. 2024a, May 20 (access date). "Artifacts—Insectothopter," https://www.cia.gov/legacy/museum/artifact/insectothopter/.

Central Intelligence Agency. 2024b, May 20 (access date). "Insectothopter: The Bug-Carrying Bug" (Youtube video). https://youtu.be/TZ3spmVqnco.

Chanute, Octave. 1891. *Aerial Navigation*. Railroad and Engineering Journal.

Cheng, Qian, et al. 2024, March. "Review of Common Hydrogen Storage Tanks and Current Manufacturing Methods for Aluminium Alloy Tank Liners," *Int. J. Lightweight Materials & Manufacture*, 7(2): 269–284. https://www.sciencedirect.com/science/article/pii/S2588840423000434.

Chennupati, Siva Raghuram Prasad. 2021, Feb. 4 (publication date). "Universal Propeller, Operating Method and

Bibliography

Favored Uses," WO2021/018353 (July 27, 2019, priority date).
Chessel, Jean-Philippe, and Jean-Pierre Prost. 2017, May 16 (issue date). "Balloon Comprising Photovoltaic Means and a Solar Concentration Device," U.S. Patent 9,650,122 (French priority application filed Nov. 22, 2011).
Chin, D. D., and D. Link. 2016. "Flapping Wing Aerodynamics: From Insects to Vertebrates," *J. Experimental Biology*, 219(7): 920–932. https://doi.org/10.1242/jeb.042317.
Choi, Sang H., et al. 2006. "Power Budget Analysis for High Altitude Airships," https://ntrs.nasa.gov/api/citations/20060012139/downloads/20060012139.pdf.
Choi, Sang H., et al. 2011, Sept. 20 (issue date). "High Altitude Airship Configuration and Power Technology and Method of Operation for Same," U.S. Patent 8,020,805 (provisional application filed July 31, 2006).
Chronister, Nathan. 2008 (5th ed.). *The Ornithopter Design Manual*. Ornithopter Zone. https://ornithopter.org/archive/ODM5.pdf.
Chronister, Nathan. 2018, Spring. "Schmid Mechanism Revealed!" *Flapping Wings: The Ornithopter Society Newsletter*, 1–2, 4. https://www.ornithopter.org/newsletter/2018.1.web.pdf.
Clements, E. W., and G. J. O'Hara. 1972, July. "The Navy Rigid Airship" (Naval Research Laboratory).
Collins, Paul. 2002, Spring. "The Beautiful Possibility: Here Comes the Sun," https://www.cabinetmagazine.org/issues/6/collins.php.
Colozza, Anthony J. (Analex Corp.). 2002, September. "Hydrogen Storage for Aircraft Applications Overview," Contract NAS3–00145. National Aeronautics and Space Administration.
Colozza, Anthony J. 2012, August. *Radioisotope Stirling Engine Powered Airship for Low Altitude Operation on Venus*. NASA/CR—2012-217665. National Aeronautics and Space Administration. https://www.researchgate.net/publication/286041992_Radioisotope_Stirling_Engine_Powered_Airship_for_Low_Altitude_Operation_on_Venus?enrichId=rgreq-d002bb5b9fbfc524cccdf610545c54de-XXX&enrichSource=Y292ZXJQYWdlOzI4NjA0MTk5MjtBUzozMDQwMjY0MjYxMTEzNjBAMTQ0OTQ5NjlNjIwNA%3D%3D&el=1_x_2&_esc=publicationCoverPdf.
Colozza, Anthony J., and Robert L. Cataldo. 2014, July. "Radioisotope Stirling Engine Powered Airship for Atmospheric and Surface Exploration of Titan," NASA/TM—2014-218321. National Aeronautics and Space Administration.
Colpan, Can Ozgur, and Ankic Kovač, eds. 2022. *Fuel Cell and Hydrogen Technologies in Aviation*. Springer Nature Switzerland.
Contact Patch. 2021, May. 6. "M.1410: Marine Propellers," https://the-contactpatch.com/book/marine/m1410-marine-propellers.
Cooper, Iver P. 2025. *Airships: Their Science, History and Future*. McFarland.
Costes, Didier. 1993, June 18 (application filed). "Planeur Aquatique Comportant un Flotteur," French Patent Pub. 2,707,588 (published Jan. 20, 1995).
Costes, Didier. 2000, July 19 (application filed). "Perfectionnement au Planeur Aquatique a Foncton de Derive pour un Bateau ou Aeronef," French Patent Pub. 2,811,958 (published Jan. 25, 2002).
Cousin, Michael, and Cory Hatch. 2024, Aug. 26. "From WWII bombers to desert drones: INL's aviation history predates atomic energy," https://inl.gov/feature-story/from-wwii-bombers-to-desert-drones-inls-aviation-history-predates-atomic-energy.
Cox, Ernest Stewart. 1969. *World Steam in the Twentieth Century*. Allan.
Crockford, Jacque. 2017, Jan. 13. "3 Rowing Workouts to Boost Strength, Endurance, and Aerobic Capacity," https://www.ideafit.com/group-fitness/rowstronger-boat-not-required/.
Crompton, Thomas Roy. 2000. *Battery Reference Book*. Elsevier Science.
Crowley, Andrew J. 1919, Nov. 11 (issue date). "Airship," U.S. Patent 1,321,722 (application filed March 22, 1918).
Curry, Marty. 2002, Feb. 6. "Solar-Powered Gossamer Penguin in Flight," https://www.dfrc.nasa.gov/Gallery/Photo/Albatross/HTML/ECN-13413.html.

Bibliography

Darbyson, Walter. 1933, Oct. 24. "Aeroplane," U.S. Patent 1,931,753 (application filed June 23, 1932).

Darnton, Robert. 2023. *The Revolutionary Temper: Paris, 1748–1789*. W. W. Norton.

Das, Sarit K. 2005. *Process Heat Transfer*. Alpha Science International.

Defense, U.S. Department of. 2020. "Chapter 15, Nuclear Fuel Cycle and Proliferation," *Nuclear Matters Handbook*. https://www.acq.osd.mil/ncbdp/nm/NMHB2020rev/chapters/chapter15.html.

Dell, R. M. 1996, July 15. "Aqueous Electrolyte Batteries," *Philosophical Transactions: Mathematical, Physical and Engineering Sciences*, 354 (1712): 1515–27.

De Lôme, Henri Dupuy. 1872. *Note sur L'Aérostat a Hélice: Construit pour le Compte de L'État* (Note on the Propeller Aerostat Built on Behalf of the State). Gauthier-Villars.

DeltaHawk Engines. 2024, June 18 (access date). "Simplicity, Carried to its Extreme, Becomes Elegance," https://www.deltahawk.com/engines/.

DeLuca, Richard. 2022, Feb. 26. "Charles Ritchel and the Dirigible," https://connecticuthistory.org/charles-ritchel-and-the-dirigible/.

Demirel, Yasar. 2007. *Nonequilibrium Thermodynamics: Transport and Rate Processes in Physical, Chemical and Biological Systems*. Elsevier Science.

De Piolenc, F. Marc. 1999, June. "Introduction to Nuclear Fission Power," *Aerostation*.

Desmond, Kevin. 2018. *Electric Airplanes and Drones: A History*. McFarland.

Deutsches Zentrum fur Luft- und Raumfahrt (German Aerospace Center). 2024, May 12 (access date). "Antares DLR-H2: Fuel cell-powered aircraft," https://www.dlr.de/en/images/2013/2/antares-dlr-h2-fuel-cell-powered-aircraft_9601.

Dewetron. 2022, Dec. 5, "The Piezoelectric and Pyroelectric Effect," https://www.dewetron.com/2022/05/the-piezoelectric-and-pyroelectric-effect/.

Diamond Aircraft. 2011, June 23. "Diamond Aircraft Proudly Presents the World's First Serial Hybrid Electric Aircraft 'DA36 E-Star,'" https://www.diamondaircraft.com/en/about-diamond/newsroom/news/article/diamond-aircraft-proudly-presents-the-worlds-first-serial-hybrid-electric-aircraft-da36-e-star/.

Dick, Harold, and Douglas Robinson. 1992. *The Golden Age of the Great Passenger Airships: Graf Zeppelin and Hindenburg*. Smithsonian.

Diesel, Rudolf. 1894. *Theory and Construction of a Rational Heat Motor*. Translated by Bryan Donkin. E. & F. N. Spon.

Diesel, Rudolf. 1912. *The Present Status of the Diesel Engine in Europe, and a Few Reminiscences of the Pioneer Work in America*. Busch-Sulzer Bros. – Diesel Engine Co.

Dipigny-Giroux, Leslie Ann, and Cary J. Mock. 2009. *Historical Climate Variability and Impacts in North America*. Springer Netherlands.

Discovery. 1933, July. Title unknown. 14(163): 220–3, as abstracted by "Besler System of Steam Power for Aircraft," on page 633 of an unidentified publication, available at https://web.archive.org/web/20190702142007/http://flyingkettle.com/besler4.htm.

Dixon, Mrs. Cromwell. 1908, April. "Airship Stock Pays Well" (advertisement), *Popular Mechanics* 10(4): 144.

Djetel, Steve, et al. 2019, May 16 (online submission date). "A Stirling Engine for Automotive Applications," Vehicle Power and Propulsion Conference, Dec. 2017, Belfort, France. https://hal.science/hal-02131002.

Domański, Jacek. 2024, Feb. 1. "2 February 1872—Maiden Flight of Dupuy de Lôme Dirigible Balloon," *Afterburner: The Aviation Magazine*. https://afterburner.com.pl/2-february-1872-maiden-flight-of-dupuy-de-lome-dirigible-balloon/.

D'Orcy, Ladislas. 1917. *D'Orcy's Airship Manual: An International Register of Airships with a Compendium of the Airship's Elementary Mechanics*. Century.

Dorrington, Graham E. 2007a, February. "Performance of Non-Rigid Airships Operating in the Neutral Buoyancy Condition," *Aeronautical J.*, 89–103.

Dorrington, Graham E. 2007b. "Performance of Battery-Powered Airships," *Proc. I Mech E* 221: 91–104. https://doi.org/10.1243/09544100JAERO41.

Bibliography

Dorsey, Gary. 1990. *The Fullness of Wings: The Making of a New Daedalus*. Viking.

Doty, Stephen R. 2004, November 12. "The History of Weather Observing in Lunenburg, Vermont, 1859–1892," http://www.uvm.edu/~vtstclim/Documents/pdfs/Lunenburg_history.pdf.

Drake, Jonah P., et al. 2024. "Modelling Human Endurance: Power Laws vs Critical Power," *Eur. J. Applied Physiology*, 124: 507–26.

Dreno, Maxime. 2014, Sept. 16. "Human-Powered Airship," https://www.behance.net/gallery/19816229/Human-powered-airship.

Dudhia, Anu. 2007, Dec. 13. "Basic Physics of Rowing," http://eodg.atm.ox.ac.uk/user/dudhia/rowing/physics/basics.html#contents.

Dudley, R., and C. P. Ellington. 1990, January 1. "Mechanics of Forward Flight in Bumblebees: II. Quasi-steady Lift and Power Requirements," *J. Experimental Biology*, 148(1): 53–88. https://journals.biologists.com/jeb/article/148/1/53/5862/-Mechanics-of-Forward-Flight-in-Bumblebees-II-QUASI.

Duke Energy. 2012, March 27. "Pressurized Water Reactors (PWR) and Boiling Water Reactors (BWR)," https://nuclear.duke-energy.com/2012/03/27/pressurized-water-reactors-pwr-and-boiling-water-reactors-bwr.

Eckhard, Dietrich. 2023. *Jet Web: Connections in the Development History of Turbojet Engines 1920–1950*. Springer Fachmedien Wiesbaden.

EEPower. 2024, May 20 (access date). "What Are Supercapacitors?," https://eepower.com/capacitor-guide/types/supercapacitor/#.

Ehrhart, Josef. 1935, Sept. 24 (issue date). U.S. Patent 2,015,514, "Device for the Control of Motion of Movable Blades on Blade Wheels" (Application filed March 23, 1935).

Einat, Moshe, and Roy Kalderon. 2014, July 14. "High Efficiency Lifter Based on the Biefeld-Brown Effect," *AIP Advances*, 4(7): 077120. https://pubs.aip.org/aip/adv/article/4/7/077120/20695/High-efficiency-Lifter-based-on-the-Biefeld-Brown.

Ellington, C. P. 1984, Feb. 24. "The Aerodynamics of Hovering Insect Flight. I. The Quasi-Steady Analysis," *Philosophical Transactions Royal Society London, Series B (Biological Sciences)*, 305 (1122): 1–15.

Elliott, Sheldon D., Jr., et al. 1965, Sept. "Tethered Aerological Balloon System," Technical Publication 3830. U.S. Naval Ordnance Test Station (NOTS).

El-Sayed, Ahmed F. 2016. *Fundamentals of Aircraft and Rocket Propulsion* (Springer).

Emsley, John W. 1883, April 17 (issue date). "Balloon," U.S. Patent 276,012 (application filed March 2, 1883).

Energy Efficiency & Renewable Energy, Office of, U.S. Department of Energy. 2024a, May 10 (access date). "Hydrogen Storage," https://www.energy.gov/eere/fuelcells/hydrogen-storage.

Energy Efficiency & Renewable Energy, Office of, U.S. Department of Energy. 2024b, May 12 (access date). "Comparison of Fuel Cell Technologies," https://www.energy.gov/eere/fuelcells/-comparison-fuel-cell-technologies.

Energy Efficiency & Renewable Energy, Office of, U.S. Department of Energy. 2024c, May 12 (access date). "Types of Fuel Cells," https://www.energy.gov/eere/fuelcells/types-fuel-cells.

Energy, U.S. Department of. 2011, January (draft). "Appendix D Military Reactors," in *Highly Enriched Uranium: Striking a Balance*. Dept. of Energy.

Engblom, William A. 2012, Sept. 13 (publication date). "Dual-Aircraft Atmospheric Platform," U.S. Patent Pub. 2012/0232721. (Provisional filing date March 7, 2011).

Engblom, William A. 2015, Jan. 13 (issue date). "Dual-Aircraft Atmospheric Platform," U.S. Patent 8,931,727 (application filed March 7, 2012).

Engineering Toolbox. 2009. "Wire Ropes—Strengths," https://www.engineeringtoolbox.com/wire-rope-strength-d_1518.html.

English Mechanic and Mirror of Science. 1869, Sept. 3. "Marriott's Aerial Steam Carriage 'Avitor,' at San Francisco," *English Mechanic and Mirror of Science*, 9(232): 511, 517.

Bibliography

Ennis, William Duane. 1915. *Applied Thermodynamics for Engineers.* Van Nostrand.

Ernouf, Baron. 1884. *Histoire de Quatre Inventeurs Français au Dix-Neuvième Siècle.* Librairie Hachette.

Ernst, William D., and Richard K. Shaltens. 1997, February. "Automotive Stirling Engine Development Project," DOE/NASN0032-34, NASA CR-190780, MTI Report 91TR15. U.S. Department of Energy.

Esfahanian, V., et al. 2006, February. "Thermal Analysis of an Si Engine Piston Using Different Combustion Boundary Condition Treatments," *Applied Thermal Engineering*, 26(2-3): 277–287. https://doi.org/10.1016/j.applthermaleng.2005.05.002.

Esmailian, Ehsan, et al. 2014. "Numerical Investigation of the Performance of Voith Schneider Propulsion," *American J. Marine Science*, 2(3): 58–62. http://pubs.sciepub.com/marine/2/3/3.

Euro Airship 2023. "Solar Airship One: Technological Challenges," https://solarairshipone.com/?page_id=1349&lang=en.

European Aviation Safety Agency. 2014, August. "Type-Certificate Data Sheet, Zeppelin LZ N07."

Experimental Department of Airplane Engineering Division. 1918, October. "Review of British Radiator Tests," *Bull. Experimental Department Airplane Engineering Division*, 2(1): 90.

Farris, Franklin E., and Woodward M. Rand. 1964, Nov. 17 (issue date). "Underwater Glider," U.S. Patent 3,157,145 (application filed Dec. 7, 1960, assigned to Oceanic Systems Corp).

Federal Aviation Administration, United States. 1995, Feb. 6. *Airship Design Criteria.* FAA-P-8110-2.

Federal Aviation Administration, United States. 2022, March 29. *Airplane Flying Handbook.* FAA-H-8083-3C. https://www.faa.gov/regulations_policies/handbooks_manuals/aviation/airplane_handbook.

Fédération Aéronautique Internationale. 2024, May 13 (access date). "Records" (Class "Experimental/New Technologies," Subclass "I-C, Human-Powered Aircraft"). https://www.fai.org/records?f%5B0%5D=field_record_sport%3A2021&f%5B1%5D=field_subclass%3A1387.

Festo AG. 2009, April 19 (Wayback Machine Access Date). "A Remote-Controlled Hybrid Construction with Flapping-Wing Mechanism," https://web.archive.org/web/20090419213425/http://www3.festo.com/__C1256D56002E7B89.nsf/html/Air_ray_en.pdf/$FILE/Air_ray_en.pdf.

Festo AG. 2018, March. "BionicFlyingFox: Ultra-Lightweight Flying object with Intelligent Kinematics," https://www.festo.com/PDF_Flip/corp/Festo_BionicFlyingFox/en/.

Ficken, N. L., and Mary C. Dickerson. 1969, July. "Experimental Performance and Steering Characteristics of Cycloidal Propellers," Report 2983. Naval Ship Research and Development Center, Navy Dept.

Flagpole Company, The. 2016, April 3 (Wayback Machine archive date). "Weather Conditions," http://www.flagpolecompany.co.uk/weather%20conditions.html.

Fleischer, William B., and Sidney Zafran. 1957, May 20. "Development of a Steam Powered Sports Car" (B. Sci., Mechanical Engineering, Massachusetts Institute of Technology).

Flying Kettle Project. 2019a, July 21 (Wayback Machine Archive Date). "Flying on Steam," https://web.archive.org/web/20190702145517/http://www.flyingkettle.com/besler5.htm.

Flying Kettle Project. 2019b, July 21 (Wayback Machine Archive Date). "Light Steam Power," https://web.archive.org/web/20190702152200/http://www.flyingkettle.com/besler2.htm.

Folkson, Richard, and Steve Sapsford. 2022 (2nd ed.). *Alternative Fuels and Advanced Vehicle Technologies for Improved Environmental Performance.* Elsevier.

Fork, Werner, and Birgit Jürgens. 2002. "How the VSP Works," 116–123, in *The Fascination of the Voith-Schneider Propeller: History and Engineering.* Koehler.

Foshag, W. F., and G. D. Boehler

Bibliography

(Aerophysics Company). 1969, March. "Review and Preliminary Evaluation of Lifting Horizontal-Axis Rotating-Wing Aeronautical Systems (HARWAS)," Contract DAAJ02-67-C-0046. USAAV-LABS Technical Report 69-13. U.S. Army Aviation Materiel Laboratories.

Fowler, Frank G. 1870, January 4 (issue date). "Improvement in Steering Propellers," U.S. Patent 98,483.

Fraas, A.P., and A.W. Savelainen. 1954, May. "ORNL Aircraft Nuclear Power Plant Designs" (Atomic Energy Commission).

Fritzche, Helmut, and Brian Schwartz. 2008. *Stanford R. Ovshinsky: The Science and Technology of an American Genius*. World Scientific.

Fuller, N. J., et al. 1992, May. "Assessment of the Composition of Major Body Regions by Dual-Energy X-Ray Absorptiometry (Dexa), with Special Reference to Limb Muscle Mass," *Clinical Physiology*, 12(3): 253–66.

Gabrielli, Georg Theodor Lagus. 1893, June 27 (issue date). "Balloon-Ship," U.S. Patent 500,326 (application filed June 16, 1892).

Gage, James P. 1859, March 8. "Balloon," U.S. Patent 23,163.

Ganapathy, V. 2001, July. "Superheaters: Design and Performance," *Hydrocarbon Processing*, 41–45. http://v_ganapathy.tripod.com/superhtr.pdf.

Garrett Motion Inc. 2020, Sept. 20. "World's First Commercial Diesel Engine with Brake Thermal Efficiency Above 50% Launched by Weichai, Boosted by Garrett," https://www.garrettmotion.com/news/newsroom/article/worlds-first-commercial-diesel-engine-with-brake-thermal-efficiency-above-50-launched-by-weichai-boosted-by-garrett/.

Garrick, I. E. 1936. "Propulsion of a Flapping and Oscillating Airfoil," NACA Report 567. National Advisory Committee for Aeronautics. https://ntrs.nasa.gov/citations/19930091642.

Garrison, Peter. 1996, March. "The Little Engine That Might," *Flying Magazine*, 123(3): 101–3.

Gau, Jeff, et al. 2023, Oct. 4. "Bridging Two Insect Flight Modes in Evolution, Physiology and Robophysics," *Nature*, 622: 767–74. https://www.nature.com/articles/s41586-023-06606-3.

Gavaghan, Helen. 1989, Dec. 23. "Technology: Pedal Power Lifts Helicopter into History...," https://www.newscientist.com/article/mg12416963-100-technology-pedal-power-lifts-helicopter-into-history/.

Gebhardt, George Frederick. 1917. *Steam Power Plant Engineering*. J. Wiley and Sons.

Geery, Daniel J. 2001, Dec. 11 (issue date). "Submersible Water Toy," USP 6,328,622 (application filed Oct. 7, 1996).

Geery, Daniel J. 2006a, Oct. 29. "Waterwing," http://www.youtube.com/watch?v=WcYFrhn6Gq8.

Geery, Daniel J. 2006b, Nov. 5. "'Waterwing' in Air," http://www.youtube.com/watch?v=9OvuVD_MqyM.

Gefa-Flug. 2015, June. *Flight Manual AS105GD*.

Geoghegan, John H. 2017, Nov. 30. "These Atomic-Powered Airships Never Made it off the Drawing Board," https://www.navytimes.com/flashpoints/2017/11/30/-these-atomic-powered-airships-never-made-it-off-the-drawing-board/.

Gerhardt, Heinz A. 1993, Nov. 30 (issue date). "Paddle Wheel Rotorcraft," U.S. Patent 5,265,827 (application filed Sept. 16, 1992).

Gillispie, Charles Coulston. 2014. *The Montgolfier Brothers and the Invention of Aviation 1783–1784*. Princeton University Press.

Gleason, Reed. 2019, Feb. 22 (Wayback Machine Archive Date). "The White Dwarf Flies Again!," https://web.archive.org/web/20190222051355/http://home.teleport.com/~reedg/whitedwarf.html.

Global Security. 2016, July 2. "S1W / S2W (Submarine Thermal Reactor Mark STR)," https://www.globalsecurity.org/military/systems/ship/systems/s1w.htm#google_vignette.

GoGreenSolar. 2022, Aug. 23. "The History of Solar Panels and Solar Energy: An Overview," https://blog.gogreensolar.com/history-of-solar-panels.

Goodheart, Benjamin H. 2011, Fall. "Tracing the History of the Ornithopter: Past, Present, and Future," *J. Aviation/*

Bibliography

Aerospace Education & Research, 21(1), article 8.

Goodyear Aircraft Corporation. 1943, September. *United States Navy K-Type Airships Pilot's Manual.*

Gorn, Michael H., and Giuseppe De Chiara. 2022. *X-Planes from the X-1 to the X-60: An Illustrated History.* Springer International.

Goss, William Freeman Myrick. 1910. *Superheated Steam in Locomotive Service.* Carnegie Institution of Washington Publ. No. 127, Carnegie Institution of Washington.

Graham, Robert W., and Arthur J. Glassman. 1980, Oct. 13–16. "Some Advantages of Methane in an Aircraft Gas Turbine," Aerospace Congress (Los Angeles, California). National Aeronautics & Space Administration.

Graver, Joshua Grady. 2005, May. "Underwater Gliders: Dynamics, Control and Design" (Dissertation, Ph.D., Mechanical and Aerospace Engineering Dept., Princeton University). https://naomi.princeton.edu/wp-content/uploads/sites/744/2021/03/jggraver-thesis-4-11-05.pdf.

Graver, Joshua Grady, et al. 2003, August. "Underwater Glider Model Parameter Identification," *Proc. 13th Int. Smp. Unmanned Untethered Submersible Technology.* https://www.researchgate.net/publication/228580445_Underwater_glider_model_parameter_identification.

Graybill, Jacob D. 1897, Oct. 20 (issue date). "Aerial Machine," U.S. Patent 592,704 (application filed May 26, 1896).

Green Car Congress. 2008, April 4. "Boeing Flies Hydrogen Fuel Cell Airplane," https://www.greencarcongress.com/2008/04/boeing-flies-hy.html.

Green Car Congress. 2010, January 13. "ENFICA-FC Fuel Cell Inter-City Aircraft Ready for Flight Testing," https://www.greencarcongress.com/2010/01/-enfica-20100113.html.

Green Car Congress. 2013, July 31. "Aviat, Aviation Foundation Unveil Concept CNG-Fueled Single-Engine Aircraft," https://www.greencarcongress.com/2013/07/aviat-20130731.html.

Grice, Gary K. 2005a, February. "History Of Weather Observing at the Naval Observatory, Washington, D.C., 1838–1913," https://web.archive.org/web/20160220203325/http://mrcc.sws.uiuc.edu/FORTS/histories/DC_Naval_Observatory_Grice.pdf.

Grice, Gary K. 2005b, February. "History of Weather Observing in Washington, D.C., 1821–1950," https://web.archive.org/web/20170517002850/http://mrcc.sws.uiuc.edu/FORTS/histories/DC_Washington_DC_Grice.pdf.

Grosser, Morton. 1981. *Gossamer Odyssey: The Triumph of Human Powered Flight.* Houghton Mifflin.

Gunston, Bill. 1998. *World Encyclopaedia of Aero Engines.* Patrick Stephens.

Gunther, Reinhard. 2024, Jan. 26. "The Efficiency of Solar Power at High Elevation," https://clouglobal.com/higher-ground-the-efficiency-of-solar-power-at-high-altitudes/.

Gur, Ohad, et al. 2010, July-August. "Full-Configuration Drag Estimation," *J. Aircraft*, 47(4): 1356-67.

Guzy, Lawrence T., et al. 1991. "A Note: Can Vehicle Speed be Estimated Accurately?," *J. Applied Social Psychology*, 21: 172–4. https://onlinelibrary.wiley.com/doi/abs/10.1111/j.1559-1816.1991.tb00495.x.

Habibnia, Mehdi, et al. 2020, June 21–24. "A Novel Propulsion System Based on Cycloidal Rotors Coupled with Pair-Wing for VTOL Aircrafts, Cyclo-Craft," *Proceedings of the Canadian Society for Mechanical Engineering International Congress*, Charlottetown, PE, Canada. https://doi.org/10.32393/csme.2020.55.

Haenlein, Paul. 1872, Aug. 27 (issue date). "Improvements in Balloon-Locomotives," U.S. Patent 130,915.

Hagerman, Fritz, and Marjorie Hagerman. 2020. "A Comparison of Energy Output and Input Among Elite Rowers," https://worldrowing.com/wp-content/uploads/2020/12/3Chapter10_English_Neutral-1.pdf.

Harrison, Mark. 2003. "The Political Economy of a Soviet Military R&D Failure; Steam Power for Aviation, 1932 to 1939," Warwick Economic Research Papers No. 611, *J. Econ. History* 63(1): 178–212.

Bibliography

http://www2.warwick.ac.uk/fac/soc/economics/research/workingpapers/publications/twerp611.pdf (2001 draft).

Harte, David, et al. 2011, June. "An Application of Paddlewheel Propulsion to a High Speed Craft," Second International Symposium on Marine Propulsors, Hamburg, Germany. http://www.marinepropulsors.com/smp/files/downloads/smp11/Paper/FA3-1_Harte.pdf.

Hatch, D. S. 1910. "Aerial Navigation," in *Cyclopedia of Automobile Engineering*, 4: 1–114. American Technical Society.

Haydon, Frederick Stansbury. 1941. *Aeronautics in the Union and Confederate Armies*, vol. 1. Johns Hopkins University.

Hays, Thomas Chadwick. 2015. "Closed Cycle Propulsion for Small Unmanned Aircraft" (Ph.D. Oklahoma State University).

Helicopter Museum. 2017, July 21. "Steam-Powered Helicopters Arrive at Helicopter Museum," https://verticalmag.com/press-releases/steam-powered-helicopters-arrive-helicopter-museum/.

Hemighaus, Greg, et al. 2007. *Aviation Fuels: Technical Review*. Chevron Corporation.

Heney, Elaine. 2021, June 9. "Speeds of a Horse: How to Understand Walk, Trot, Canter & Gallop," https://elaineheneyhorses.com/speeds-of-a-horse/.

Henry, Charles J. 1959, December. "A Survey of Cycloidal Propulsion," Report No. 728. Office of Naval Research.

Heppe, Stephen. 2014. Oct. 21 (issue date). "Tethered Airships," U.S. Patent 8,864,063. (US Patent Pub 2012/0312918, 2012, Dec. 13; application filed June 13, 2011).

Hermeus Corp. 2024, June 10 (access date). "Chimera," https://www.hermeus.com/chimera.

Heung, L. Kit. 2003. "Using Metal Hydride to Store Hydrogen," Contract No. DE-AC09-96SR18500, U.S. Department of Energy. https://core.ac.uk/download/pdf/71214152.pdf.

Heung, L. Kit, et al. 2001, July 23 (PDF last modified date). "Hydrogen Storage Development for Utility Vehicles," https://core.ac.uk/download/pdf/71206305.pdf.

High Pressure Steam Locomotive Technology. 2018, July 22 (Wayback Machine archive date). https://web.archive.org/web/20180722215651/http://www.aqpl43.dsl.pipex.com/MUSEUM/LOCOLOCO/hptech.htm.

Hirschberg, Mike. 2012, July/August. "Human Powered Helicopters Take Off," *VERTIFLITE*, 58(4): 38–40.

Hirschel, Ernst Heinrich, et al. 2012. *Aeronautical Research in Germany: From Lilienthal Until Today*. Springer Berlin Heidelberg.

Hodgson, John Edmund. 1924. *The History of Aeronautics in Great Britain: From the Earliest Times to the Latter Half of the Nineteenth Century*. Oxford University Press; H. Milford.

Hoerner, Sighard F. 1965. *Fluid-Dynamic Drag*. Hoerner Fluid Dynamics.

Holloszy, J. O., and E. F. Coyle. 1984, April. "Adaptations of Skeletal Muscle to Endurance Exercise and Their Metabolic Consequences," *J. Applied Physiology: Respiratory, Environmental & Exercise Physiology*, 56(4): 831–8. https://pubmed.ncbi.nlm.nih.gov/6373687/.

H3X. 2023. "200kW in a 18kg Package" https://www.h3x.tech/.

Huber, John T., and John S. Noyes. 2013, April 24. "A New Genus and Species of Fairyfly, *Tinkerbella nana* (Hymenoptera, Mymaridae), with Comments on its Sister Genus *Kikiki*, and Discussion on Small Size Limits in Arthropods," *J. Hymenoptera Research*, 32: 17–44. https://jhr.pensoft.net/articles.php?id=1635.

Hudson, Dreyfuss. 2011, March 24. "American Steam Locomotive Efficiency—the Effect of Blastpipe Size and Superheat Levels," cs.trains.com/TRCCS/forums/t/189535.aspx.

Huler, Scott. 2004. *Defining the Wind: The Beaufort Scale and How a 19th-Century Admiral Turned Science into Poetry*. Crown.

Hultgren, Thor. 1948. *American Transportation in Prosperity and Depression*. National Bureau of Economic Research. http://www.nber.org/chapters/c4617.pdf.

Bibliography

Hush-Kit. 2021, Aug. 23. "Top Ten Human-Powered Aircraft," https://hushkit.net/2021/08/23/top-ten-human-powered-aircraft/.

Hydrogen Tools. 2024, May 10 (access date). "Basic Hydrogen Properties," https://h2tools.org/hyarc/hydrogen-data/basic-hydrogen-properties.

HyLight. 2024, Feb. 7. "Sustainable Aerial Inspections," https://www.arec-idf.fr/fileadmin/DataStorageKit/AREC/Event/Hyvolution_2024/Hylight_-_drone_dirigeable_H2_surveillance_aerienne.pdf.

IFBF. International Flow Battery Forum. 2024, May 7 (access date). "What Is a Flow Battery?," https://flowbatteryforum.com/what-is-a-flow-battery/.

Ivanov, N. S., et al. 2022. "Electric Machines with High Specific Power," *Russian Electrical Engineering*, 93(10): 621–30.

Jabbar, Hamid, et al. 2017, Dec. 11. "Sustainable Micro-Power Circuit for Piezoelectric Energy Harvesting Tile," *Integrated Ferroelectrics*, 183(1): 193–209, https://doi.org/10.1080/10584587.2017.1376964.

James, Carolyn C. 2000, Spring. "The Politics of Extravagance: The Aircraft Nuclear Propulsion Project," *Naval War College Review*, 53(2): 158–190. https://www.jstor.org/stable/44638305.

Jobe, Charles E. 1984, July. "Prediction of Aerodynamic Drag" (Air Force Wright Aeronautical Laboratories).

Johansen, Herbert O. 1962, Nov. "Behold the Dirigible!," *Popular Science* 60–3, 202, 204, 207.

Johnson, V. E. 1912, Feb. 10. "Steam-Driven Models," *Flight and the Aircraft Engineer*, 4(6) (whole 163): 131.

Johnstone, David. 2018, June 7. "How Does Your Cycling Power Output Compare?," https://www.cyclinganalytics.com/blog/2018/06/how-does-your-cycling-power-output-compare.

Jordi, C., et al. 2010, June. "Fish-Like Propulsion of an Airship with Planar Membrane Dielectric Elastomer Actuators," *Bioinspiration & Biomimetics*, 5(2010): 026007. http://iopscience.iop.org/1748-3190/5/2/026007.

Jude, Alexander. 1906. *The Theory of the Steam Turbine*. C. Griffin, Limited.

Jürgens, Dirk. 2006. "Voith Schneider Propeller–Current Applications and New Developments," Voith Turbo, Brochure G 1949. https://www.semanticscholar.org/paper/Voith-Turbo-The-Voith-Schneider-Propeller-Current-J%C3%BCrgens/b2d78bedbdff5893120de12a7a1d128045e8712d.

Jurich, Leo. 1960, April. "The Nuclear Powered Airship," ABAC Acquisition No. 1025. Reprinted in *Aerostation*, June 1999, 4–8.

Kalogiru, Soteris A. 2023. *Solar Energy Engineering: Processes and Systems*. Elsevier Science.

Kantor, George, et al. 2001, October 28–29. "Collection of Environmental Data from an Airship Platform," *Proc. SPIE Conf. Sensor Fusion & Decentralized Control IV*, 4571: 76–83. http://citeseerx.ist.psu.edu/viewdoc/download?doi=10.1.1.15.7169&rep=rep1&type%http://www.ri.cmu.edu/pub_files/pub3/kantor_george_a_2001_1/kantor_george_a_2001_1.pdf.

Kaplan, Philip. 2005. *Big Wings: The Largest Aeroplanes Ever Built* (Pen and Sword).

Karas, J. 1959. "Science in Court," *J. American Judicature Soc'y*, 42: 186–191, 195.

Karasek, Matej, et al. 2018, Sept. 14. "A Tailless Aerial Robotic Flapper Reveals That Flies Use Torque Coupling in Rapid Banked Turns," *Science*, 361(6407): 1089–1094. https://www.science.org/doi/10.1126/science.aat0350?ijkey=AzT6TTb7S5us6&keytype=ref&siteid=sci.

Katnur, Fuad, et al. 2024, April. "Cyclo Rotor Propulsion Equipped Drone," https://www.researchgate.net/publication/379697019_Cyclo_Rotor_Propulsion_Equipped_Drone?enrichId=rgreq-b8a9a94c1ca06c1ccb8483cb22b1a054-XXX&enrichSource=Y292ZXJQYWdlOzM3OTY5NzAxOTtBUzoxMTQxMTI4MTIzODExMzg2OEAxNzEzNTY5NjU0el=1_x_2&_esc=publicationCoverPdf.

Katz, Joseph, et al. 1982, July. "Cooling Air Inlet and Exit Geometries on Aircraft Engine Installations," *J. Aircraft*, 19(7): 525–530, AIAA 80-1242R.

Kays, William Morrow, and Alexander

Bibliography

Louis London. 1998 (3rd ed.). *Compact Heat Exchangers*. Krieger.

Kelly, Maurice. 2006. *Steam in the Air: The Application of Steam Power in Aviation During the 19th and 20th Centuries*. Pen & Sword Books Limited.

Kenealey, James. 2018, Sept. 12. "The Fastest Aircraft You Didn't Know About," https://www.morson.com/the-fastest-aircraft-you-didnt-know-about.

Khalin, Anatolii, and Natalya Kizilova. 2019, May. "Performance Comparison of Different Aerodynamic Shapes for Autonomous Underwater Vehicles," *Archive Mechanical Engineering*, 66(2): 171–189. https://www.researchgate.net/publication/335526761_Performance_comparison_of_different_aerodynamic_shapes_for_autonomous_underwater_vehicles.

Khosravi, Maryam, et al. 2013, April. "Single and Concurrent Effects of Endurance and Resistance Training on Pulmonary Function," *Iranian J. Basic Medical Sciences*, 16(4); 628–34. https://www.ncbi.nlm.nih.gov/pmc/articles/PMC3821882/.

Khoury, Gabriel Alexander, ed. 2012 (2nd ed.). *Airship Technology*. Cambridge University Press.

King, James Wilson. 1878 (2nd ed.). *Report of Chief Engineer J.W. King, United States Navy on European Ships of War and Their Armament, Naval Administration and Economy, Marine Constructions and Appliances, Dockyards, Etc.* GPO.

Kirsten, Kurt F. J. 1922, Oct. 17 (issue date). "Propeller," U.S. Patent 1,432,700 (application filed Dec. 1, 1921).

Kirsten, Kurt F. J. 1929, Dec. 24 (issue date). "Engine-Driven Marine Vessel," U.S. Patent 1,740,820 (application filed April 10, 1924).

Kirsten, Kurt F. J. 1936, June 23 (issue date). "Propeller for Aircraft," U.S. Patent 2,045,233 (application filed Aug. 17, 1934).

Kirsten, Kurt F. J. 1937, Aug. 17 (issue date). "Aircraft," U.S. Patent 2,090,052 (application filed Aug. 20, 1934).

Klopčič, Nejc, et al. 2023, Nov. "A Review on Metal Hydride Materials for Hydrogen Storage," *J. Energy Storage*, 72 (Part B): 108456. https://www.sciencedirect.com/science/article/pii/S2352152X23018534.

Knotts, Rob. C. F. 2014, Summer. "Ritchel's Flying Machine of 1878," *Dirigible: The Journal of the Airship Trust*, 72: 7–10.

Konrad, Captain John. 2009, "Skysails," *Mariners Weather Log*, 53(1). https://www.vos.noaa.gov/MWL/apr_09/skysails.shtml.

Krawetz, Barton, and Leo Celniker. 1989, July 25 (issue date). "Propulsion System for a Buoyant Vehicle," USP 4,850,551 (application filed Dec. 14, 1987, assigned to Lockheed Corp.).

Kretov, A. S., and V. V. Glukhov. 2021, Dec. 11. "Alternative Fuel in Transport Aviation and Estimation of Its Application Efficiency," *Russian Aeronautics*, 64(3): 365–75. https://www.ncbi.nlm.nih.gov/pmc/articles/PMC8665699/.

Kroo, Ilan. 2016, Dec. 3 (Wayback Machine archive date). "Engine Placement," Stanford University, course AA241, "Aircraft Design: Synthesis and Analysis," https://web.archive.org/web/20161203020212/http://adg.stanford.edu/aa241/propulsion/engineplacement.html.

Kumar, R. Vasant, and Thapanee Sarakonsri. 2010. "Introduction to Electrochemical Cells," https://application.wiley-vch.de/books/sample/3527324070_c01.pdf.

Kuttenkeuler, Jakob. 2010, May 21. "KTH Underwater Glider," http://www.youtube.com/watch?v=QZylIBK7vIw.

La Fon, A. F. 1934, Aug. 14. "Aircraft Construction," U.S. Patent 1,969,804 (application filed March 25, 1931).

Lamb, J. Parker. 2003. *Perfecting the American Steam Locomotive*. Indiana University Press.

Lambert, Casey Marcel. 2002. "Dynamics Modeling and Conceptual Design of a Multi-tethered Aerostat System" (Thesis, M. Appl. Sci., Dept. Mechanical Engineering, University of Victoria).

Lana, Francisco. 1910. *The Aerial Ship*. Aeronautical Classics—No. 4. Aeronautical Society of Great Britain. English translation of the 5th and 6th chapters Francisco Lana de Terzi's *Prodromo overo Saggio di alcune inventione nuove premesso all'arte maestra* (Brescia 1670).

Bibliography

Lange Aviation GmbH. 2024. "RED.3 Battery System with Cells of Type 21700," https://www.lange-aviation.com/en/battery-system/.

Langford, John S., et al. 1986. "Final Report of the Daedalus Project Working Group," Massachusetts Institute of Technology.

Law, Daniel C., et al. 2009, Aug. 11 (PDF last modified date). "Lightweight, Flexible, High-Efficiency III-V Multijunction Cells," https://www.spectrolab.com/pv/support/Law%20et%20al.,%20%20WCPEC-4%202006,%20Thin,%20Flexible%20III-V%20MJ%20-%20Final.pdf.

Leclert, Emile. 1872. "M. Dupuy de Lôme's Aërial Ship," *Naval Science*, 1: 280–5.

Lee, Jonathan P., and Adam P. Bruckner. 2017, Jan. 5. "Let No New Improvement Pass Us By: The History of the Kirsten-Boeing Engineering Company," 55th AIAA Aerospace Sciences Meeting, Jan. 9–13, 2017, Grapevine, Texas. https://arc.aiaa.org/doi/abs/10.2514/6.2017-0114.

Lee, Russell. 2010, Aug. 7. "First Public Demonstration of Solar-Powered Gossamer Penguin," https://airandspace.si.edu/stories/editorial/first-public-demonstration-solar-powered-gossamer-penguin.

Lentink, David, et al. 2010. "Chapter 14: The Scalable Design of Flapping Micro-Air Vehicles Inspired by Insect Flight," in *Flying Insects and Robots*, pp. 185–205, edited by Dario Floreano et al. Springer Berlin Heidelberg.

Levinson, Mark. 1992, March. "Frederick Kurt Kirsten: A Biographical Sketch," https://uw-s3-cdn.s3.us-west-2.amazonaws.com/wp-content/uploads/sites/103/2022/07/13113604/UW-Kirsten-Mark-Levinson-bio.pdf.

Li, Jiaqi, et al. 2021. "Triboelectric Nanogenerators for Harvesting Wind Energy: Recent Advances and Future Perspectives," *Energies*, 14: 6949. https://doi.org/10.3390/en14216949.

Li, Jin. 1991, May. "Theoretical and Experimental Study of Cycloidal Propellers" (M. Engineering, Memorial University of Newfoundland).

Li, Xiaojian, et al. 2011, August. "Research on Thermal Characteristics of Photovoltaic Array of Stratospheric Airship," *J. Aircraft*, 48(4): 1380–6.

Liberatore, Eugene K. 1954. *Special Types of Rotary Wing Aircraft*. (Rotary Wing Aircraft Handbooks and History, vol. 11) U.S. Dept. of Commerce.

Library of Congress. 2024a, May 14 (access date). "Le Trans-Ether, Aéro-Moteur de la Navigation Atmosphérique / F. Ducroz, breveté S.G. du Gt., 25, rue du Buloi; Harent, lith." Call No. LOT 13404, no. 23 [P&P]. Repro No. LC-DIG-ppmsca-02523. https://www.loc.gov/resource/ppmsca.02523/.

Library of Congress. 2024b, July 5 (access date). "Navigation aérienne. Solution d'un grand problème par l'emploi des voiles mobiles ... Systéme Augte. Lanteigne, menuisier m'ecen., ... / dessiné par l'auteur," Call No. LOT 13404, no. 20 [P&P]. Repro No. LC-DIG-ppmsca-02520. https://www.loc.gov/resource/ppmsca.02520/.

Liggett, Paul E. 2011, Feb. 1 (issue date). "Piezoelectric and Pyroelectric Power-Generating Laminate for an Airship Envelope," U.S. Patent 7,878,453 (application filed Jan. 28, 2008).

Liggett, Paul E., et al. 2013, Sept. 3 (issue date). "Metallized Flexible Laminate Material for Lighter-than-Air Vehicles," U.S. Patent 8,524,621. (PCT Application filed Sept. 20, 2006).

Lin, Yuexia Luna, et al. 2023, Sept. 13. "Fluid–Structure Interactions of Bristled Wings: The Trade-Off Between Weight and Drag," *J. Royal Society Interface*, 20: 20230266 http://doi.org/10.1098/rsif.2023.0266.

Lindeburg, Michael R. 2010. *Core Engineering Concepts for Students and Professionals*. Professional Publications, Inc.

Lippincott, Matthew. 2022, June 19. "Sailing the Sky: Endless Gliding Takes Shape," https://www.headfullofair.com/post/sailing-the-sky/.

Liu, Yangmin, et al. 2021. "A High Sensitivity Self-Powered Wind Speed Sensor Based on Triboelectric Nanogenerators (TENGs)," *Sensors* 21: 2951. https://doi.org/10.3390/s21092951.

Lobner, Peter. 2022a, March 10. "TAO

Bibliography

Group Airships," https:/lynceans.org/-wp-content/uploads/2021/04/TAO-Group-airships-converted.pdf.

Lobner, Peter. 2022b, March 18. "Sunrise—Solar-Powered Thermal Airship," https://lynceans.org/wp-content/uploads/2019/08/Sunrise-solar-thermal-airship-converted.pdf.

Lobner, Peter. 2022c, March 18. "Sterling Solar-Electric Thermal Airship Concept," https://lynceans.org/wpcontent/uploads/2019/08/Sterling-solar-thermal-airship-converted.pdf.

Lobner, Peter. 2022d, September 3. "Aérial Concept Group & Transoceans – IRIS Challenger & Lélio," https://lynceans.org/wp-content/uploads/2022/02/-Aerial-Concept-Group-Transoceans-converted.pdf.

Lobner, Peter. 2023, Oct. 27. "ISL Aeronautical & Space Systems (Formerly Bosch Aerospace Inc.)—UAV Blimps and Tethered Aerostats," https://lynceans.org/wp-content/uploads/2022/07/ISL-BOSCH-Aerospace-1.pdf.

Lobner, Peter. 2024, Jan. 5. "Walden Aerospace / LTAS – Electro-Kinetic (EK) Propulsion Airships," https://lynceans.org/wp-content/uploads/2021/05/-Walden-LTAS_Exotic-hybrid-airships_R1-converted.pdf.

Locke, F.W.S., Jr. 1954. "A Preliminary Study of a Nuclear-Powered AEW Airship," Report DR-1649 (Navy Dept. Bur. Aeronautics).

Loening, Grover C. 1920, June. "Engine Shape as Affecting Airplane Operation," *J. Soc'y Automotive Engineers*, 6(6): 417–21.

Loftus, Elizabeth F. 1996. *Eyewitness Testimony*. Harvard University Press.

Loftus, Elizabeth F., and J. C. Palmer. 1974. "Reconstruction of Auto-Mobile Destruction: An Example of the Interaction Between Language and Memory," *J. Verbal Learning and Verbal Behaviour*, 13: 585–589. (As summarized at https://web.archive.org/web/20130122101256/http://www.holah.co.uk/study-detail.php?slug=loftus.)

Logan, Earl, Jr., and Ramendra Joy. 2003 (2nd ed.). *Handbook of Turbomachinery*. Taylor & Francis.

Logothetis, I., et al. 2017. "Triboelectric Effect in Energy Harvesting," *IOP Conf. Ser.: Mater. Sci. Eng.* 254: 042021. https://doi.org/10.1088/1757-899X/254/4/042021.

Lovegrove, Keith, and Wes Stein. 2020. *Concentrating Solar Power Technology: Principles, Developments, and Applications*. Elsevier Science.

Lowry, John T. 1999. *Performance of Light Aircraft*. AIAA.

Lubkowski, Steven, et al. 2010, April 5 (PDF creation date). "Trade-Off Analysis of Regenerative Power Source for Long Duration Loitering Airship," http://catsr.ite.gmu.edu/SYST490/SolarEnergy_HighAltitudeAirship.pdf.

Luchter, Stephen, and Roy A. Renner. 1977, April. "An Assessment of the Technology of Rankine Engines for Automobiles," ERDA-77–54. U.S. Energy Research and Development Administration.

Lycoming. 2006, October (3rd ed.). *Operator's Manual Lycoming O-320 Series*. Lycoming.

Lycoming. 2009, December (8th ed., 2005, October). *Operator's Manual Lycoming O-360, HO-360, IO-360, AIO-360, HIO-360 & TIO-360 Series*. Lycoming. https://www.lycoming.com/content/operator%27s-manual-O-360-HO-360-IO-360-AIO-360-HIO-360-TIO-360-60297-12.

Lynch, James, et al. 2022, Feb. 3 (PDF last modified date). "Autonomous Actuation of Flapping Wing Robots Inspired by Asynchronous Insect Muscle," https://sponberg.gatech.edu/wp-content/uploads/2022/08/Gau-et-al-2022_02.pdf.

Ma, Kevin H., et al. 2013, March 28. "Controlled Flight of a Biologically Inspired, Insect-Scale Robot," *Science*, 340: 603–7.

MacCready, Paul. 1985, November. "The Great Pterodactyl Project," *Engineering & Science*, 49(2): 18–24, https://calteches.library.caltech.edu/3471/1/MacCready.pdf.

Magnan, Antoine. 1934. *La Locomotion Chez Les Animaux. 1, Le Vol Des Insectes*. Librairie Scientifique Hermann & Co.

Bibliography

Mahdi, Khaled, and Nadir Bellel. 2014. "Development of a Spherical Solar Collector with a Cylindrical Receiver," *Energy Procedia*, 52: 438–448. https://www.researchgate.net/publication/280567992_Development_of_a_Spherical_Solar_Collector_with_a_cylindrical_receiver.

Maimun, Adi, et al. 2010. "Influence of Twin Hulls Geometry on Aerodynamic Characteristics of WIG Catamaran During Ground Effect," *Proceedings of the 9th WSEAS International Conference on Applications of Computer Engineering*. http://www.wseas.us/e-library/conferences/2010/Penang/ACE/ACE-24.pdf.

Majeski, J. 2002, October. "Stirling Engine Assessment" (Electric Power Research Institute), https://www.engr.colostate.edu/~marchese/mech337-10/epri.pdf.

Marcy, William L., and Ralph O. Hockway (Martin Marietta Corp.). 1979, Sept. 15. "Propulsion Options for the Hi Spot Long Endurance Drone Airship" (Final Report). Report MCR 79-632. Contract N62269-79-C-0204. Naval Air Development Center.

Marks, Lionel Simeon, and Theodore Baumeister. 1916. *Mechanical Engineers' Handbook*. McGraw-Hill.

Marlow Ropes. 2023, June. "Industrial & Utility Ropes," https://www.marlowropes.com/us/wp-content/uploads/2023/06/industrial__utility.pdf.

Martin, Marvin. 1935, November. "Marriott and His Flying Avitor," *Flying Magazine*, 17(5): 289–290, 318.

Mason, Lee. 2023, May 2. "Small Closed Brayton Cycle Engines for Space Applications," MIT Gas Turbine Workshop. https://ntrs.nasa.gov/api/citations/20230006422/downloads/MIT%2520Gas_Turbine_Workshop_Mason_final.pdf.

Mateo-March, et al. 2022. "The Record Power Profile in Professional Female Cyclists: Normative Values Obtained from a Large Database," *Int. J. Sports Physiology & Performance*, 17(5): 682–6.

Maybach, Wilhelm A. 1902, Sept. 16 (issue date). "Cooling and Condensing Apparatus," U.S. Patent 709,416 (application filed March 28, 1901).

Mayer, Helmut. 2022, Feb. 1. "The Initial Research and Testing Phase," https://aviationh2.com.au/the-initial-research-and-testing-phase/.

Mazda. 2023. "Five Things You Need to Know About the World's First Commercial Compression Ignition Engine," https://insidemazda.mazdausa.com/the-mazda-way/technology/-five-things-need-know-worlds-first-compression-ignition-engine/.

Mazer, Lawrence F., et al. 1994, January. "Expert Testimony Regarding the Speed of a Vehicle: The Status of North Carolina Law and the State of the Art," *Campbell Law Review*, 16(2): 191–204. https://core.ac.uk/reader/232782940.

McIntyre, John. 2016, Jan. 18. "Human Powered Flight, What Can the Past Tell Us About the Future," https://www.humanpoweredflight.co.uk/hpfMedia/media/7/2016-RAeS-HPFG-lecture.pdf.

McKee, Eric Michael. 2012, December. "Novel Airframe Design for the Dual-Aircraft Atmospheric Platform Novel Airframe Design for the Dual-Aircraft Atmospheric Platform Flight Concept" (M.S. Mechanical Engineering, Embry-Riddle Aeronautical University). https://commons.erau.edu/edt/104/.

McNabb, Michael Lynn. 2001, December. "Development of a Cycloidal Propulsion Computer Model and Comparison with Experiment" (M.S. Aerospace Engineering, Mississippi State University).

McNeil, Ian. 2002. *An Encyclopedia of the History of Technology*. Taylor & Francis.

McPhee. John. 1973. *The Deltoid Pumpkin Seed*. Farrar Straus Giroux.

Meade, Richard Kidder. 1918. *The Chemist's Pocket Manual*. Chemical Publishing Company.

Mechanical Technology Incorporated. 1979, September. "Assessment of the State of Technology of Automotive Stirling Engines," National Aeronautics and Space Administration.

Merritt, Frederick R. 1898, Dec. 6 (issue date). "Air-Ship," U.S. Patent 615,569 (Application filed April 7, 1898).

Michel, Silvain, et al. 2008, May. "Feasibility Studies for a Bionic Propulsion System of a Blimp Based on Dielectric

Bibliography

Elastomers," *Proc. SPIE* (International Society for Optical Engineering) 6927: 69270S-1 to 62970S-14. https://www.researchgate.net/publication/228752086.

Micro Air Vehicles Laboratory (Delft University of Technology). 2024. "Delfly," https://www.delfly.nl/home/ (and daughter pages).

Miller, Richard. 1967. *Without Visible Means of Support*. Printed by Parker.

Millikan, Frank Rives. 2007. "Joseph Henry: Father of Weather Service," https://web.archive.org/web/20090730024508/http://siarchives.si.edu/history/jhp/joseph03.htm.

Miner, S. S. 1966, Feb. "New Revolver-Like Steam Engine," *Pop. Sci. Monthly*, 188(2): 84–88.

Mingjing, Qi, et al. 2023. "Asynchronous and Self-Adaptive Flight Assembly via Electrostatic Actuation of Flapping Wings," *Advanced Intelligent Systems*, 3(11): 210048. https://onlinelibrary.wiley.com/doi/epdf/10.1002/aisy.202100048.

Mitchell, Matthew P. 2011, Feb. 15 (issue date). "High-Altitude Long-Endurance Airship," U.S. Patent 7,887,007.

Mollenhauer, Klaus, and Helmut Tschoeke. 2010. *Handbook of Diesel Engines*. Springer.

Muzzi, Muzio. 1844, Oct. 16 (issue date)., "Flying Machine," U.S. Patent 3,799.

Myers, Carl E. 1897a, Sept. 2. "An Aerial Navigation Problem," *Leslie's Weekly Illustrated*, 85 (1190): 154.

Myers, Carl Edgar. 1897b, April 20. U.S. Patent No. 581,218, "Sky-Cycle" (Application filed March 13, 1889).

Myers, Carl Edgar. 1902, Feb. "Progress in Automobile Motors and Airships," *Automobile Review*, 6(2): 33–4.

Myers, Carl E., and Carlotta Myers. 1885, May 26 (issue date). U.S. Patent 318,575, "Guiding Apparatus for Balloons" (Application filed Dec. 18, 1884).

Nakonechny, B. V. 1961, January. "Experimental Performance of a Six-Bladed Vertical Axis Propeller," report no. 1446. David Taylor Model Basin.

Nanda, Ankit. 2011, Fall. "The Propulsive Design Aspects on the World's First Direct Drive Hybrid Airplane" (Thesis, M.S. Aerospace Engineering, Embry-Riddle Aeronautical University). https://commons.erau.edu/edt/110.

National Air and Space Museum, Smithsonian. 2024, May 25 (access date). "Besler Steam Engine, Reproduction," https://airandspace.si.edu/collection-objects/-besler-steam-engine-reproduction/nasm_A19650253000.

National Meteorological Library and Archive (U.K.). 2018, Dec. 7 (PDF last modified date). "Fact Sheet 6—the Beaufort Scale, version 1," https://www.metoffice.gov.uk/binaries/content/assets/metofficegovuk/pdf/research/library-and-archive/library/publications/factsheets/factsheet_6-the-beaufort-scale.pdf.

National Museum of American History (Smithsonian Institution). 2024 (access date). "Patent Model for a Feathering Paddle Wheel, 1877," Catalog 325944. (Associated with the patent of Henry Williams, issued April 3, 1877, U.S. Patent 189,164). https://americanhistory.si.edu/collections/nmah_843821.

National Renewable Energy Laboratory, Department of Energy. 2023, October 25 (access date). "Interactive Best Research-Cell Efficiency Chart," https://www.nrel.gov/pv/interactive-cell-efficiency.html

National Weather Service. 2017, Aug. 19 (Wayback Machine archive date). "History of the National Weather Service," 1800–1899 tab. https://web.archive.org/web/20170819055332/http://www.weather.gov/timeline.

Nature. 1872, Feb. 22. "Aerial Navigation in France," *Nature*, 334. (Article reprinted from the *Daily News*).

Navy, U.S. Dept. of, Bureau of Engineering. 1929, April 1. "Blau Gas Replaces Gasoline as Fuel in the 'Graf Zeppelin,'" *Bulletin of Engineering Information*, 39: 5–6.

Naymark, Captain Sherman. 1970, April. "'Underway on Nuclear Power': The Development of the Nautilus," *Proc. U.S. Naval Inst.* 96/4/806, https://www.usni.org/magazines/proceedings/1970/april/underway-nuclear-power-development-nautilus.

Nelson, Jenny A. 2003. *The Physics of Solar Cells*. World Scientific Publishing Company.

Bibliography

New York Herald. 1863, Sept. 8. "Aerial Navigation," no. 9853, p. 3. https://www.loc.gov/resource/sn83030313/1863-09-08/ed-1/?sp=3&st=image.

New York Times. 1866, May 26. "Ascent and Return of the Aereon," https://www.nytimes.com/1866/05/26/archives/ascent-and-return-of-the-aereon.html.

New York Times. 1866, June 7. "Local Intelligence: The Aereon. Her Second Trip," https://www.nytimes.com/1866/06/07/archives/local-intelligence-the-aereon-her-second-tripsix-thousand-feet.html.

NH_3 Fuel Association 2024. "Introduction to NH_3 Fuel," https://nh3fuelassociation.org/introduction/.

Norberg, U. M. Lindhe. 2006. *WIT Transactions on State of the Art in Science and Engineering,* 3: 120–154, https://web.archive.org/web/20170817105435/https://www.witpress.com/Secure/elibrary/papers/1845640012/1845640012204FU1.pdf.

Noth, André. 2008, July 17 (PDF creation date). "History of Solar Flight," https://ethz.ch/content/dam/ethz/special-interest/mavt/robotics-n-intelligent-systems/asl-dam/documents/projects/History_of_Solar_Flight_Skysailor.pdf.

Novella, Steven. 2020, March 16. "Perpetual Flying Machine," NEUROLOGICAblog. https://theness.com/neurologicablog/perpetual-flying-machine/.

Nozaki, Hirohito, et al. 2007, Dec. 12–14. "Thrusting Test of Cycloidal Propeller for 20 Meter-Class Airship-Type Aerial Base Robot," *Proceedings of the 16th Transportation and Logistics Conference of the Japan Society of Mechanical Engineers,* Paper 3210, 119–120 (in Japanese).

Nozaki, Hirohito, et al. 2009, May 4. "Research and Development on Cycloidal Propellers for Airships," 18th AIAA Lighter-than-Air Systems Technology Conference, May 4–7, 2009, Seattle, Washington. https://doi.org/10.2514/6.2009-2850.

Odougherty, Patrick. 2018. *St. Patrick, the Green Revolution and the Hydrogen Conversion Project.* lulu.com.

Off-Grid Europe. 2021, Aug.2 (Wayback Machine Archive Date). "Lead-Acid Battery," https://web.archive.org/web/20210802001304/https://www.off-grid-europe.com/info/lead-acid-battery/.

Ogawa, Toshio, and Yoshikazu Tanaka. 1967. "Balloon Measurement of Atmospheric Electric Potential Gradient," *J. Geomagnetism & Geoelectricity,* 19(4): 307–13.

Ohajianya A. C., et al. 2020, June. "Design and Construction of a Membraneless Zinc-Chlorine Electric Cell," *J. Sustainable Energy,* 11(1): 6–8.

Olis, Stephen. 2017, April 27. "A First Principles Analysis of Alternative Marine Propulsion Mechanisms" (Major Qualifying Project Report, Worcester Polytechnic Institute).

Olley, Jane. 2008, October. "Human-Powered Handpumps for Water Lifting," https://old2019.sswm.info/sites/default/files/reference_attachments/OLLEY%202008.%20Humanpowered%20handpumps.pdf.

Onda, Mashiko, and Yasushi Morikawa. 1991. "An Acrobatic Airship 'ACROSTAT,'" SAE Technical Paper 911994, International Pacific Air & Space Technology Conference 1991, https://doi.org/10.4271/911994; also SAE. 1991. Transactions, *J Aerospace, Sec 1,* 100 (Part 2): 2101–5.

Onda, Mashiko, et al. 2003, November. "Cycloidal Propeller and its Application to Advanced LTA Vehicles," AIAA's 3rd Annual Aviation Technology, Integration, and Operations (ATIO) Forum. https://www.researchgate.net/publication/268573799_Cycloidal_Propeller_and_its_Application_to_Advanced_LTA_Vehicles.

Orr, Mathew W. 2000, Sept. 19. "Aerodynamic Properties of the Inboard Wing Concept" (M.Sci. Aerospace Engineering, Virginia Polytechnic Institute), https://www.google.com/url?sa=t&source=web&rct=j&opi=89978449&url=https://citeseerx.ist.psu.edu/document%3Frepid%3Drep1%26type%3Dpdf%26doi%3D316812e4cd357b08f02080f1039cbc4ab4cf0364&ved=2ahUKEwjbt_zC3piHAxXBFlkFHcM-CPoQFnoECBkQAQ&usg=AOvVaw2im6kSrrAxwcf7vBl4DoK8.

Otago Witness. 1866, Sept. 28. "Dr. Andrews's Flying Ship in New York," Issue 774, p. 4.

Bibliography

Otto, Marcel, et al. 2023, June 19. "Ammonia as an Aircraft Fuel: A Critical Assessment from Airport to Wake," *ASME Open J. Engineering*, 2: 021033-1–021033-12. https://doi.org/10.1115/1.4062626.

Ozoroski, Thomas A., et al. 2015, January. "High Altitude Long Endurance UAV Analysis Model Development and Application Study Comparing Solar Powered Airplane and Airship Station-Keeping Capabilities," NASA/TM-2015-218677. National Aeronautics and Space Administration.

Page, Robin, and Steve Jenkins. 2005. *Animals in Flight*. Houghton Mifflin Harcourt.

Parker, James F., Jr., and Vita R. West. 1973 (2nd ed.). *Bioastronautics Data Book*. NASA SP-3006. National Air and Space Administration. https://ntrs.nasa.gov/api/citations/19730006364/downloads/19730006364.pdf.

Parry-Williams, Gemma, and Sanjay Sharma. 2020. "The Effects of Endurance Exercise on the Heart: Panacea or Poison?," *Nature Reviews Cardiology*, 17: 402–12 https://www.nature.com/articles/s41569-020-0354-3.

Parsons, Samuel R. 1920, June. "Design Factors for Airplane Radiators," *J. Soc'y Automotive Engineers*, 6(6): 437–440.

Phan, Hoang Vu, et al. 2020a, July 1. "Towards the Long-Endurance Flight of an Insect-Inspired, Tailless, Two-Winged, Flapping-Wing Flying Robot," *IEEE Robotics and Automation Letters*. https://arxiv.org/abs/2005.06715.

Phan, Hoang Vu, et al. 2020b, Dec. 4. "Mechanisms of Collision Recovery in Flying Beetles and Flapping-Wing Robots," *Science*, 370 (6521): 1214–9 https://www.science.org/doi/10.1126/science.abd3285.

Phillips, Del. 2009, Autumn. "The World's Youngest Aviator: Cromwell Dixon," *Montana: The Magazine of Western History*, 59(3): 50–66, notes 95–96.

Piancastelli, Luca, and Marco Pelligrini. 2007, December. "The Bonus of Aircraft Piston Engines, an Update of the Meredith Effect," *Int. J. Heat & Technology*, 25(2): 51–56. https://www.researchgate.net/publication/253649721_The_bonus_of_aircraft_piston_engines_an_update_of_the_Meredith_effect.

Pistoia, Gianfranco. 2005. *Batteries for Portable Devices*. Elsevier Science.

Planas. Oriol. 2018, March 21. "Advantages and Disadvantages of the Stirling Engine," https://en.demotor.net/stirling-engine/advantages-disadvantages.

Pocock, George. 1851. *A Treatise on the Aeropleustic Art*. Longman, Brown, and Co.

Pornsin-Sirirak, T. Nick, et al. 2000. "Microbat: A Palm-Sized Electrically Powered Ornithopter," https://citeseerx.ist.psu.edu/document?repid=rep1&type=pdf&doi=8b7f7d16bd6b629f390503434d9b83c5c56aee65.

Prieto, J. I., et al. 2000. "A New Equation Representing the Performance of Kinematic Stirling Engines," *Proc. Inst. Mech. Engrs.* 214 Part C: 449–64.

Pulman, Chris. 2004, April 26 (PDF creation date). "The Physics of Rowing," https://eodg.atm.ox.ac.uk/user/dudhia/rowing/physics/rowing.pdf.

Purandare, Ravi Yeshvant. 2007, May. "A Buoyancy-Propelled Airship" (Dissertation, Ph.D., Mechanical Engineering, New Mexico State University).

Quick, Darren. 2010, March 17. "Rocket Powered Dragonfly DF1 Helicopter Cleared for Take-Off," https://newatlas.com/dragonfly-df1-helicopter/14539/.

Rae, Andrew. 2020, June 30. "No Propeller? No Problem. This Blimp Flies on Buoyancy Alone," *IEEE Spectrum*. https://spectrum.ieee.org/no-propeller-no-problem-this-blimp-flies-on-buoyancy-alone. (Originally published in the print edition of *IEEE Spectrum*, July 2020, under the title "This Blimp Flies on Buoyancy Alone).

Ragan, Sean Michael. 2010, March 17. "Helicopter with Hydrogen-Peroxide-Rocket-Powered Blades," https://makezine.com/article/science/energy/helicopter-with-hydrogen-peroxide-r/.

Ragheb, M. 2025, Jan. 26. "Nuclear Marine Propulsion," https://mragheb.com/NPRE%20402%20ME%20405%20Nuclear%20Power%20Engineering/Nuclear%20Marine%20Propulsion.pdf.

Ramezani, Alireza, et al. 2016, May 16. "Bat

Bibliography

Bot (B2), a Biologically Inspired Flying Machine," *2016 IEEE International Conference on Robotics and Automation (ICRA)*, 3219–26. IEEE. https://secemu.org/wp-content/uploads/2022/10/13-Bat-Box-B2.pdf.

Ramos, Eli. 2023, Dec. 5. "Robotic Insect Reveals Evolutionary Secrets of the Fastest Flapping Fliers," https://news.mongabay.com/2023/12/robotic-insect-reveals-evolutionary-secrets-of-the-fastest-flapping-fliers/.

Rathke, P., et al., 2013. "Long Distance Flight Testing with the Fuel Cell Powered Aircraft Antares DLR-H2," DLR Document ID 30219, https://www.dglr.de/publikationen/2014/301219.pdf.

Reay, David Anthony. 1977. *The History of Man-Powered Flight*. Pergamon.

Recks, Robert J. 2002. An Introduction to Muscle Powered Ultra-Light Gas Blimps. Association of Balloon and Airship Constructors (ABAC).

RED Aircraft GmbH. 2017, Aug. 9 (Wayback Machine Archive Date). "RED A05 - V6–3550cc/216 cu in," https://web.archive.org/web/20170809172108/https://www.red-aircraft.com/wp-content/uploads/2012/07/RED-A05I.pdf.

Reed, Daniel. 1897, October 12 (issue date). "Air Ship," U.S. Patent 591,692 (application filed June 10, 1896).

Reefsteamers. 2018, Jan. 30 (Wayback Machine Archive Date). "25NC No.3472 'Elize,'" https://web.archive.org/web/20180130164459/http://www.reefsteamers.com/css/Rolling%20Stock/25NC%203472.html.

Reik, Oliver. 2018, Sept. 23. Post, Rotax 912 ULS Installed Weight, in Rotax Engine Forum, online community of Zenith Aircraft builders and flyers. https://zenith.aero/forum/topics/rotax-912-uls-installed-weight.

Reiman, Major Adam D. 2009, June. "AMC's Hydrogen Future: Sustainable Air Mobility" (Graduate Research Project, M.Sci. Engineering and Environmental Management, Air Force Institute of Technology, Air University).

Reynolds, Alva L. 1906, April. "The Aerial Rowboat," *Pop. Mech.* 8(4): 427–8.

Rhodes, John. 2024, April 4 (access date).

"Steam Vs. Diesel: A Comparison of Modern Steam and Diesel in the Class I Railroad Environment," http://www.internationalsteam.co.uk/trains/newsteam/modern50.htm.

Riaz, Omair, et al. 2013. "Piezoelectric Energy Harvesting for Airships and Investigation of Bio-Inspired Energy Harvesters," 5th European Conference for Aeronautics and Space Sciences (EUCASS). https://www.eucass.eu/component/docindexer/%3Ftask%3Ddownload%26id%3D4237.

Ridden, Paul. 2010, June 28. "Zeppy 3: Wind-Powered Airship to Attempt Mediterranean Crossing," https://newatlas.com/zeppy3-sail-balloon-mediterranean-crossing-attempt/15552/.

Riddle, William Nelson. 1892, April 19 (issue date). "Aerial Ship," U.S. Patent 473,344 (application filed July 11, 1891).

Ritchel, Charles F. 1878, March 12 (issue date). U.S. Patent 201,200, "Improvement in Flying-Machines."

Robinson, Douglas. 1982. *Up Ship!: A History of the U.S. Navy's Rigid Airships 1919–1935*. Naval Institute Press.

Rodgers, Vice Admiral William Ledyard. 1937. *Greek and Roman Naval Warfare*. Naval Institute Press.

Rompokos, Pavlos. 2020, Nov. 13. "Liquefied Natural Gas for Civil Aviation," *Energies 2020*, 13(22): 5925. https://doi.org/10.3390/en13225925.

Rose, Alexander. 2021. *Empires of the Sky: Zeppelins, Airplanes, and Two Men's Epic Duel to Rule the World*. Random House.

Roth, Emanuel M. 1966. *Bioenergetics of Space Suits for Lunar Exploration*. NASA SO-84. National Aeronautics and Space Administration.

Rousson, Stephane. 2007, July 4. "Make Me Fly...," https://www.youtube.com/watch?v=8F6pQ07rD-A&t=37s.

Rousson, Stephane. 2014a, January. "Dossier Technique Aerosail," https://www.rousson.org/Stephane_Rousson/Aerosail_files/Dossier%20Technique%20Ae%CC%81rosail%20copie.pdf.

Rousson, Stephane. 2014b, March 19. "Aérosail Voilier des airs," http://

Bibliography

www.rousson.org/Stephane_Rousson/Aerosail_files/Aerosail.pdf.

Rowing Level. 2024a, May 22 (access date). "2000m Row Times: Rowing Standards by Age and Ability," https://rowinglevel.com/rowing-times/2000m-times.

Rowing Level. 2024b, May 22 (access date). "Marathon Row Times; Rowing Standards by Age and Ability," https://rowinglevel.com/rowing-times/marathon-times.

Royal Magazine. 1905. "The Latest Thing in Airships: An Aerial Skiff." *The Royal Magazine*, 15: 340.

Saab. 2015, March 24. "The secret to the world's most silent submarine," https://www.saab.com/newsroom/stories/2015/march/the-secret-to-the-worlds-most-silent-submarine.

Sachse, H. 1926, February. "Kirsten-Boeing Propeller," NACA Technical Memorandum 351. Translated by Dwight M. Miner from *Zeitschrift für Flugtechnik und Motorluftschiffahrt*, January 14, 1926, pp. 1–4. https://ntrs.nasa.gov/citations/19930090732.

Sadraey, Mohammed H. 2013. *Aircraft Design: A Systems Engineering Approach*. Wiley.

Sane, Sanjay P. 2003, Dec. 1. "The Aerodynamics of Insect Flight," *J. Experimental Biology*, 206(23): 4191–4208. https://journals.biologists.com/jeb/article/206/23/4191/13945/The-aerodynamics-of-insect-flight.

Santos-Dumont, Alberto. 1973 (1904). *My Airships: The Story of My Life*. Dover Publications.

Saponara, Sergio, and Lucian Mihet-Popa. 2020. *Energy Storage Systems and Power Conversion Electronics for E-Transportation and Smart Grid*. Mdpi AG.

Schirber, Michael. 2020, April 27. "Flying Insects and Their Robot Imitators," https://physics.aps.org/articles/v13/60.

Schmidt, Theodore. 2001. "J. H. Hagedoorn—Inventing the Hapa: A Review of a Geophysicist's 'Other' Work and How It Inspired Others," *Geophysical Prospecting*, 49: 735–45.

Schoeberl, Ernst. 2004, May 21 (PDF creation date). "The Musculair 1 & 2 Human-Powered Aircraft and Their Optimization." Translated by Heinz Altherr and Dave Wilson.

Schoeberl, Ernst. 2008, August. "From Sunrise to Solar-Impulse: 34 Years of Solar Powered Flight," *Technical Soaring: Int J*, 32(4): 115–121. Presented at the XXIX OSTIV Congress, 6–13 August 2008, Lüsse, Germany. https://journals.sfu.ca/ts/index.php/ts/article/view/88.

Schwaiger, Meinhard, and David Wills. 2016, September. "D-Dalus VTOL—Efficiency Increase in Forward Flight," *Aircraft Engineering and Aerospace Technology*, 88(5): 594–604, https://www.researchgate.net/publication/308940213.

Schwartz, Stephen I. 2011 (1998). *Atomic Audit: The Costs and Consequences of U.S. Nuclear Weapons Since 1940*. Rowman & Littlefield Publishers.

Schweers, Johann G., and John D. Schweers. 1905, June 20 (issue date). "Air Ship," U.S. Patent 702,933 (application filed Oct. 10, 1903).

Science Daily. 2019, Nov. 14. "New Material Breaks World Record Turning Heat into Electricity," https://www.sciencedaily.com/releases/2019/11/191114115851.htm.

Science History Institute. 2024, June 15 (access date). "Ballon à Voile de Guyot" postcard, by A. Molynk, Box 287. https://digital.sciencehistory.org/works/k643b2505.

Scientific American. 1866, May 26. "'Experiments in Aerial Navigation," *Scientific American*, 14: 363.

Scientific American. 1933, Sept. "A Steam Driven Airplane Engine," *Scientific American*, 149(3): 124–5. https://web.archive.org/web/20190702144417/http://flyingkettle.com/besler3.htm.

Scott, Jeff. 2006, Jan. 29. "NACA 0012 Lift Characteristics," https://aerospaceweb.org/question/airfoils/q0259c.shtml.

Seifert, Jost. 2012. "A Review of the Magnus Effect in Aeronautics," *Progress Aerospace Sciences*, 55: 17–45.

Seifert, Jost. 2013, Sept. 10. "Magnus and Transverse Flow Hybrid Rotor," U.S. Patent 8,528,855 (application filed Dec. 21, 2011).

Seifert, Jost. 2018, April 17 (issue date). "Stirling Engine for an Emission-Free Aircraft," U.S. Patent 9,945,361.

Bibliography

Self, Douglas. 2008, Oct. 6. "Rotary Steam Boilers," http://www.douglas-self.com/MUSEUM/POWER/rotaryboil/rotaryboil.htm.

Self, Douglas. 2018, Dec. 9. "The Cyclogyros," http://www.douglas-self.com/MUSEUM/TRANSPORT/cyclogyro/cyclogyro.htm.

Self, Douglas. 2022, Sept. 20. "Steam Aeroplanes," http://www.douglas-self.com/MUSEUM/TRANSPORT/steamplane/steamplane.htm.

Semmens, Peter William Brett, and Alan J. Goldfinch. 2000. *How Steam Locomotives Really Work*. Oxford University Press.

Senate, United States. 1968, May 27–28. Joint Hearings before the Committee on Commerce, and the Subcommittee on Air and Water Pollution of the Committee on Public Works, United States Senate (90th Congress, 2d Session) on "The Automobile Steam Engine and Other External Combustion Alternatives to the Internal Combustion Engine," serial no. 90–82. GPO.

Senate, United States. 1974, July 16 and 18. "Advanced Aeronautical Concepts," Hearings, Committee Aeronautical and Space Sciences, 93rd Cong. 2d Sess.

Shipman, Pat. 1998. *Taking Wing: Archaeopteryx and the Evolution of Bird Flight* (Simon & Schuster).

Shyy, Wei, et al. 2013. *An Introduction to Flapping Wing Aerodynamics*. Cambridge University Press.

Sigler, Dean. 2011, Aug. 26. "Embry Riddle Begins GFC Test Flights," https://sustainableskies.org/embry-riddle-begins-gfc-test-flights/.

Sigler, Dean. 2020, Sept. 14. "Eather One—When Friction is a Good Thing," https://sustainableskies.org/eather-one-when-friction-good-thing/.

Simonin, Louis. 1876, Sept. "Industrial Applications of Solar Heat," *Pop. Sci. Monthly*, 9(33): 550–560.

Sinor, J. E. 1992, January. "Comparison of CNG and LNG Technologies for Transportation Applications," Final Subcontract Report June 1991–December 1991. National Renewable Energy Laboratory. https://afdc.energy.gov/files/pdfs/2451.pdf.

Skaarup, Harold. 2012. *California Warplanes*. iUniverse.

Sloop, John L. 1978. *Liquid Hydrogen as a Propulsion Fuel, 1945–1959*. NASA SP-4404. National Air and Space Administration.

Smart Microsystems. 2012, May 6. "Fish-Like Underwater Glider Taking a Dive," http://www.youtube.com/watch?v=fPlmbqQYvk4.

Smith, Paul. 2001, Feb. 11. "The South African Class '25' Condensing Locomotive," https://web.archive.org/web/20100523211622/http://stanleys-steamers.gen.nz/Class%2025%20-%20an%20analysis.htm.

SNL. 1959, May 23. "Nuclear-Powered Blimp," *Science News-Letter*, 75(21): 322.

Snyder, Bernard J. 1996, May 3. "Aircraft Nuclear Propulsion: An Annotated Bibliography" (USAF History and Museums Program).

Sockel, Helmut. 2013. "Essential Contributions of Austria to Fluid Dynamics Prior to the End of World War II," in *The History of Theoretical, Material and Computational Mechanics—Mathematics Meets Mechanics and Engineering*, pp. 355–384, edited by Erwin Stein. Spring Berlin Heidelberg.

Solar Energy Technologies Office, Department of Energy. 2023, October 25 (access date). "Copper Indium Gallium Diselenide," https://www.energy.gov/eere/solar/copper-indium-gallium-diselenide.

Solar Flight 2024. "Sunseeker Duo—First Two Seat Solar Powered Aircraft," https://www.solar-flight.com/sunseeker-duo/.

Solar Impulse Foundation. 2023, October 26 (accessed). "Historic Flight: Our Adventure," https://aroundtheworld.solarimpulse.com/adventure.

Solomon, Brian. 1998. *American Steam Locomotive*. Motorbooks International.

Solomon, Brian. 2000. *The American Diesel Locomotive*. Voyageur Press.

Southampton, University of. 1995a, August 7. "Airship Crosses the Solent," originally published in the *New Reporter*, 10(5): n.p. (Nov. 11, 1992). https://web.archive.org/web/20051201050609/http://www.soton.ac.uk/~newrep/vol10/nxbe004.htm.

Bibliography

Southampton, University of. 1995b, August 7. "Up, Up and Away," originally published in the *New Reporter*, 9(15): n.p. (June 5, 1992). https://web.archive.org/web/20051201044930/http://www.soton.ac.uk/~newrep/vol9/nxab003.htm.

Spearman, M. Leroy. 2003, April 7–10. "An Inboard-Wing Arrangement for High-Capacity Airlift and Sealift Vehicles," Applied Vehicle Technology Panel Symposium on Novel Vehicle Concepts and Emerging Vehicle Technologies, Brussels, Belgium. https://www.cs.odu.edu/~mln/ltrs-pdfs/NASA-2003-avtps-mls.pdf.

Spektor, Rostislav, and Karen L. Jones. 2021, March. "A Breath of Fresh Air: Air-Scooping Electric Propulsion in Very Low Earth Orbit," *Game Changer*, Center for Space Policy and Strategy. https://aerospace.org/sites/default/files/2021-03/Spektor-Jones_AirBreathing_20210318.pdf.

Srinivas, Tangellapalli. 2007. "Generalized Thermodynamic Analysis of Steam Power Cycles with 'N' Number of Feedwater Heaters," *Int. J. Thermodynamics*, 10: 177–85.

Steam Automobile Club of America, Inc. 1965. "Some Particulars of the Williams Steam Car," *Steam Automobile*, 7(4): 19.

Steam Car Club of Great Britain, The. 2024, May 5 (access date). "Uniflow Steam Engine Road Vehicles," http://www.steamcar.net/uniflow-doble.html.

Steam Car Developments & Steam Aviation. 1934, June. "The Besler Steam-Driven Aeroplane," Steam Car Developments & Steam Aviation, 3(28): n.p. Pages copied by Self 2022.

Steam Power Club News. 1981, April. "Flying by Steam," Steam Power Club News, 38–40. https://web.archive.org/web/20190702132819/http://flyingkettle.com/besler1.htm.

Stewart, John D. 1944, Feb. 15 (issue date). "Airship," U.S. Patent 2,341,577 (application filed May 6, 1942).

Stilley, Faye. 1999, February. "Spencer's Ornithopter," *Model Airplane News*, 40–44. https://ornithopter.org/archive/orniplane.article.pdf.

Stommel, Henry. 1989, April. "The Slocum Mission," *Oceanography*, 22–25. https://seatrec.com/wp-content/uploads/2020/09/Stommel-Slocum-Mission-Article.pdf.

Strack, W. C. 1970, May. "Condensers and Boilers for Steam-Powered Cars: A Parametric Analysis of Their Size, Weight and Required Fan Power," NASA Tech Note D-5813.

Sullivan, Callum R. 2007, Sept. 4 (issue date). "Tri-Cycloidal Airship," U.S. Patent 7,264,202. (Application filed Nov. 1, 2005).

Sullivan, Charles A. 1880, Nov. 30 (issue date). "Flying-Machine," U.S. Patent 235,040 (application filed Aug. 23, 1880).

SunPlower Propeller. 2022. "Impossible for 100 Years," https://www.sunplower.de/technology.

Suppes, Glaen J., and Truman Storvick. 2006. *Sustainable Nuclear Power* (Academic Press).

Sutton, George Paul. 2006. *History of Liquid Propellant Rocket Engines*. American Institute of Aeronautics and Astronautics.

Syroco. 2020, Oct. 31. "Speedcraft Features," https://www.youtube.com/watch?v=ZRBEggA3gVw.

Syroco. 2022a, March 3. "Prototype First Flight," https://www.youtube.com/watch?v=EAj7uYNjfkk.

Syroco. 2022b, Dec. 30. "On the Road to the Sailing World Speed Record | Syroco — Footage from the Journey!," https://www.youtube.com/watch?v=WpmgVO5uSs8.

Syroco. 2024. "L'Aile d'Eau and the Weightless Yacht Concept," https://syro.co/en/news/laile-deau-and-the-weightless-yacht-concept/.

Talbot, Frederick A. 1901. "Cycling Through the Air: A Marvellous Airship Described," *Harmsworth Magazine*, 6: 341–7.

TAO Group. 2023. "The First Autonomously Flying Solar Airship in the World," https://www.tao-group.de/en_solarluftschiff_lotte.html.

Tartière, Thomas, and Marco Astolfi. 2023, August. "ORC World Map," https://orc-world-map.org/.

Technical World Magazine. 1910, March. "The Boy Aviator," *Technical World Magazine*, 13(1): 155.

Bibliography

Terpitz, Julian. 2019, April. "LNG for Aircrafts," 19th Int. Conference & Exhibition on Liquefied Natural Gas, Shanghai, China. https://www.gti.energy/training-events/events-overview/past-events/-lng2019-conference/.

Thesee, Gilles. 2024. "Aerodynamics of the Radiator," http://contrails.free.fr/engine_aerodyn_radia_en.php.

Thome, Emma. 2012, July 11. "World Record for Rowers Who Generated Enough Electricity to Power a House for a Day," https://phys.org/news/2012-07-world-rowers-electricity-power-house.html.

Thompson, James M., and Oscar J. Niegenfind. 1925, June 2 (issue date). "Aeroplane," U.S. Patent 1,540,667.

Time and Tide. 1952, Sept. 27. 33(Pt. 2): 1098.

Tissandier, Gaston. 1872. *Les Ballons Dirigeables: Expériences de M. Henri Girddard en 1852 et en 1855, et de M. Dupuy de Lome en 1872.* E. Dentu.

Tissandier, Gaston. 1885. *Les Ballons Dirigeables: Application de L'Électricité a la Navigation Aérienne.* Gauthier-Villars.

Tomatore, Cinzia, et al. 2022, July 22. "Ammonia as Green Fuel in Internal Combustion Engines: State-of-the-Art and Future Perspectives," *Frontiers Mechanical Engineering*, 8: 944201. https://doi.org/10.3389/fmech.2022.944201.

Torenbeek, Egbert. 1982. *Synthesis of Subsonic Airplane Design*, 2nd ed. (Kluwer Academic).

Torenbeek, Egbert. 2013 (1976). *Synthesis of Subsonic Airplane Design.* Springer Netherlands.

Toronto, University of. 2010, Sept. 22. "Human-Powered Ornithopter Becomes First Ever to Achieve Sustained Flight (w/ Video)," https://phys.org/news/2010-09-human-powered-ornithopter-sustained-flight-video.html.

Tung, Jul-Min, et al. 2007, June 11. "Design of an Underwater Glider with Fore and Aft Buoyancy Engines," in *2007 Symposium on Underwater Technology and Workshop on Scientific Use of Submarine Cables and Related Technologies*, Tokyo, Japan, pp. 446–450, https://doi.org/10.1109/UT.2007.370770; https://ieeexplore.ieee.org/document/4231100.

ULPower. 2024. "Why Develop a Gasoline Aircraft Engine and Not a Diesel?," https://ulpower.com/en/engines/faq/why-no-diesel.

Union of Concerned Scientists. 2018, March 14. "Series vs Parallel vs Series/Parallel Drivetrains," https://www.ucsusa.org/resources/all-about-drivetrains.

United States Air Force. 1964, Jan. 15. *Guided Missiles Fundamentals.* AF Manual 52–31.

United States Centennial of Flight Commission. 2024. "Early Helicopter Technology," https://www.centennialofflight.net/essay/Rotary/early_helicopters/HE1.htm.

United States Submarine School. 1963. *Basic Enlisted Submarine Text, Part 1.* GPO.

United States v. Sowards. 2012, June 26. United States Court of Appeals, Fourth Circuit. http://caselaw.findlaw.com/us-4th-circuit/1604482.html.

UPSBatteryCenter.com. 2022, Nov. 20. "World's First Zinc Chlorine Flow Battery," https://blog.upsbatterycenter.com/worlds-first-zinc-chlorine-flow-battery/.

Urieli, Israel. 2020, Dec. 12. Stirling Cycle Machine Analysis (Ohio University) https://ohioopen.library.ohio.edu/opentextbooks/9/.

Valentine, Harry. 2015. "Researching a Heat-Pumped Condensing Steam Locomotive," http://www.martynbane.co.uk/modernsteam/hvalentine/condense.htm.

Valenzuela P. L., et al. 2022, "The Record Power Profile of Male Professional Cyclists: Normative Values Obtained from a Large Database," *Int. J. Sports Physiology & Performance*, 17(5): 701-710.

Vance, Jason Thomas. 2009, August. "Experimental and Natural Variation in Hovering Flight Capacity in Bees, Hymenoptera: Apidae" (Ph.D., Biological Sciences, University of Nevada, Las Vegas).

Van der Vlugt, Rolf. 2009, October. "Aero- and Hydrodynamic Performance

Bibliography

Analysis of a Speed Kiteboarder: Breaking the World Speed Sailing Record" (Master's Thesis, Aerospace Engineering, Delft University of Technology). https://www.google.com/url?sa=t&source=web&rct=j&opi=89978449&url=https://repository.tudelft.nl/islandora/object/uuid%253A9e0c7a62-149c-4fab-8d27-afe15c1a8795&ved=2ahUKEwiMktm8kpqHAxVeFVkFHct6BJsQFnoECBUQAQ&usg=AOvVaw2AkubY9IIecOseagDRq3fJ.

Van Orden, Jack E. 1957. "The Nuclear Powered Zeppelin," reprinted in *Aerostation*, June 1999, 9–14.

Vergara. Julio A., and Chris B. McKesson. 2002, January. "Nuclear Propulsion in High-Performance Cargo Vessels," Marine Technology and SNAME News, https://www.researchgate.net/publication/233626256.

Veziroğlu, T. Nejat. 1995. "Twenty Years of the Hydrogen Movement: 1974–1994," *Int. J. Hydrogen Energy*, 20(1): 1–7.

Vineeth, C.S. 2012 (Rev. ed.). *Stirling Engines: A Beginners Guide*, https://www.researchgate.net/publication/362215201_Stirling_Engines_A_Beginners_Guide.

Virtual Steam Car Museum. 2015. "Williams Engine Company, Inc" (citing an October 1967 article in *Road Test*). http://www.virtualsteamcarmuseum.org/makers/williams_engine_company.html.

Volland, H. 2013. *Atmospheric Electrodynamics*. Spring Berlin Heidelberg.

Wade, John. 2022. *Transport Curiosities, 1850-1950: Weird and Wonderful Ways of Travelling by Road, Rail, Air and Sea*. Pen & Sword Books.

Walters, E. W. 1917. *Heroic Airmen and Their Exploits*. C. H. Kelly.

Wang, Meng, et al. 2018. "Air-Flow-Driven Triboelectric Nanogenerators for Self-Powered Real-Time Respiratory Monitoring," *ACS Nano*. XX:xx. https://doi.org/10.1021/acsnano.8b02562. https://www.ncbi.nlm.nih.gov/pmc/articles/PMC6279609/.

Wang, Shuhua, et al. 2015. "Elasto-Aerodynamics-Driven Triboelectric Nanogenerator for Scavenging Air-Flow Energy," *ACS Nano*, 9(10): 9554–63.

https://pubs.acs.org/doi/10.1021/acsnano.5b04396.

War Dept. 1898. *Drill Regulations for Cavalry, United States Army*. GPO.

War Dept. 1941, Feb. 11. *Technical Manual of Airship Aerodynamics*. TM 1–320. GPO.

Wardale, David. 1998. *The Red Devil and Other Tales from the Age of Steam*. Self-published.

Weatherbug. 2020, November 3. "The Albuquerque Box—Mystery Explained," https://www.weatherbug.com/news/-The-Albuquerque-Box-%E2%80%93-Mystery-Explained.

Wegener, Peter P. 2012. *What Makes Airplanes Fly?: History, Science, and Applications of Aerodynamics*. Springer.

Weisstein, Eric W. 2025. "Curtate Cycloid," https://mathworld.wolfram.com/CurtateCycloid.html.

Weitering, Hanneke. 2023, March 1. "Universal Hydrogen Flies Hydrogen-Powered Dash 8," https://www.ainonline.com/news-article/-2023-03-02/universal-hydrogen-flies-hydrogen-powered-dash-8.

Wertheim, Eric. 2023, October. "Sweden's Gotland-class Subs: AIP pioneers of the Baltic Sea," *Proc. U.S. Naval Inst.*, 149/10/1, 448, https://www.usni.org/magazines/proceedings/2023/october/-swedens-gotland-class-subs-aip-pioneers-baltic-sea.

Wertheim, Margaret. 2004, Dec. 5. "Lower, Slower, Nearer," *Los Angeles Times*. https://www.latimes.com/archives/la-xpm-2004-dec-05-tm-airship49-story.html.

Whale, George. 1919. *British Airships: Past, Present and Future*. John Lane.

Whitfield, Bethany. 2011, June 23. "EADS/Diamond Unveil Electric Hybrid," https://www.flyingmag.com/news-eadsdiamond-unveil-electric-hybrid/.

Whitman, Roger B. 1920, May. "An Airship of '63: A Forgotten Page of Aeronautical History," *U.S. Air Service*, 3: 29–32.

Whitman, Roger B. 1932, January. "He Flew an Airship Before the Wrights Were Born!," *Pop. Sci. Monthly*, 120(1): 15–18, 123–5.

Wilkinson, Paul Howard. 1940. *Diesel Aviation Engines*. National Aeronautics

Bibliography

Council. Chapters 1-6 are available as separate PDFs at https://www.enginehistory.org/Piston/Diesels/diesels.shtml. The full text of the 1942 edition is available as page images at https://catalog.hathitrust.org/Record/001040354.

Williams, Phillip. 2014. *Empire and Holy War in the Mediterranean: The Galley and Maritime Conflict Between the Habsburgs and Ottomans.* Bloomsbury Publishing.

Wilson, David Gordon. 1986a, July-August. "A Short History of Human-Powered Vehicles," *American Scientist,* 74(4): 350-7.

Wilson, David Gordon. 1986b. "Understanding Pedal Power," technical paper no. 51. VITA (Volunteers in Technical Assistance). https://ocw.mit.edu/courses/ec-711-d-lab-energy-spring-2011/15286019b5a06fde2d43af6c00f460d4_MITEC_711S11_lab1_pedal.pdf.

Wilson, David Gordon. 2004 (3rd ed.). *Bicycling Science.* MIT Press.

Wilson, E. E. 1926, June. "Steam Power Plants in Aircraft," National Advisory Committee for Aeronautics Technical Notes No. 239.

Wilson, Jack, et al. 2009, Dec. 1. "An Investigation of Ionic Wind Propulsion," https://ntrs.nasa.gov/citations/20100000021.

Windsor, H. H. 1907, December. "International Balloon Race of 1907," *Popular Mechanics,* 9(12): 1325-1332.

Wise, David Burgess. 1973. *Steam on the Road.* Hamilyn Publishing Group Ltd.

Woodward, D. E. 1958. "Proposal for a Large Rigid Airship Design for Airborne Early Warning and Control Operations," reprinted in *Aerostation,* June 1999, 15-20.

World Nuclear Association. 2021, Aug. 26. "Fast Neutron Reactors," https://world-nuclear.org/information-library/current-and-future-generation/fast-neutron-reactors.

World Nuclear Association. 2024a, April 30. "Nuclear Power Reactors," https://world-nuclear.org/information-library/nuclear-fuel-cycle/nuclear-power-reactors/nuclear-power-reactors.

World Nuclear Association. 2024b, May 16. "Physics of Uranium and Nuclear Energy," https://world-nuclear.org/information-library/nuclear-fuel-cycle/introduction/physics-of-nuclear-energy.

Wright, A. Dean. 1966, Dec. "The Performance of Ground Observers in Detecting, Recognizing and Estimating speed to Low-Altitude Aircraft," Tech. Report 66-19 (GWU HumRRO). https://apps.dtic.mil/sti/tr/pdf/AD0645537.pdf.

Wright, G. J. 1803. "V. Remarks on the Present State of Aerostation," *Philosophical Magazine,* 15: 19-32.

Wu, Xiaotao, et al. 2009, September. "Modelling and Linear Control of a Buoyancy-Driven Airship," Asian Control Conference. https://www.researchgate.net/publication/224598820_Modelling_and_Linear_Control_of_a_Buoyancy-Driven_Airship.

Wu, Xiaotao, et al. 2010, Sept1-3. "Modelling and Control of a Complex Buoyancy-Driven Airship," 8th IFAC Symposium on Nonlinear Control Systems, Bologna, Italy. https://www.sciencedirect.com/science/article/pii/S1474667015371172.

Wu, Xiaotao, et al. 2011. "Modelling and Control of a Buoyancy Driven Airship," https://hal.archives-ouvertes.fr/tel-01146532.

Wu, Yuping. 2015. *Lithium-Ion Batteries: Fundamentals and Applications.* CRC Press.

Xisto, Carlos M., et al. 2016. "Parametric Analysis of a Large-Scale Cycloidal Rotor in Hovering Conditions," *J. Aerospace Engineering,* 30(1). http://publications.lib.chalmers.se/publication/235793.

Xu, Hanfeng, et al. 2018, Nov. 21. "Flight of an Aeroplane with Solid-State Propulsion," *Nature,* 563: 532-5.

Xuan, Haibin, et al. 2020, Feb. 11. "Recent Progress in Aerodynamic Modeling Methods for Flapping Flight," *AIP Advances,* 10: Article 020701, https://pubs.aip.org/aip/adv/article/10/2/020701/21833/Recent-progress-in-aerodynamic-modeling-methods.

Yenne, Bill. 2001. *The World's Worst Aircraft.* Barnes & Noble.

Yirka, Bob. 2020, Dec. 4. "Copying Beetle Wings to Design MAVs that Can

Bibliography

Recover from Midair Collisions," https://techxplore.com/news/2020-12-beetle-wings-mavs-recover-midair.html.

Young, A.D. 1939, April 27. "The Calculation of the Total and Skin Friction Drags of Bodies of Revolution at Zero Incidence," Rept. 1874 (Great Britain, Air Ministry).

Yu, Hu (username: huyu0711). 2011, Oct. 5. "Test Flight of Cyclogyro," https://www.youtube.com/watch?v=9ZYRii4MjLY.

Zahm, Albert Francis. 1911. *Aërial Navigation: A Popular Treatise on the Growth of Air Craft and on Aëronautical Meteorology.* D. Appleton.

Zakaria, Mohamed Yehia, et al. 2015, June. "Design Optimization of Flapping Ornithopters: The Pterosaur Replica in Forward Flight," *J. Aircraft*, 53(1): 1-12. https://www.researchgate.net/publication/279252445.

Zhang, Jun, et al. 2019, Jan. 16 (PDF last modified date). "Robotic Artificial Muscles: Current Progress and Future Perspectives," https://projects.iq.harvard.edu/files/biodesignlab/files/2019_zhang_ieee_transactions_on_robotics_-_robotic_artificial_muscles_current_progress_and_future_perspectives.pdf.

Zheng, Peng, et al. 2020, Oct. 7. "A Comprehensive Review of Atmosphere-Breathing Electric Propulsion Systems," *Int. J. Aerospace Engineering*, 2020: Article ID 8811847, https://doi.org/10.1155/2020/8811847.

Zi, Yunlong, and Zhong Lin Wang. 2017, March 1. "Nanogenerators: An Emerging Technology Towards Nanoenergy," *APL Materials*, 5: 074103.

Author's Preexisting Work

As noted in the front matter, portions of this book were previously published in the *Grantville Gazette*, which ceased publication in July 2022. That online magazine presented fiction set in and nonfiction relating to the fictional literary universe created by the late Eric Flint's alternate-history sci-fi novel *1632*. In that novel, a new time line is created when a fictional West Virginia town (Grantville) is moved from the year 2000 to Thuringia, Germany, during the Thirty Years' War. The nonfiction considered the limited knowledge and resources that would have been available to the townspeople and proposed how they might cope. Naturally, the fictional aspects have been omitted from the present work!

Cooper, Iver P. 2012. "Airship Propulsion: Part 1: Thrust and Drag," *Grantville Gazette* 41.

Cooper, Iver P. 2012. "Airship Propulsion, Part 2: Revving Up," *Grantville Gazette* 42.

Cooper, Iver P. 2012. "Airship Propulsion, Part 3: Steaming Along," *Grantville Gazette* 43.

Cooper, Iver P. 2012. "Airship Propulsion, Part 4: The Aereon," *Grantville Gazette* 44.

Cooper, Iver P. 2021. "Tethered Balloons and Kites in the 1632 Universe, Part 2," *Grantville Gazette* 96.

Index

Ader, Clement 36
Aerial Steam Transit Company 33
Aero Turbines Ltd. 38
aerodynamics modeling 213–16; Aereon 217–21
airplane power see under power
airplane propulsion see under propulsion
airplanes, specific: Aerodrome No. 6 36; Aerovironment Global Observer 114; AeroVironment Nano Hummingbird 192; Antares 20E 114; Antares DLR-H2 114–15; Aviat Husky CND demonstrator 117; B-57B 110–12; Bat Bot 193; Bell X-1 205; Besler (1933) 37–38, 244; Blohm & Voss BV 138 104; Convair NB-36H 95; Cycloplane 17; Daedalus 88 19, 26, 28; Dash 8-300 115; Delfy (various models) 195–96; Diamond DA36 E-Star 76; Dimona motor flider 114; Dornier DO 18 104; Dornier DO 26 105; Eather One 121; Eco-Eagle 76–77; Eole 36; Festo AG Air_ray 196; Gossamer Albatross 18–19, 26; Gossamer Condor 18; Gossamer Penguin 84; Grumman Cheetah 112; Grunau Baby IIa 192; Hatfield Puffin 18; Heinkel HE 176 204; Hurricane 59; Insectothopter 193–95; Junkers F-24 104; Junkers G-38 104; Junkers Ju 42 104; Junkers Ju 86 104; KUBeetle-S 196; Lange Antares 75; Light Eacle 19; Lockheed X-7 207; Mauro Solar Riser 83–84; Messerscrhmitt Bf 109f 59; Microbat 193; Militsky-Birditschka MB-E1 75; Mufli 18; Musculair 2 19, 26, 29; Mustang P-51D 59; Pipistel Velis Electro 211; Potez 25 106; Rapid 200-FC 115; Republic XF-91 Thunderceptor 205; Robobee 196; Skybird 192; Snowbird 191; Solar Challenger 84–85; Solar Impulse 85; Solar Impulse II 85; Spencer Orniplane 192; Spitfire 59; SUNPAC 18; Sunrise I 83; Sunrise II 83; Sunseeker Duo 85; Sunseeker I 85; Toucan 19; TU-154 112; TU-155 112, 117; Wright Flyer 211; X-15 204; X-43A 112; Zeroavia plane 115
airship power see under power
airship propulsion see under propulsion
airships, specific: Acrostat 178–79; Aereon I 123–24, 129, 131–8, 140–2, 211, 217–26, 247; Aereon II 125–26, 247; Aereon III 128; Aereon 7 128; Aereon 26 128; Aerosail 151–52; Akron 39; Avitor Hermes Jr. 33–35; D2 16; De Lome 9–11, 20–21; Dirigible-4 74; Dirigicycle 11; Enbryo 190; Giffard 31–32; Graf Zeppellin II (LZ130) 106; Hindenburg (LZ129) 106, 109, 115; Hylighter 35 drone 113–14; Iris Challenger 2 75; K-class 6, 20–21; La France 73–4; Lockheed Martin HALE-D 85; Lotte 74, 85; Macon 138; Mademoiselle Louise 150–51; Moon 14–15; Phoenix 131, 142; Pilstrom 190–91; R101 106; Shenandoah 249; Sky-Cycle 14–15; Snoopy 16; Solar Airship One 86; Velocipde 13; Walden Aerospace XEM-1 85, 209; White Diamond 74; White Dwarf 16, 21; Windream One 150–51; Zeppelin NT 3; Zeppy-1 16, 243, 248; Zeppy-3 16
airships vs. airplanes 1–2
airships, winged 128–30, 145–46
Allen, Bryan 18
Alloymyrina dichotoma 196
Andrews, Solomon 123–26

bats 193
battery power 69–82; history, airplanes, battery electric 75; history, airplanes, hybrid gas-electric 75–77; history, airships 69–75; overview 77–78;

281

Index

performance characteristics 78–79; recharageable battery comparison 79–81; see also motors; supercapacitors
Becquerel, Edmond 83
Bell, Hugh 9
Besler, William J. 37–38
biomimetic propulsion 212; birds vs. humans 188–89; history, airships 190–91; history, bird-inspired 188–192; history, insect-inspired 193–97; history, manned airplanes, engine-powered 191–2; history, manned airplanes, human-powered 191; history, pterosaur-inspired 192–93; history, unmanned airplanes 192–97; insect flight 197–200; transmission 200–1; undulation 201–2; wing design 200
birds 124, 175, 188–93, 197–99, 201
Blanchard, Jean-Pierre 165
Bockrath, T. A. 97
Boeing, William 175
boilers, rotating steam 38
Brayton cycle 67–68, 98
Breguet Aircraft Works 38
buoyancy-driven propulsion 212; analysis 131–47; history, airships 123–131; underwater glides and 128–30
Burgess, Charles P. 149, 155–58

Carnot cycle 40, 46, 62, 98
Cataldo, Robert L. 103
Cayley, George 30–31, 127, 142–43
Charles, Jacques 165
chien de mer 150–3, 159–60, 248
CIA 193–95
Clements, E. W. 97
Colozza, Anthony J. 103
Condensers 48–49, 53–55, 230–31
Congreve, William 169, 171
Conrad, Bill 112
cooling drag 58–58
Costes, Didier 150
cyclogyros see cycloidal propulsion
cycloidal propulsion 173–87; see also paddlewheel propulsion

D'Amecout, Gustave Ponton 43
Danilewski, Konstantin 16–17,190–91
DeLaurier, James 192
De Lome, Henri Dupuy 9–11, 20–21
De Terzi, Francisco Lana 147
Dewar, James 109
Diesel, Rudolf 104
diesel power 211–12; analysis 107–8;

history, airplanes 104–6; history, airships 106–7
Dixon, Cromwell 14–16
Doble (steam car manufacturer) 37–38
Dorrington, Graham 16, 74
Du Temple de la Croix, Felix 35

electrokinetic propulsion 208–9
Eneas, A. G. 86
engines: airplane, commercial and military 4–5; airplane, general aviation 3–4; cooling 3; fuel consumption see engines, fuel efficiency; gasoline (see also engines, Otto cycle; engines, spark ignition); internal combustion 3; Otto cycle 3; performance considerations 5–7; piston 6–7; ramjet 5; rocket 5; scramjet 112, 246; spark ignition 3; thermal efficiency 6–7; turbofan 5–7; turbojet 5–7; turboprop 5–7; see also fuels; power; propulsion
engines, steam 40–41; Besler (1958) 42–43
Ericsson, John 86
Erres, Rudolf A. 108

flapping see biomimetic propulsion
Flettner, Anton 207
Forlanini, Enrico 43
Fowler, Frank G. 175–77
Fritts, Charles 83
fuel cells see battery power
fuels: ammonia 117–18; Blau gas 117; diesel see diesel power; external combustion of see Rankine cycle, organic; steam power; Stirling cycle; gasoline see Otto cycle; power, conventional; hydrogen see hydrogen fuel power; internal combustion of see power, conventional; kerosene see power, conventional; natural gas 116–17; see also engines, power

Geery, Daniel J. 129–30
Geherhardt, William 17
Giffard, Henri 30–33
Goddard, Robert 110, 206
Graver, Joshua Grady 131, 217–19
Great Lakes Aircraft Corporation 39–40
Groves, H. H. 36
Gurney, Goldsworthy 31

Haenlein, Paul 116
Haessler, Helmut 17
Harrington, Mabel 11

282

Index

Harris, Jeremy 192
helicopters, specific: Atlas 19; Da Vinci III 19; Gamera II 19; Swisscopter Dragonfly DF1 205, 206; Yuri I 19
Henson, William Samuel 33, 35
Huttner 38
hydrogen fuel power 211; fuel cells 114–15; history, airplanes 110–12; history, airships 108–9, 113–14; safety 115–16; storage 109–10, 112–13

insects 193–96, 197–200

Kanellopoulos, Kanellos 19
Kaplan, Meilin 87
Kikiki huna (fairyfly wasp) 197
Kirsten, Frederick 175
Kiselev, Valentin 192
Krebs, Arthur Constantin 71
Kremer Prize 18, 19

Langley, Samuel Pierrpont 36
Lanteigne, Auguste 166
Lassie, Jean Baptiste Justin 210
LeMay, Curtis 115
lifting body shape 146
Lilienthal, Otto 17
Lippisch, Alexander 191, 203
Locke, F. W., Jr. 96, 101
Lunardi, Vincenso 165

Magnan, Antoine 198
Magnus effect propulsion 207–8, 249
manta ray 196
Marriott, Frederick 33–35
Massachusetts Institute of Technology (MIT) 19
Maxim, Hiram 36
McCallin, Lois 19
McConaghy, Robert 64–65
Meerwein, Karl Friedrich 17
Meredith effect 59
Merritt, Frederick R. 172
Meyer, P. 110
Mitchell, Matthew D. 65
Montgolfier Joseph-Michel and Etienne 164
Morse, Francis 96–97
motors 82
Mouchot, Augustin 86
Moy, Thomas 35
Mozhaiskii, Alexander Fedorovich 35–36
muscle power 9–17, 212; analysis 21–29;

history, airplanes 17–19, 21; history, airships 9–17, 20–21; history, helicopters 19
Myers, Carl E. 12–14

Norton, Tony 16
nuclear power 211; analysis 97–103; history, airplanes 95–96; history, airships 96–97

oar propulsion 164–69
Opel, Fritz von 203–4
ornithopters see biomimetic propulsion

paddlewheel propulsion 169–73; see also cycloidal propulsion
piezoelectric power 118–20
Pifre, Abel 86
Plante, Gaston 69
Pocock, George 148
power: alternative external combustion (see Rankine cycle, organic; Stirling cycle, Brayton cycle); battery see battery power; Brayton cycle engine see Brayton cycle; conventional 3–7; diesel see diesel power; hydrogen see hydrogen power; muscle see muscle power; nuclear see nuclear power; piezoelectric see piezoelectric power; solar-electric see piezoelectric power; solar-thermal see solar-thermal power; steam (working fluid) see steam power; steam analogues (working fluid) see Rankine cycle, organic; Stirling cycle engine see Stirling Cycle; thermoelectric see thermoelectric power; triboelectric see triboelectric power; weight and 5–6; see also engines; fuels
power, external combustion as source see Brayton cycle; Rankine cycle, organic; steam power; Stirling cycle
power, required propulsive 5
propulsion: biomimetic see biomimetic propulsion; buoyancy-differential see buoyancy-differential propulsion; conventional 3–7; cycloidal propeller see cycloidal propulsion; electrokinetic see electrokinetic propulsion; flapping see biomimetic propulsion; Magnus effect see Magnus effect propulsion; oars see oar propulsion; paddlewheels see paddlewheel propulsion; ramjet see ramjet propulsion; rocket see rocket

283

Index

propulsion; undulating see biomimetic propulsion; wind see wind propulsion
pterosaurs 192–93
Purandare, Ravi Yeshwant 131, 139–40, 217–19

Queen Alexandra's Birdwing butterfly 197
Quetzalcoatlus northropi (pterosaur) 192
Quinlan, Mark 11

Radeamakers, Laurens 87
Raebiger, Horst 192
ramjet propulsion 206–7
Rankine cycle, organic 60–61
Rankine cycle, steam 45–48, 98, 217–18
Reichert, Todd 19, 191
Renard, Charles 71
Reynolds, Alva 167
Ritchel, Charles Francis 11–13
Robert, Nicolas-Louis and Anne-Jean 165
Rochelt, Holger 19
rocket propulsion 203–6
ropes and cables, strength and weight of 158
Rousettus aegyptiacus (Egyptian fruit bat) 193
Rousson, Stephane 16, 150–54
Roziere, Jean-Francois Pilatre de 142

Schmid, Adalbert 191–92
Schneider, Ernst 177
Sikorsky Prize 19
Simonin, Louis 86
solar-electric power 211; analysis 88–90; history, airplanes 83–85; history, airships 85–86
solar power 83, 87–88; concentration 92–94
solar-thermal power 86–87, 90–93; history 86–87, 93–94
Southampton University 18
steam power 30–59, 211; analysis 43–59; history, airplanes 35–; history, airships 30–35; history, helicopters 43; solar heat see solar power; solar-thermal power; steam locomotive data 229–31; thermal efficiency 45–48, 229–36; thermal performance 50–52; weight and 52–53, 55–58
Stirling, Robert 62
Stirling cycle 61–67, 98, 211; analysis 65–67, 92; history, airplanes 64–65; history, airships 65, 87, 103
Stommel, Henry 128
Stringfellow, John 33, 35
supercapacitors 81

thermodynamic cycles see Brayton cycle; Carnot cycle; Rankine cycle; Stirling cycle
thermodynamics modeling 217–18
thermoelectric power see solar-thermal power
Tissandier, Albert 69–71
Tissandier, Gaston Albert 69–71
triboelectric power 120–21
Tsiolkovskiy, Konstantin Eduwardovich 205–6

undulating see biomimetic propulsion
Ursinus, Oskar 24

Vaeth, Gordon 100, 102
Voith-Schneider propeller 177–78, 181, 183–85
Von Linde, Carl 107
Von Ohain, Hans 110

Watson, Bill 16
wind propulsion 212; analysis 148–66; history, airships 148–55; wind-differntial tacking 160–63
wing loading 29
Wright, G. J. 165

www.ingramcontent.com/pod-product-compliance
Lightning Source LLC
Chambersburg PA
CBHW032033300426
44117CB00009B/1039